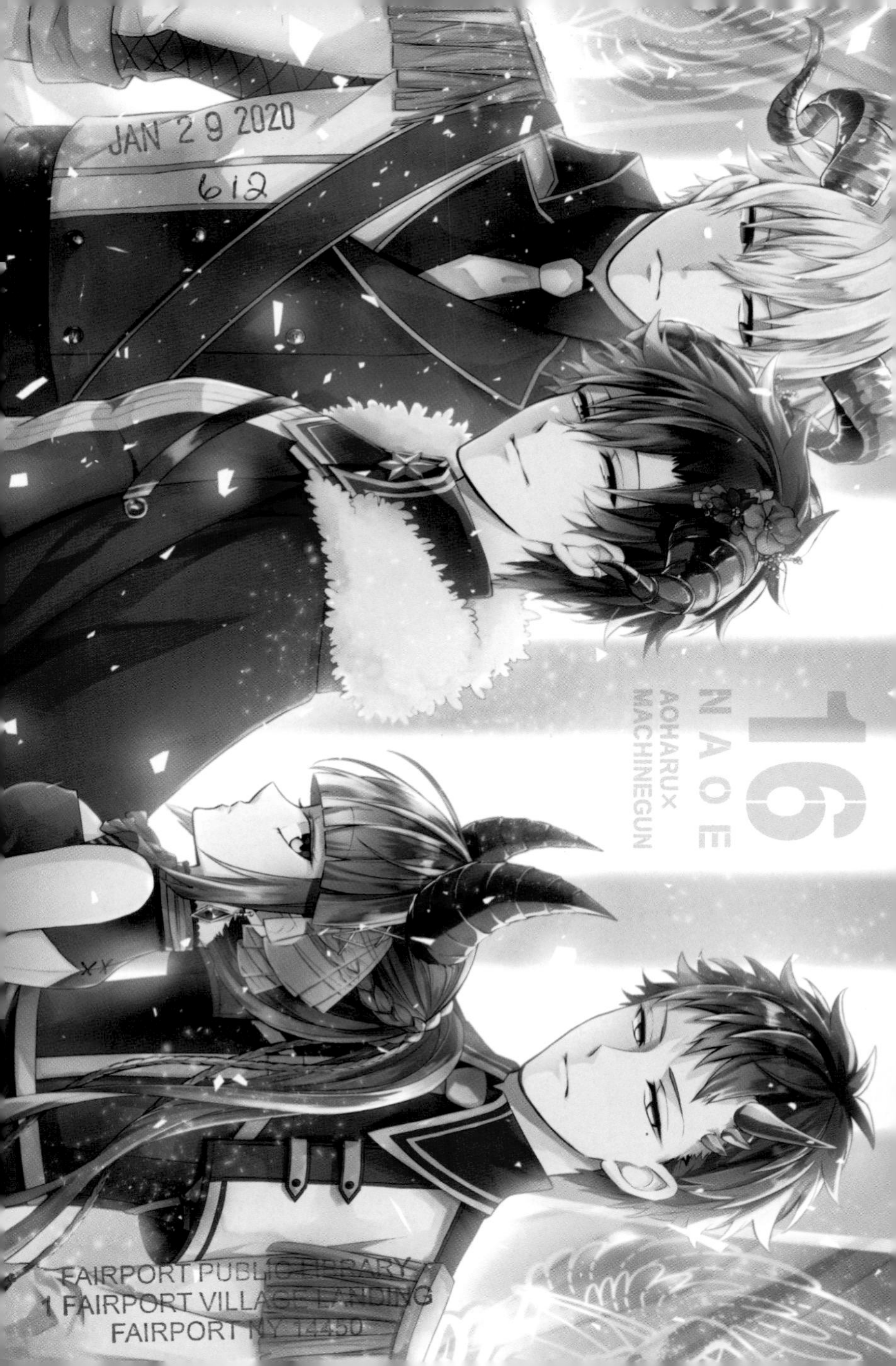
16
NAOE
AOHARU×
MACHINEGUN

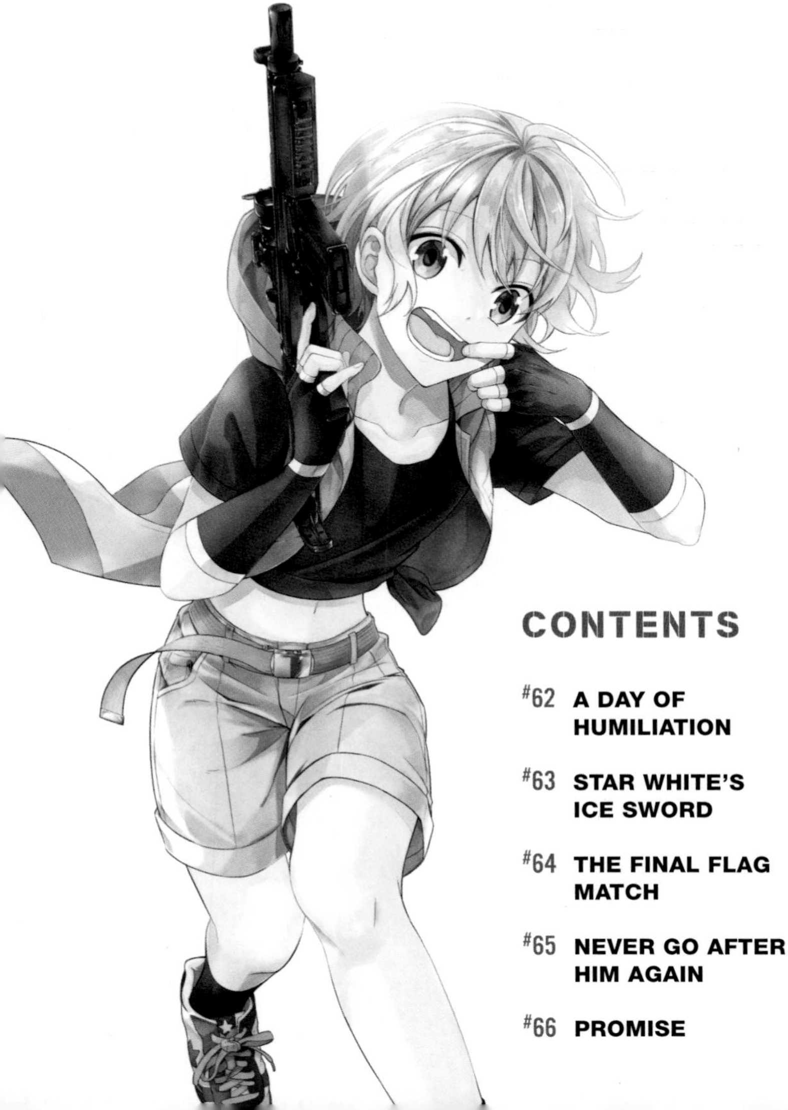

CONTENTS

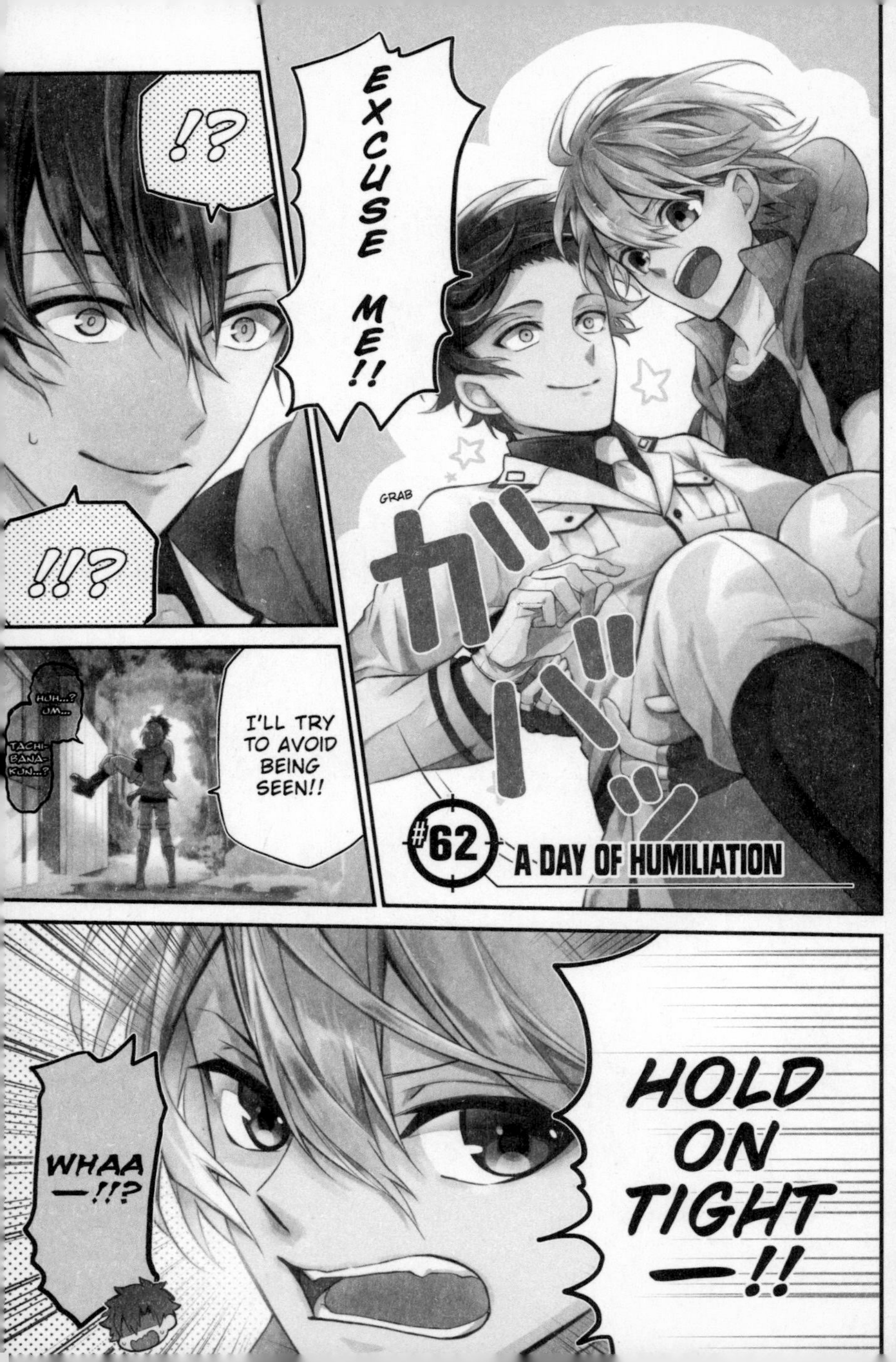
EXCUSE ME!!
GRAB
ガバッ
#62 A DAY OF HUMILIATION
!?
!!?
I'LL TRY TO AVOID BEING SEEN!!
HUH...? UM...
TACHIBANA-KUN...?
HOLD ON TIGHT—!!
WHAA—!!?

AOHARU
MACHINE
GUN

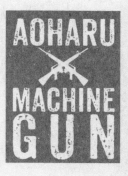

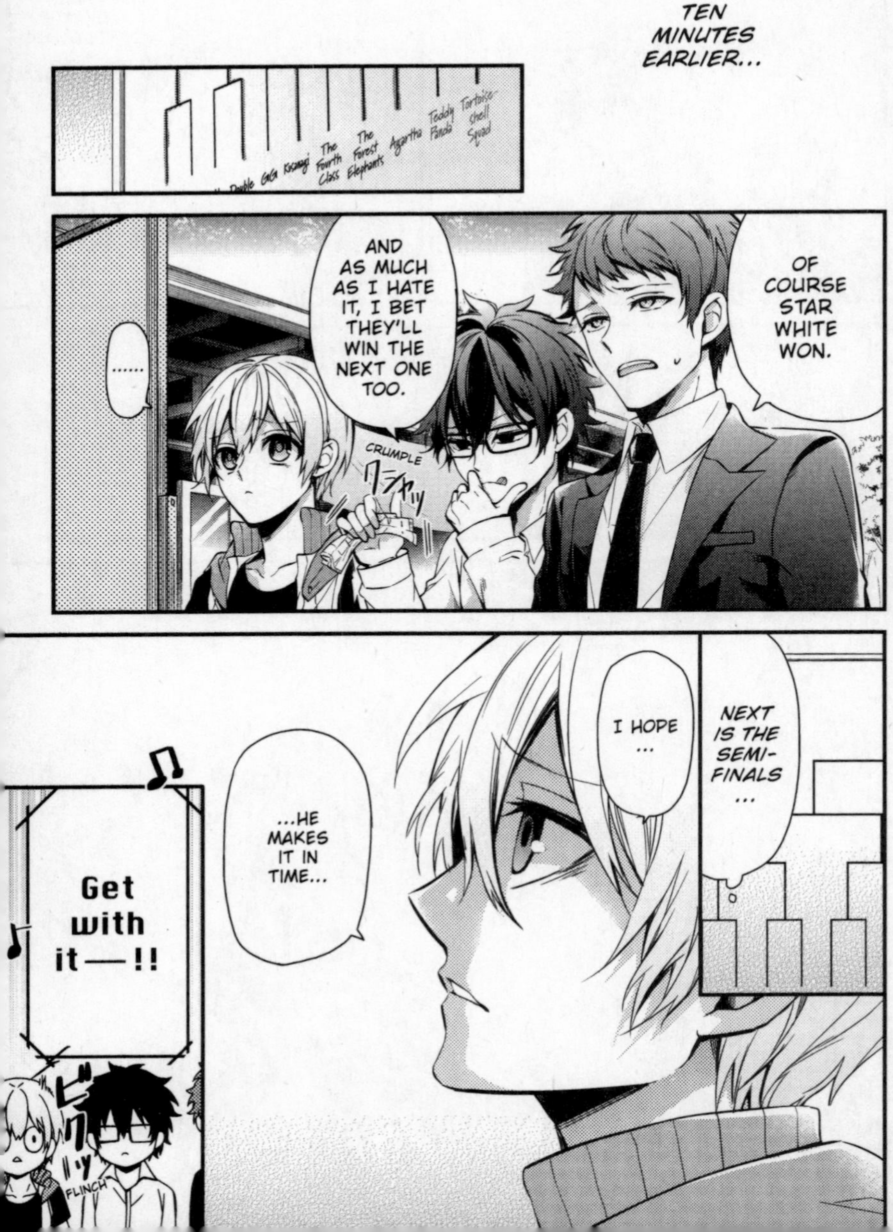
TEN MINUTES EARLIER...
Double
GaGa
Kisaragi
The Fourth Class
The Forest Elephants
Agartha
Teddy Panda
Tortoise-shell Squad
OF COURSE STAR WHITE WON.
AND AS MUCH AS I HATE IT, I BET THEY'LL WIN THE NEXT ONE TOO.
CRUMPLE
......
NEXT IS THE SEMI-FINALS...
I HOPE...
...HE MAKES IT IN TIME...
Get with it—!!
FLINCH

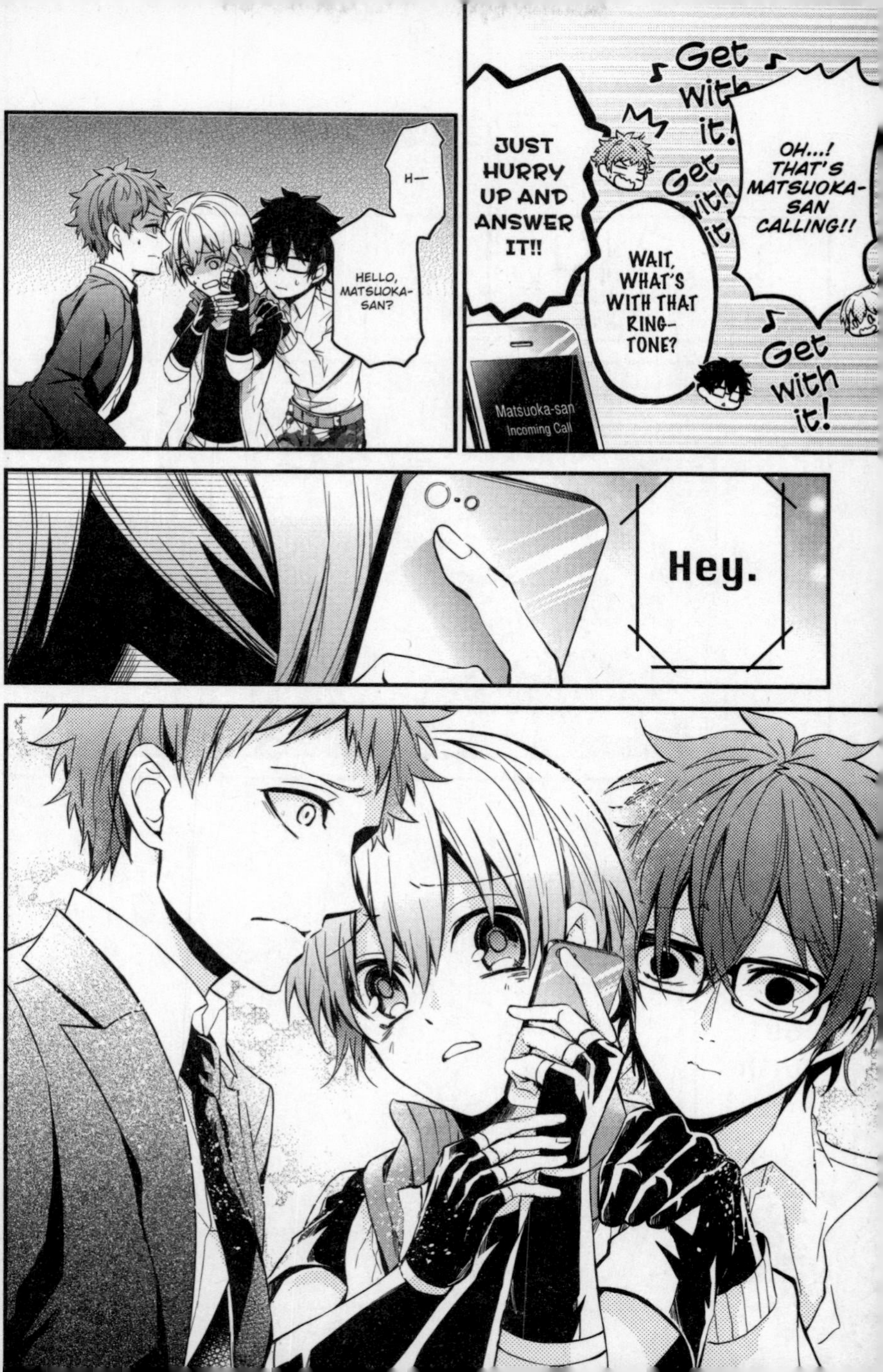
OH...! THAT'S MATSUOKA-SAN CALLING!!
Get with it! Get with it!
JUST HURRY UP AND ANSWER IT!!
WAIT, WHAT'S WITH THAT RING-TONE?
Get with it!
Matsuoka-san
Incoming Call
H—
HELLO, MATSUOKA-SAN?
Hey.

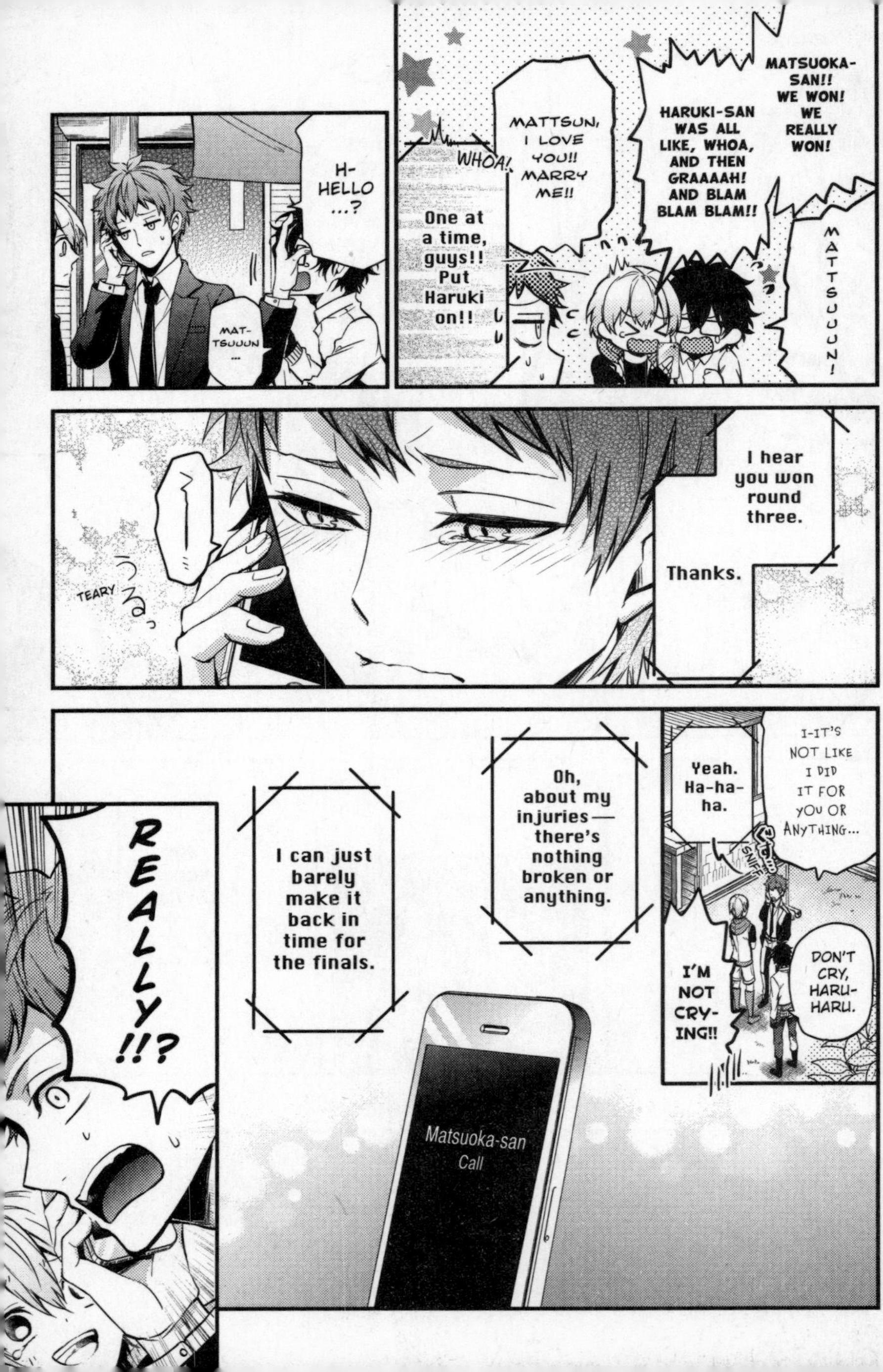
MATSUOKA-SAN!! WE WON! WE REALLY WON!
HARUKI-SAN WAS ALL LIKE, WHOA, AND THEN GRAAAAH! AND BLAM BLAM BLAM!!
MATTSUUUN!
MATTSUN, I LOVE YOU!! MARRY ME!!
WHOA!
One at a time, guys!! Put Haruki on!!
H-HELLO ...?
MAT-TSUUUN ...
I hear you won round three.
Thanks.
TEARY
I-IT'S NOT LIKE I DID IT FOR YOU OR ANYTHING...
Yeah. Ha-ha-ha.
SNIFF
DON'T CRY, HARU-HARU.
I'M NOT CRY-ING!!
Oh, about my injuries—there's nothing broken or anything.
I can just barely make it back in time for the finals.
Matsuoka-san
Call
REALLY!!?

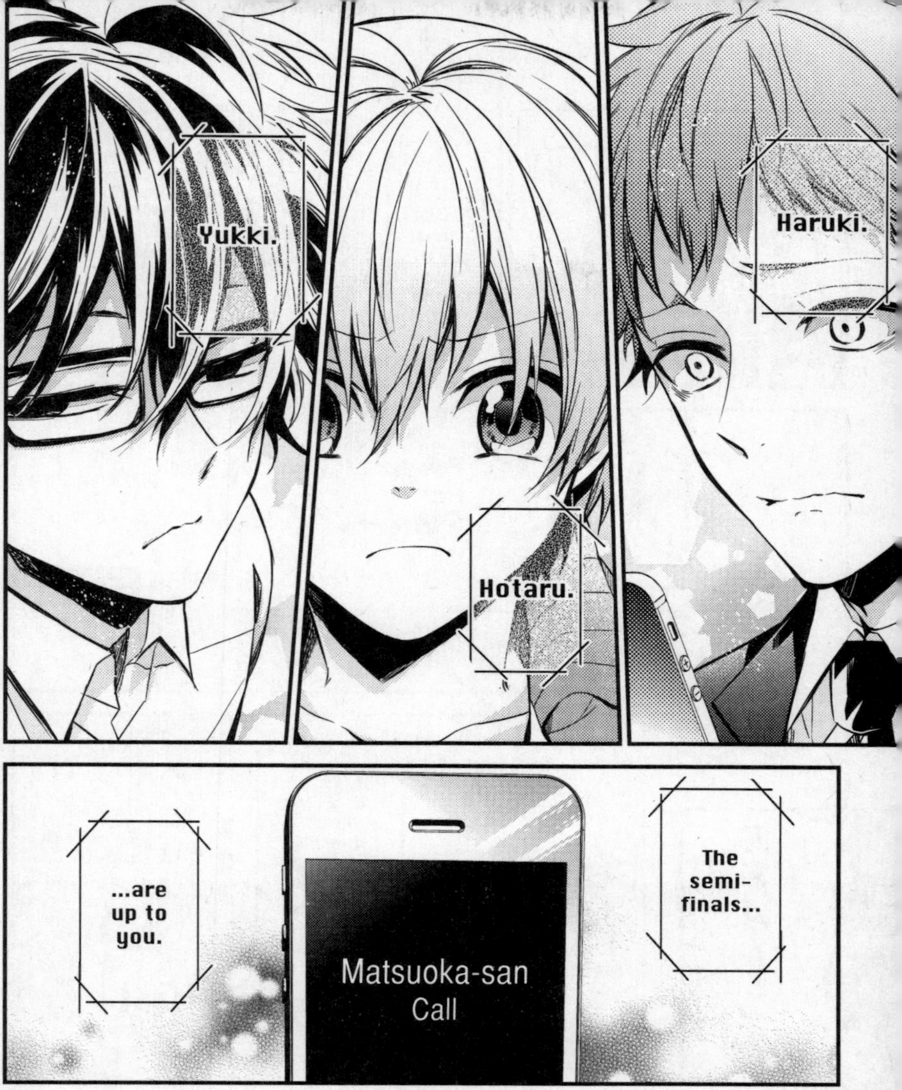
Haruki.
Hotaru.
Yukki.
The semi-finals...
Matsuoka-san
Call
...are up to you.
CLICK

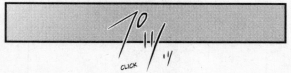

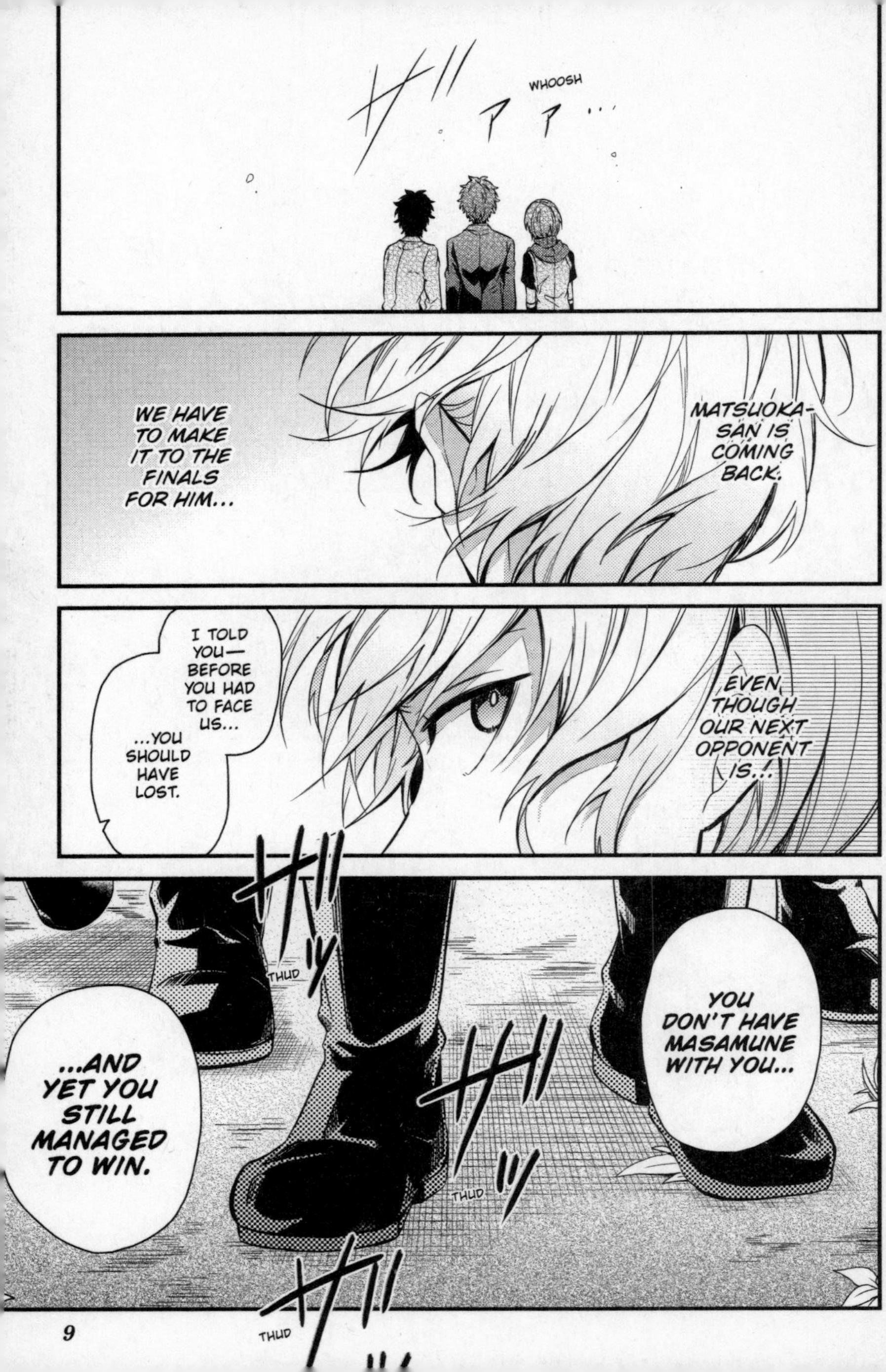
ザァァ…
WHOOSH
MATSUOKA-SAN IS COMING BACK.
WE HAVE TO MAKE IT TO THE FINALS FOR HIM...
EVEN THOUGH OUR NEXT OPPONENT IS...
I TOLD YOU—BEFORE YOU HAD TO FACE US...
...YOU SHOULD HAVE LOST.
YOU DON'T HAVE MASAMUNE WITH YOU...
...AND YET YOU STILL MANAGED TO WIN.
ザッ
THUD
ザッ
THUD
ザッ
THUD

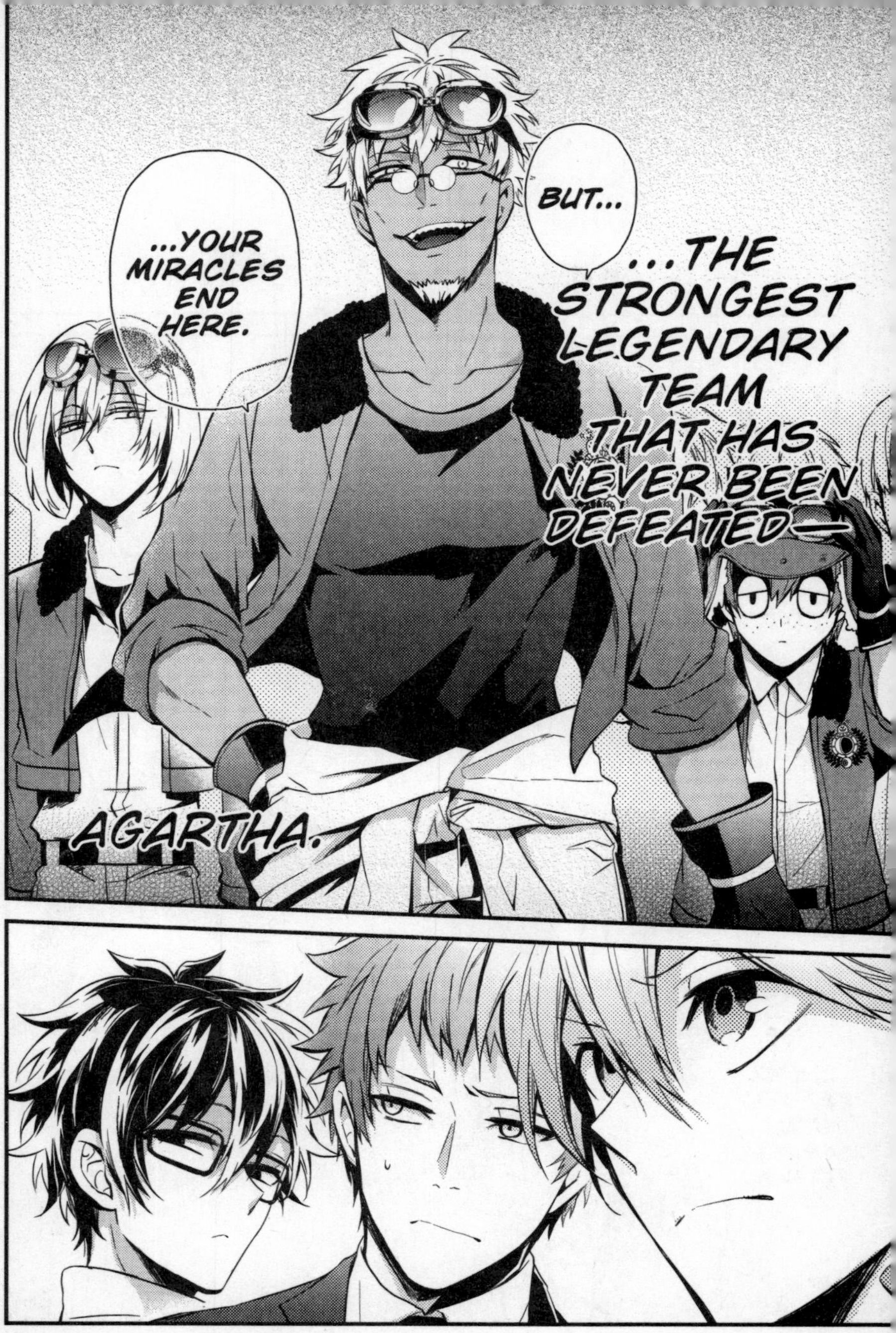
BUT...
...THE STRONGEST LEGENDARY TEAM THAT HAS NEVER BEEN DEFEATED—
...YOUR MIRACLES END HERE.
AGARTHA.

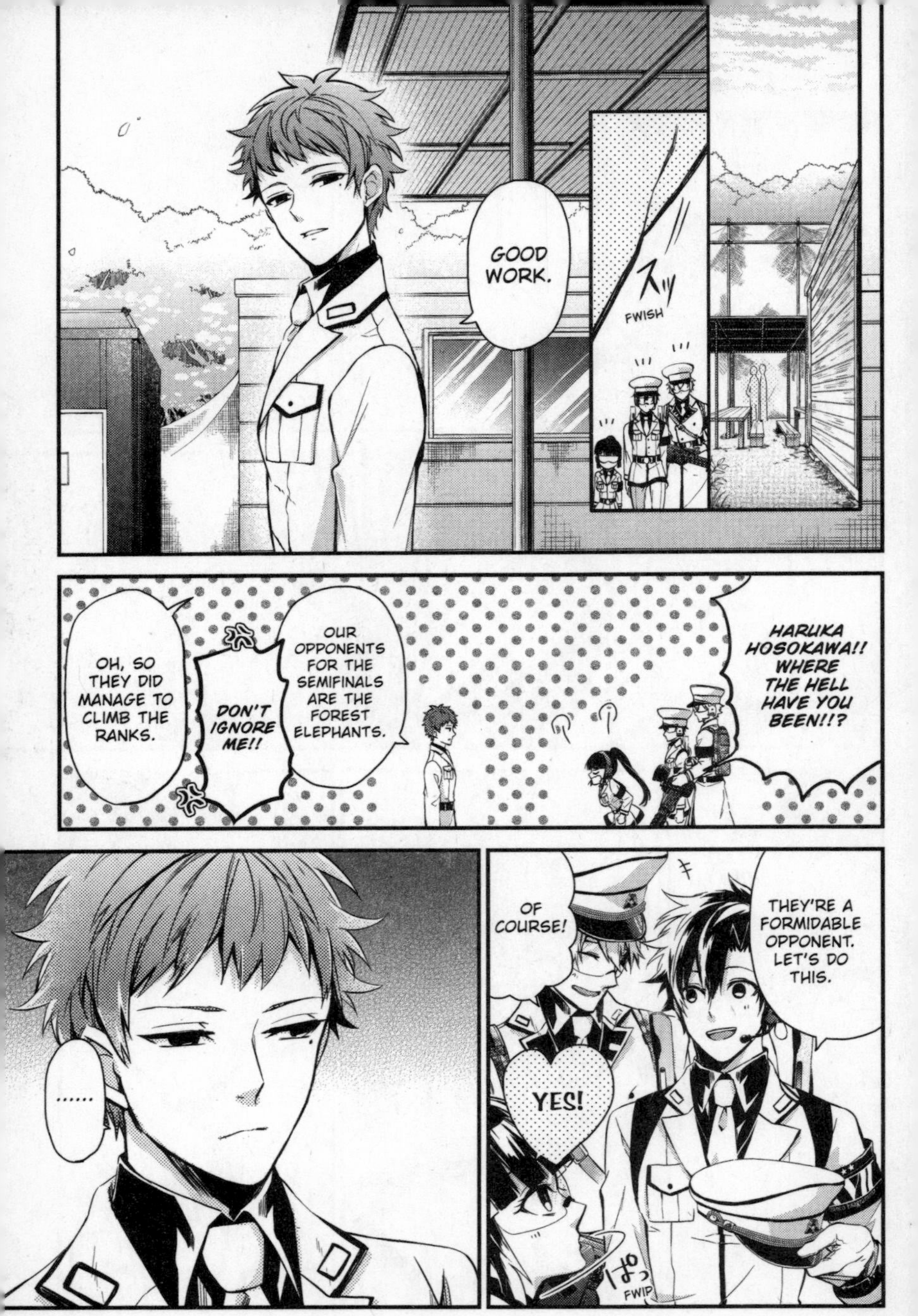
スッ
FWISH
GOOD WORK.
HARUKA HOSOKAWA!! WHERE THE HELL HAVE YOU BEEN!!?
OUR OPPONENTS FOR THE SEMIFINALS ARE THE FOREST ELEPHANTS.
DON'T IGNORE ME!!
OH, SO THEY DID MANAGE TO CLIMB THE RANKS.
THEY'RE A FORMIDABLE OPPONENT. LET'S DO THIS.
OF COURSE!
YES!
ぱっ
FWIP
......

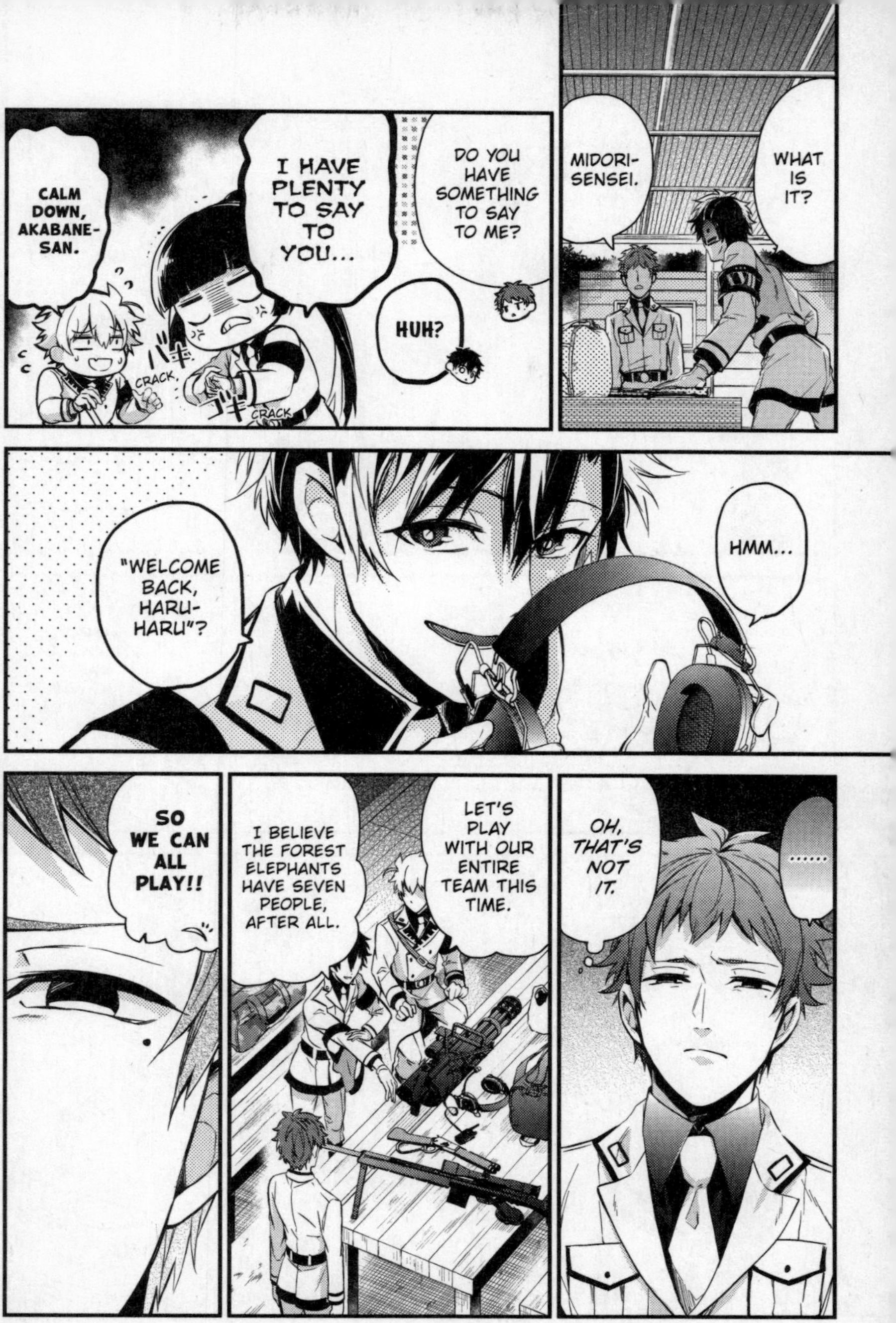
MIDORI-SENSEI.
WHAT IS IT?
DO YOU HAVE SOMETHING TO SAY TO ME?
HUH?
I HAVE PLENTY TO SAY TO YOU...
CALM DOWN, AKABANE-SAN.
CRACK
CRACK
HMM...
"WELCOME BACK, HARU-HARU"?
......
OH, THAT'S NOT IT.
LET'S PLAY WITH OUR ENTIRE TEAM THIS TIME.
I BELIEVE THE FOREST ELEPHANTS HAVE SEVEN PEOPLE, AFTER ALL.
SO WE CAN ALL PLAY!!

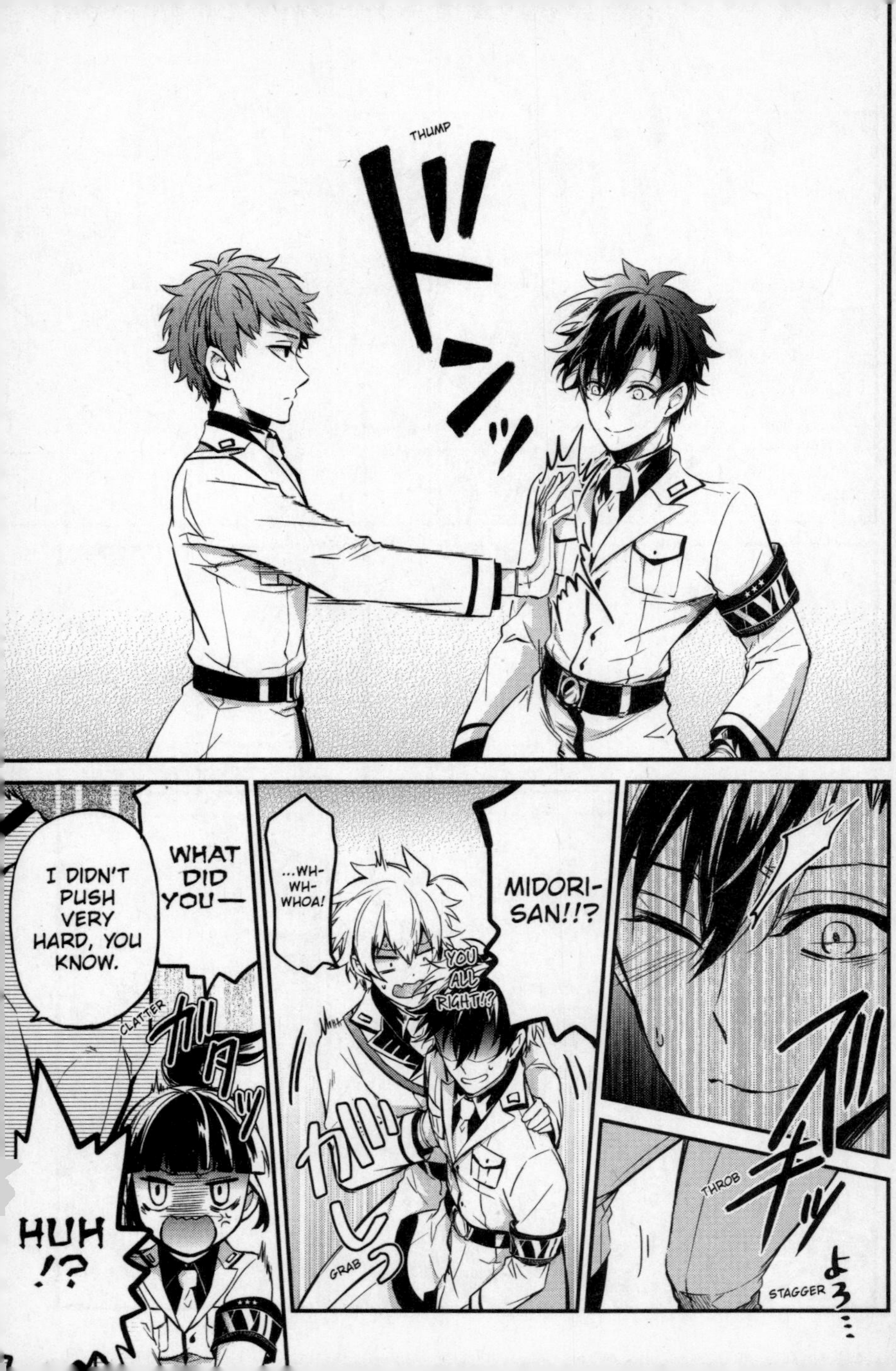
THUMP
THROB
STAGGER
MIDORI-SAN!!?
...WH-WH-WHOA!
YOU ALL RIGHT!?
GRAB
WHAT DID YOU—
I DIDN'T PUSH VERY HARD, YOU KNOW.
CLATTER
HUH!?

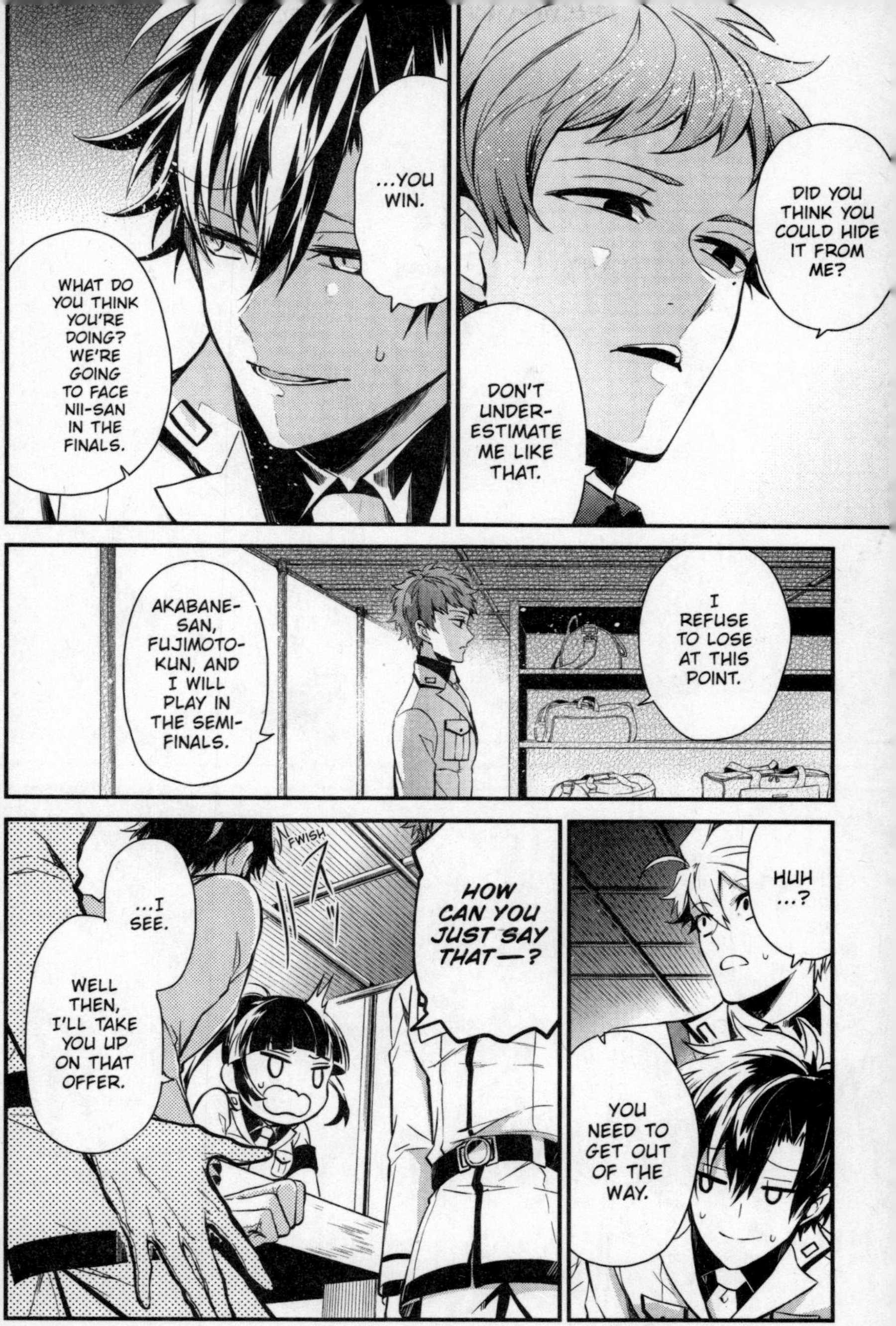
DID YOU THINK YOU COULD HIDE IT FROM ME?
DON'T UNDER-ESTIMATE ME LIKE THAT.
...YOU WIN.
WHAT DO YOU THINK YOU'RE DOING? WE'RE GOING TO FACE NII-SAN IN THE FINALS.
I REFUSE TO LOSE AT THIS POINT.
AKABANE-SAN, FUJIMOTO-KUN, AND I WILL PLAY IN THE SEMI-FINALS.
HUH ...?
YOU NEED TO GET OUT OF THE WAY.
HOW CAN YOU JUST SAY THAT—?
FWISH
...I SEE.
WELL THEN, I'LL TAKE YOU UP ON THAT OFFER.

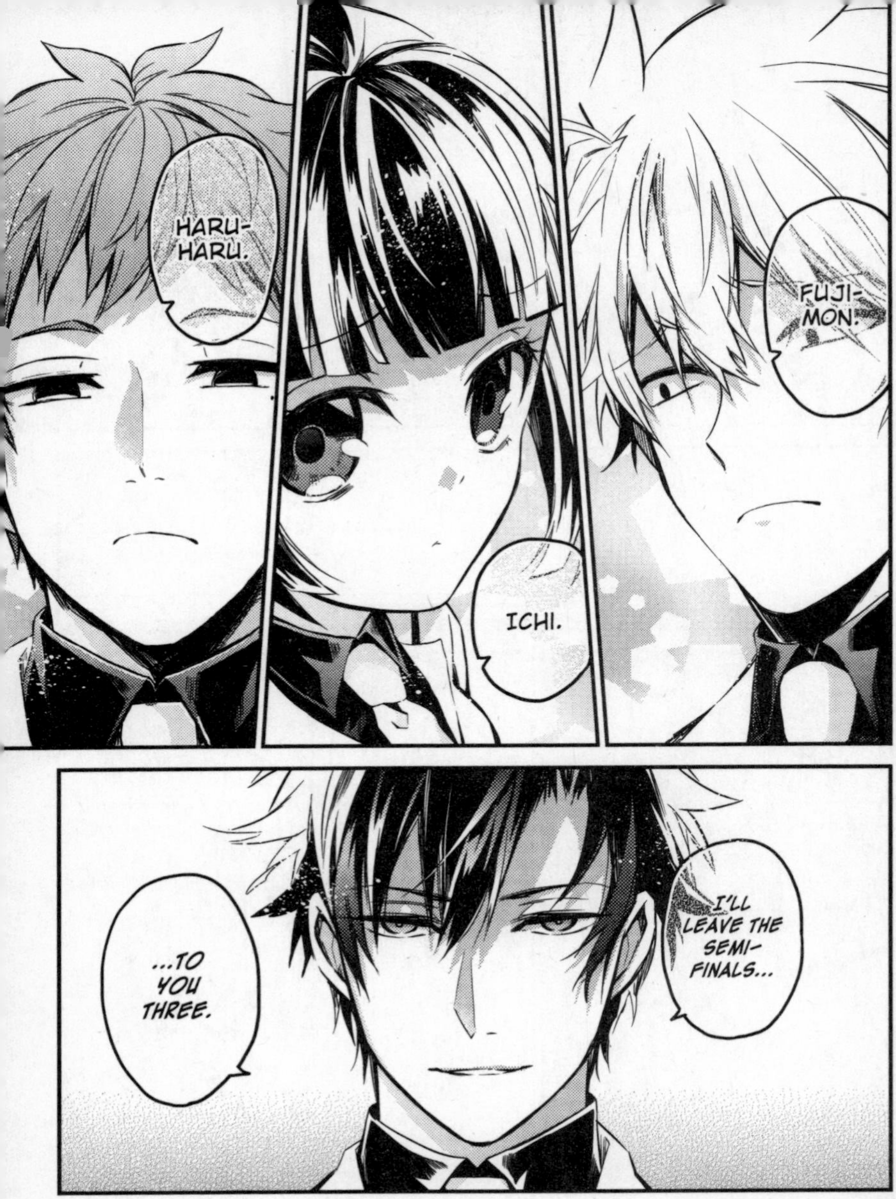
FUJI-MON.
ICHI.
HARU-HARU.
I'LL LEAVE THE SEMI-FINALS...
...TO YOU THREE.

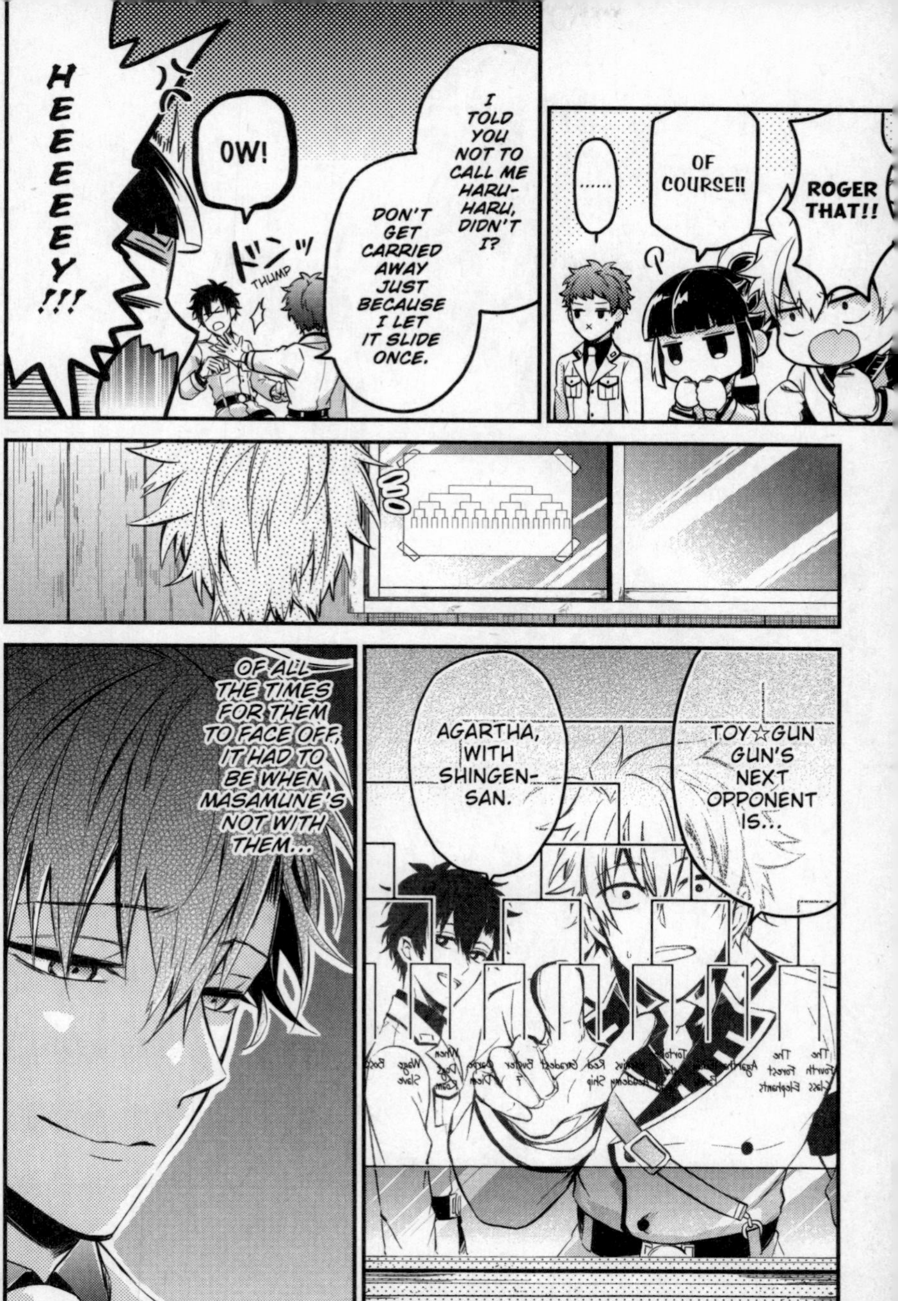
ROGER THAT!!
OF COURSE!!
......
I TOLD YOU NOT TO CALL ME HARU-HARU, DIDN'T I?
DON'T GET CARRIED AWAY JUST BECAUSE I LET IT SLIDE ONCE.
OW!
ドンッ
THUMP
HEEEEEEY!!!
TOY☆GUN GUN'S NEXT OPPONENT IS...
AGARTHA, WITH SHINGEN-SAN.
OF ALL THE TIMES FOR THEM TO FACE OFF, IT HAD TO BE WHEN MASAMUNE'S NOT WITH THEM...

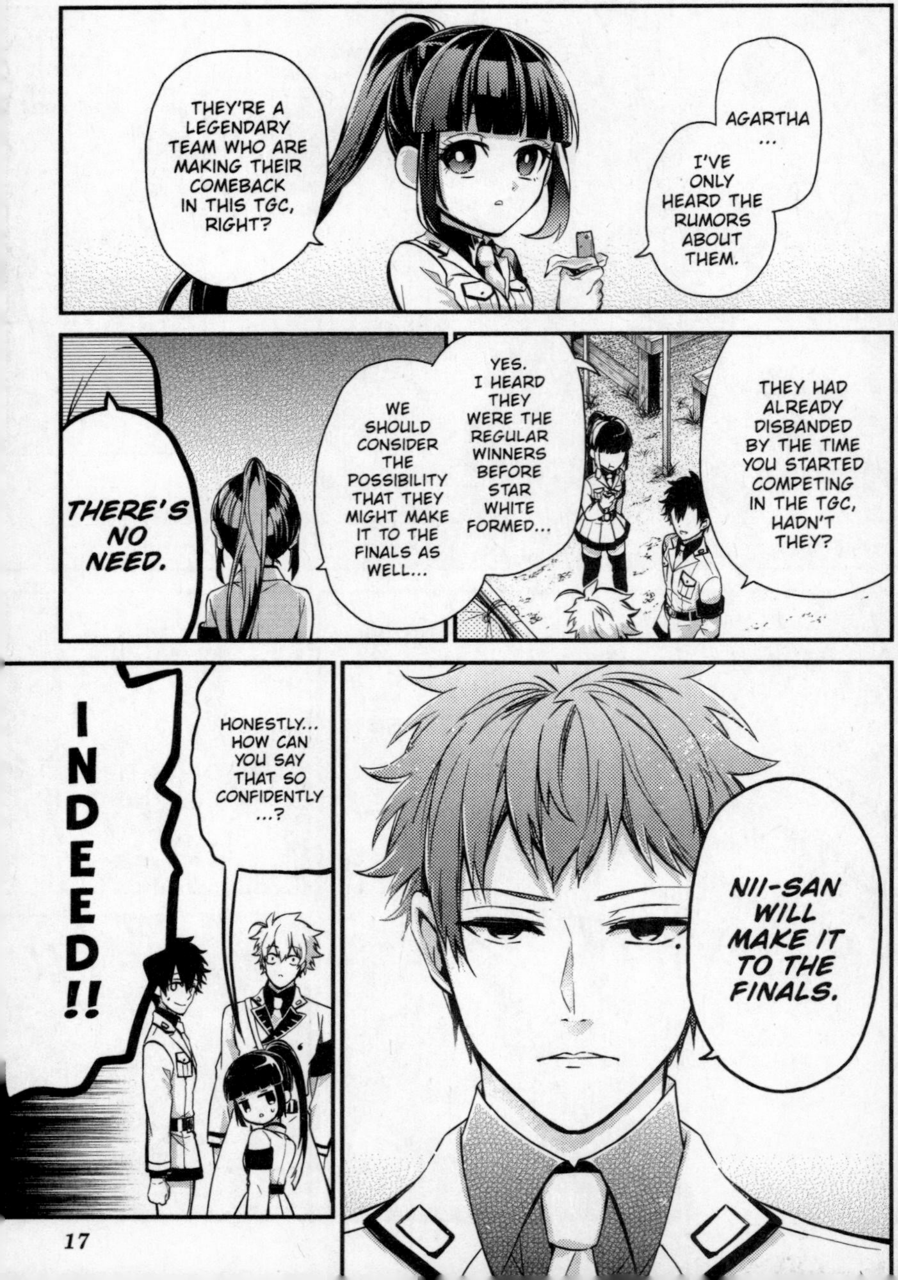
AGARTHA... I'VE ONLY HEARD THE RUMORS ABOUT THEM.
THEY'RE A LEGENDARY TEAM WHO ARE MAKING THEIR COMEBACK IN THIS TGC, RIGHT?
THEY HAD ALREADY DISBANDED BY THE TIME YOU STARTED COMPETING IN THE TGC, HADN'T THEY?
YES. I HEARD THEY WERE THE REGULAR WINNERS BEFORE STAR WHITE FORMED...
WE SHOULD CONSIDER THE POSSIBILITY THAT THEY MIGHT MAKE IT TO THE FINALS AS WELL...
THERE'S NO NEED.
NII-SAN WILL MAKE IT TO THE FINALS.
HONESTLY... HOW CAN YOU SAY THAT SO CONFIDENTLY...?
INDEED!!

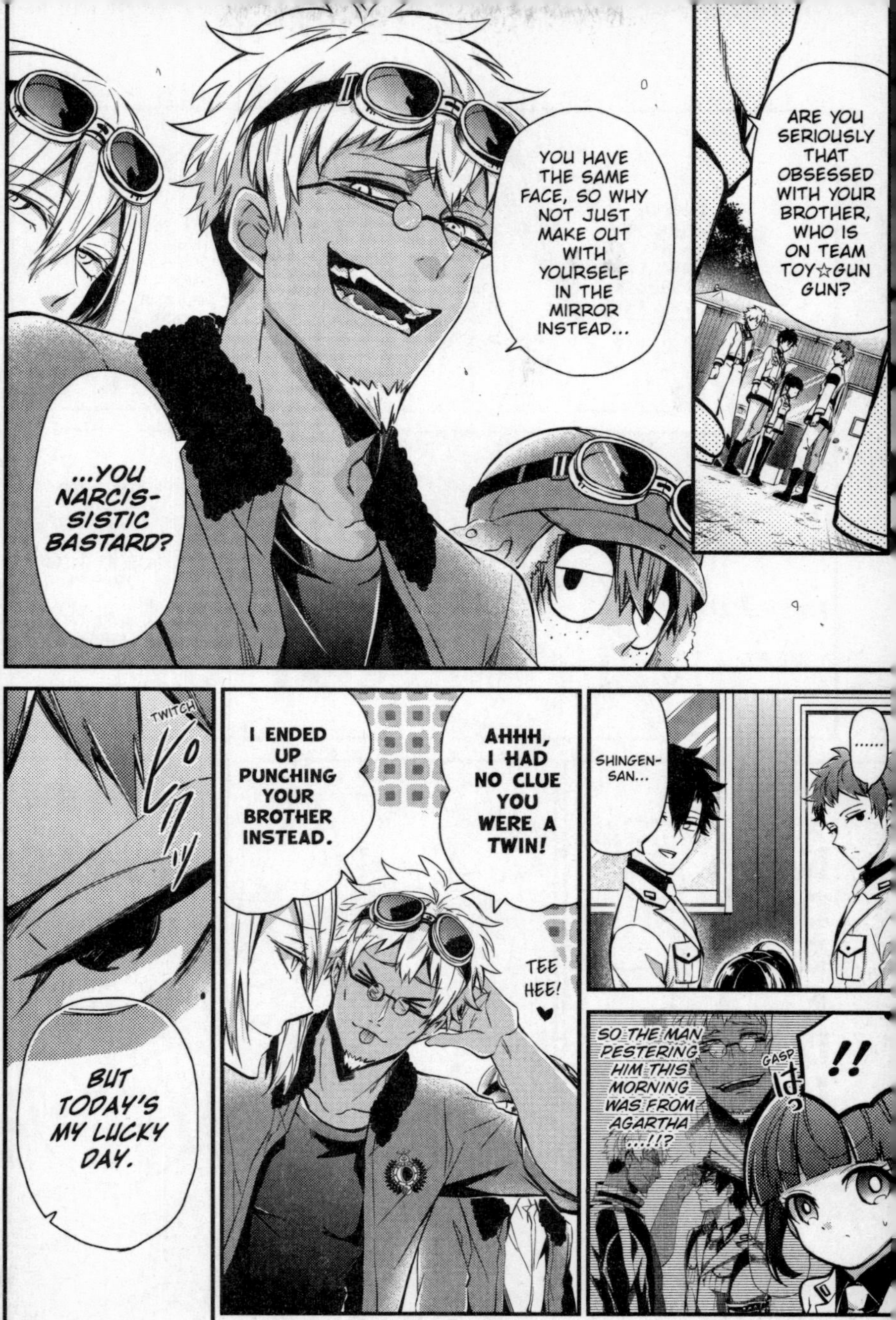
ARE YOU SERIOUSLY THAT OBSESSED WITH YOUR BROTHER, WHO IS ON TEAM TOY☆GUN GUN?
YOU HAVE THE SAME FACE, SO WHY NOT JUST MAKE OUT WITH YOURSELF IN THE MIRROR INSTEAD...
...YOU NARCIS-SISTIC BASTARD?
......
SHINGEN-SAN...
SO THE MAN PESTERING HIM THIS MORNING WAS FROM AGARTHA ...!!?
!!
GASP
はっ
AHHH, I HAD NO CLUE YOU WERE A TWIN!
I ENDED UP PUNCHING YOUR BROTHER INSTEAD.
TEE HEE! ♥
TWITCH
BUT TODAY'S MY LUCKY DAY.

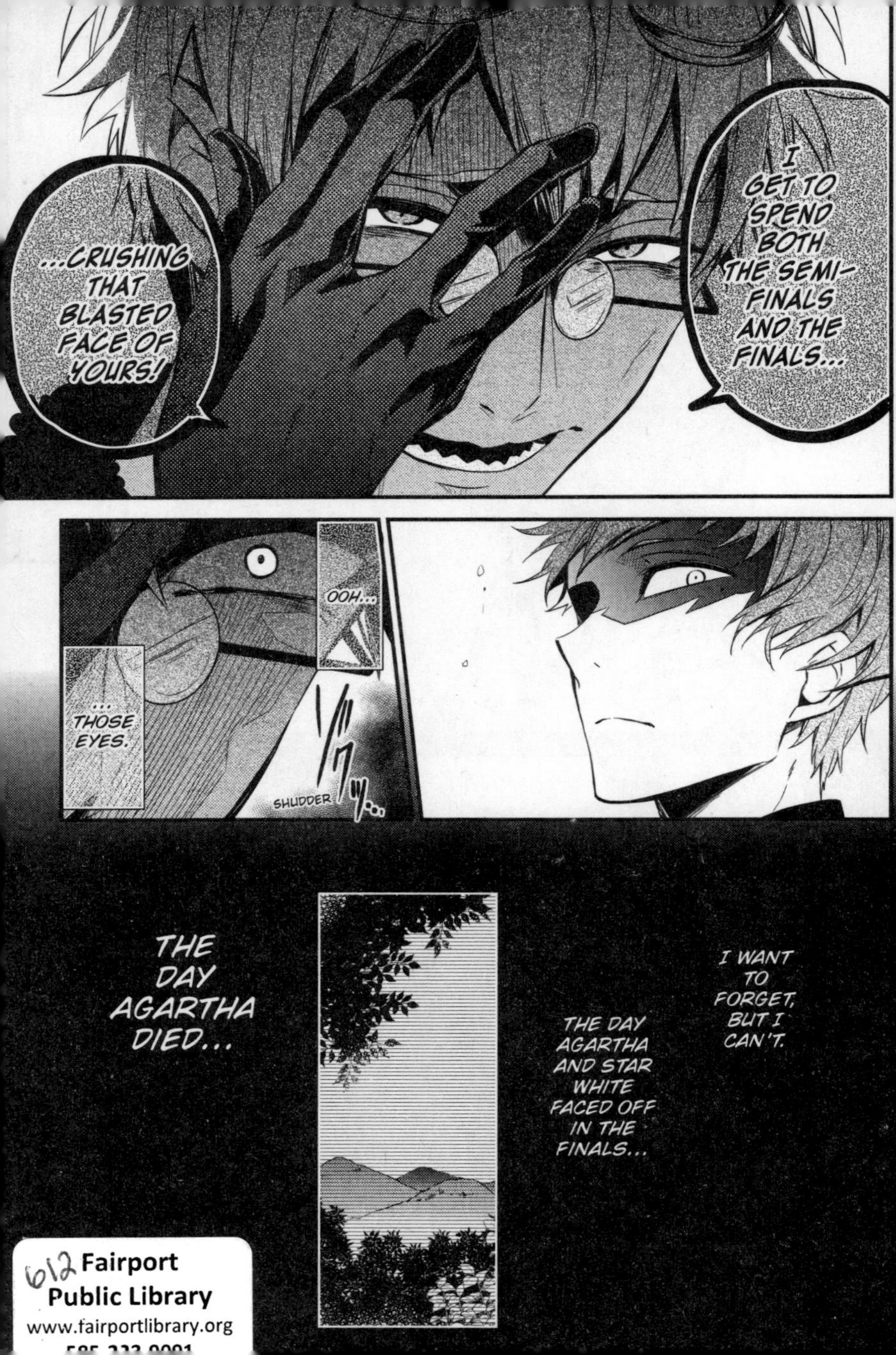
I GET TO SPEND BOTH THE SEMI-FINALS AND THE FINALS...
...CRUSHING THAT BLASTED FACE OF YOURS!
OOH...
...THOSE EYES.
SHUDDER
I WANT TO FORGET, BUT I CAN'T.
THE DAY AGARTHA AND STAR WHITE FACED OFF IN THE FINALS...
THE DAY AGARTHA DIED...

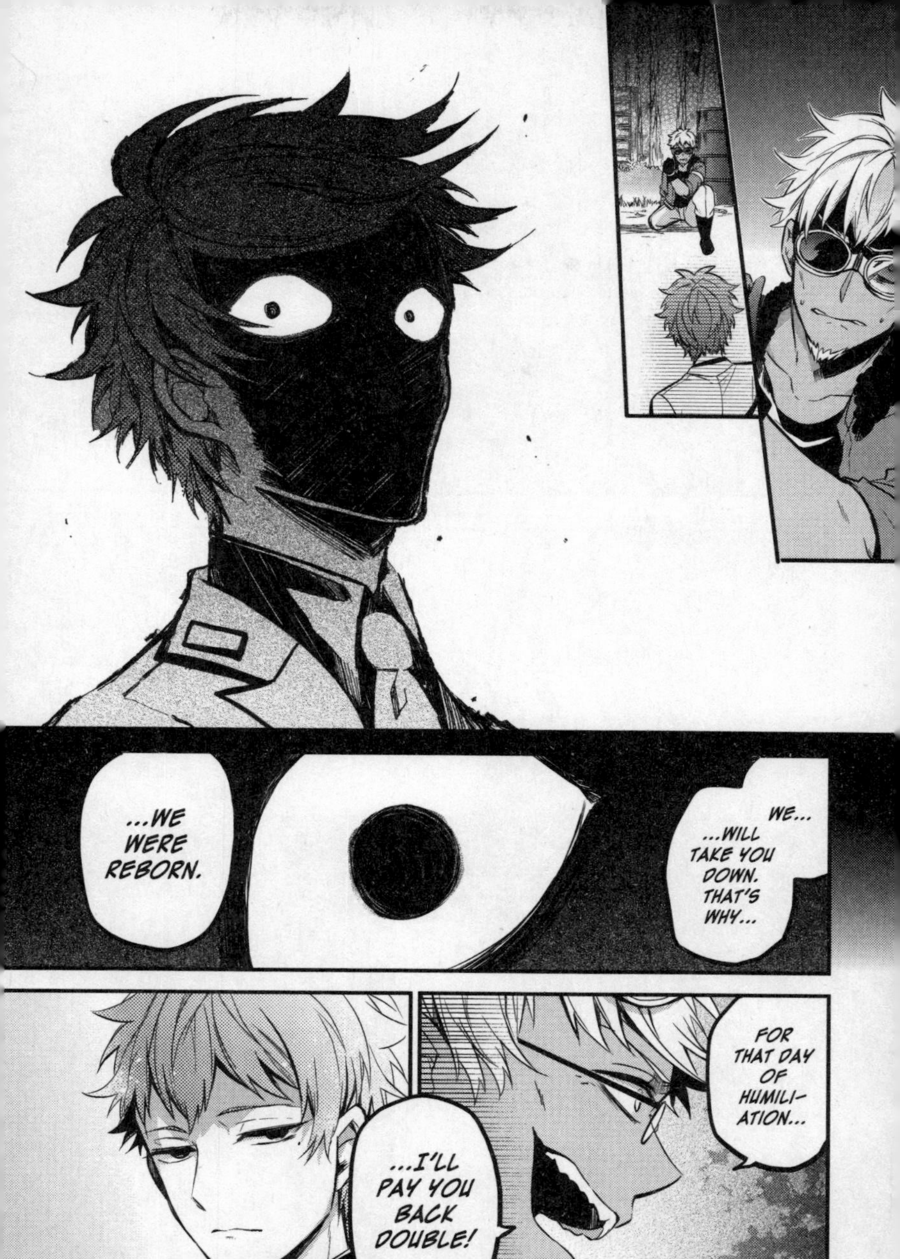
WE... ...WILL TAKE YOU DOWN. THAT'S WHY...
...WE WERE REBORN.
FOR THAT DAY OF HUMILI-ATION...
...I'LL PAY YOU BACK DOUBLE!

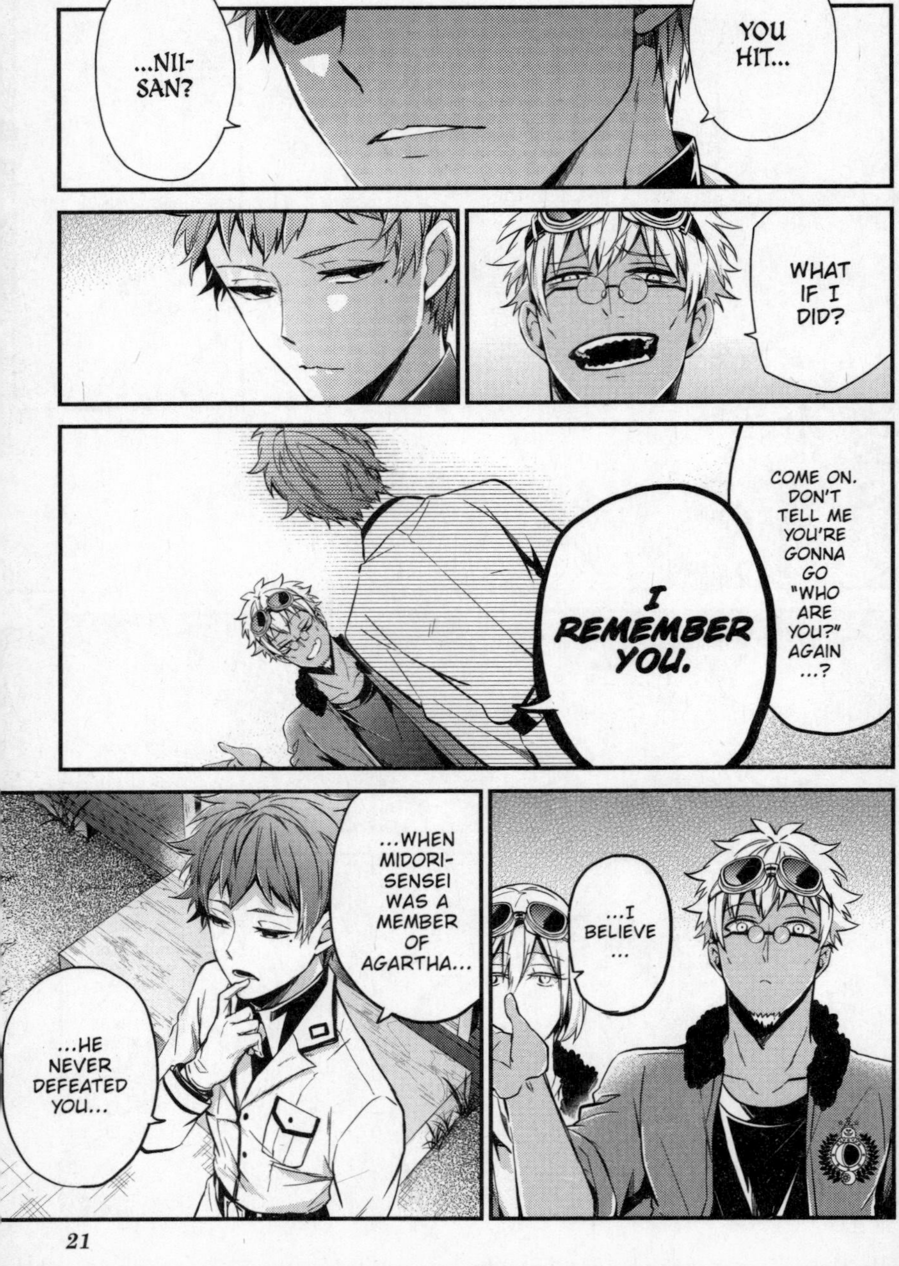
YOU HIT...
...NII-SAN?
WHAT IF I DID?
COME ON. DON'T TELL ME YOU'RE GONNA GO "WHO ARE YOU?" AGAIN ...?
I REMEMBER YOU.
...I BELIEVE ...
...WHEN MIDORI-SENSEI WAS A MEMBER OF AGARTHA...
...HE NEVER DEFEATED YOU...

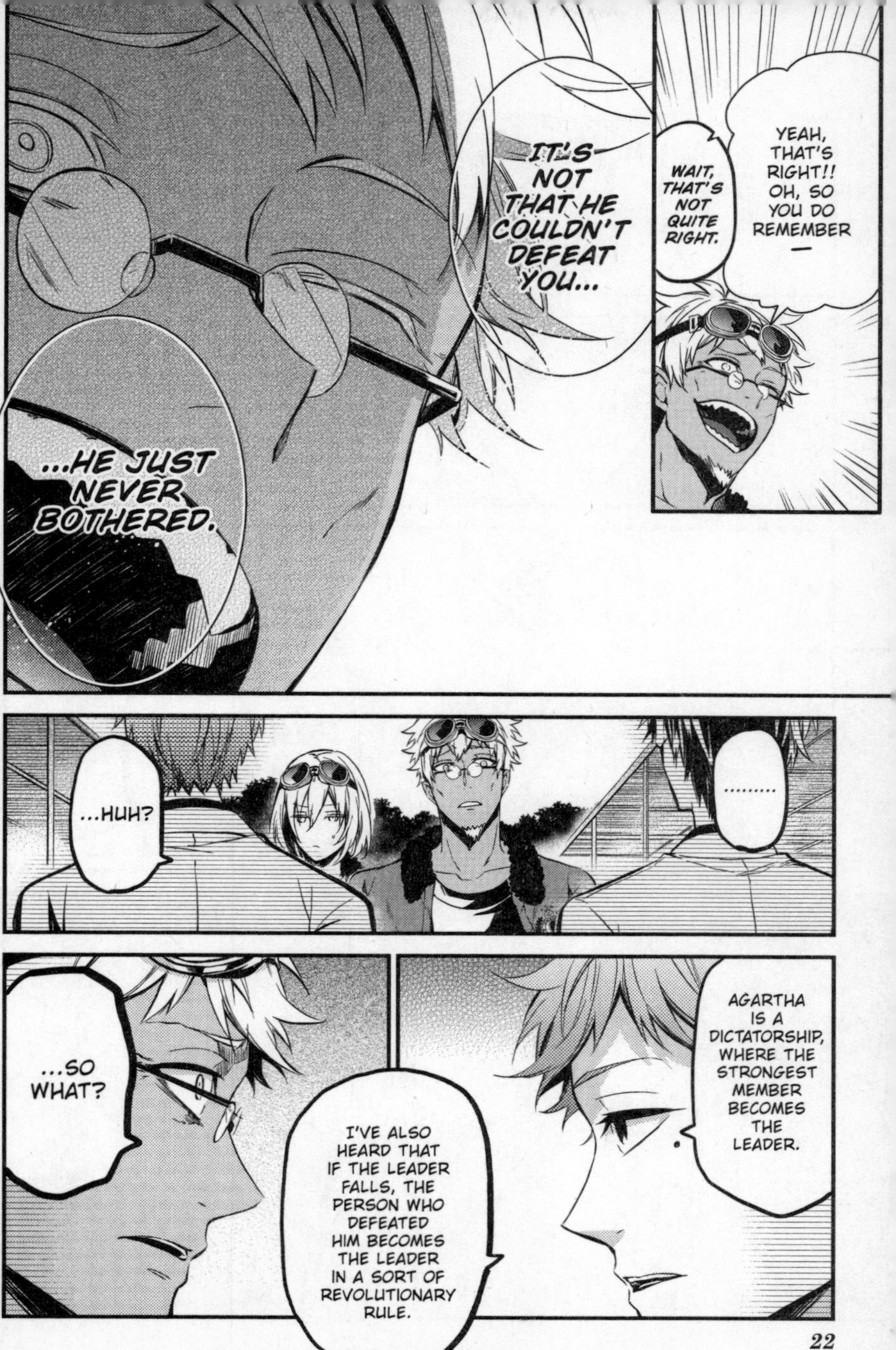
YEAH, THAT'S RIGHT!! OH, SO YOU DO REMEMBER—
WAIT, THAT'S NOT QUITE RIGHT.
IT'S NOT THAT HE COULDN'T DEFEAT YOU...
...HE JUST NEVER BOTHERED.
....
...HUH?
AGARTHA IS A DICTATORSHIP, WHERE THE STRONGEST MEMBER BECOMES THE LEADER.
I'VE ALSO HEARD THAT IF THE LEADER FALLS, THE PERSON WHO DEFEATED HIM BECOMES THE LEADER IN A SORT OF REVOLUTIONARY RULE.
...SO WHAT?

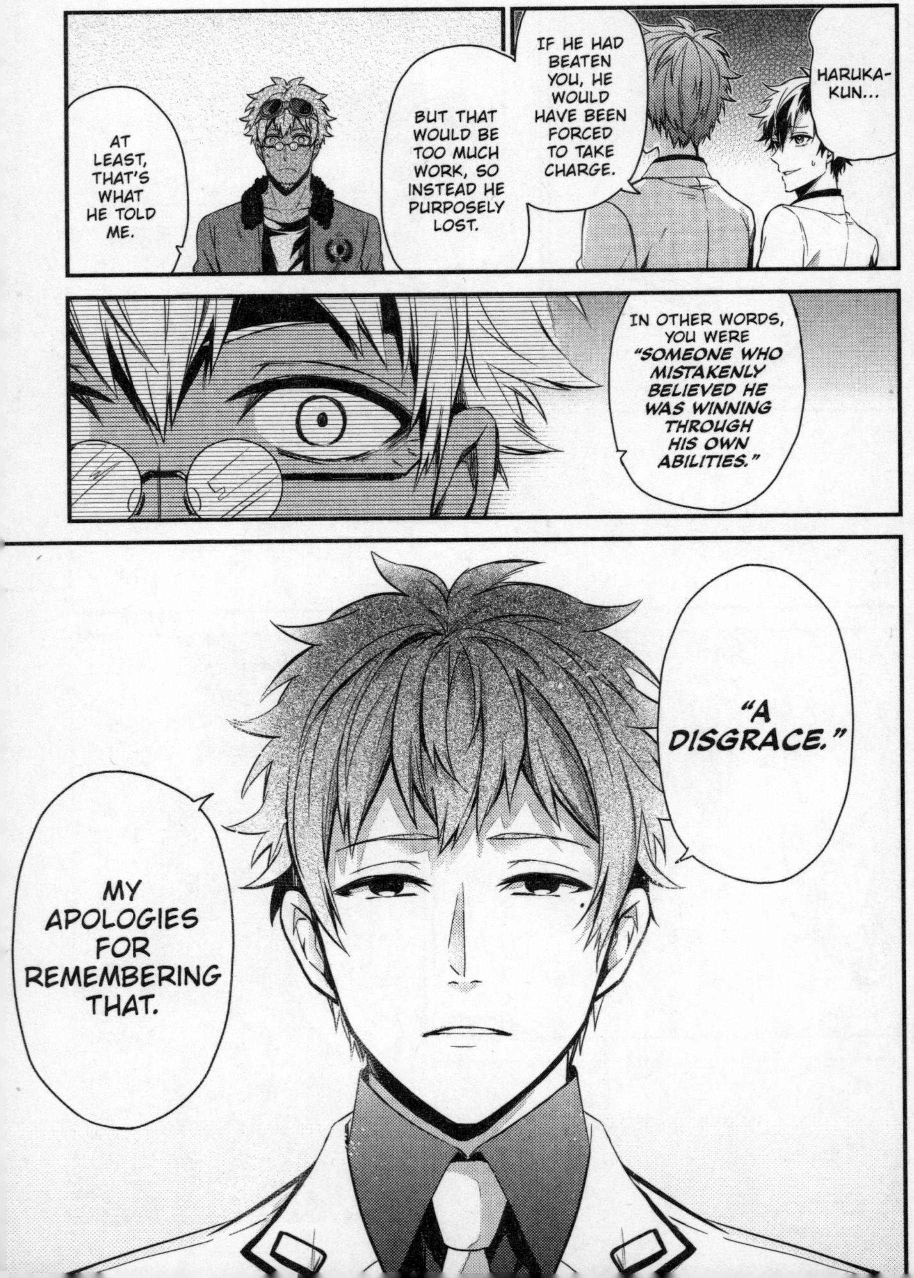
HARUKA-KUN...
IF HE HAD BEATEN YOU, HE WOULD HAVE BEEN FORCED TO TAKE CHARGE.
BUT THAT WOULD BE TOO MUCH WORK, SO INSTEAD HE PURPOSELY LOST.
AT LEAST, THAT'S WHAT HE TOLD ME.
IN OTHER WORDS, YOU WERE *"SOMEONE WHO MISTAKENLY BELIEVED HE WAS WINNING THROUGH HIS OWN ABILITIES."*
"A DISGRACE."
MY APOLOGIES FOR REMEMBERING THAT.

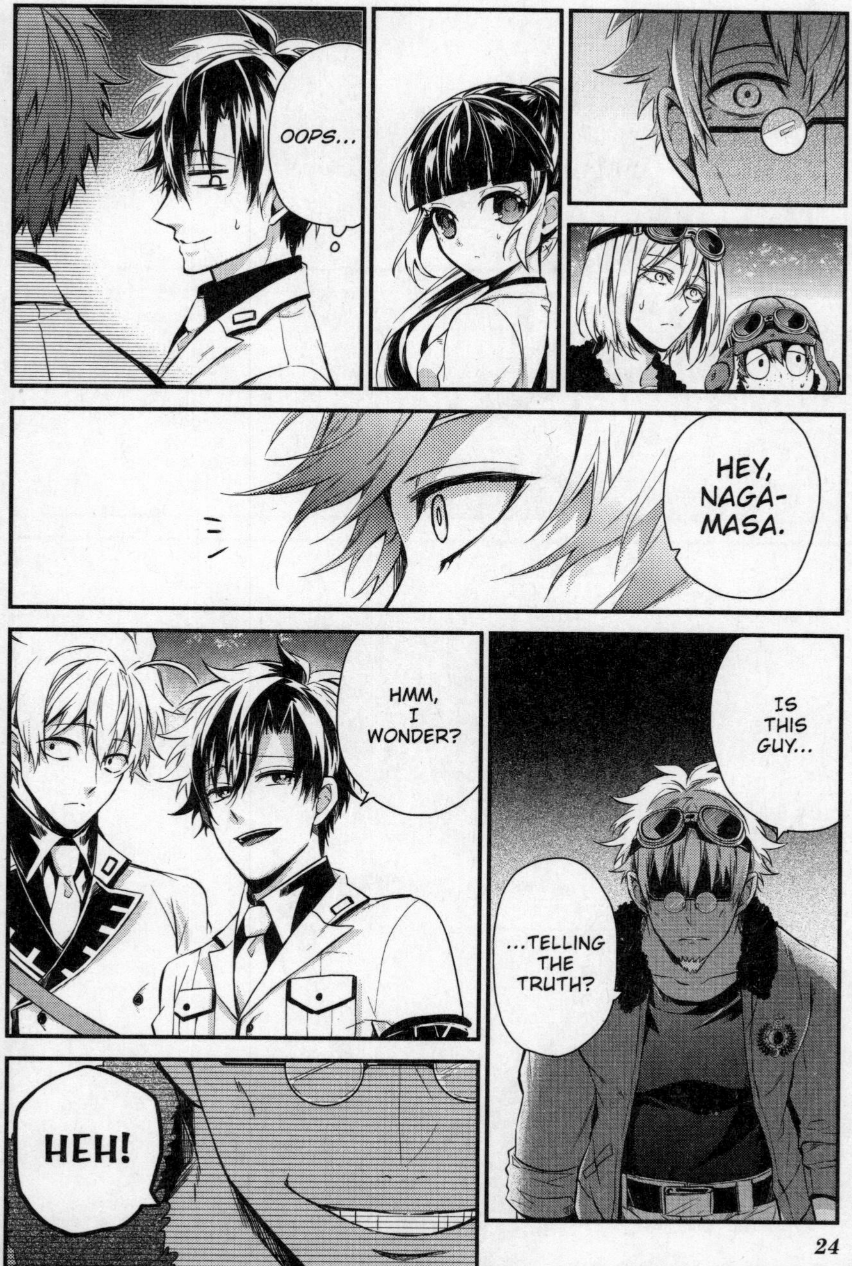
OOPS...
HEY, NAGA-MASA.
IS THIS GUY...
...TELLING THE TRUTH?
HMM, I WONDER?
HEH!

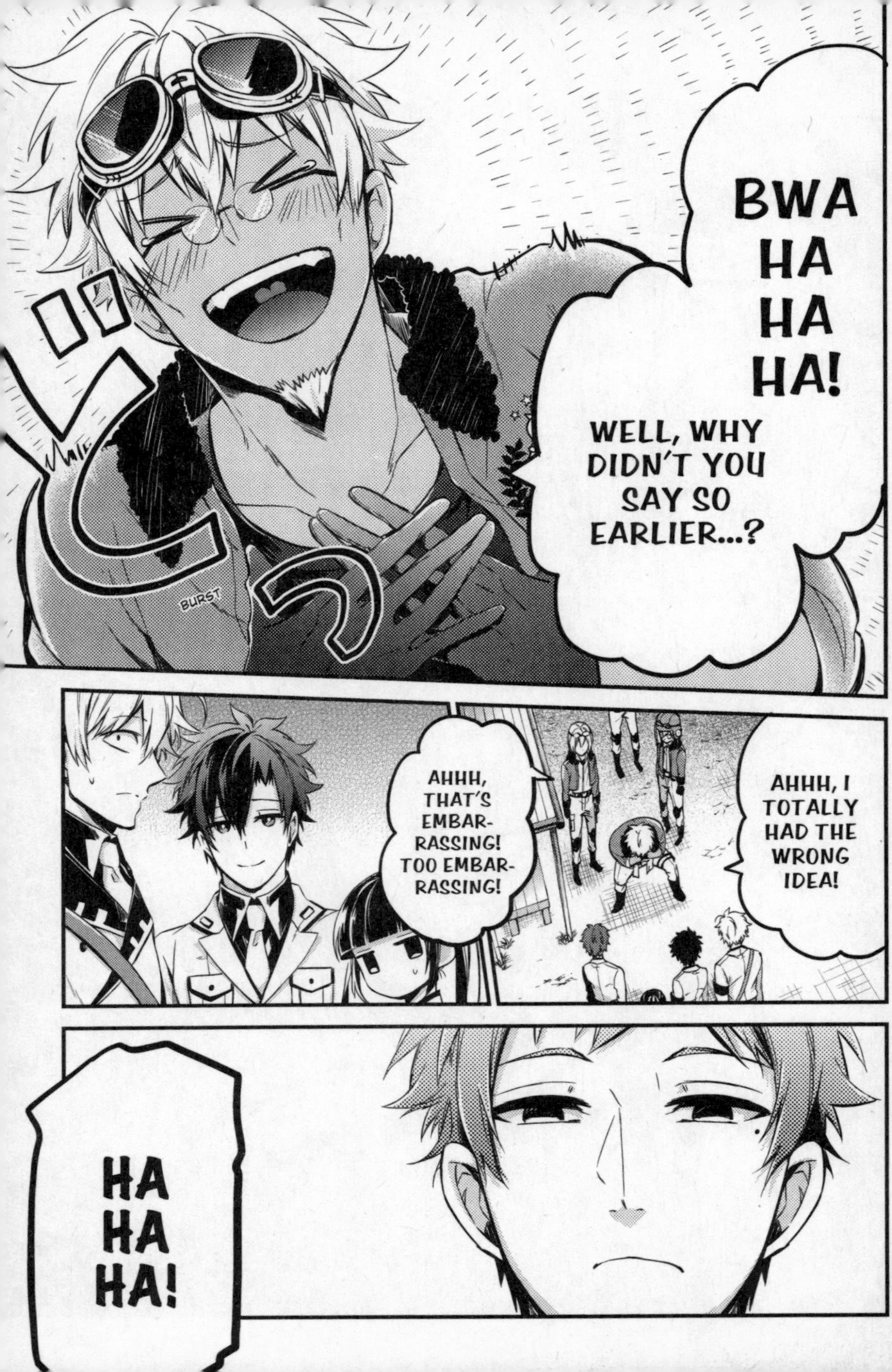
BWA HA HA HA!
WELL, WHY DIDN'T YOU SAY SO EARLIER...?
BURST
AHHH, I TOTALLY HAD THE WRONG IDEA!
AHHH, THAT'S EMBAR-RASSING! TOO EMBAR-RASSING!
HA HA HA!

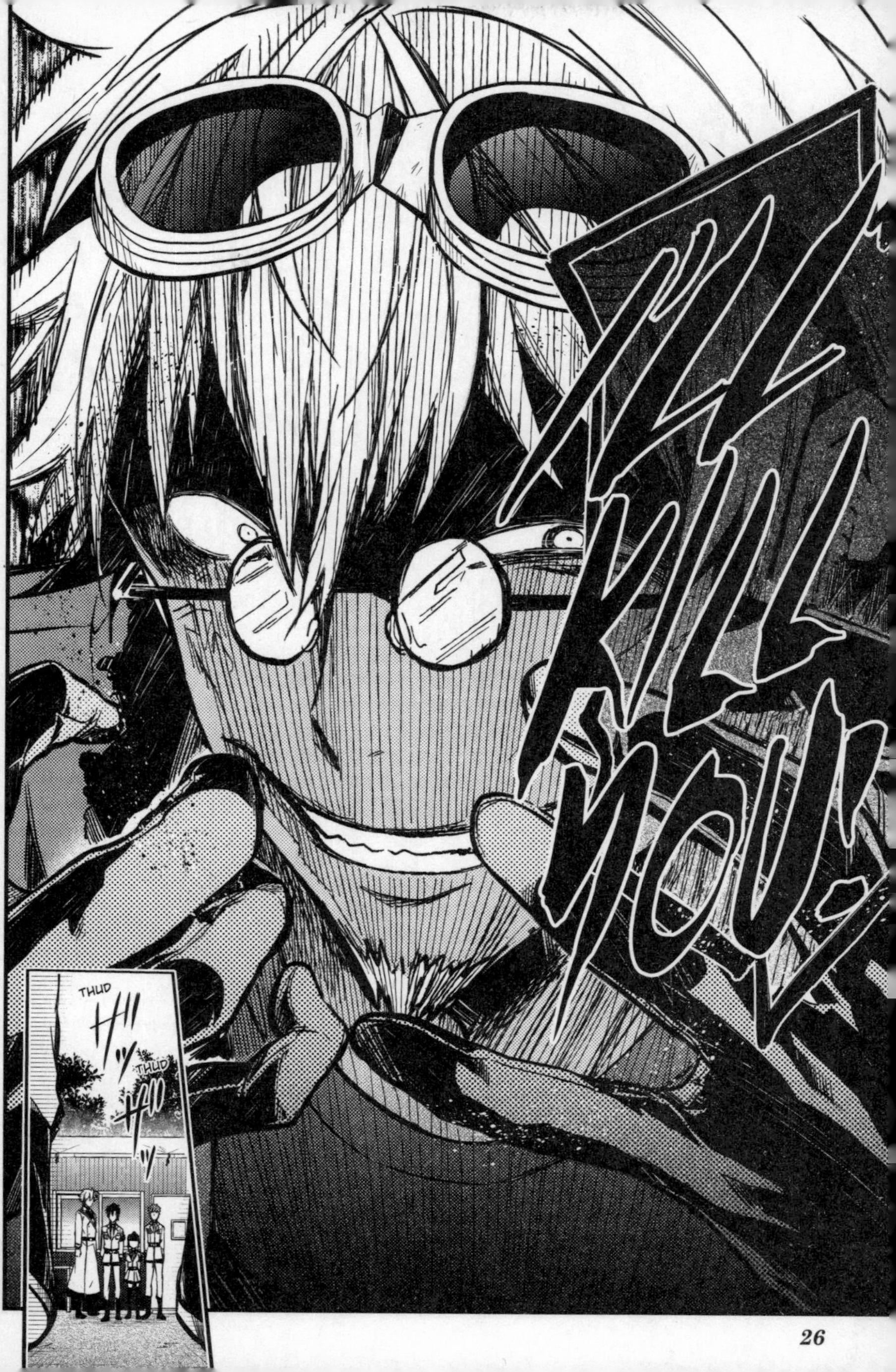
I'LL KILL YOU!
THUD
THUD

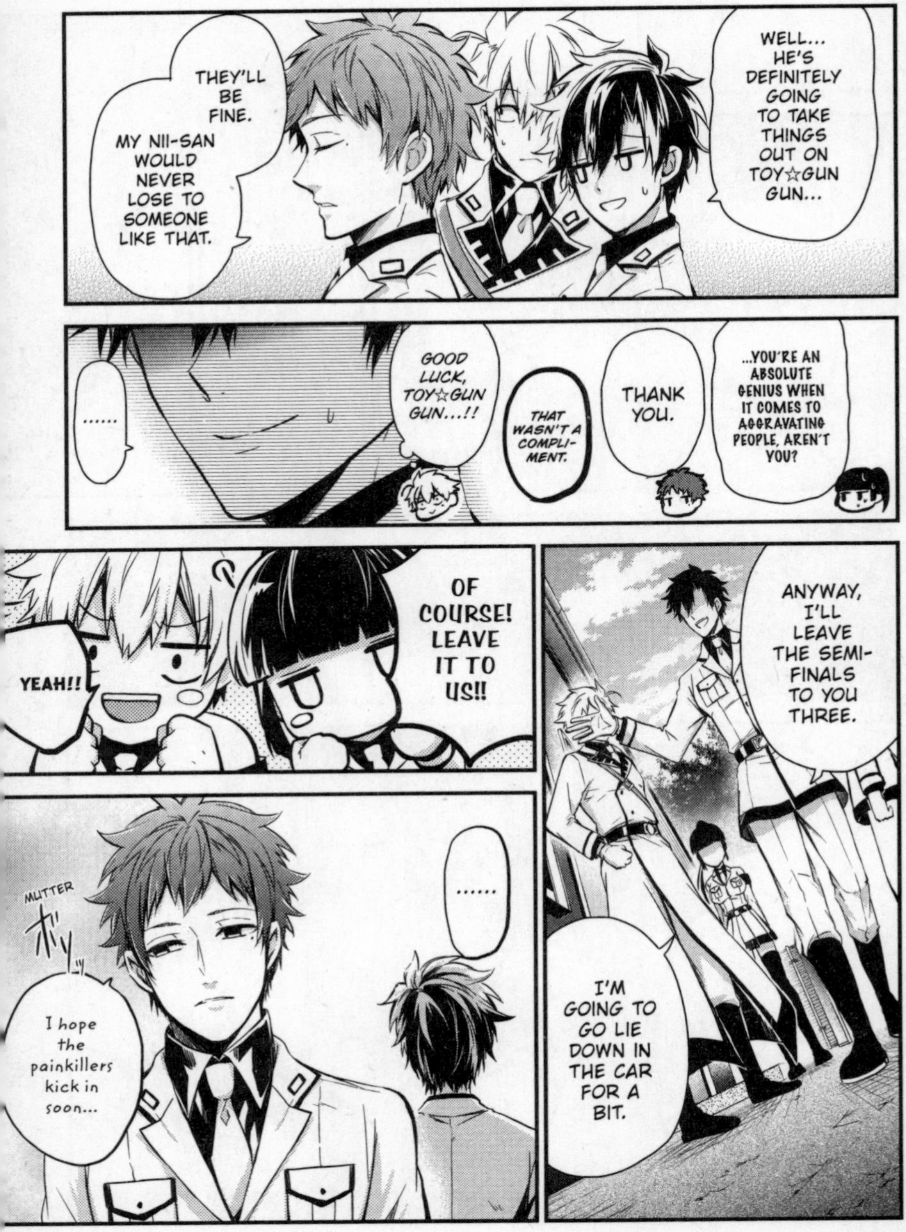
WELL... HE'S DEFINITELY GOING TO TAKE THINGS OUT ON TOY☆GUN GUN...
THEY'LL BE FINE.
MY NII-SAN WOULD NEVER LOSE TO SOMEONE LIKE THAT.
...YOU'RE AN ABSOLUTE GENIUS WHEN IT COMES TO AGGRAVATING PEOPLE, AREN'T YOU?
THANK YOU.
THAT WASN'T A COMPLIMENT.
GOOD LUCK, TOY☆GUN GUN...!!
......
ANYWAY, I'LL LEAVE THE SEMI-FINALS TO YOU THREE.
I'M GOING TO GO LIE DOWN IN THE CAR FOR A BIT.
OF COURSE! LEAVE IT TO US!!
YEAH!!
......
MUTTER
ボソッ
I hope the painkillers kick in soon...

SLIDE
ズル...

......

PANT
はっ...

You went
a little too
far there,
Haruka-kun
...

...Oww.

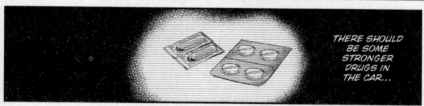

THERE SHOULD
BE SOME
STRONGER
DRUGS IN
THE CAR...

I'LL
HAVE TO
TAKE
ANOTHER
DOSE...

MIDORI-
SAN?

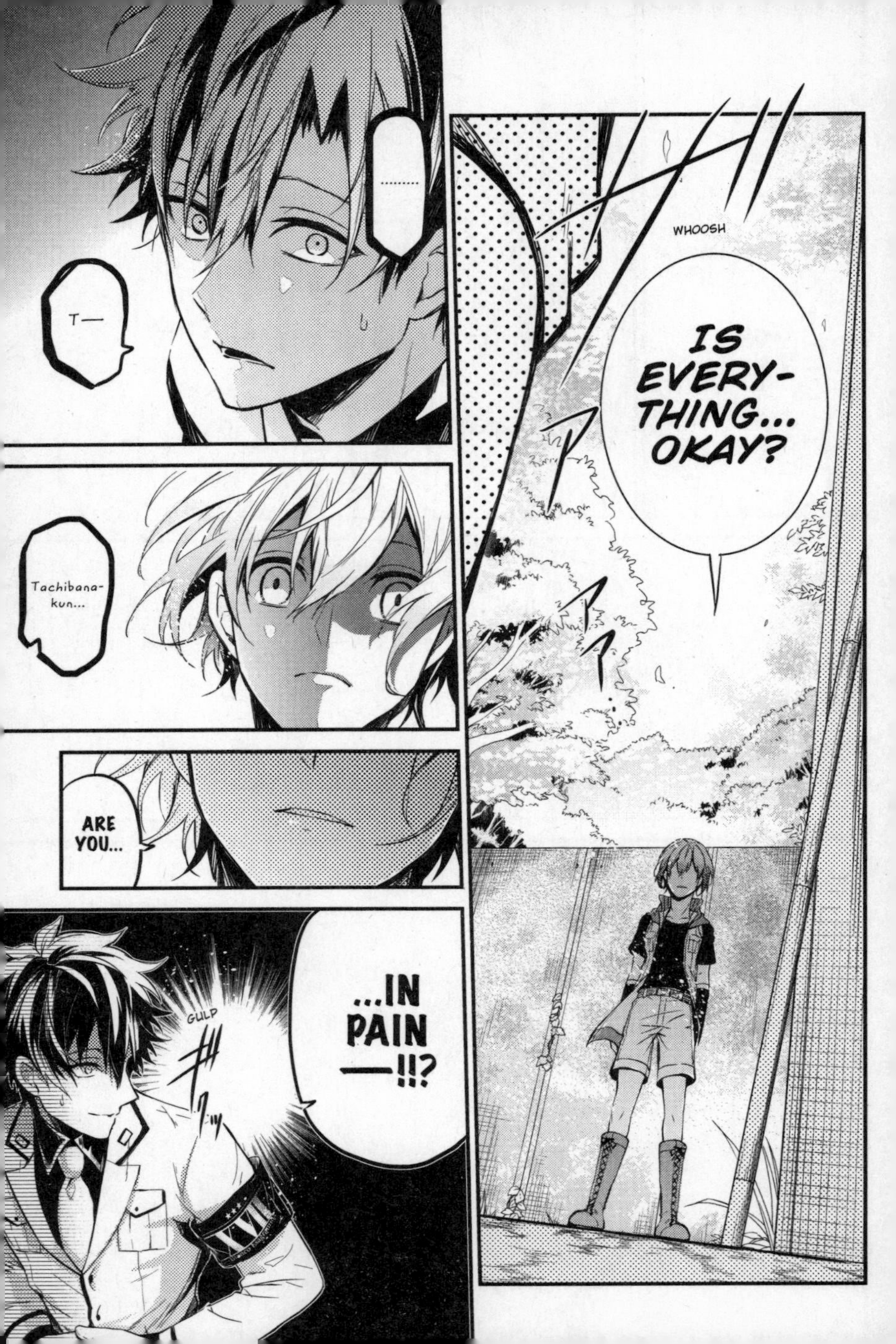
WHOOSH
IS EVERY-THING... OKAY?
......
T—
Tachibana-kun...
ARE YOU...
...IN PAIN—!!?
GULP

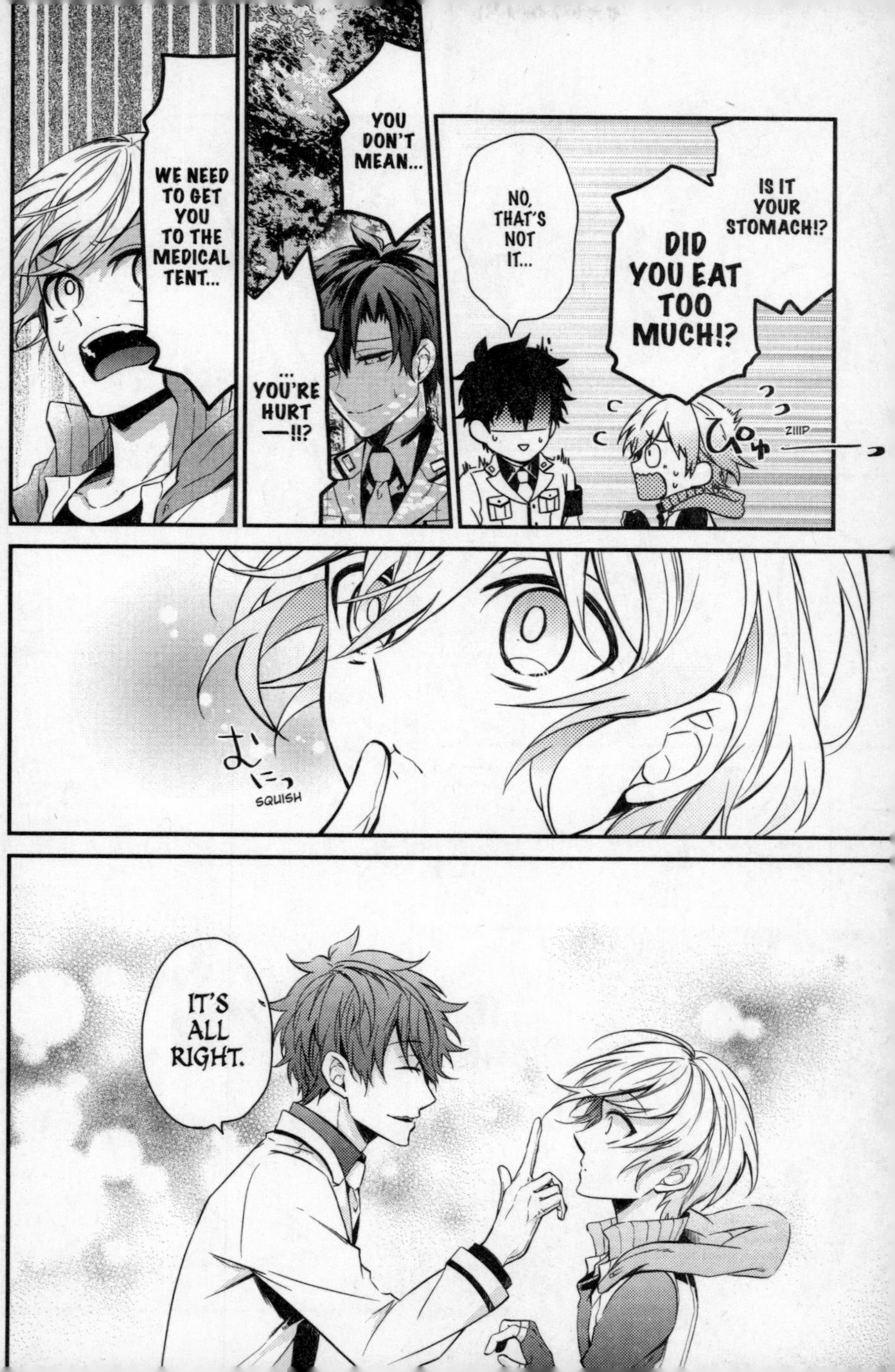
IS IT YOUR STOMACH!?
DID YOU EAT TOO MUCH!?
NO, THAT'S NOT IT...
ZIIIP
YOU DON'T MEAN...
...YOU'RE HURT—!!?
WE NEED TO GET YOU TO THE MEDICAL TENT...
SQUISH
IT'S ALL RIGHT.

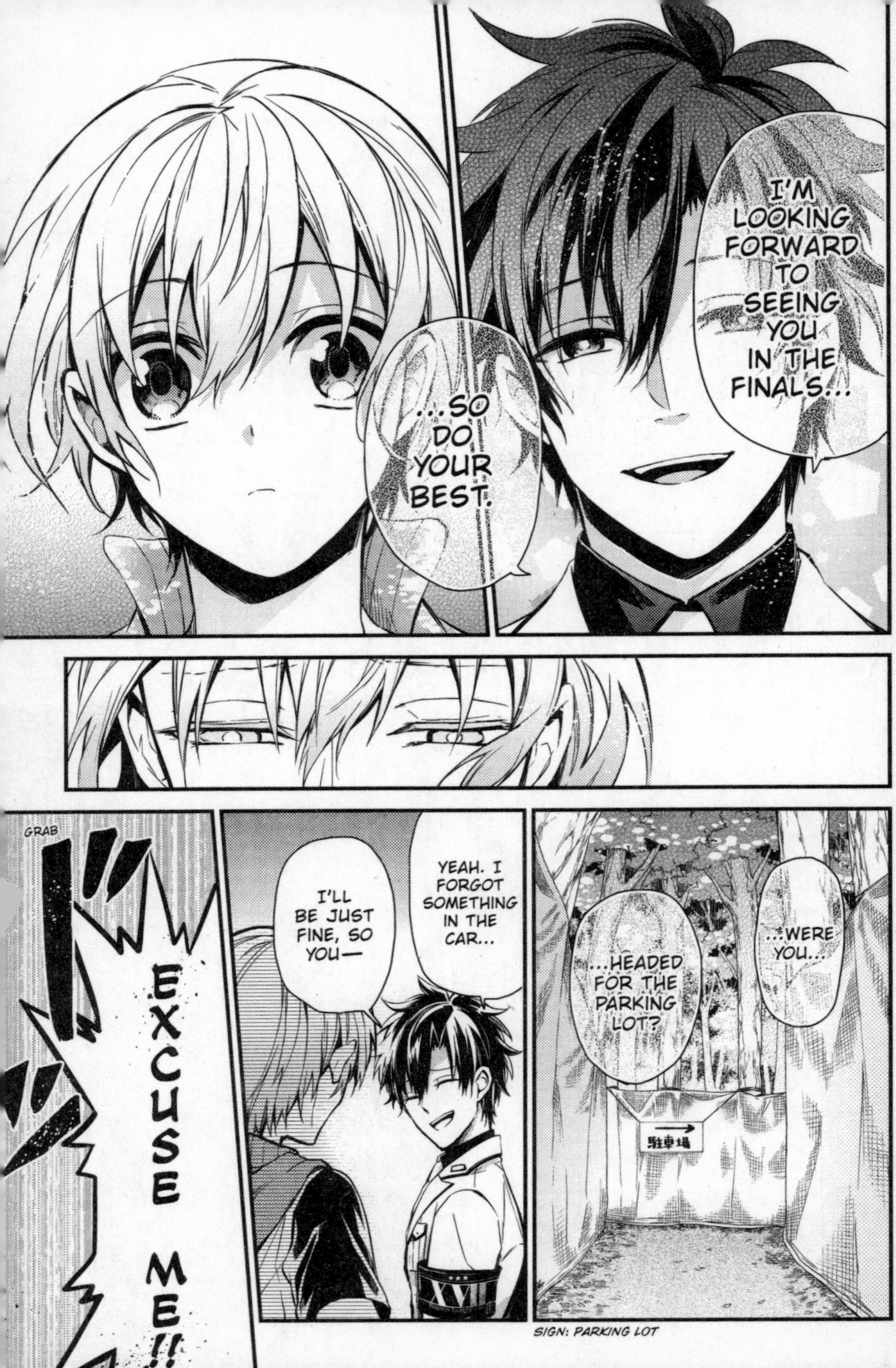
I'M LOOKING FORWARD TO SEEING YOU IN THE FINALS...
...SO DO YOUR BEST.
...WERE YOU...
...HEADED FOR THE PARKING LOT?
駐車場
YEAH. I FORGOT SOMETHING IN THE CAR...
I'LL BE JUST FINE, SO YOU—
GRAB
EXCUSE ME!!

SIGN: PARKING LOT

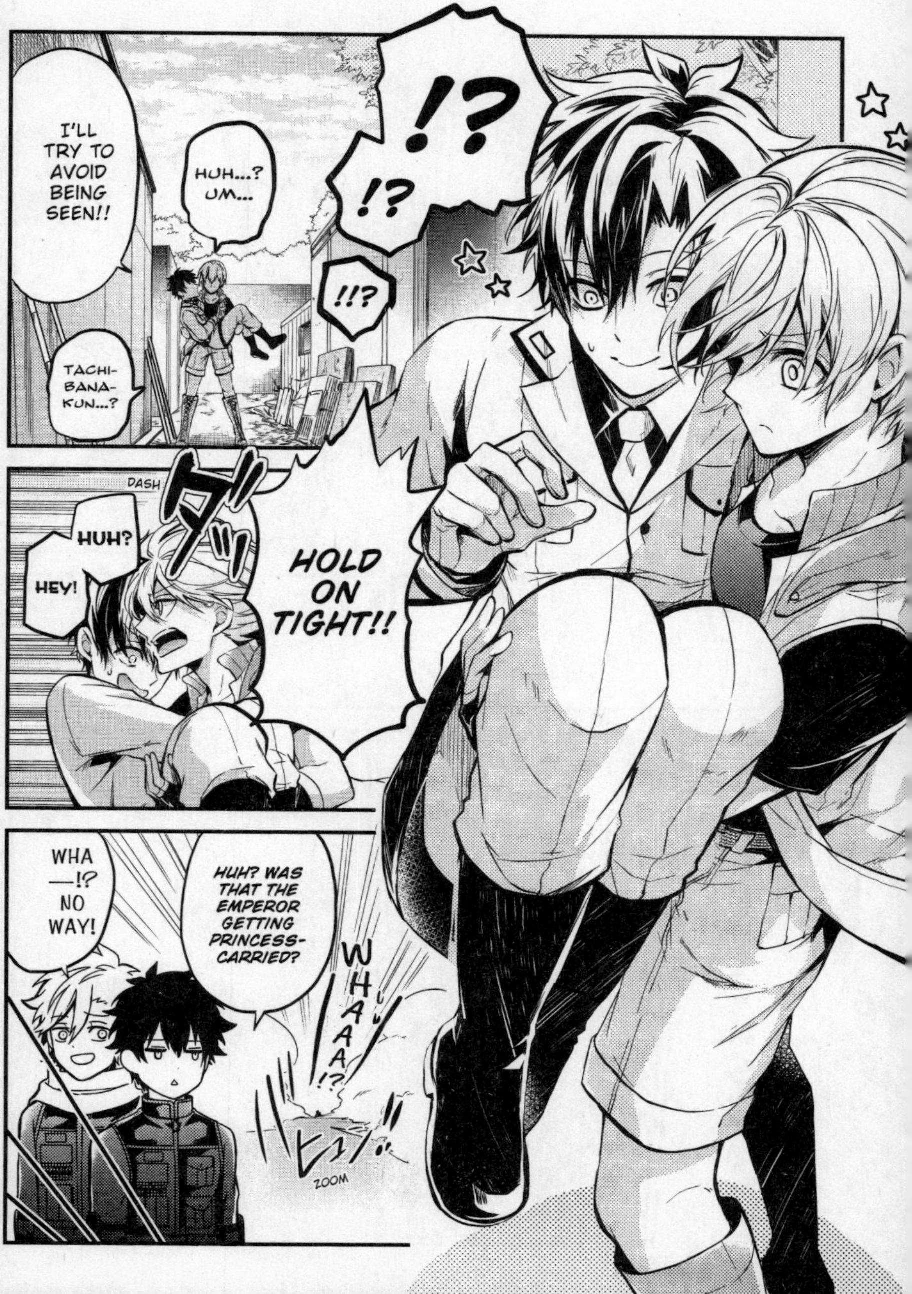
!?
!?
!!?
HOLD ON TIGHT!!
I'LL TRY TO AVOID BEING SEEN!!
HUH...? UM...
TACHIBANA-KUN...?
DASH
HUH?
HEY!
HUH? WAS THAT THE EMPEROR GETTING PRINCESS-CARRIED?
WHA—!? NO WAY!
WHAAAA!?
ZOOM

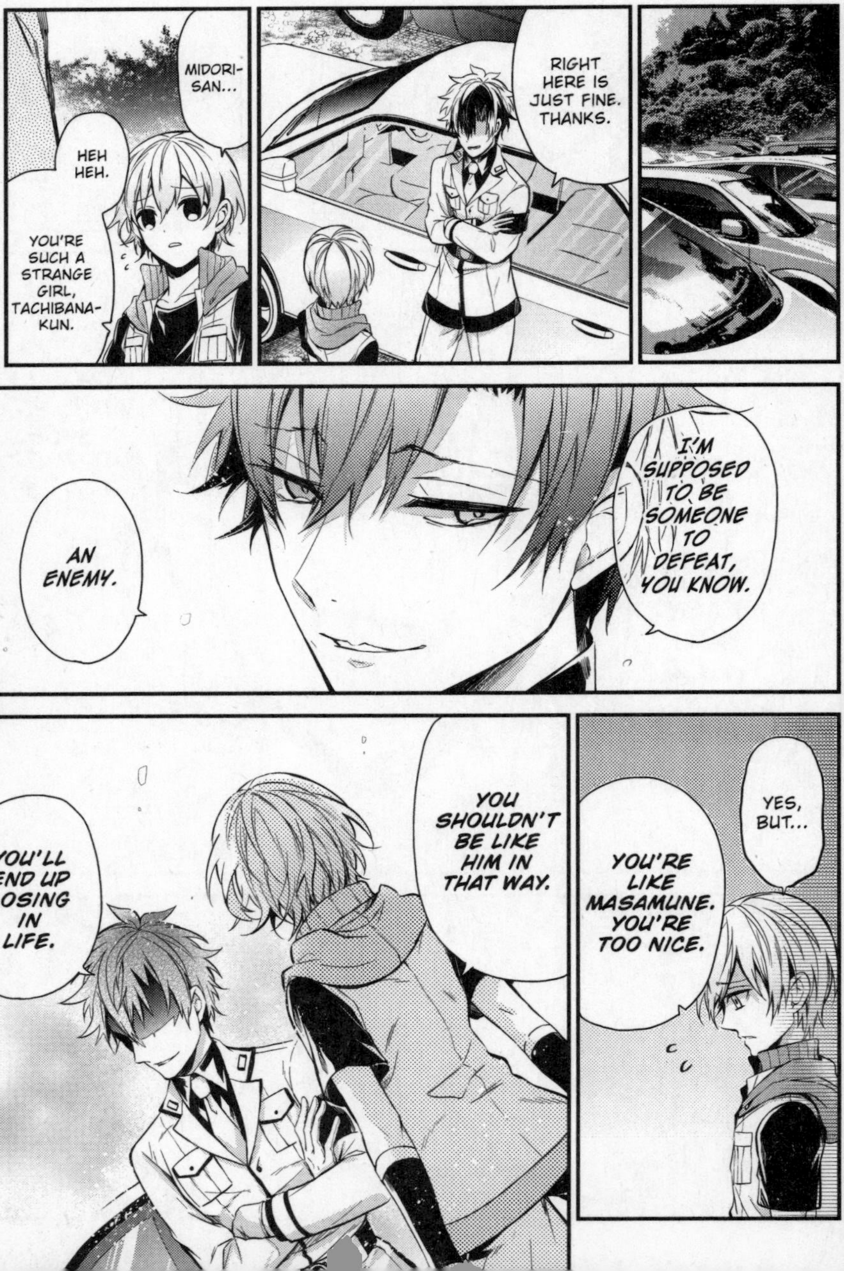
RIGHT HERE IS JUST FINE. THANKS.
MIDORI-SAN...
HEH HEH.
YOU'RE SUCH A STRANGE GIRL, TACHIBANA-KUN.
I'M SUPPOSED TO BE SOMEONE TO DEFEAT, YOU KNOW.
AN ENEMY.
YES, BUT...
YOU'RE LIKE MASAMUNE. YOU'RE TOO NICE.
YOU SHOULDN'T BE LIKE HIM IN THAT WAY.
YOU'LL END UP LOSING IN LIFE.

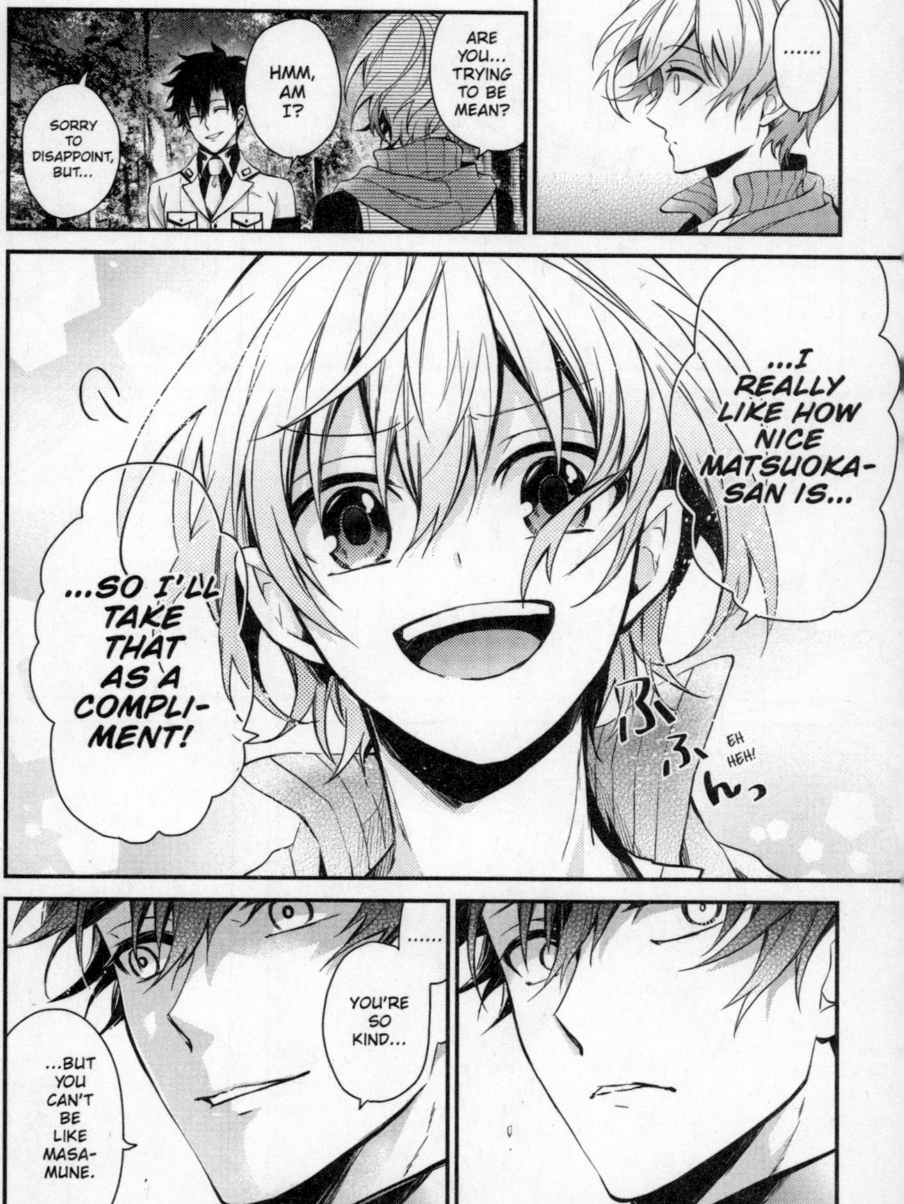
……
ARE YOU... TRYING TO BE MEAN?
HMM, AM I?
SORRY TO DISAPPOINT, BUT...
...I REALLY LIKE HOW NICE MATSUOKA-SAN IS...
...SO I'LL TAKE THAT AS A COMPLIMENT!
ふふんっ
EH HEH!
……
YOU'RE SO KIND...
...BUT YOU CAN'T BE LIKE MASAMUNE.

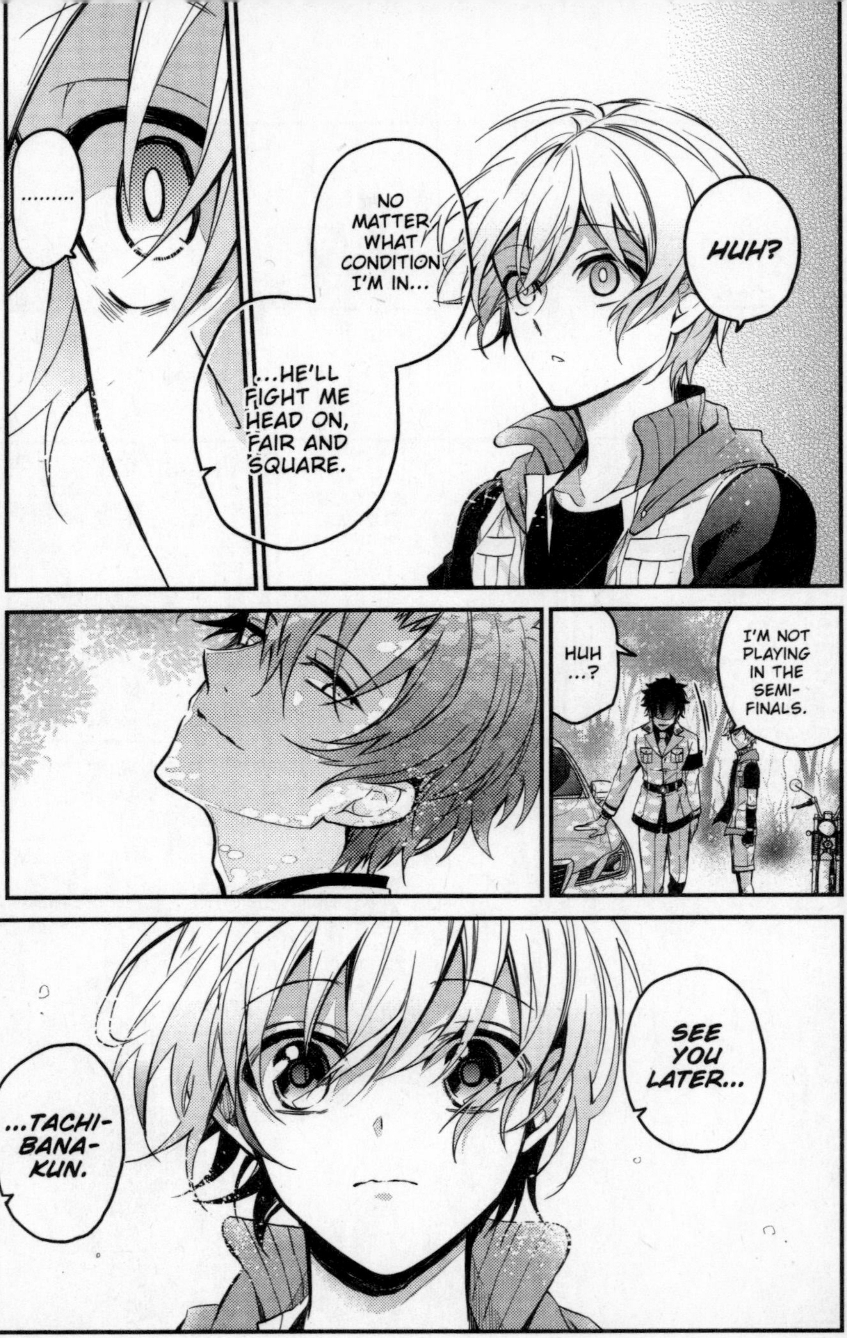
HUH?
NO MATTER WHAT CONDITION I'M IN...
...HE'LL FIGHT ME HEAD ON, FAIR AND SQUARE.
....
I'M NOT PLAYING IN THE SEMI-FINALS.
HUH ...?
SEE YOU LATER...
...TACHI-BANA-KUN.

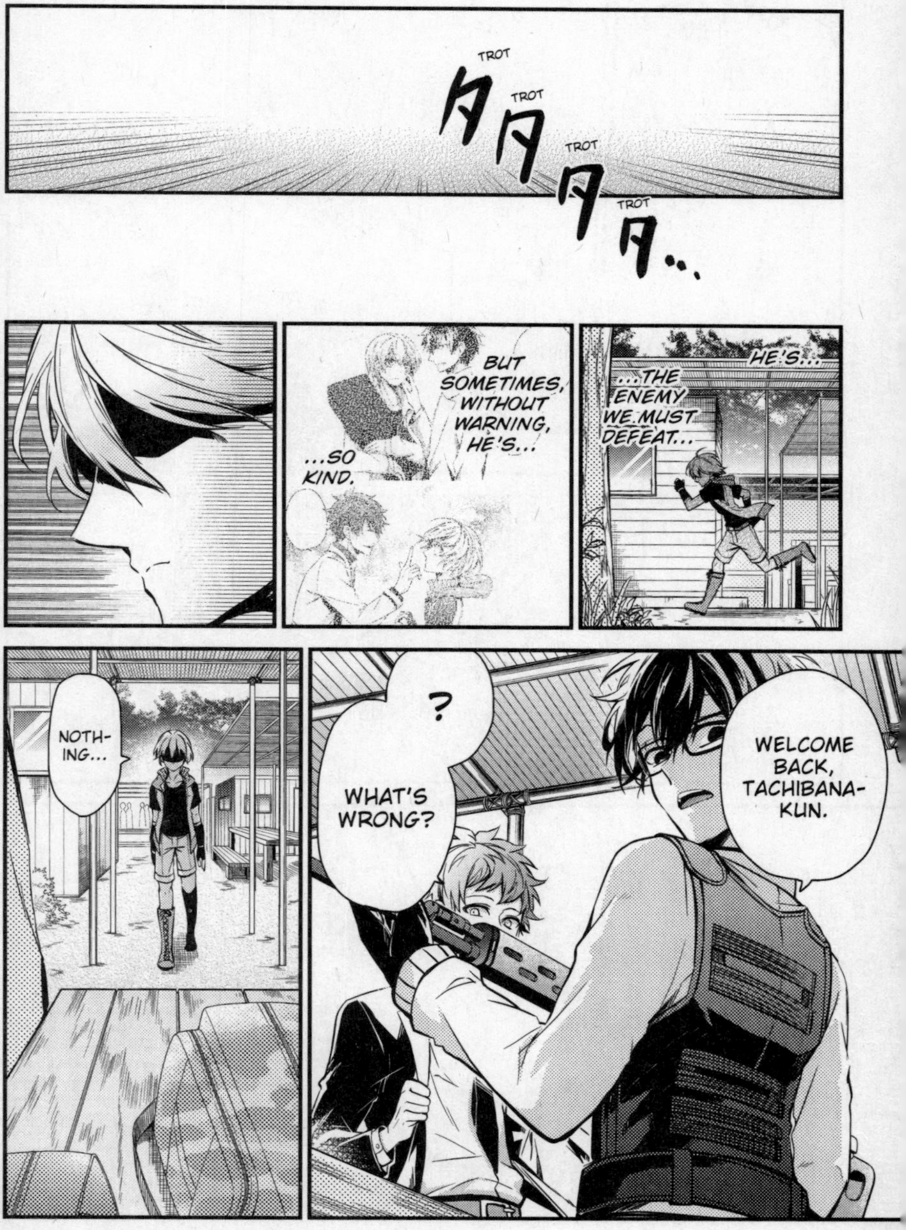
TROT
TROT
TROT
TROT
タタタタ…
HE'S...
...THE ENEMY WE MUST DEFEAT...
BUT SOMETIMES, WITHOUT WARNING, HE'S...
...SO KIND.
WELCOME BACK, TACHIBANA-KUN.
?
WHAT'S WRONG?
NOTH-ING...

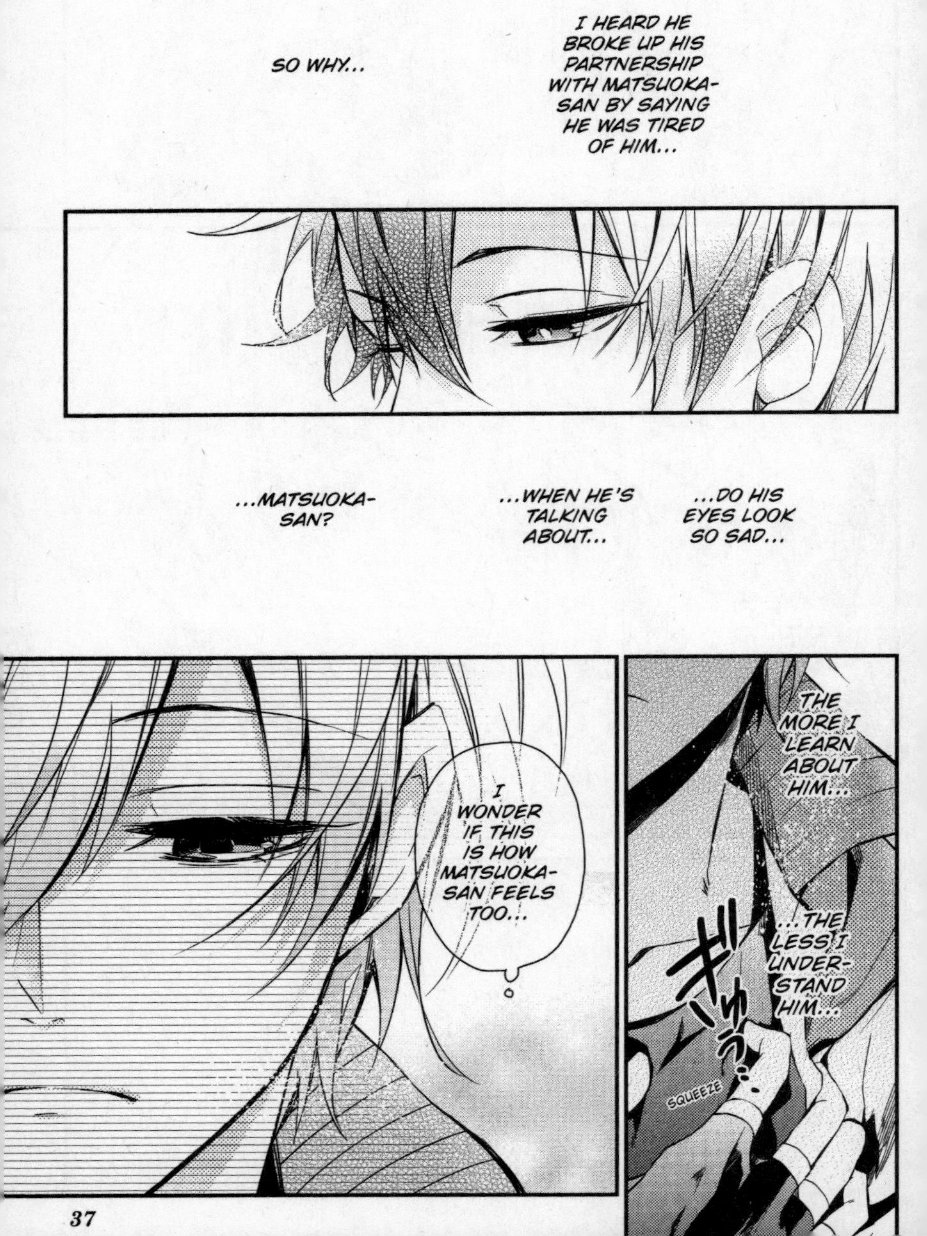
I HEARD HE BROKE UP HIS PARTNERSHIP WITH MATSUOKA-SAN BY SAYING HE WAS TIRED OF HIM...
SO WHY...
...DO HIS EYES LOOK SO SAD...
...WHEN HE'S TALKING ABOUT...
...MATSUOKA-SAN?
THE MORE I LEARN ABOUT HIM...
...THE LESS I UNDER-STAND HIM...
ぎゅう
SQUEEZE
I WONDER IF THIS IS HOW MATSUOKA-SAN FEELS TOO...

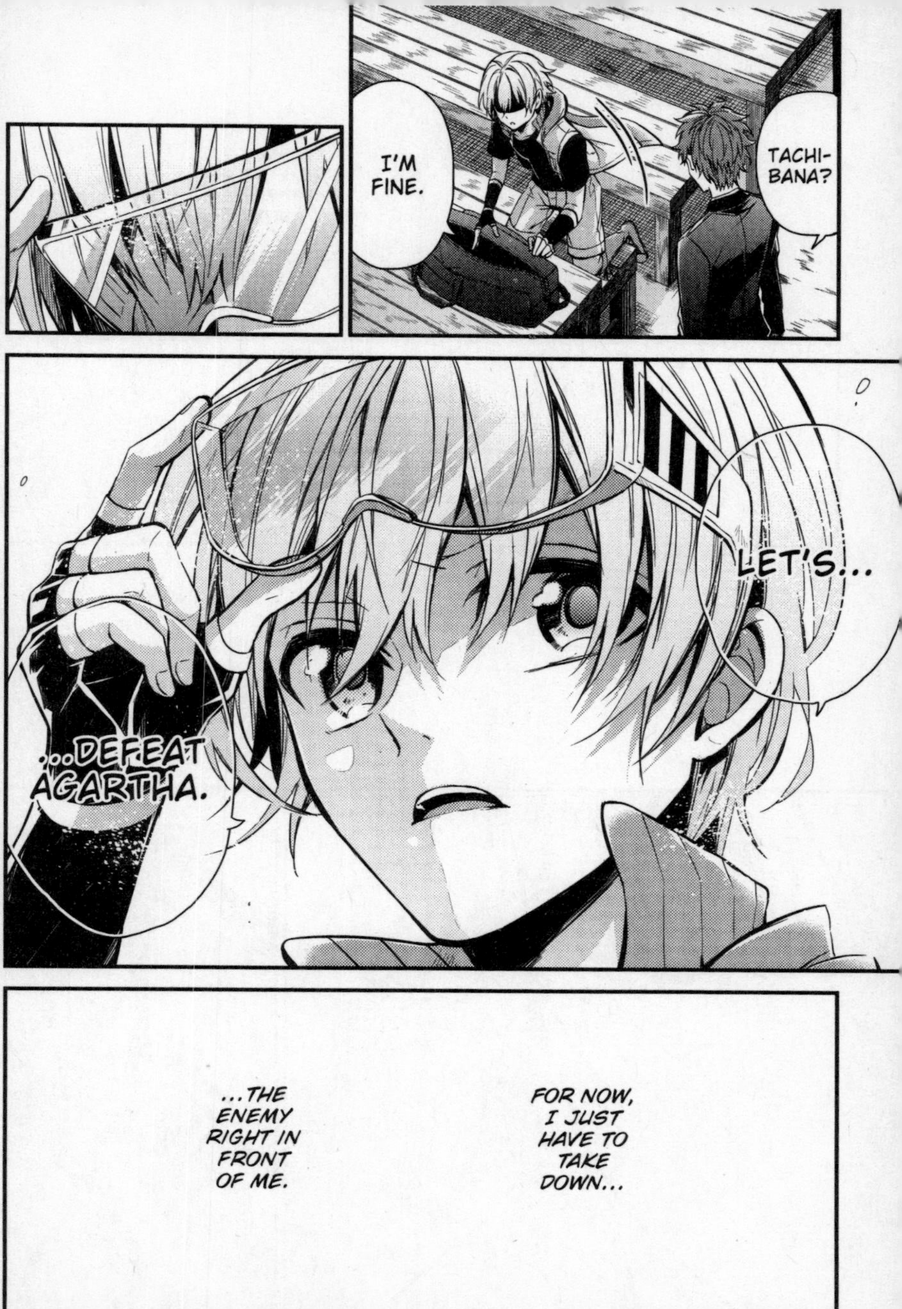
TACHI-
BANA?
I'M
FINE.
LET'S...
...DEFEAT
AGARTHA.
FOR NOW,
I JUST
HAVE TO
TAKE
DOWN...
...THE
ENEMY
RIGHT IN
FRONT
OF ME.

*EXTRA VALENTINE'S STORY FROM TWITTER
~MATSUOKA EDITION~

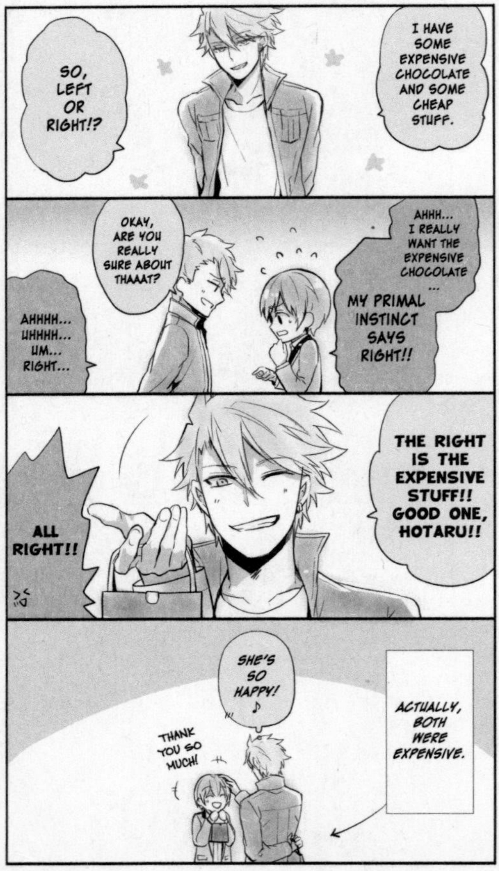
I HAVE SOME EXPENSIVE CHOCOLATE AND SOME CHEAP STUFF.
SO, LEFT OR RIGHT!?
AHHH... I REALLY WANT THE EXPENSIVE CHOCOLATE...
MY PRIMAL INSTINCT SAYS RIGHT!!
OKAY, ARE YOU REALLY SURE ABOUT THAAAT?
AHHHH... UHHHH... UM... RIGHT...
THE RIGHT IS THE EXPENSIVE STUFF!! GOOD ONE, HOTARU!!
ALL RIGHT!!
ACTUALLY, BOTH WERE EXPENSIVE.
SHE'S SO HAPPY! ♪
THANK YOU SO MUCH!

*EXTRA VALENTINE'S STORY FROM TWITTER ~YUKIMURA EDITION~

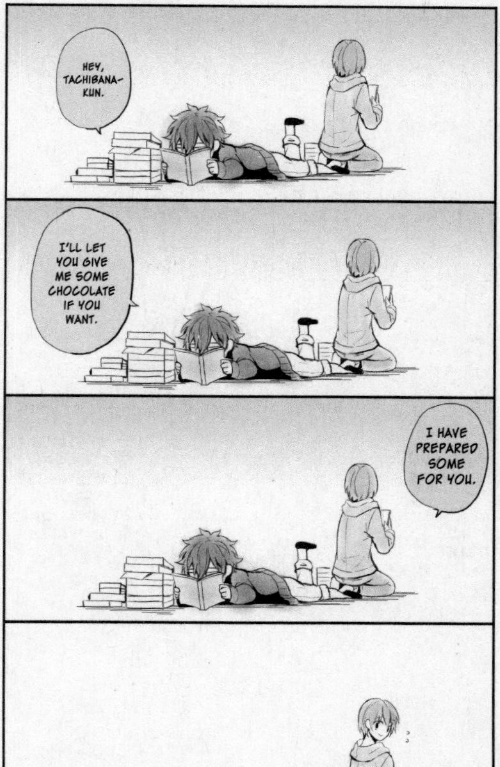
HEY, TACHIBANA-KUN.
I'LL LET YOU GIVE ME SOME CHOCOLATE IF YOU WANT.
I HAVE PREPARED SOME FOR YOU.

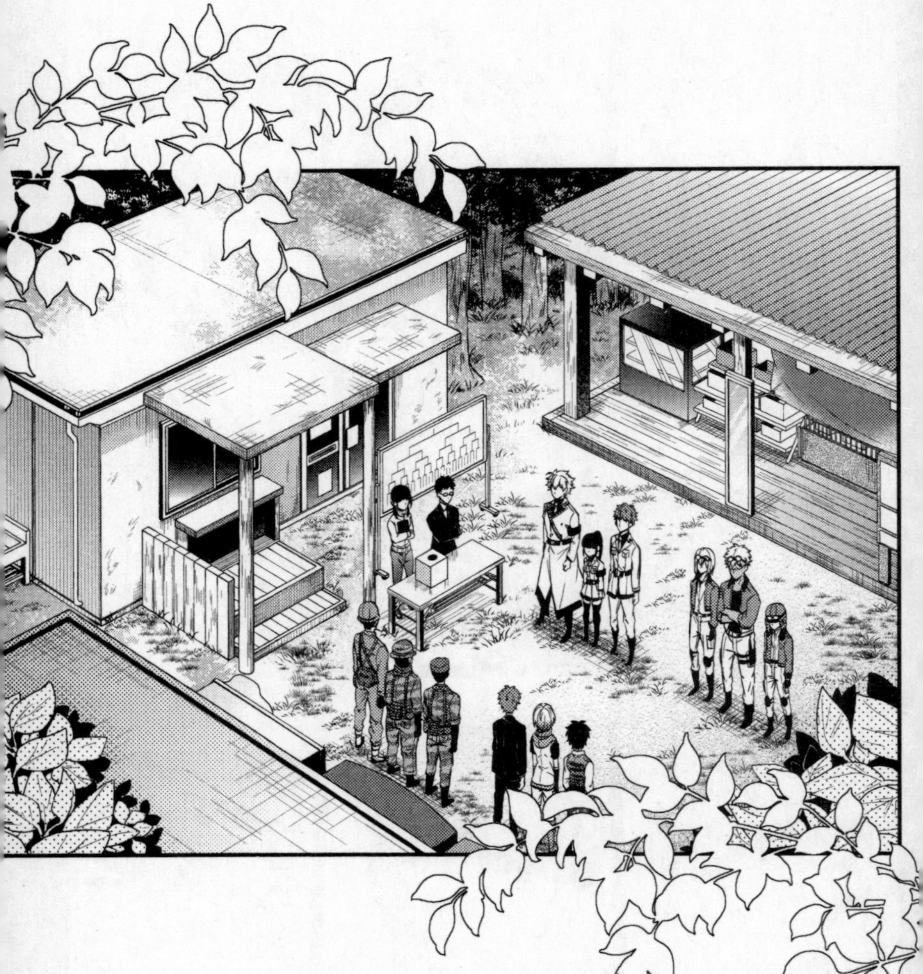

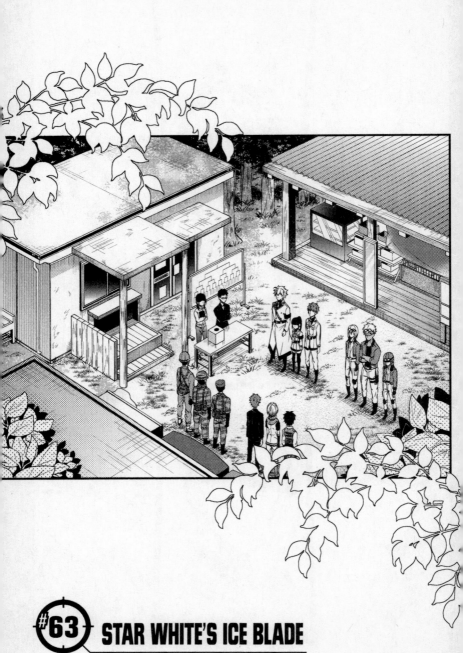

#63 STAR WHITE'S ICE BLADE

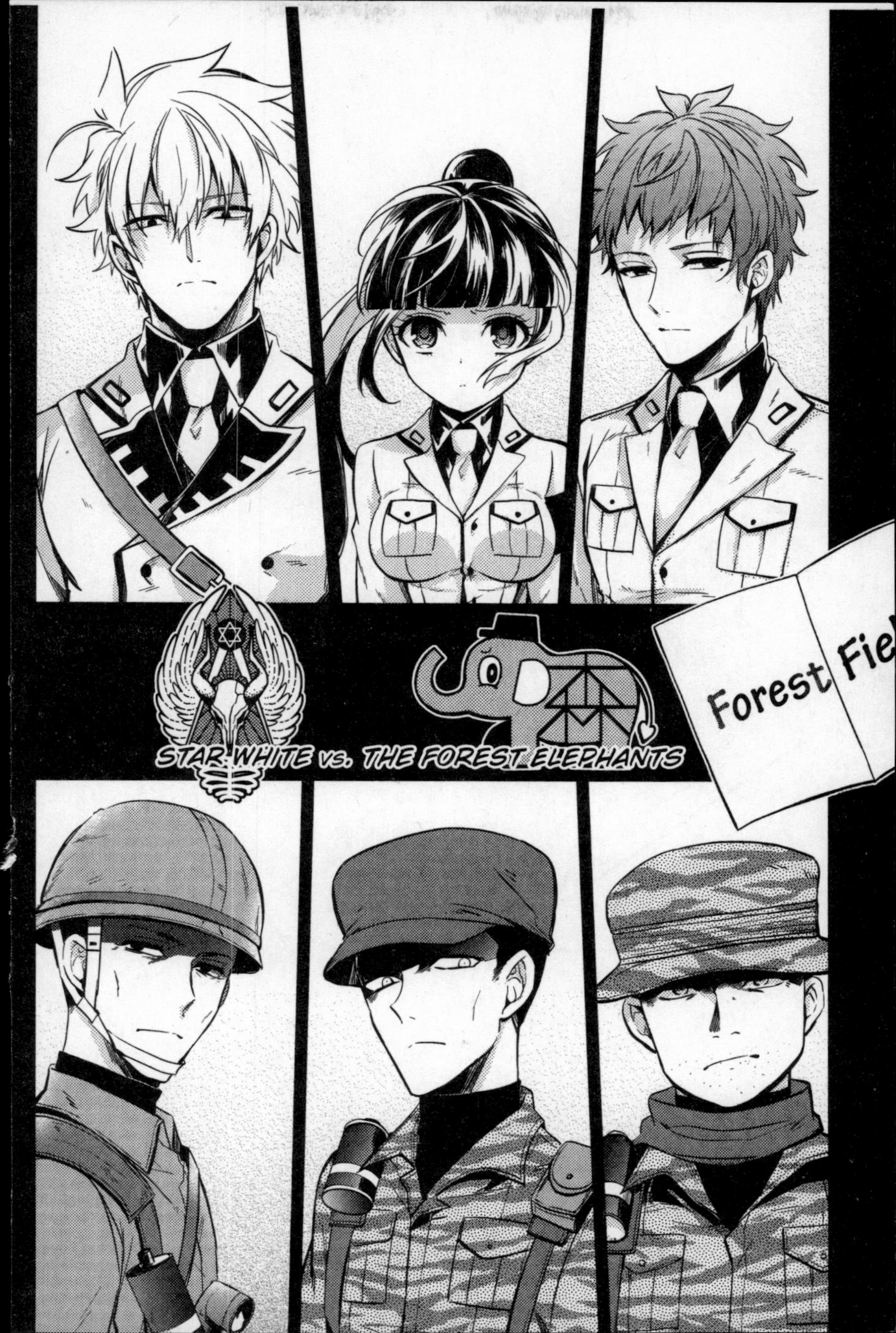
Forest Fie
STAR WHITE vs. THE FOREST ELEPHANTS

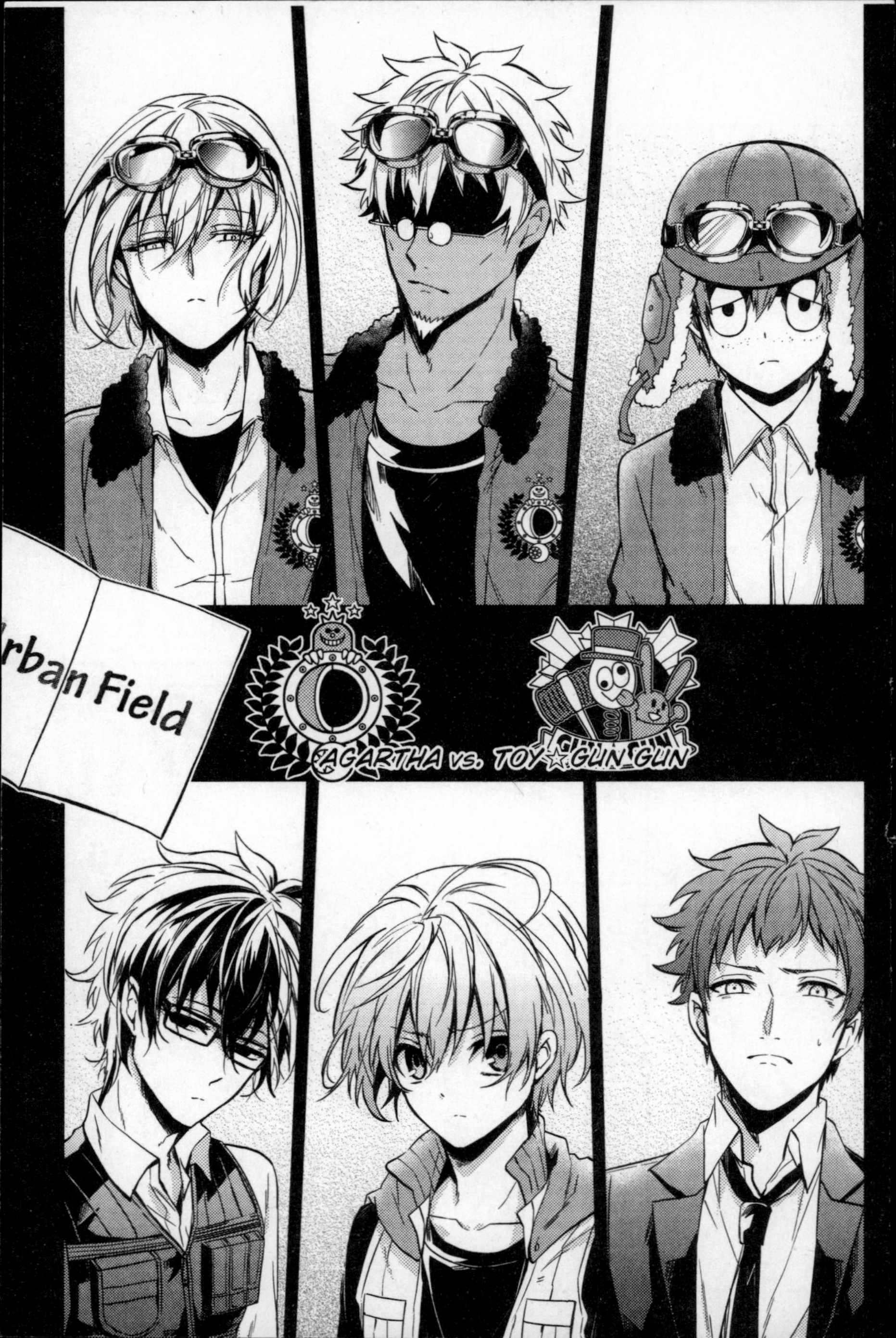
Urban Field
AGARTHA vs. TOY☆GUN GUN

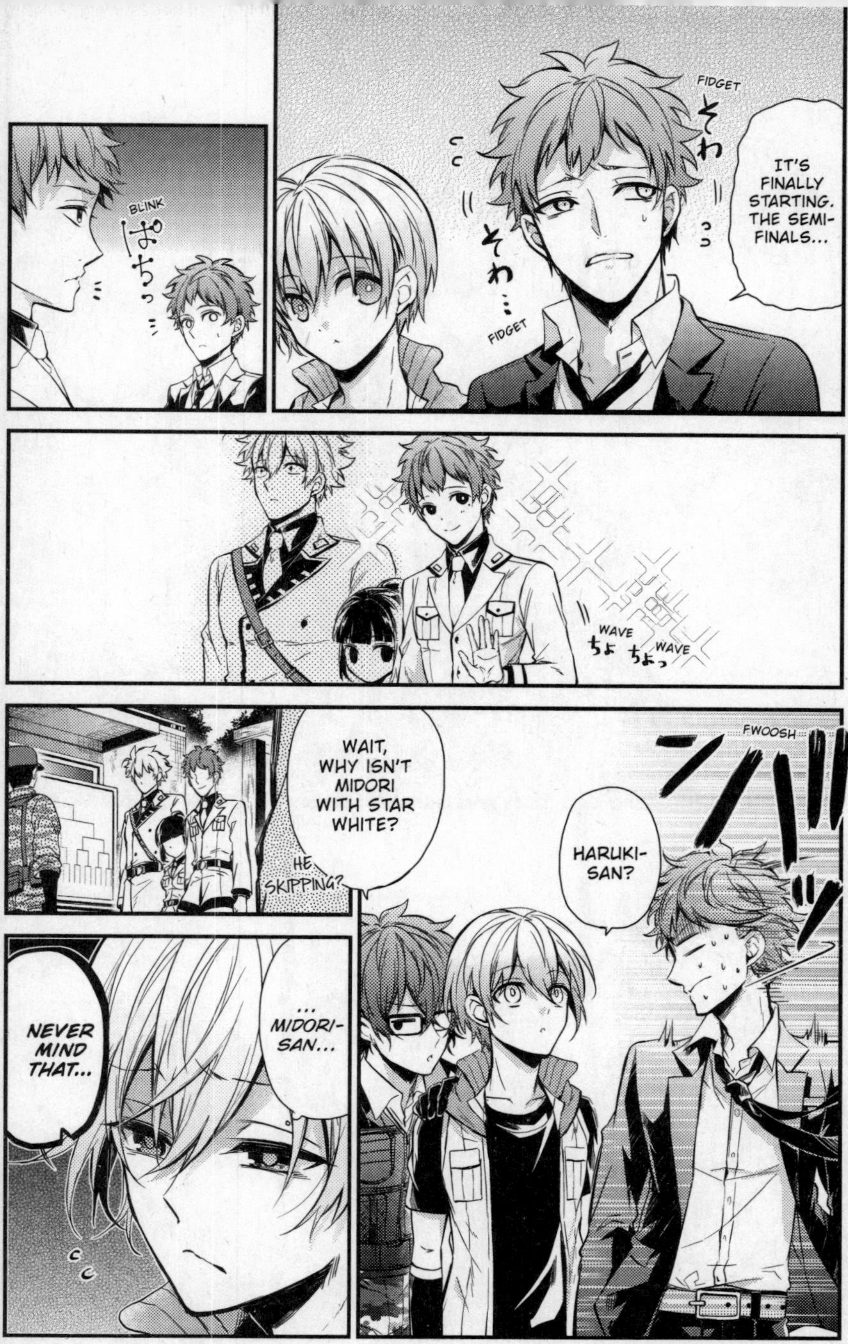
FIDGET
そわーっ
IT'S FINALLY STARTING. THE SEMI-FINALS...
そわ…
FIDGET
BLINK
ぱちっ
WAVE
ちょ
ちょっ
WAVE
FWOOSH
HARUKI-SAN?
WAIT, WHY ISN'T MIDORI WITH STAR WHITE?
HE SKIPPING?
...MIDORI-SAN...
NEVER MIND THAT...

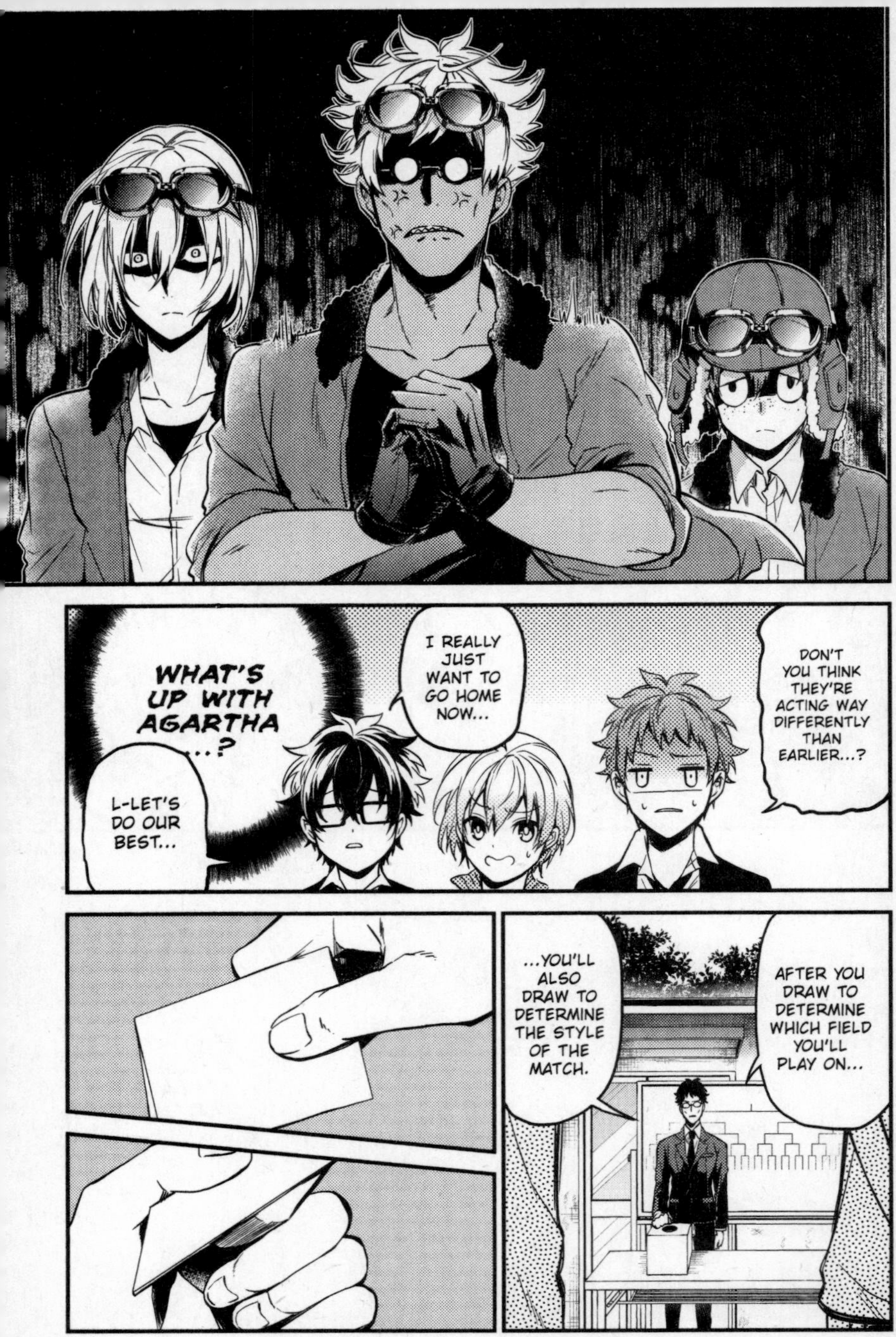
DON'T YOU THINK THEY'RE ACTING WAY DIFFERENTLY THAN EARLIER...?
I REALLY JUST WANT TO GO HOME NOW...
WHAT'S UP WITH AGARTHA ...?
L-LET'S DO OUR BEST...
AFTER YOU DRAW TO DETERMINE WHICH FIELD YOU'LL PLAY ON...
...YOU'LL ALSO DRAW TO DETERMINE THE STYLE OF THE MATCH.

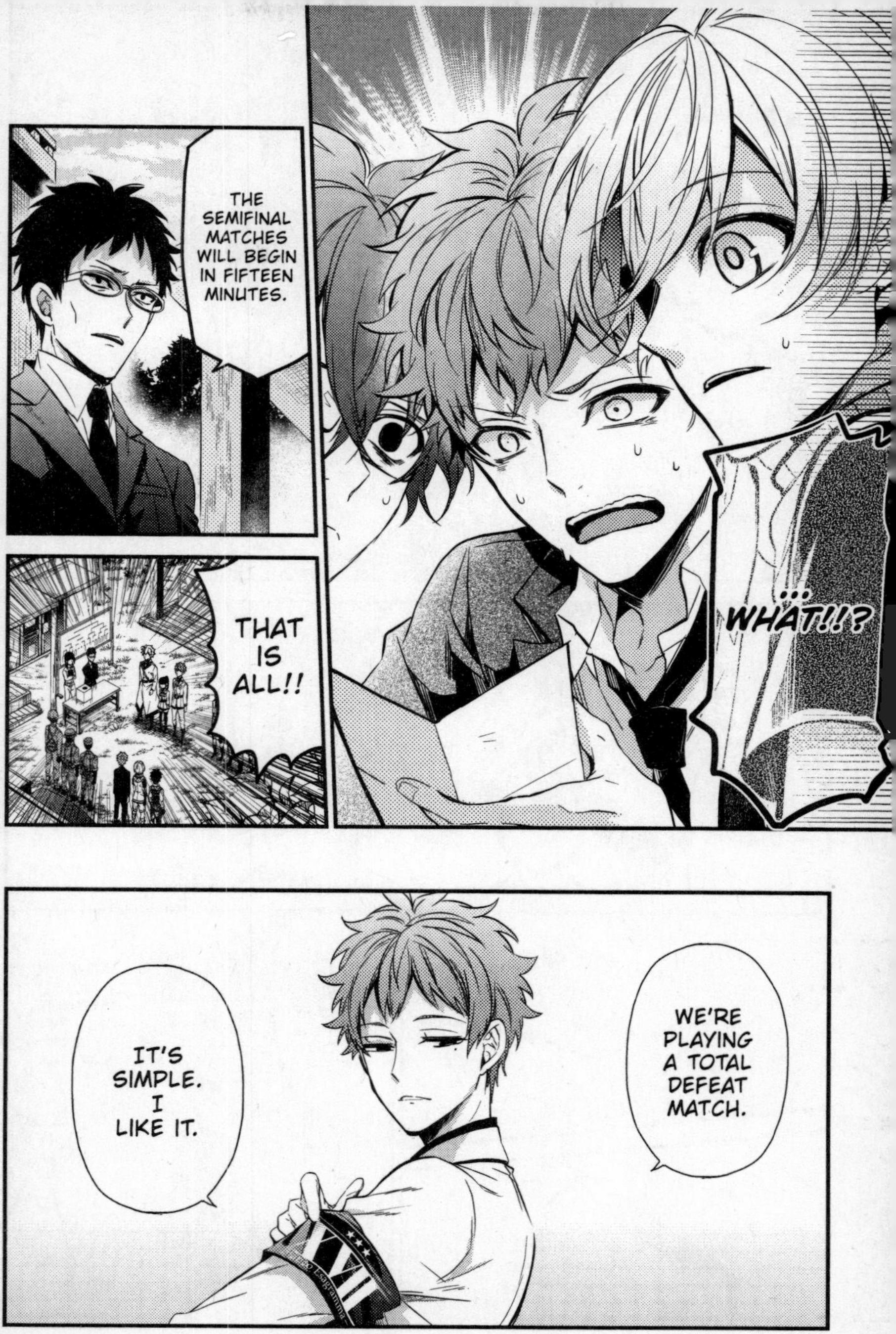
...WHAT!!?
THE SEMIFINAL MATCHES WILL BEGIN IN FIFTEEN MINUTES.
THAT IS ALL!!
WE'RE PLAYING A TOTAL DEFEAT MATCH.
IT'S SIMPLE. I LIKE IT.

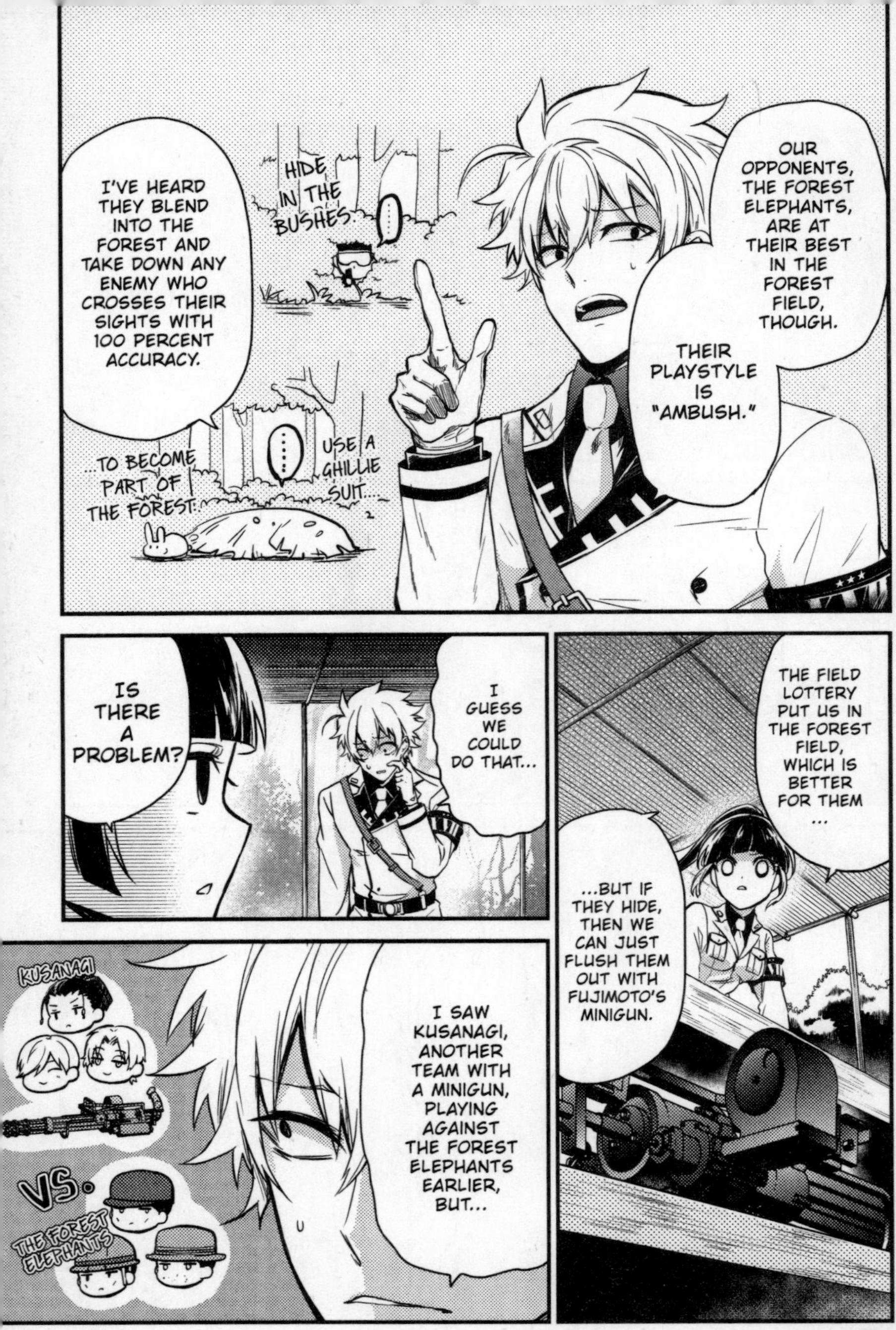
OUR OPPONENTS, THE FOREST ELEPHANTS, ARE AT THEIR BEST IN THE FOREST FIELD, THOUGH.
THEIR PLAYSTYLE IS "AMBUSH."
I'VE HEARD THEY BLEND INTO THE FOREST AND TAKE DOWN ANY ENEMY WHO CROSSES THEIR SIGHTS WITH 100 PERCENT ACCURACY.
HIDE IN THE BUSHES.
...
USE A GHILLIE SUIT...
...TO BECOME PART OF THE FOREST.
......
THE FIELD LOTTERY PUT US IN THE FOREST FIELD, WHICH IS BETTER FOR THEM ...
...BUT IF THEY HIDE, THEN WE CAN JUST FLUSH THEM OUT WITH FUJIMOTO'S MINIGUN.
I GUESS WE COULD DO THAT...
IS THERE A PROBLEM?
I SAW KUSANAGI, ANOTHER TEAM WITH A MINIGUN, PLAYING AGAINST THE FOREST ELEPHANTS EARLIER, BUT...
KUSANAGI
VS.
THE FOREST ELEPHANTS

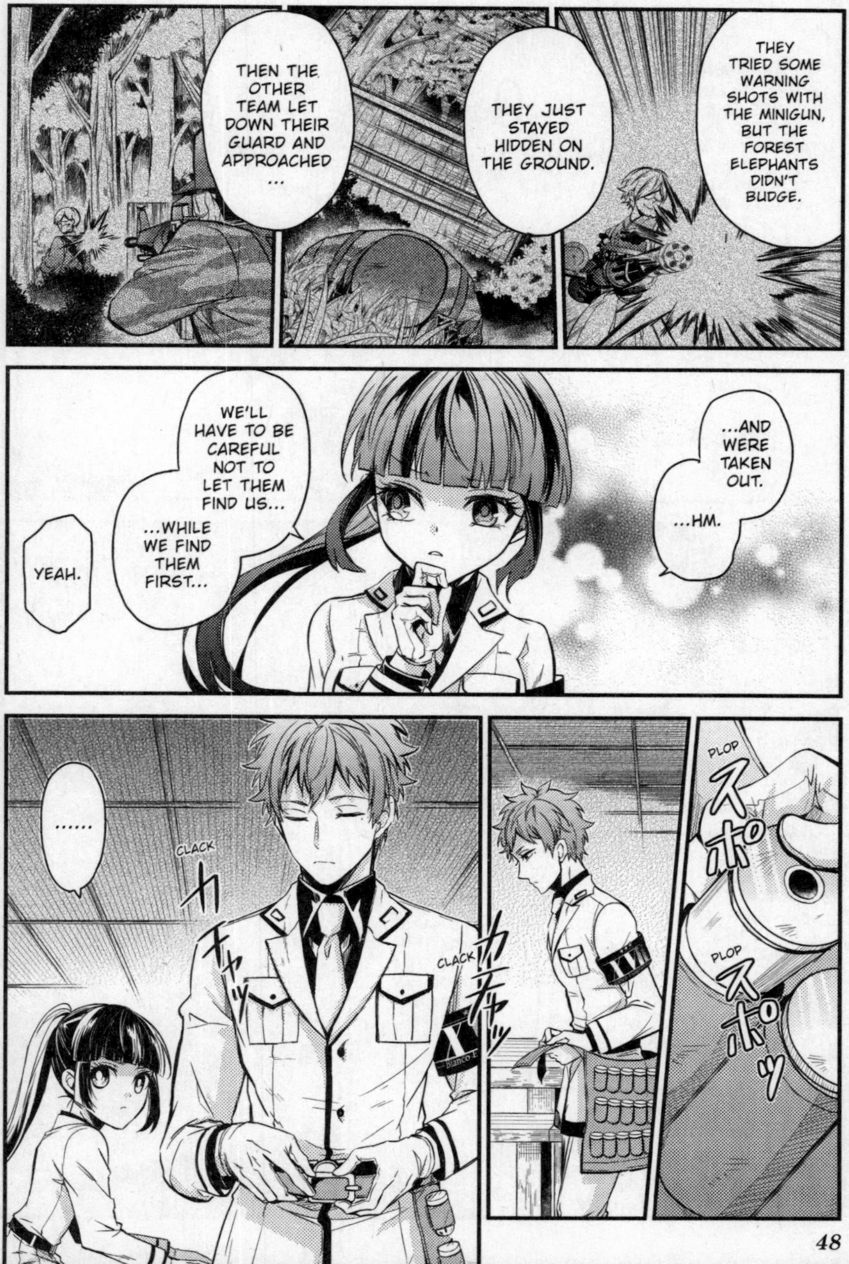
THEY TRIED SOME WARNING SHOTS WITH THE MINIGUN, BUT THE FOREST ELEPHANTS DIDN'T BUDGE.
THEY JUST STAYED HIDDEN ON THE GROUND.
THEN THE OTHER TEAM LET DOWN THEIR GUARD AND APPROACHED ...
...AND WERE TAKEN OUT.
...HM.
WE'LL HAVE TO BE CAREFUL NOT TO LET THEM FIND US...
...WHILE WE FIND THEM FIRST...
YEAH.
PLOP
スポ
PLOP
スポッ
......
CLACK
カチャッ
CLACK
カチャッ

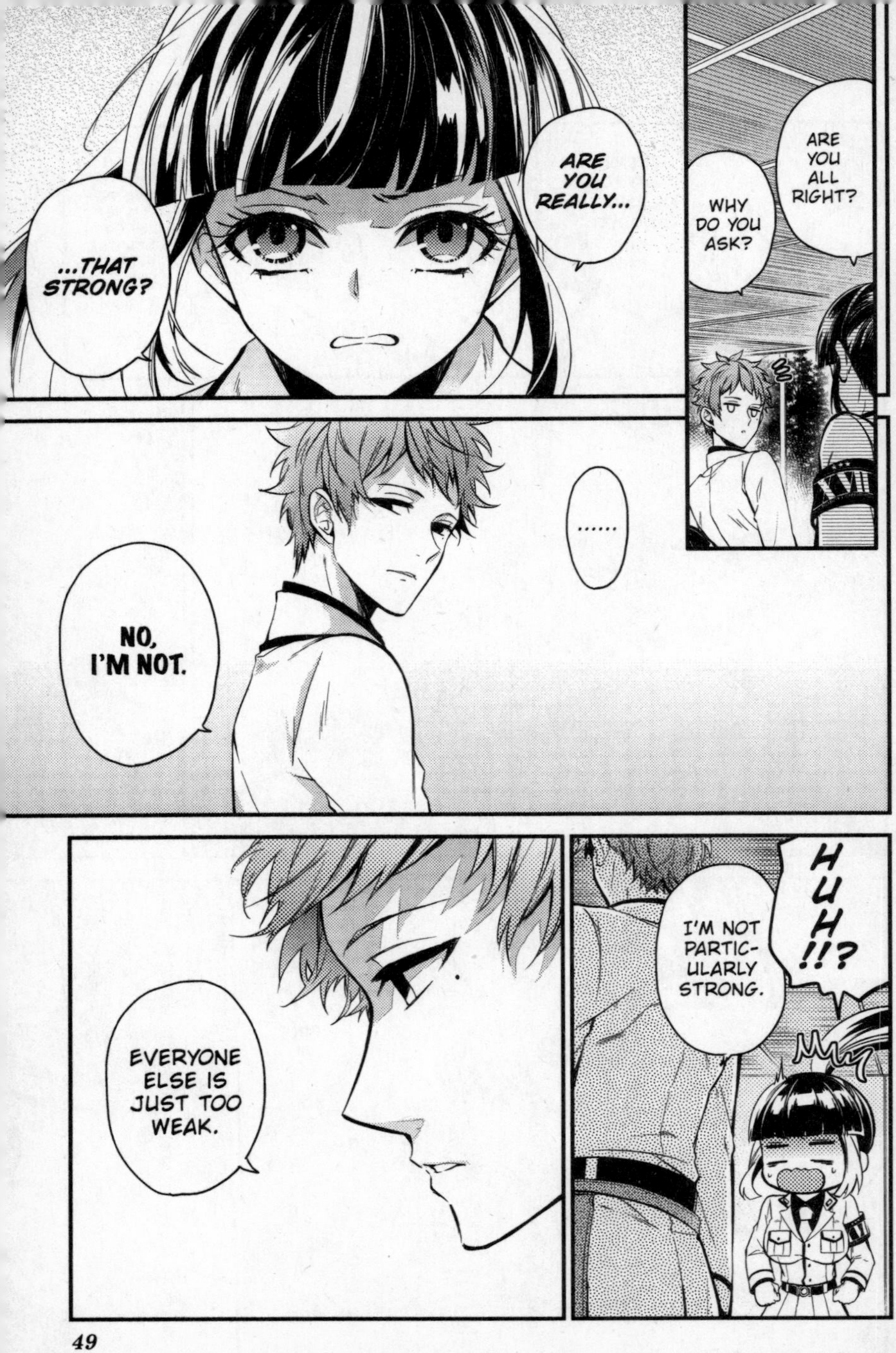
ARE YOU ALL RIGHT?
WHY DO YOU ASK?
ARE YOU REALLY...
...THAT STRONG?
......
NO, I'M NOT.
I'M NOT PARTIC-ULARLY STRONG.
HUH!!?
MMM
EVERYONE ELSE IS JUST TOO WEAK.

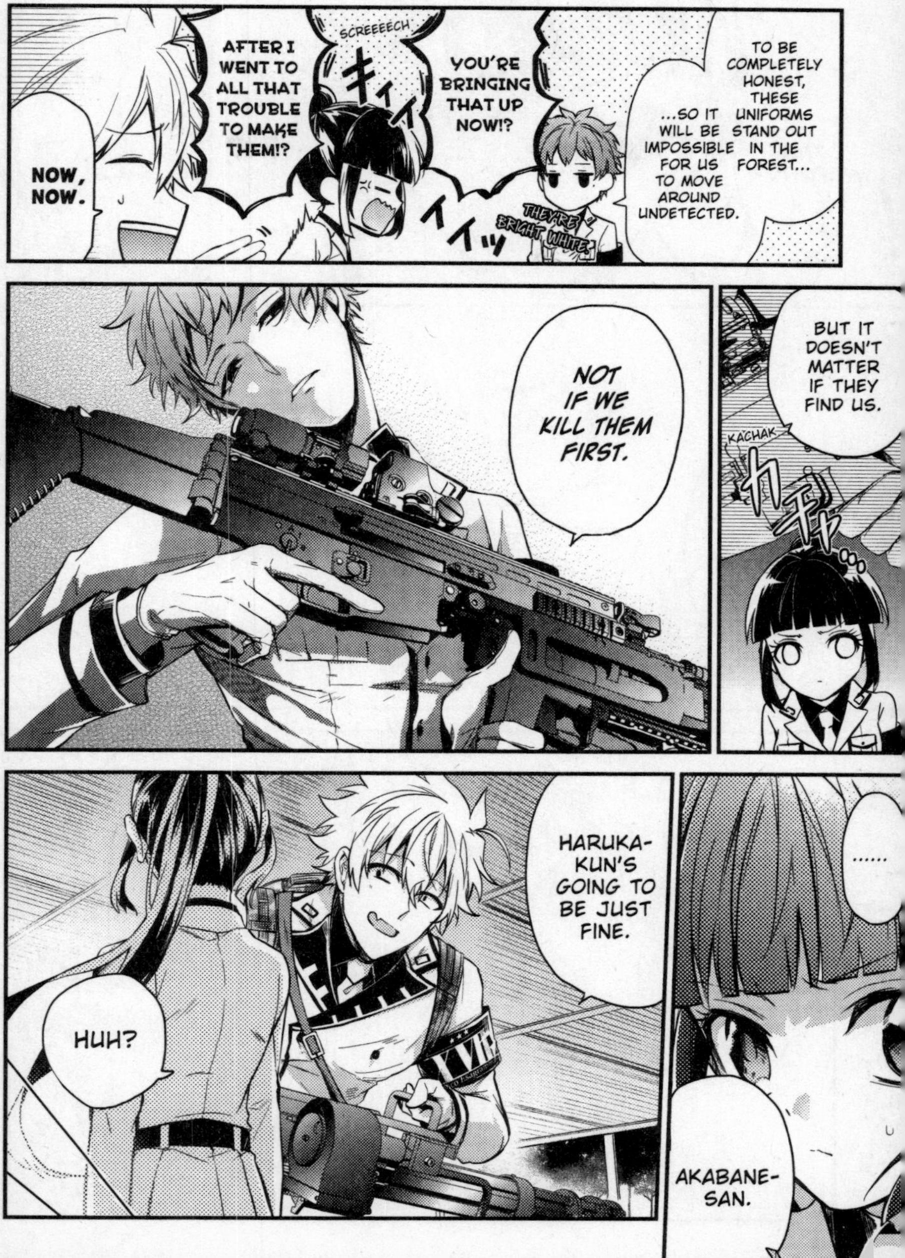

TO BE COMPLETELY HONEST, THESE UNIFORMS STAND OUT IN THE FOREST...
...SO IT WILL BE IMPOSSIBLE FOR US TO MOVE AROUND UNDETECTED.
THEY'RE BRIGHT WHITE.
YOU'RE BRINGING THAT UP NOW!?
SCREEEECH
AFTER I WENT TO ALL THAT TROUBLE TO MAKE THEM!?
NOW, NOW.
BUT IT DOESN'T MATTER IF THEY FIND US.
KACHAK
NOT IF WE KILL THEM FIRST.
......
AKABANE-SAN.
HARUKA-KUN'S GOING TO BE JUST FINE.
HUH?

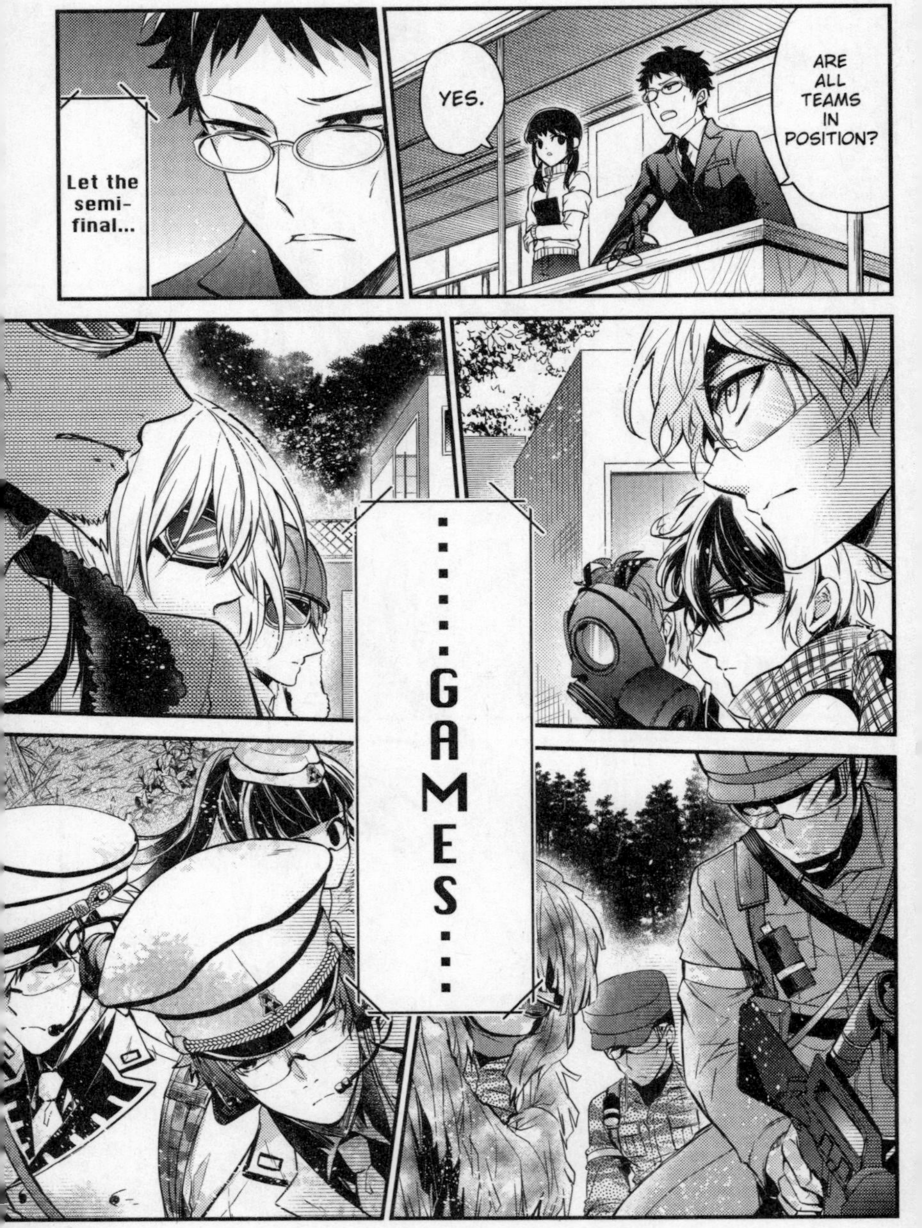
ARE ALL TEAMS IN POSITION?
YES.
Let the semi-final...
...GAMES...

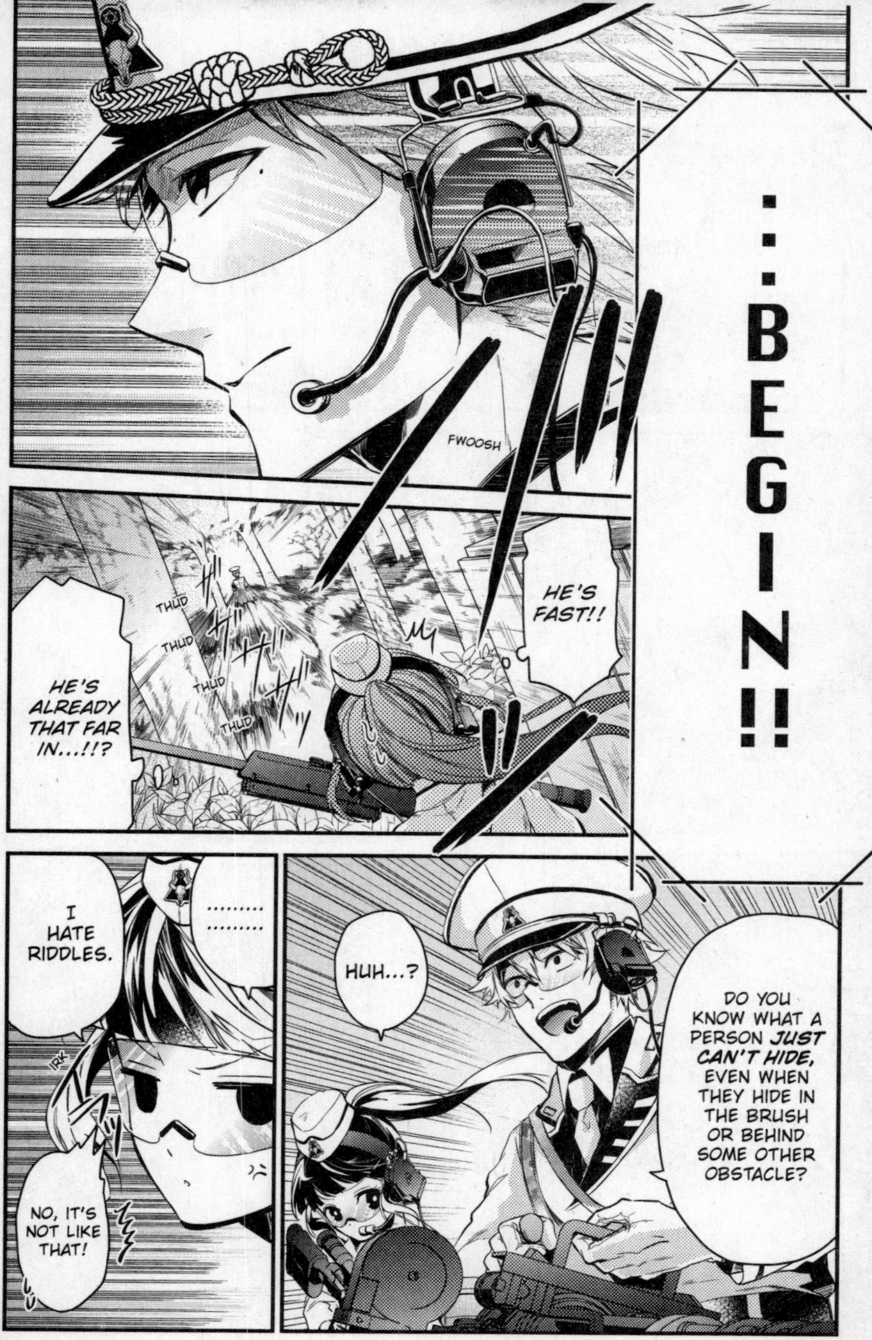

...BEGIN!!
FWOOSH
HE'S FAST!!
THUD
THUD
THUD
THUD
HE'S ALREADY THAT FAR IN...!!?
DO YOU KNOW WHAT A PERSON JUST CAN'T HIDE, EVEN WHEN THEY HIDE IN THE BRUSH OR BEHIND SOME OTHER OBSTACLE?
HUH...?
....
....
I HATE RIDDLES.
IRK
NO, IT'S NOT LIKE THAT!

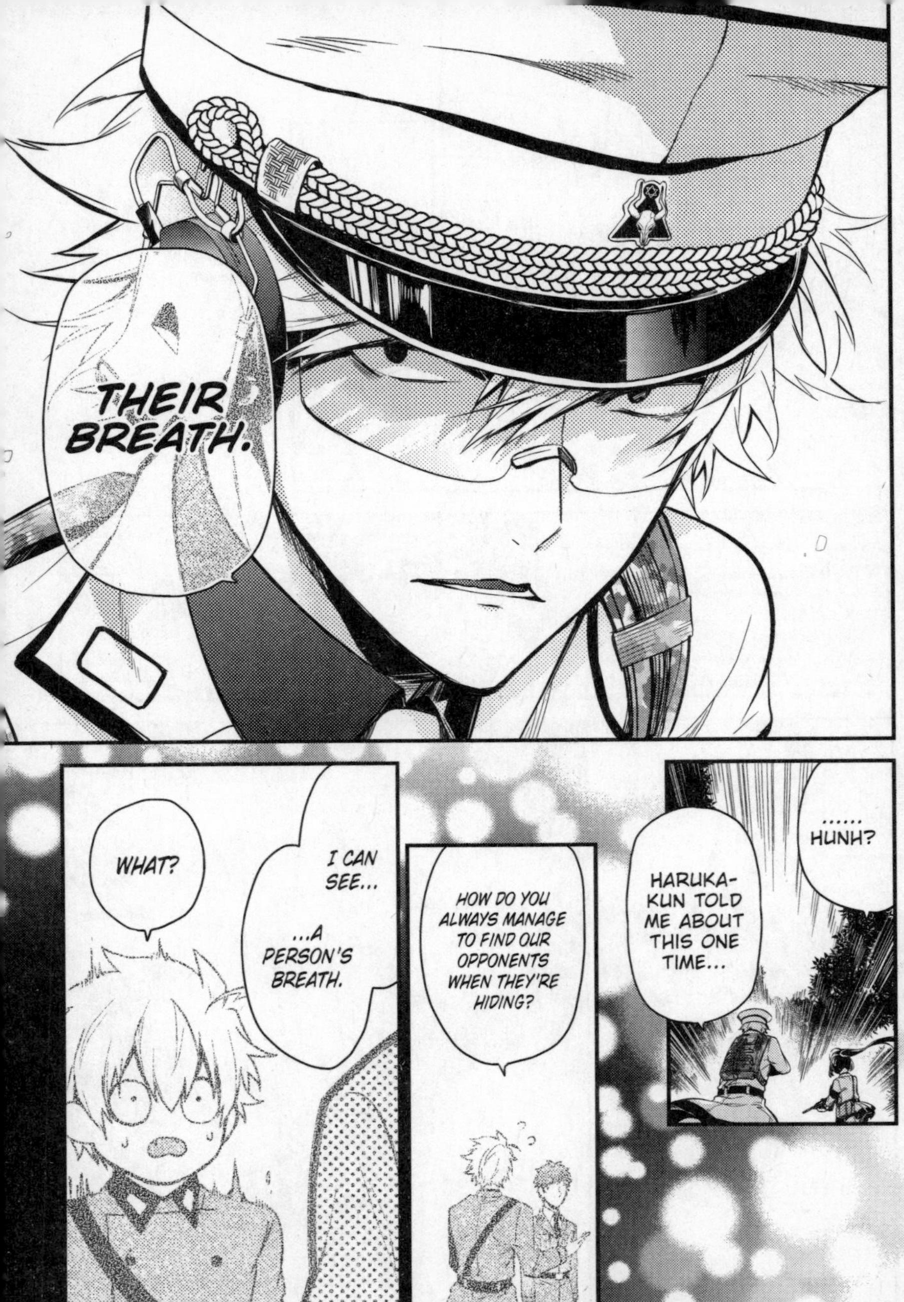
THEIR BREATH.
......HUNH?
HARUKA-KUN TOLD ME ABOUT THIS ONE TIME...
HOW DO YOU ALWAYS MANAGE TO FIND OUR OPPONENTS WHEN THEY'RE HIDING?
I CAN SEE...
...A PERSON'S BREATH.
WHAT?

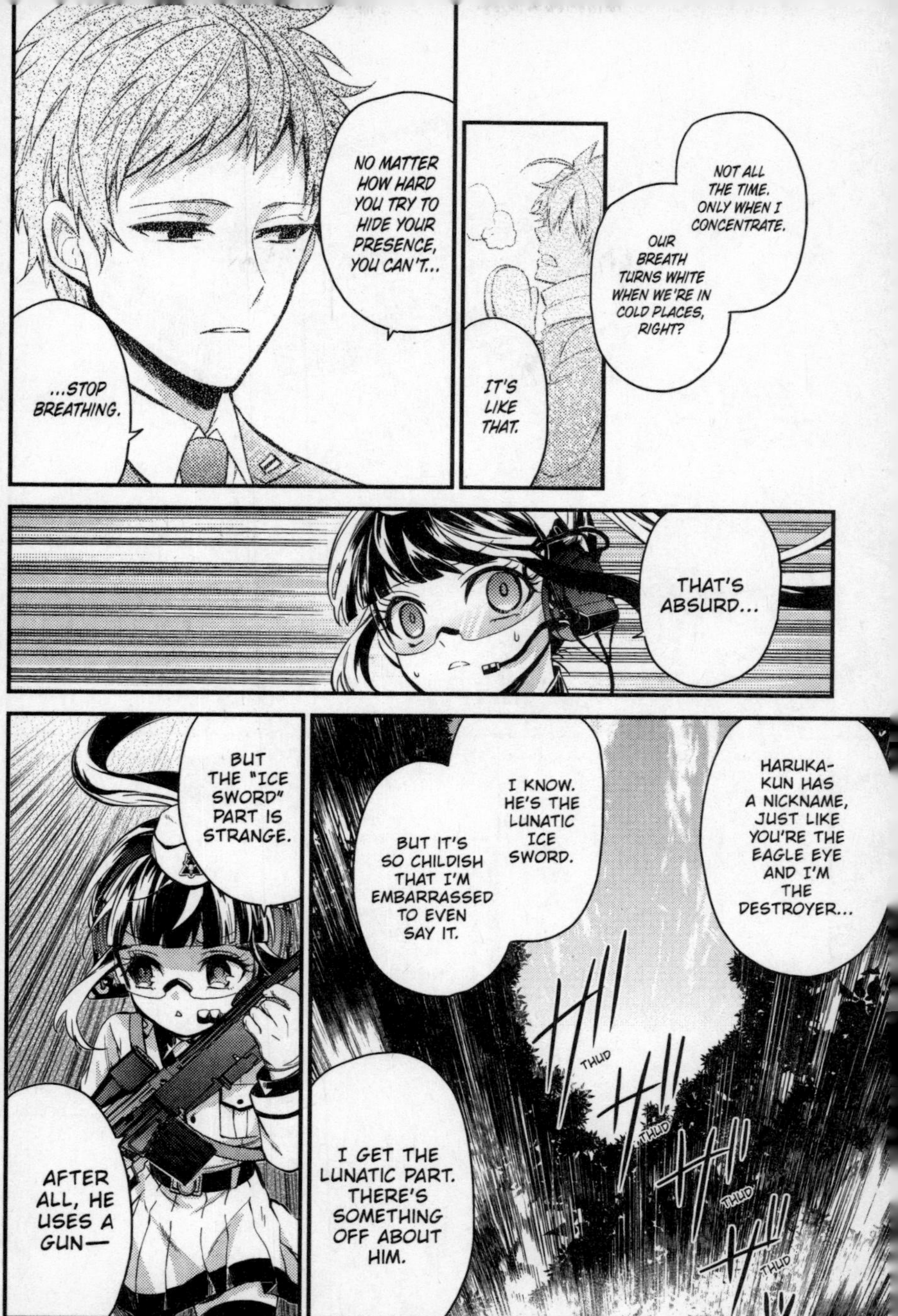
NOT ALL THE TIME. ONLY WHEN I CONCENTRATE.
OUR BREATH TURNS WHITE WHEN WE'RE IN COLD PLACES, RIGHT?
IT'S LIKE THAT.
NO MATTER HOW HARD YOU TRY TO HIDE YOUR PRESENCE, YOU CAN'T...
...STOP BREATHING.
THAT'S ABSURD...
HARUKA-KUN HAS A NICKNAME, JUST LIKE YOU'RE THE EAGLE EYE AND I'M THE DESTROYER...
I KNOW. HE'S THE LUNATIC ICE SWORD.
BUT IT'S SO CHILDISH THAT I'M EMBARRASSED TO EVEN SAY IT.
THUD
THUD
THUD
THUD
I GET THE LUNATIC PART. THERE'S SOMETHING OFF ABOUT HIM.
BUT THE "ICE SWORD" PART IS STRANGE.
AFTER ALL, HE USES A GUN—

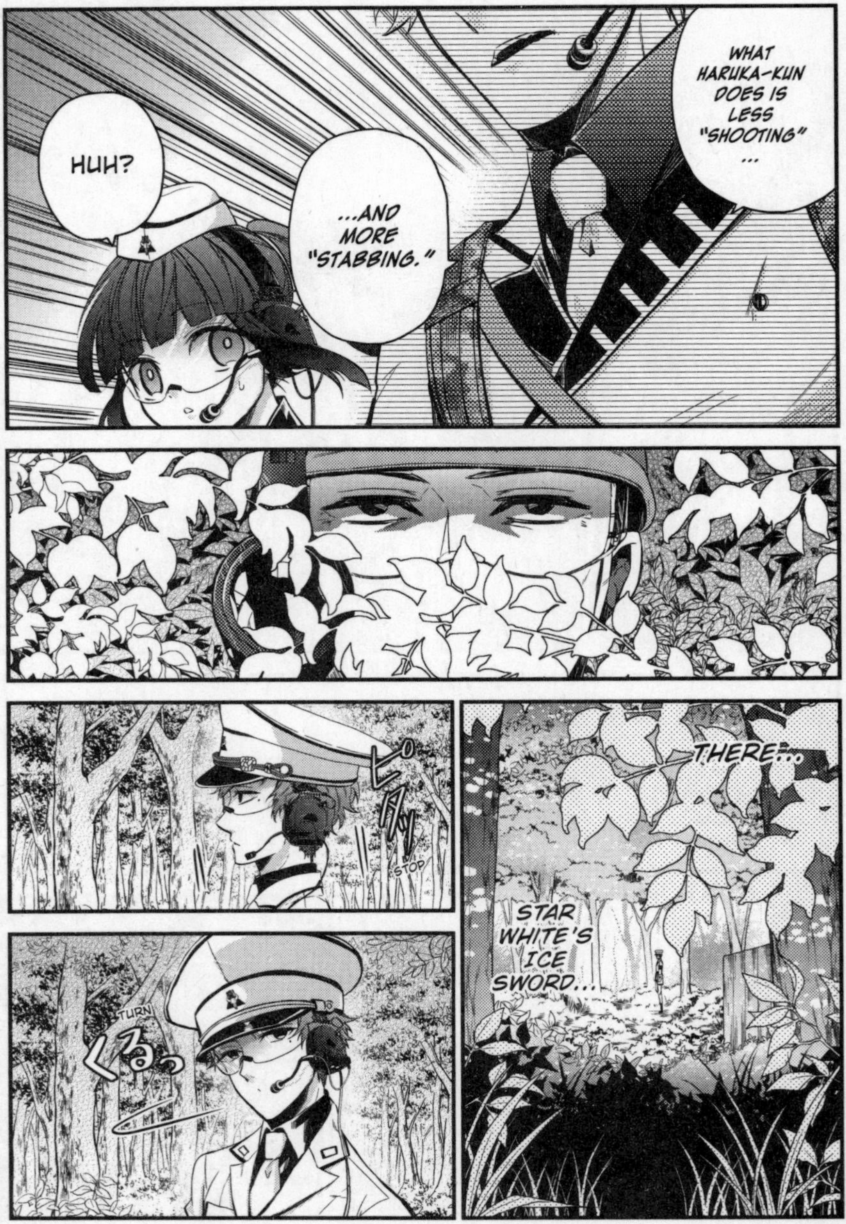
WHAT HARUKA-KUN DOES IS LESS "SHOOTING" ...
...AND MORE "STABBING."
HUH?
THERE...
STAR WHITE'S ICE SWORD...
ピタッ
STOP
TURN
くるっ

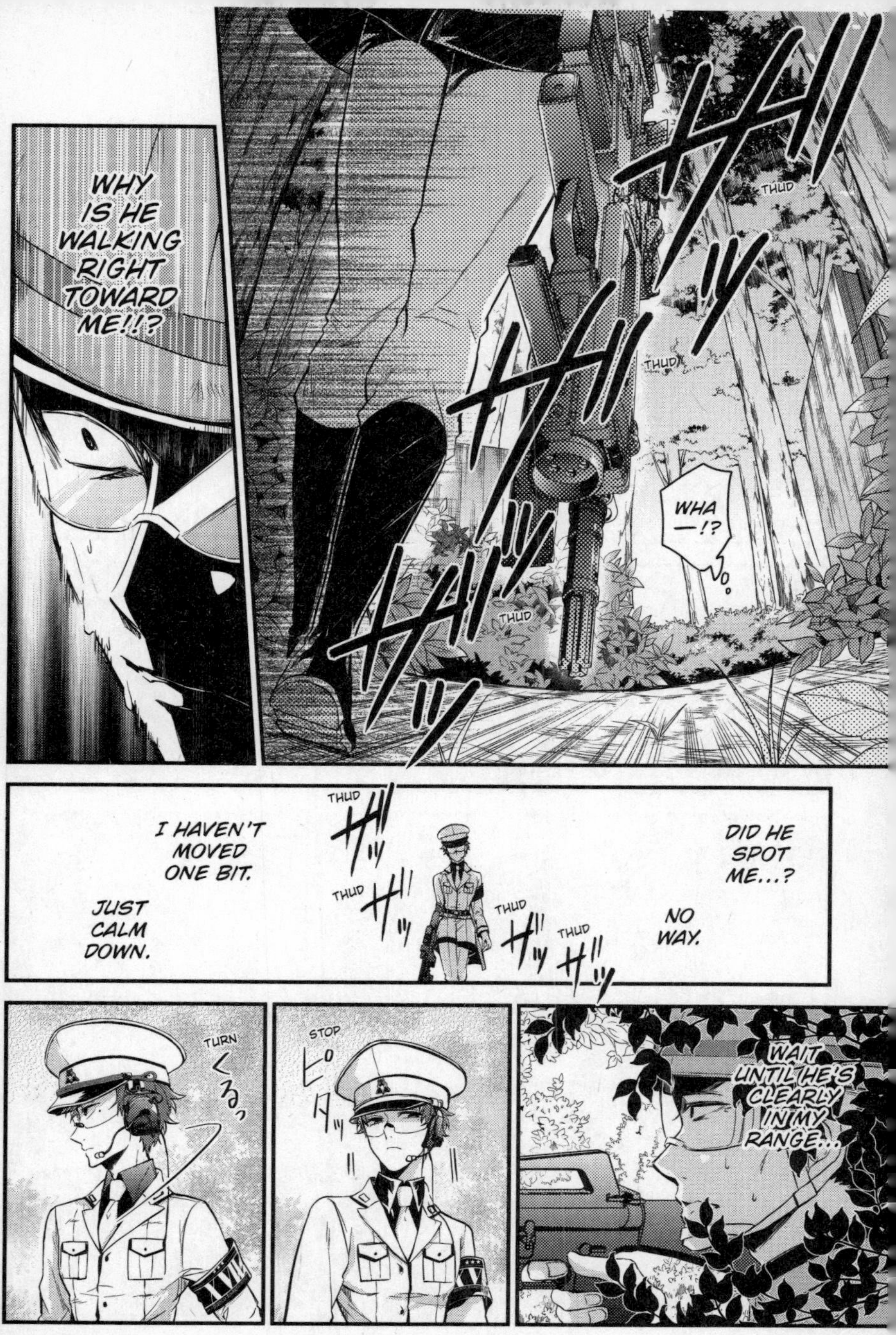
THUD
THUD
WHA—!?
THUD
WHY IS HE WALKING RIGHT TOWARD ME!!?
DID HE SPOT ME...?
NO WAY.
THUD
THUD
THUD
THUD
I HAVEN'T MOVED ONE BIT.
JUST CALM DOWN.
WAIT UNTIL HE'S CLEARLY IN MY RANGE...
STOP
TURN

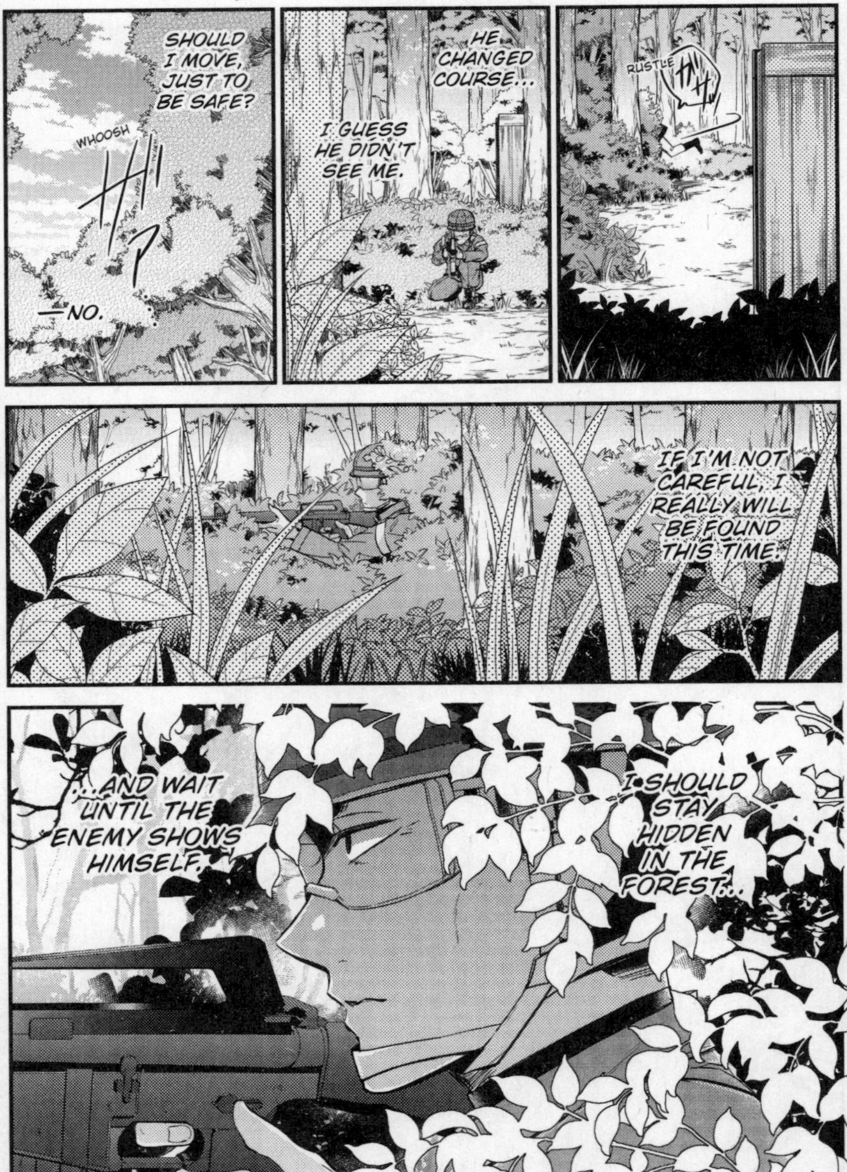
RUSTLE
HE CHANGED COURSE...
I GUESS HE DIDN'T SEE ME.
SHOULD I MOVE, JUST TO BE SAFE?
WHOOSH
—NO.
IF I'M NOT CAREFUL, I REALLY WILL BE FOUND THIS TIME.
I SHOULD STAY HIDDEN IN THE FOREST...
...AND WAIT UNTIL THE ENEMY SHOWS HIMSELF.

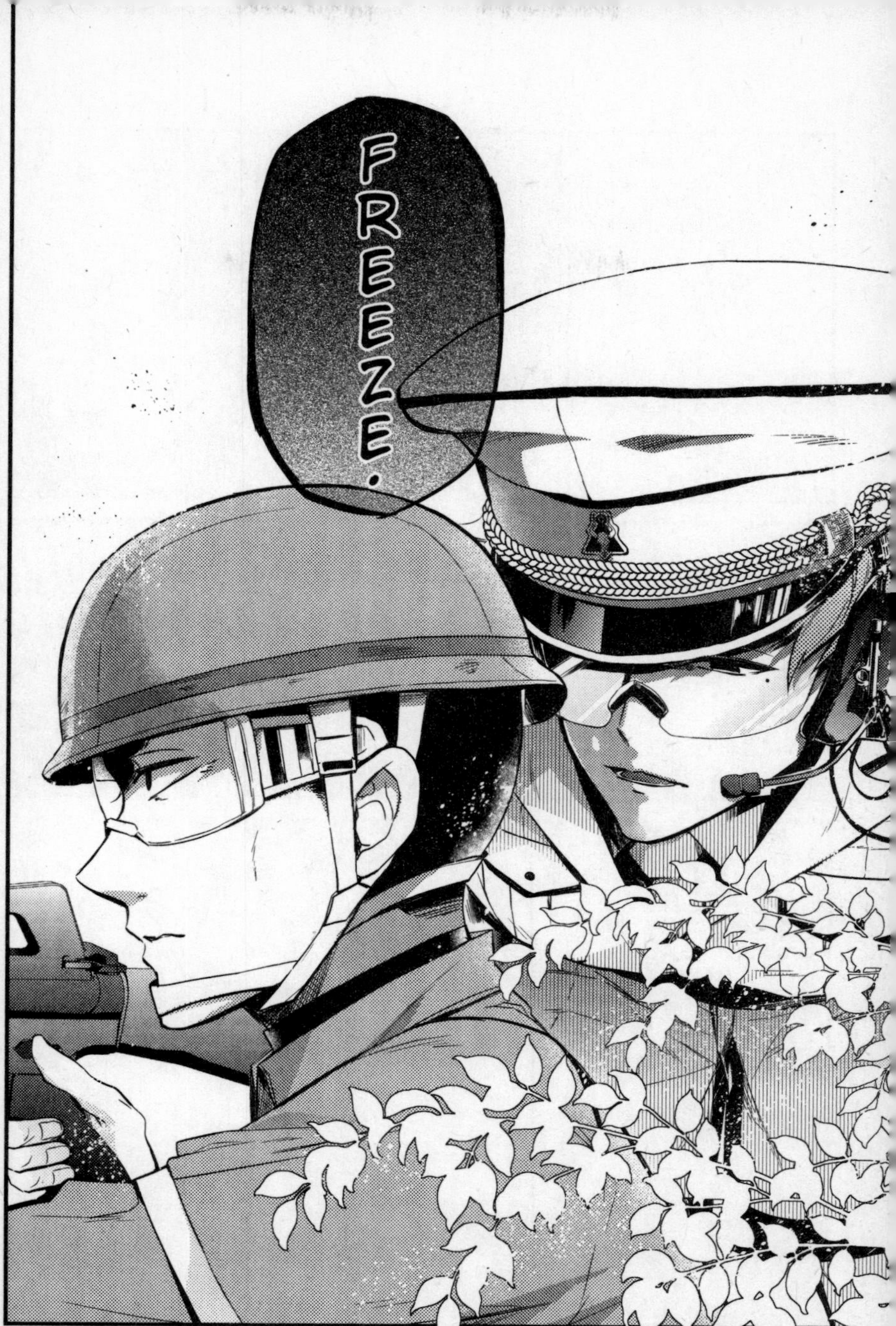
FREEZE.

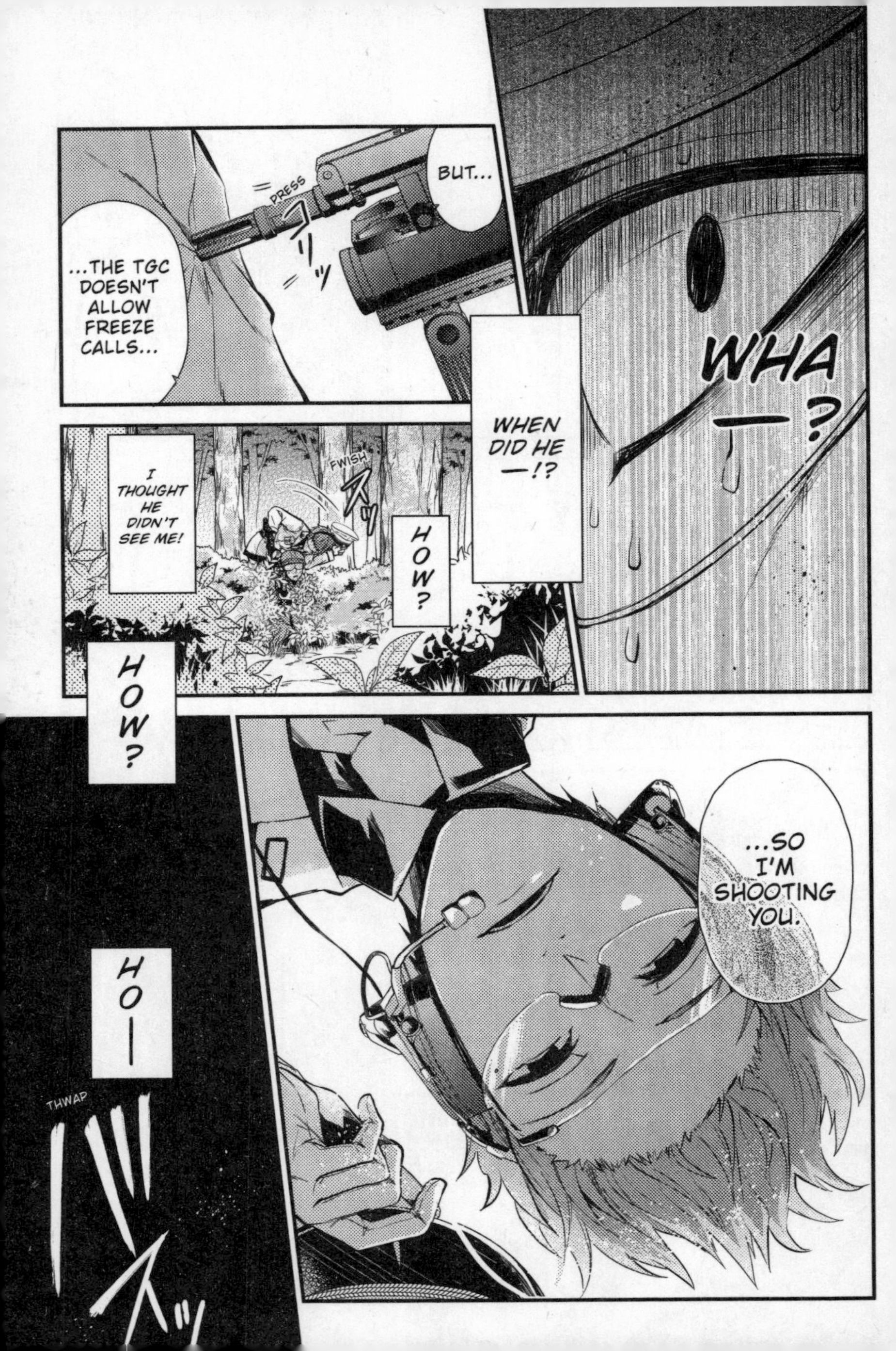
WHA—?
WHEN DID HE—!?
BUT...
PRESS
...THE TGC DOESN'T ALLOW FREEZE CALLS...
HOW?
FWISH
I THOUGHT HE DIDN'T SEE ME!
HOW?
...SO I'M SHOOTING YOU.
HO—
THWAP

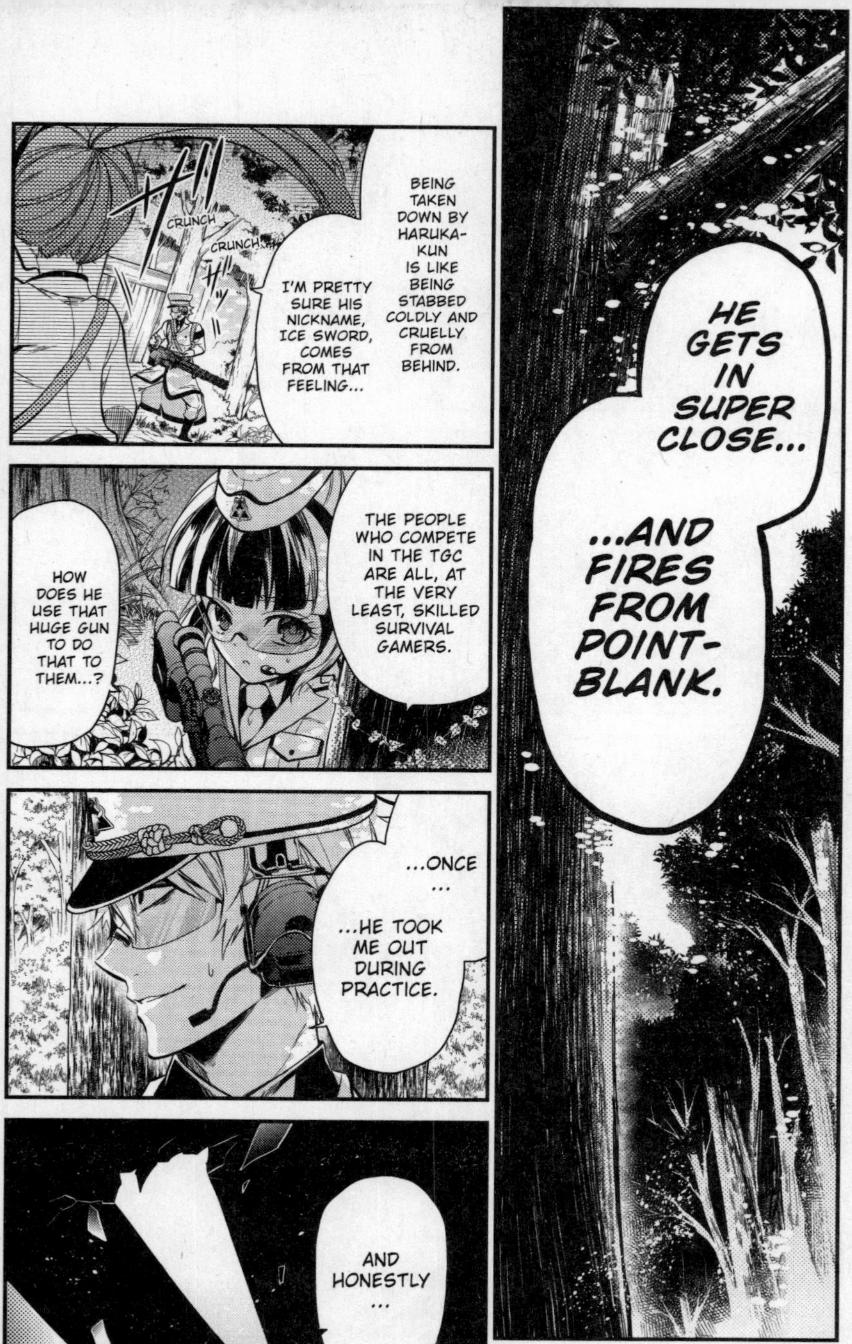
HE GETS IN SUPER CLOSE...
...AND FIRES FROM POINT-BLANK.
BEING TAKEN DOWN BY HARUKA-KUN IS LIKE BEING STABBED COLDLY AND CRUELLY FROM BEHIND.
I'M PRETTY SURE HIS NICKNAME, ICE SWORD, COMES FROM THAT FEELING...
CRUNCH
CRUNCH
THE PEOPLE WHO COMPETE IN THE TGC ARE ALL, AT THE VERY LEAST, SKILLED SURVIVAL GAMERS.
HOW DOES HE USE THAT HUGE GUN TO DO THAT TO THEM...?
...ONCE ...
...HE TOOK ME OUT DURING PRACTICE.
AND HONESTLY ...

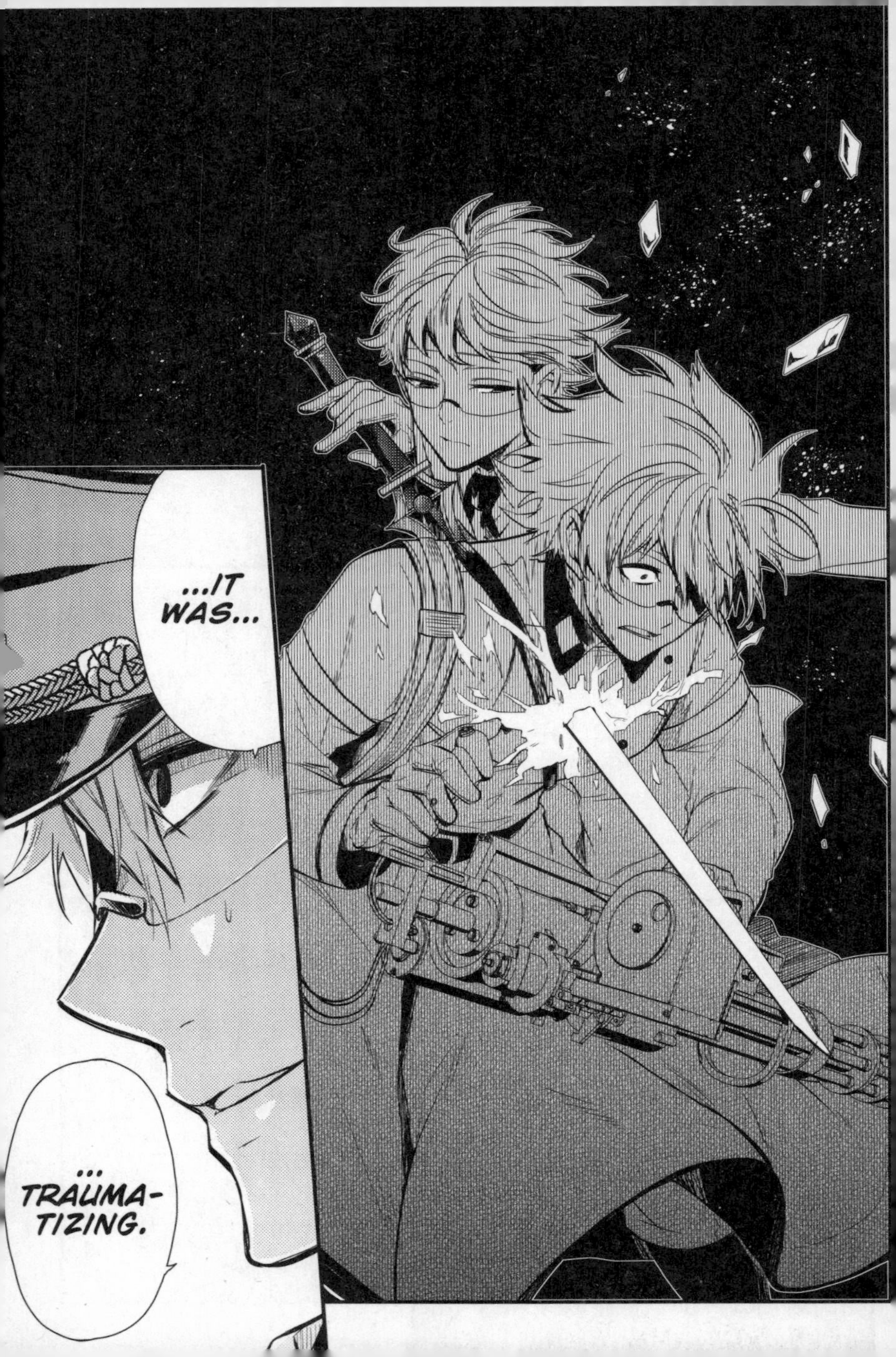
...IT WAS...
...TRAÜMA-TIZING.

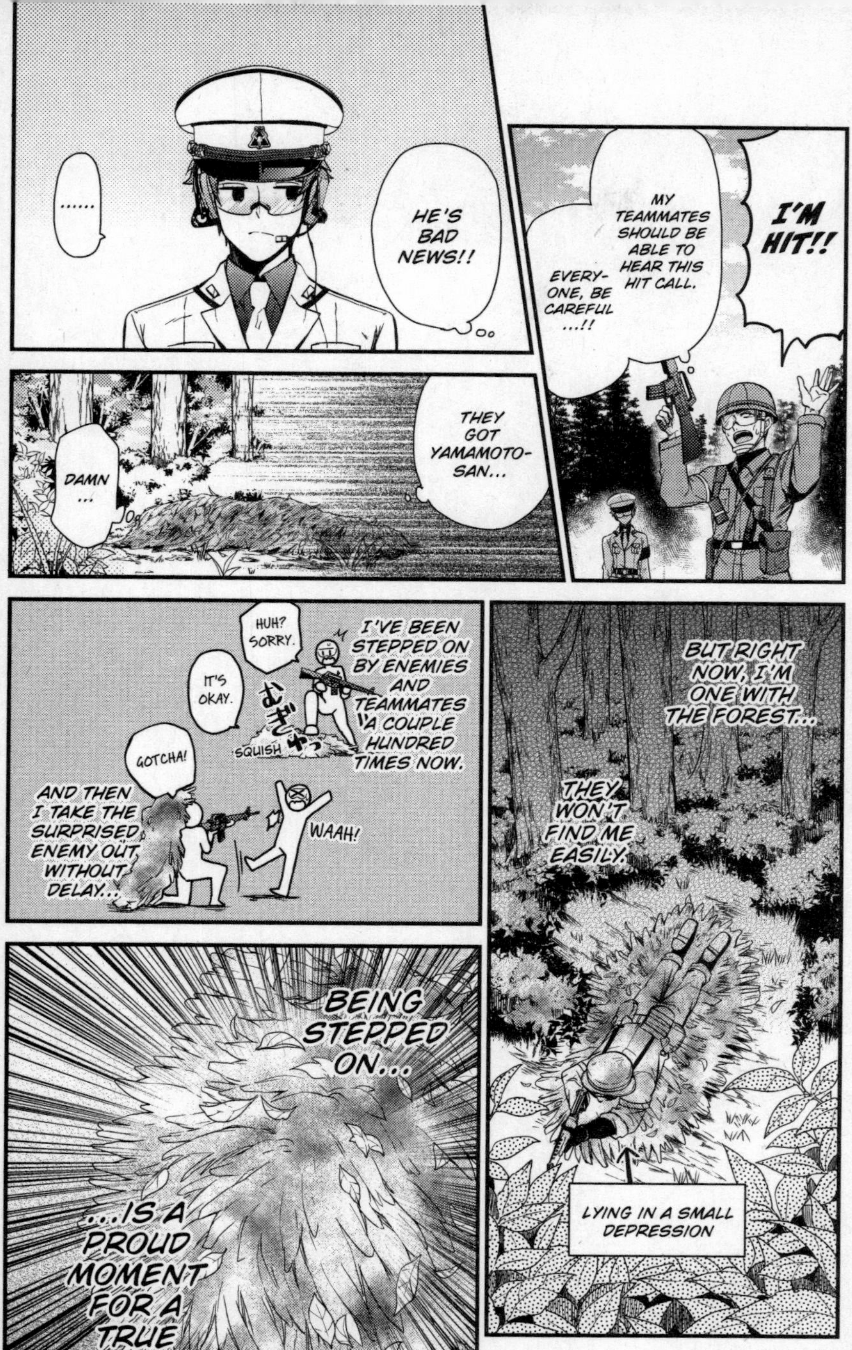
I'M HIT!!
MY TEAMMATES SHOULD BE ABLE TO HEAR THIS HIT CALL.
EVERY-ONE, BE CAREFUL ...!!
HE'S BAD NEWS!!
......
THEY GOT YAMAMOTO-SAN...
DAMN...
BUT RIGHT NOW, I'M ONE WITH THE FOREST...
THEY WON'T FIND ME EASILY.
LYING IN A SMALL DEPRESSION
I'VE BEEN STEPPED ON BY ENEMIES AND TEAMMATES A COUPLE HUNDRED TIMES NOW.
HUH? SORRY.
IT'S OKAY.
むぎゅっ
SQUISH
GOTCHA!
WAAH!
AND THEN I TAKE THE SURPRISED ENEMY OUT WITHOUT DELAY...
BEING STEPPED ON...
...IS A PROUD MOMENT FOR A TRUE MIMIC!!!

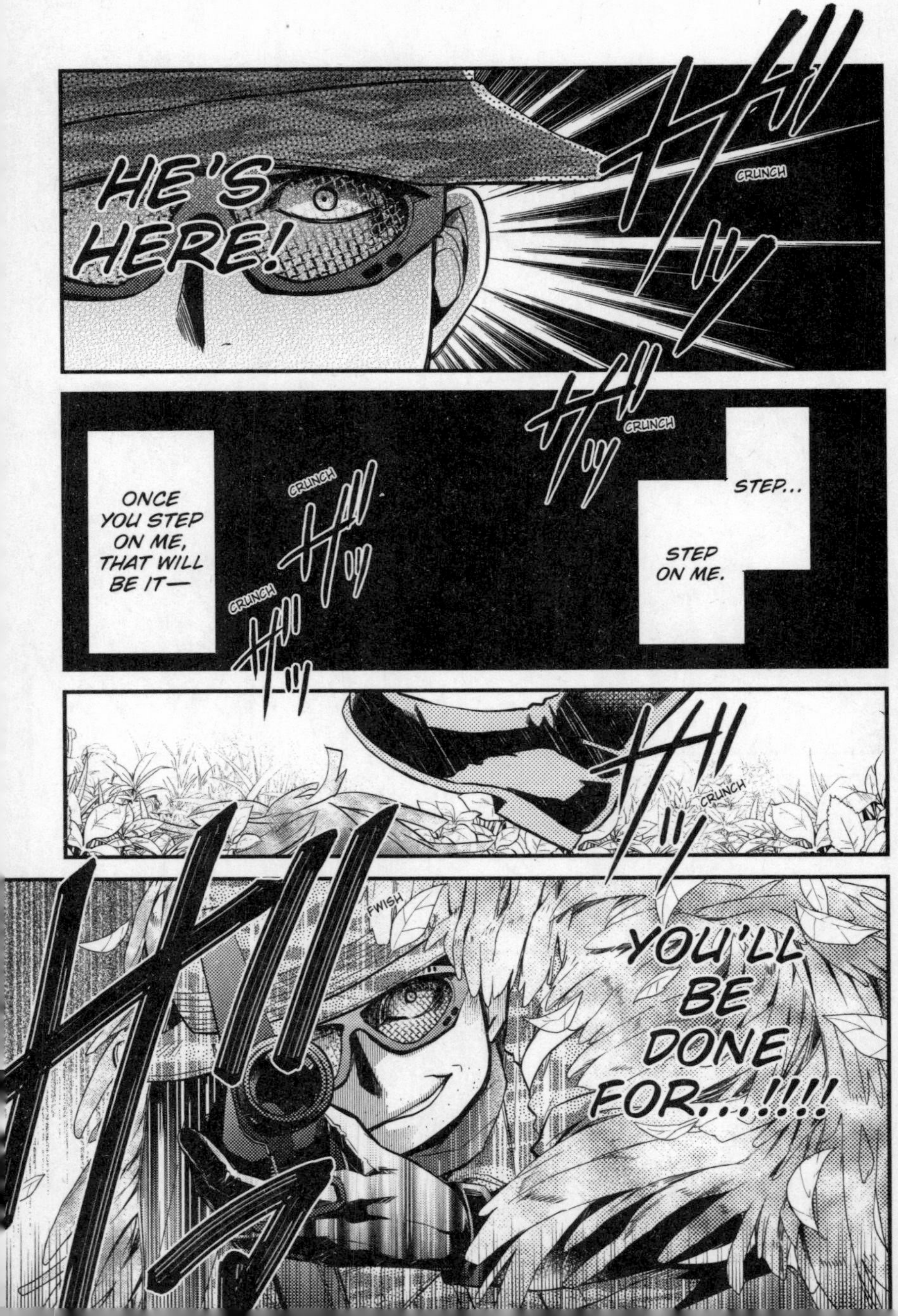

CRUNCH
HE'S HERE!
CRUNCH
STEP...
STEP ON ME.
CRUNCH
ONCE YOU STEP ON ME, THAT WILL BE IT—
CRUNCH
CRUNCH
FWISH
YOU'LL BE DONE FOR...!!!!

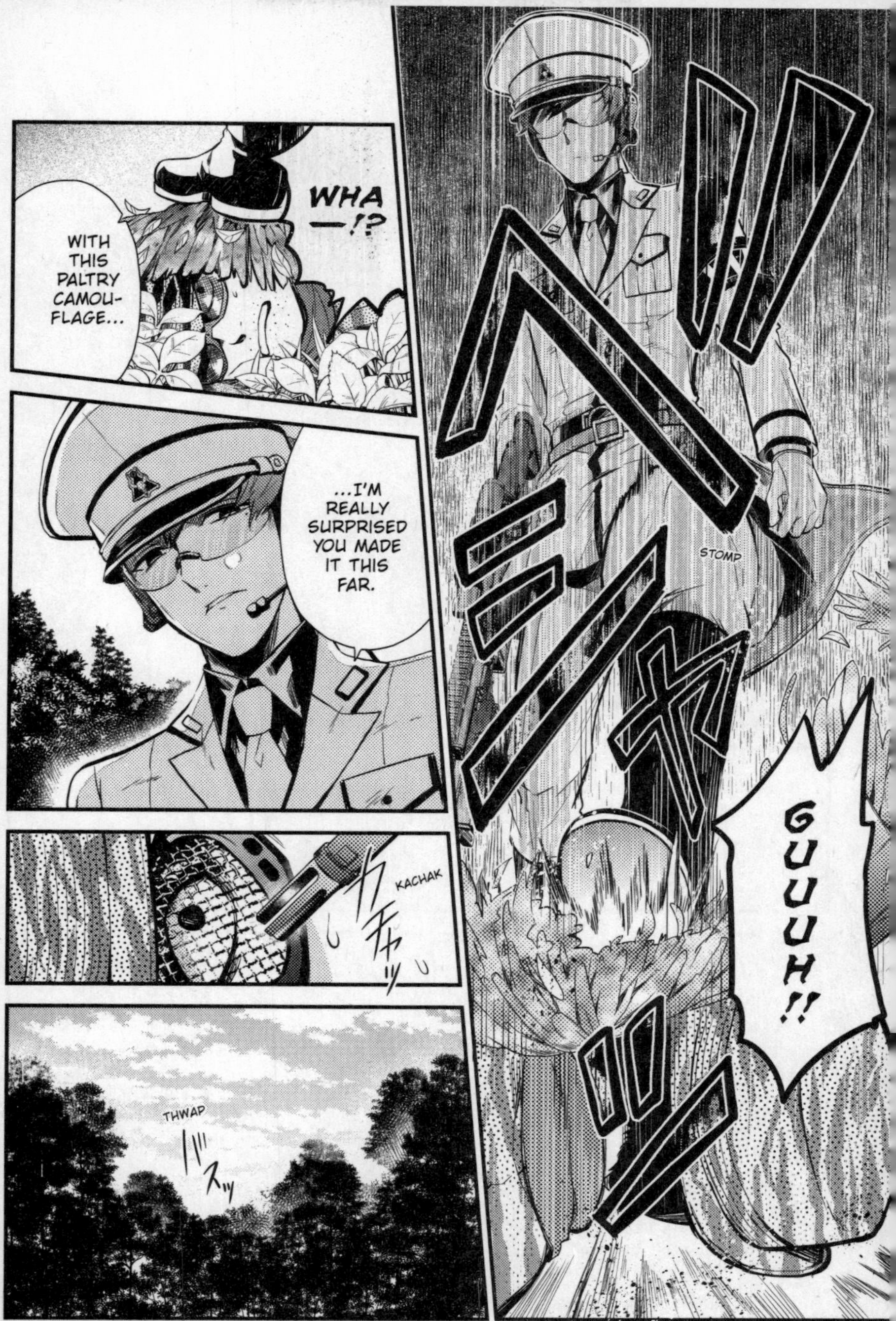
STOMP
GUUUH!!
WHA—!?
WITH THIS PALTRY CAMOUFLAGE...
...I'M REALLY SURPRISED YOU MADE IT THIS FAR.
KACHAK
THWAP

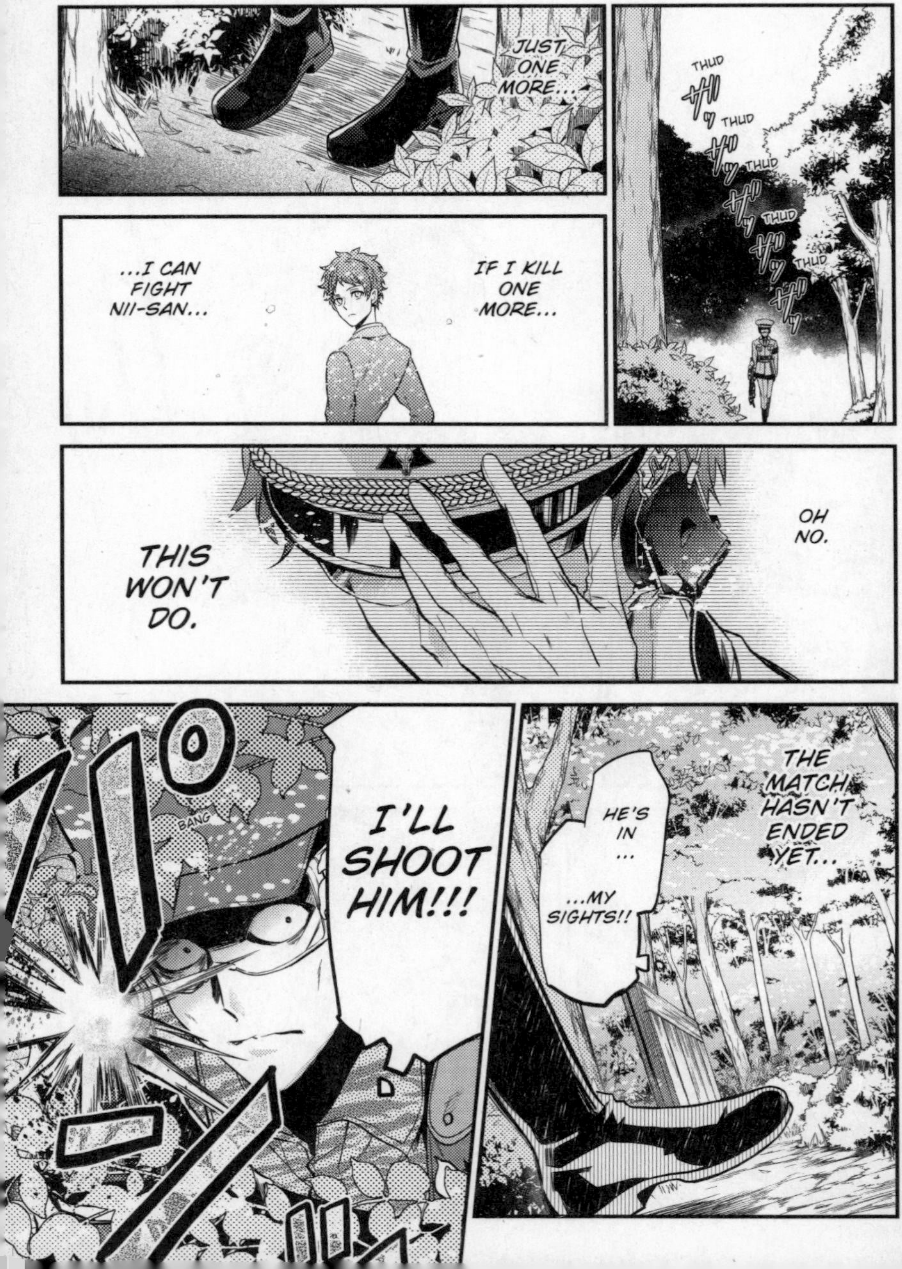
THUD
THUD
THUD
THUD
THUD
JUST ONE MORE...
IF I KILL ONE MORE...
...I CAN FIGHT NII-SAN...
OH NO.
THIS WON'T DO.
THE MATCH HASN'T ENDED YET...
HE'S IN...
...MY SIGHTS!!
I'LL SHOOT HIM!!!
BANG

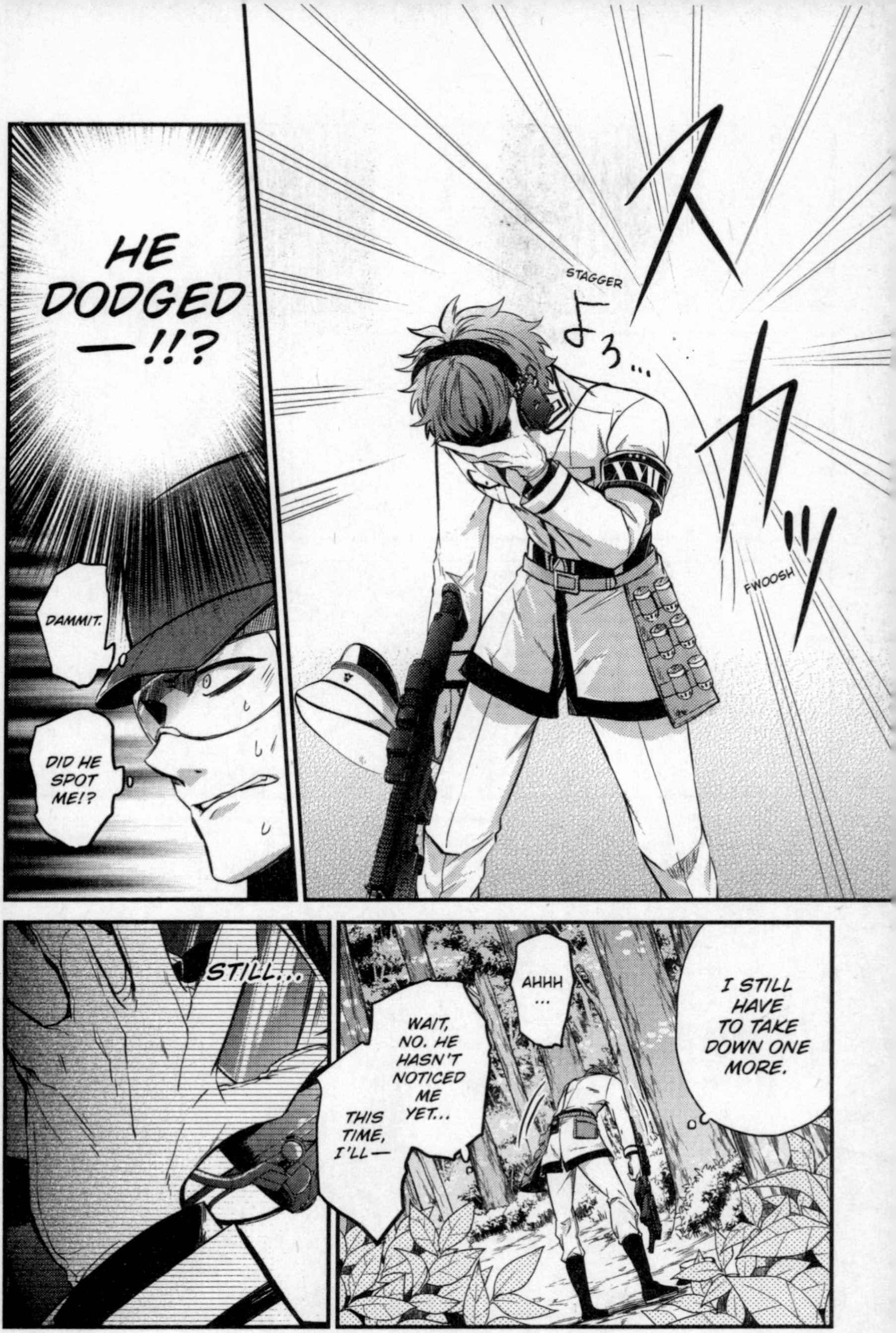
スカッ
FWOOSH
STAGGER
よろ...
HE DODGED—!!?
DAMMIT.
DID HE SPOT ME!?
I STILL HAVE TO TAKE DOWN ONE MORE.
AHHH...
WAIT, NO. HE HASN'T NOTICED ME YET...
THIS TIME, I'LL—
STILL...

...I CAN'T HELP...

...BUT SMILE!

OH...

OH?

SHUDDER

67

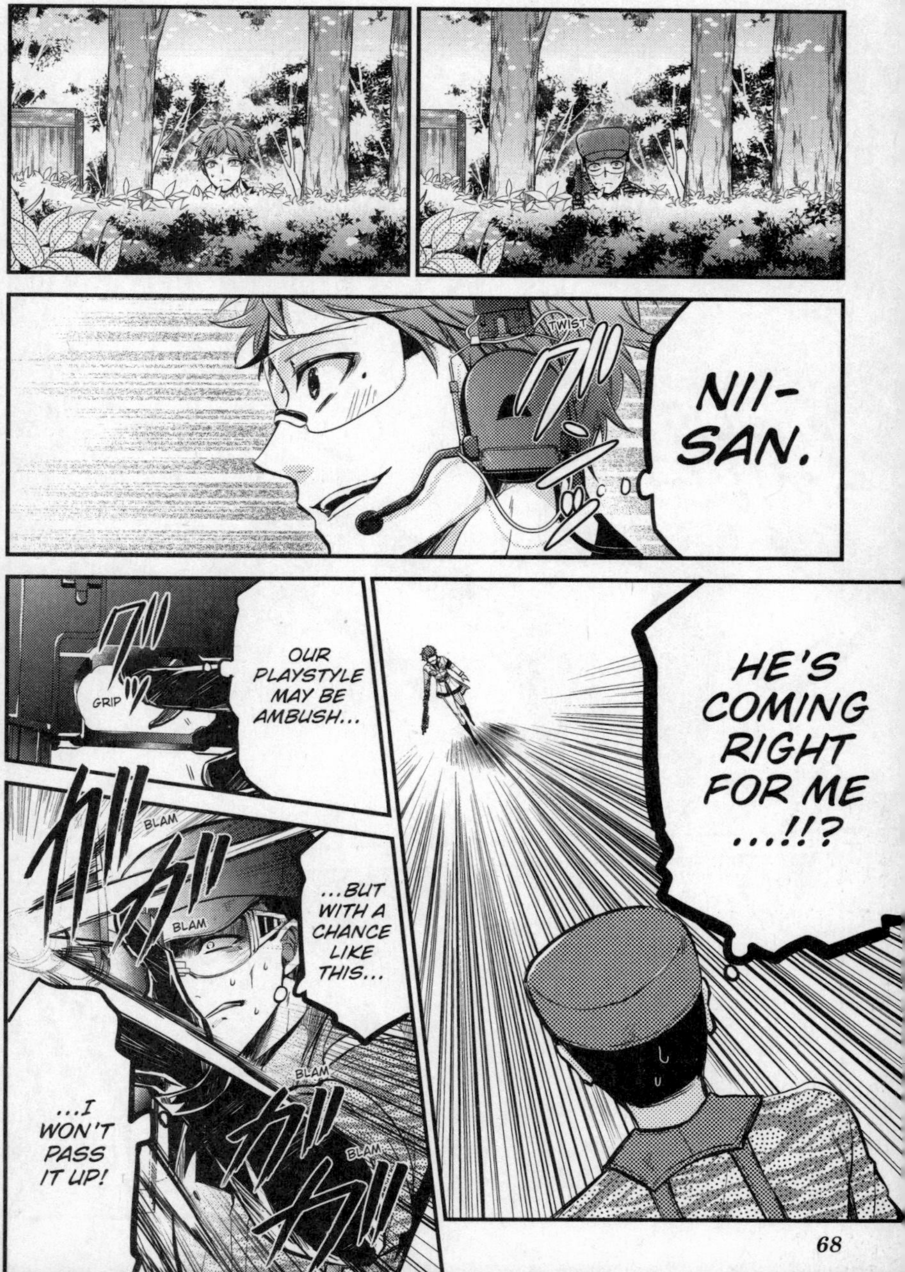
TWIST
NII-SAN.
HE'S COMING RIGHT FOR ME ...!!?
GRIP
OUR PLAYSTYLE MAY BE AMBUSH...
BLAM
BLAM
...BUT WITH A CHANCE LIKE THIS...
BLAM
BLAM
...I WON'T PASS IT UP!

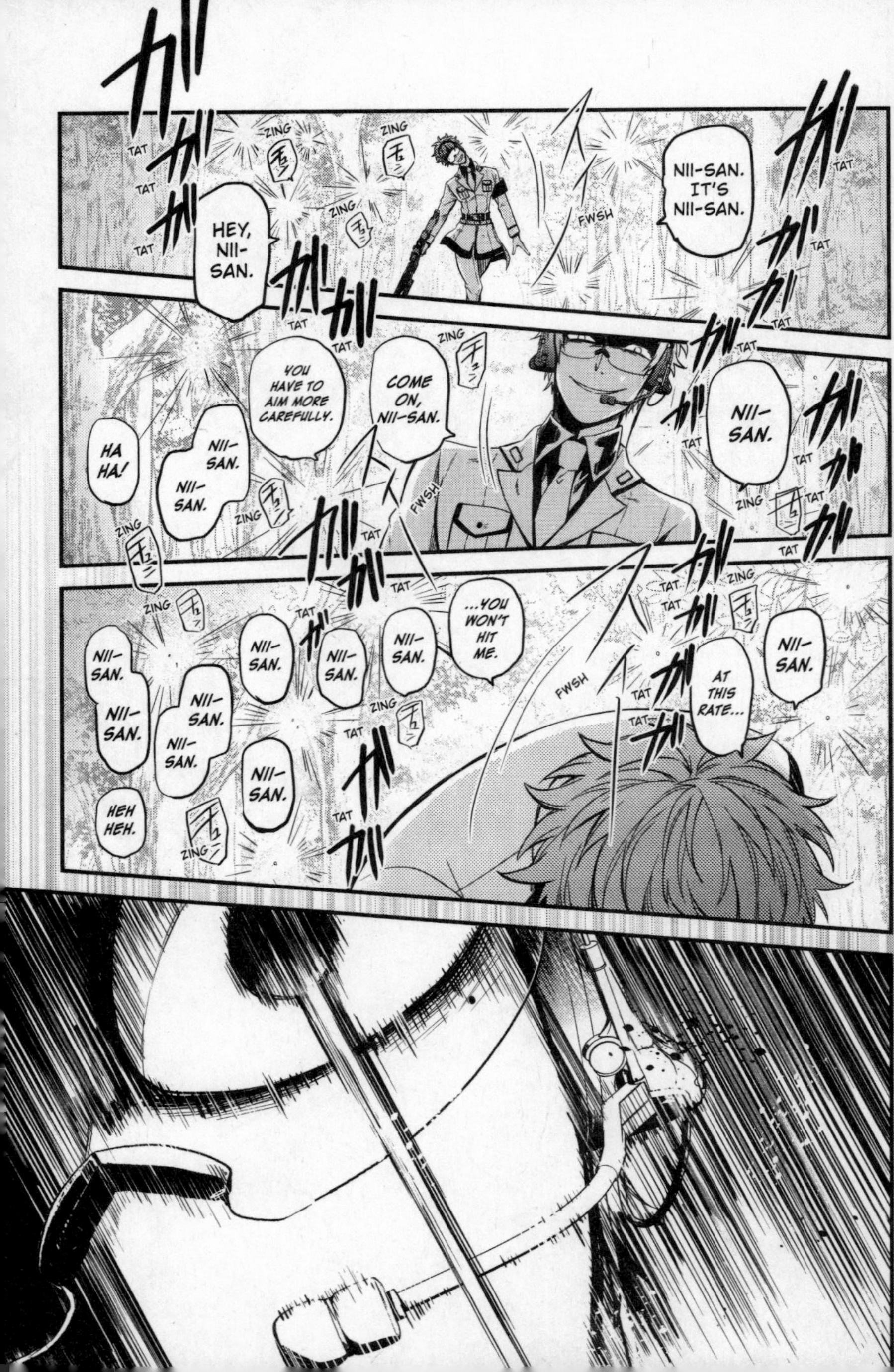

TAT
NII-SAN. IT'S NII-SAN.
FWSH
ZING
ZING
TAT
ZING
HEY, NII-SAN.
TAT
TAT
TAT
NII-SAN.
ZING
COME ON, NII-SAN.
YOU HAVE TO AIM MORE CAREFULLY.
FWSH
NII-SAN. NII-SAN.
ZING
HA HA!
ZING
TAT
ZING
NII-SAN.
AT THIS RATE...
FWSH
TAT
...YOU WON'T HIT ME.
NII-SAN.
NII-SAN.
NII-SAN.
ZING
NII-SAN. NII-SAN.
NII-SAN.
NII-SAN. NII-SAN.
HEH HEH.
ZING
TAT

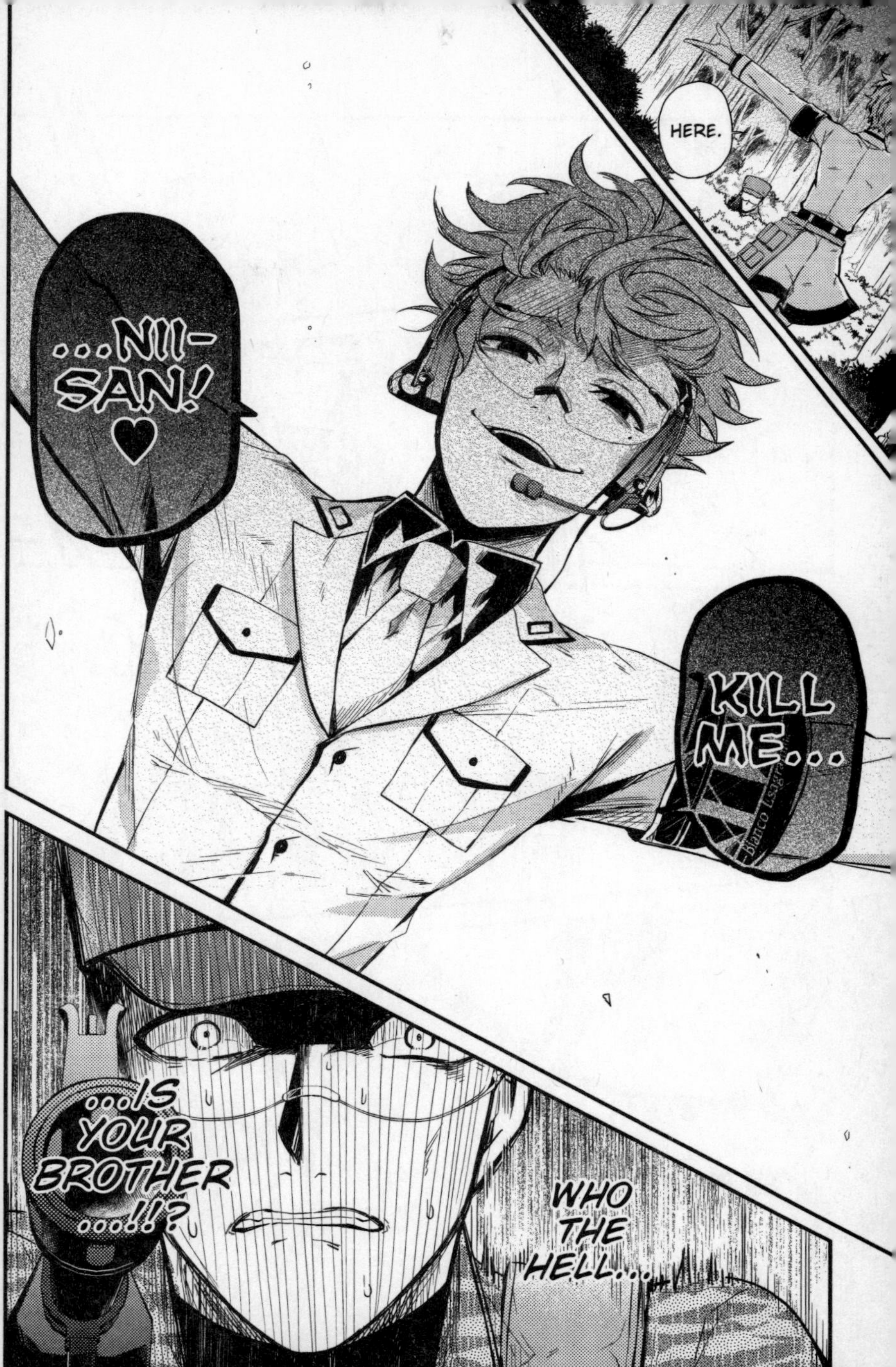
HERE.
...NII-SAN! ♥
KILL ME...
WHO THE HELL...
...IS YOUR BROTHER ...!!?

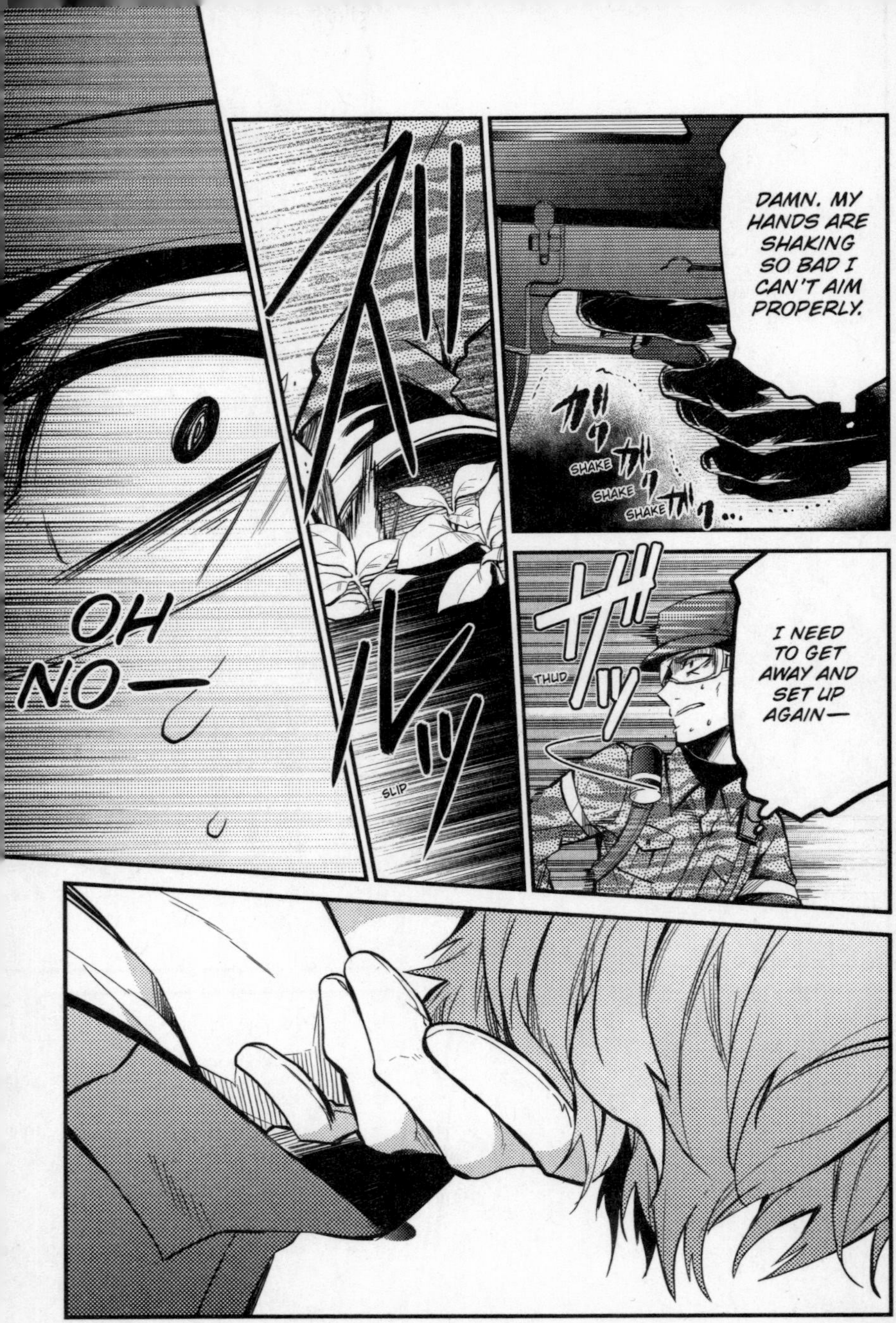
DAMN. MY HANDS ARE SHAKING SO BAD I CAN'T AIM PROPERLY.
SHAKE
SHAKE
SHAKE
THUD
I NEED TO GET AWAY AND SET UP AGAIN—
SLIP
OH NO—

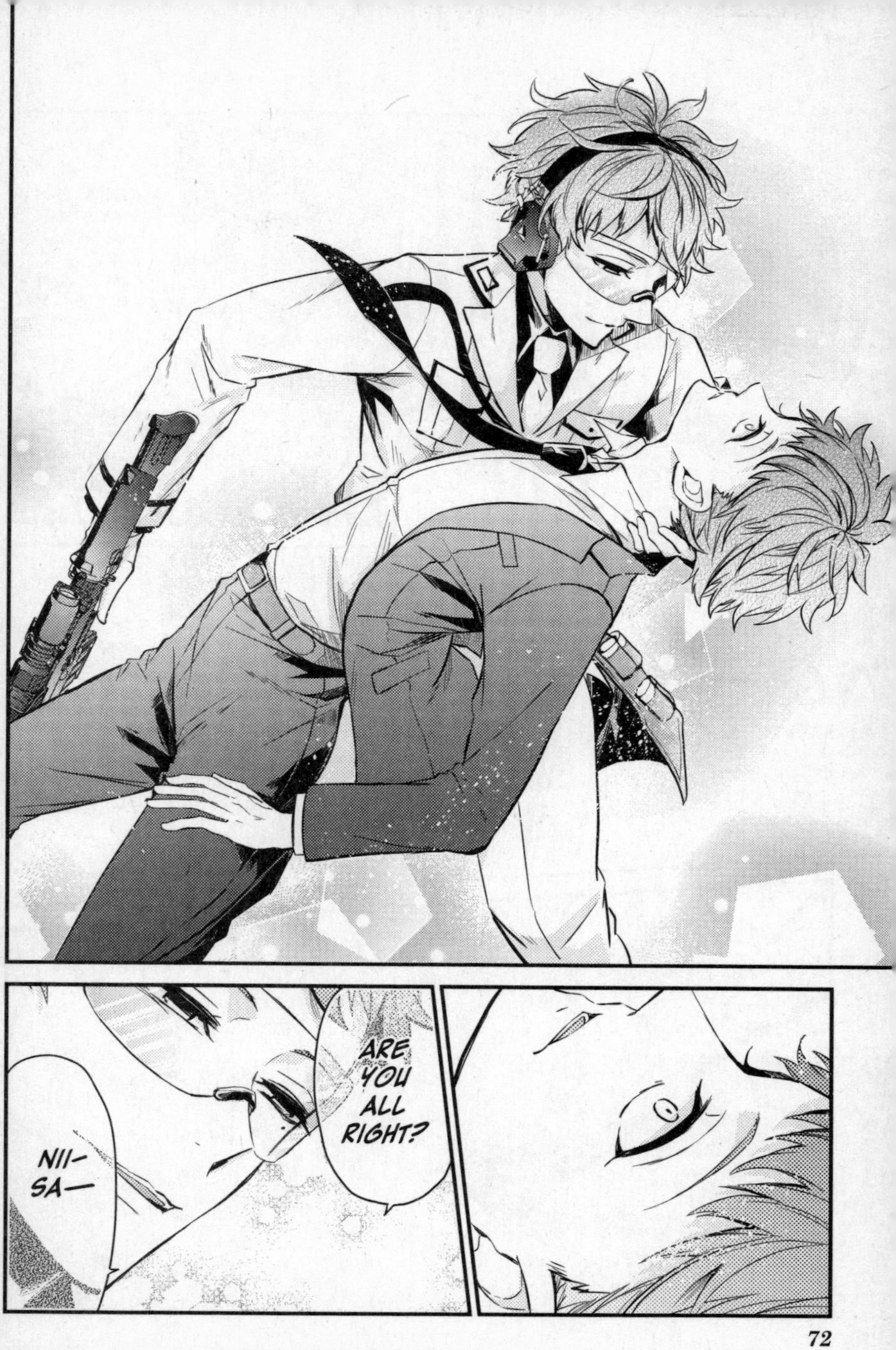
ARE YOU ALL RIGHT?
NII-SA—

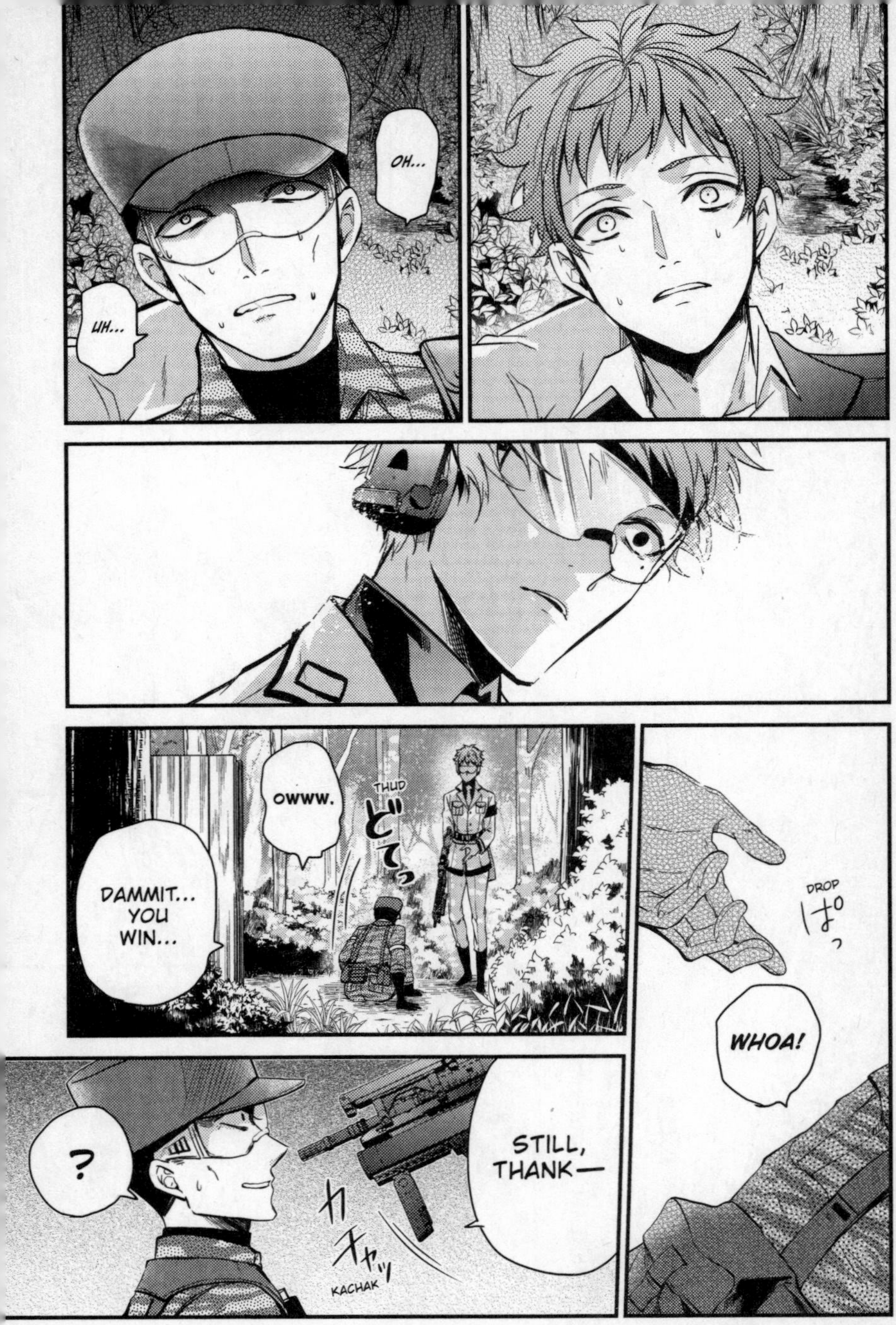
OH...
UH...
DROP
ぱっ
WHOA!
THUD
どてっ
OWWW.
DAMMIT... YOU WIN...
STILL, THANK—
カチャッ
KACHAK
?

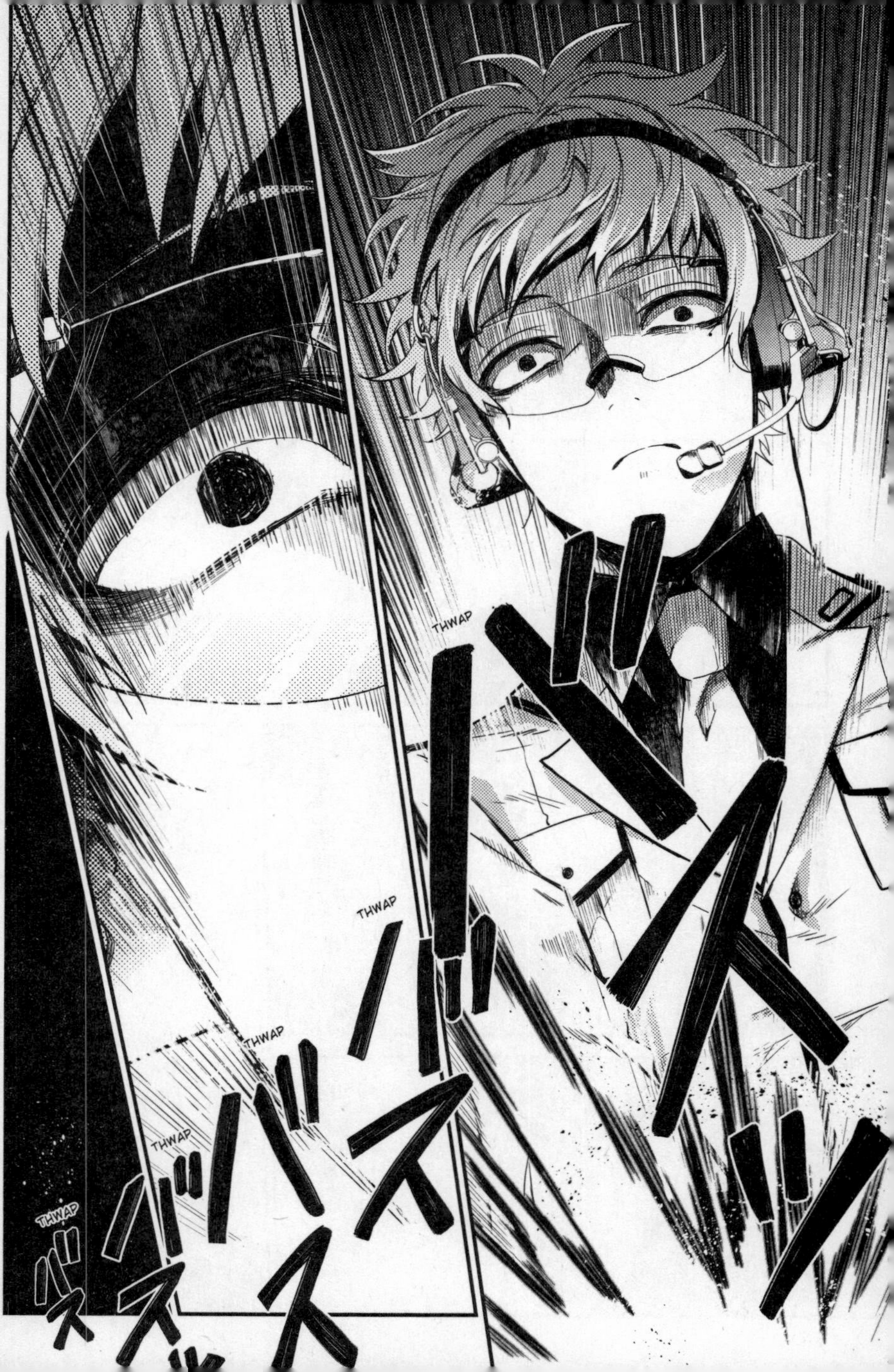
THWAP
THWAP
THWAP
THWAP
THWAP

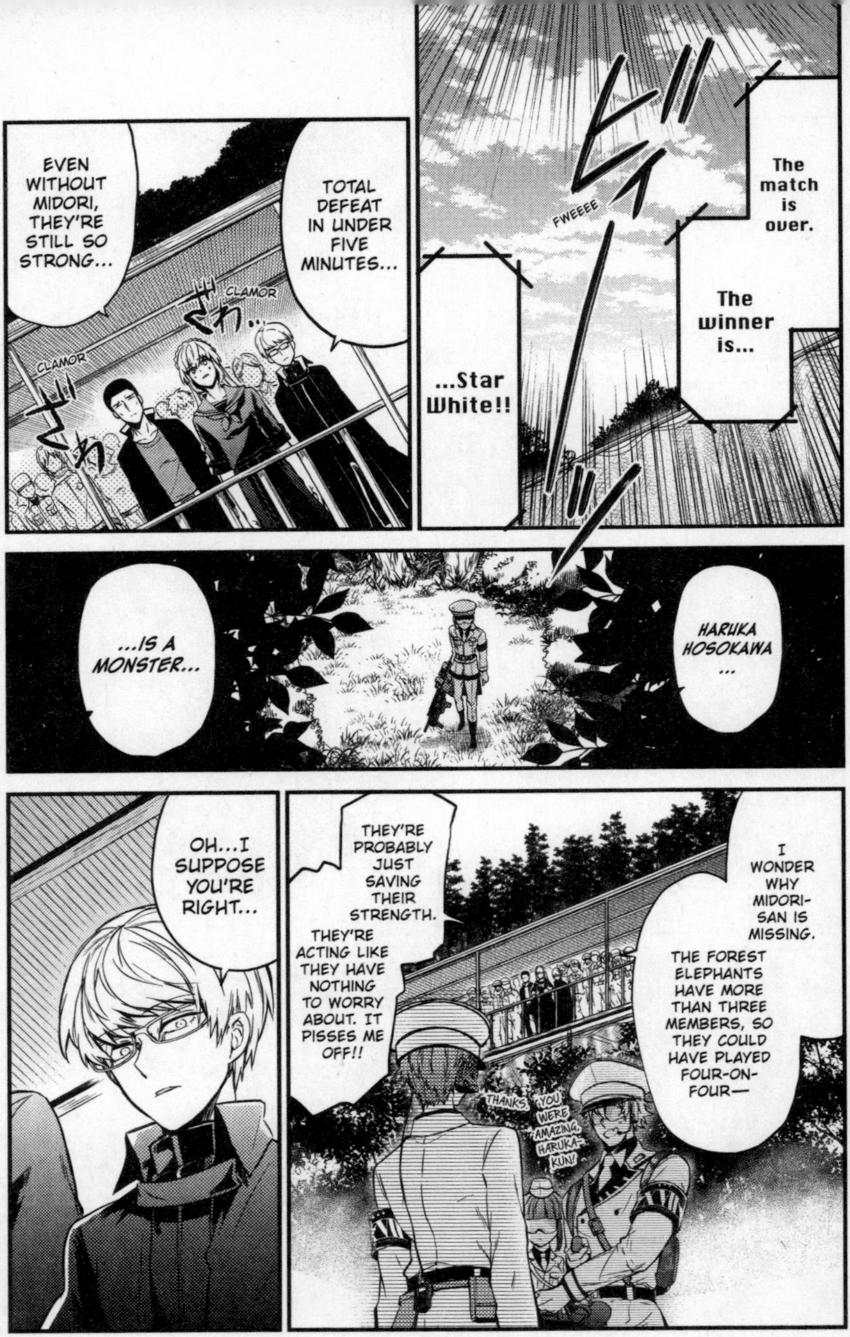
FWEEEE
The match is over.
The winner is...
...Star White!!
TOTAL DEFEAT IN UNDER FIVE MINUTES...
CLAMOR
EVEN WITHOUT MIDORI, THEY'RE STILL SO STRONG...
CLAMOR
HARUKA HOSOKAWA...
...IS A MONSTER...
I WONDER WHY MIDORI-SAN IS MISSING.
THE FOREST ELEPHANTS HAVE MORE THAN THREE MEMBERS, SO THEY COULD HAVE PLAYED FOUR-ON-FOUR—
YOU WERE AMAZING, HARUKA-KUN!
THANKS.
THEY'RE PROBABLY JUST SAVING THEIR STRENGTH.
THEY'RE ACTING LIKE THEY HAVE NOTHING TO WORRY ABOUT. IT PISSES ME OFF!!
OH...I SUPPOSE YOU'RE RIGHT...

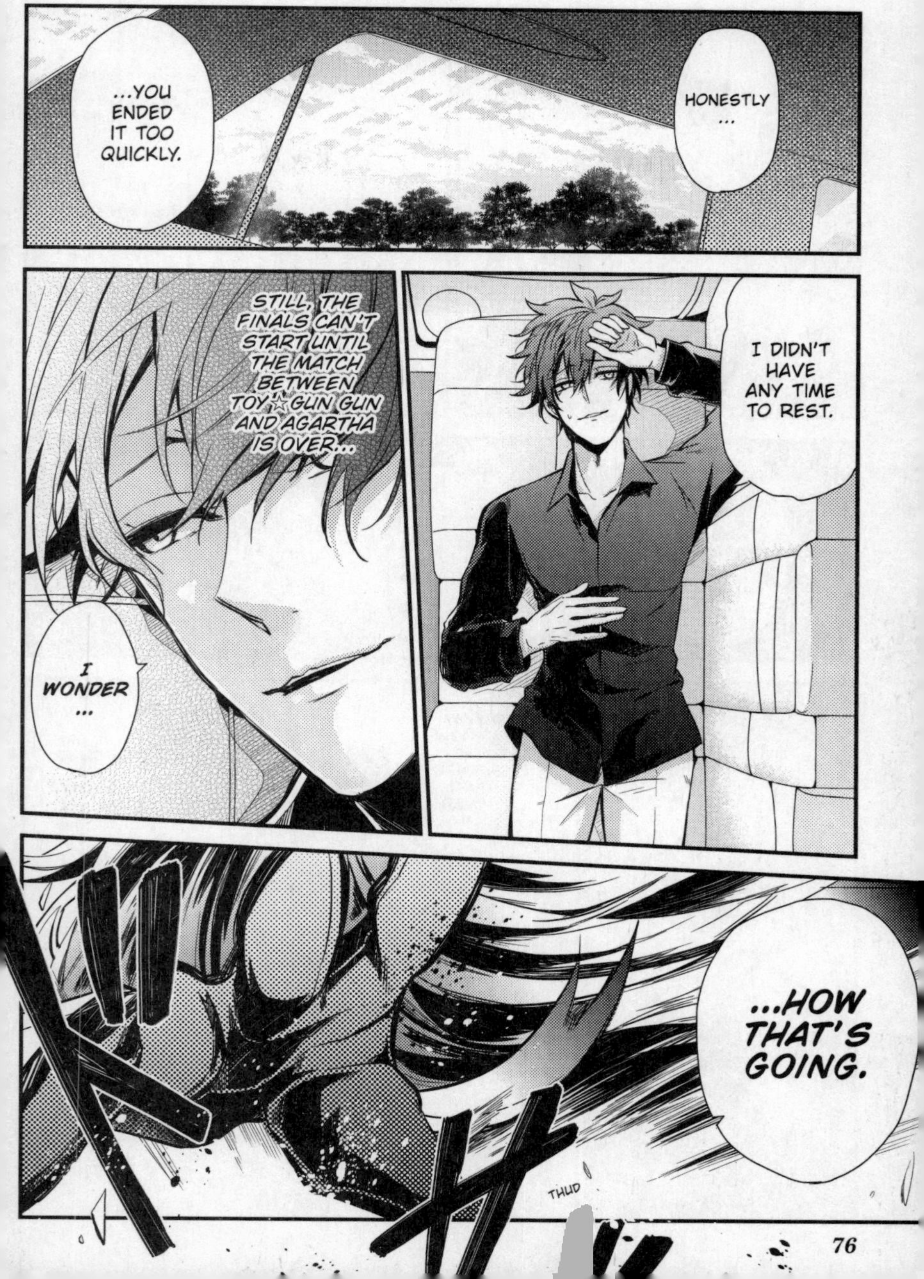
HONESTLY...
...YOU ENDED IT TOO QUICKLY.
I DIDN'T HAVE ANY TIME TO REST.
STILL, THE FINALS CAN'T START UNTIL THE MATCH BETWEEN TOY☆GUN GUN AND AGARTHA IS OVER...
I WONDER...
...HOW THAT'S GOING.
THUD

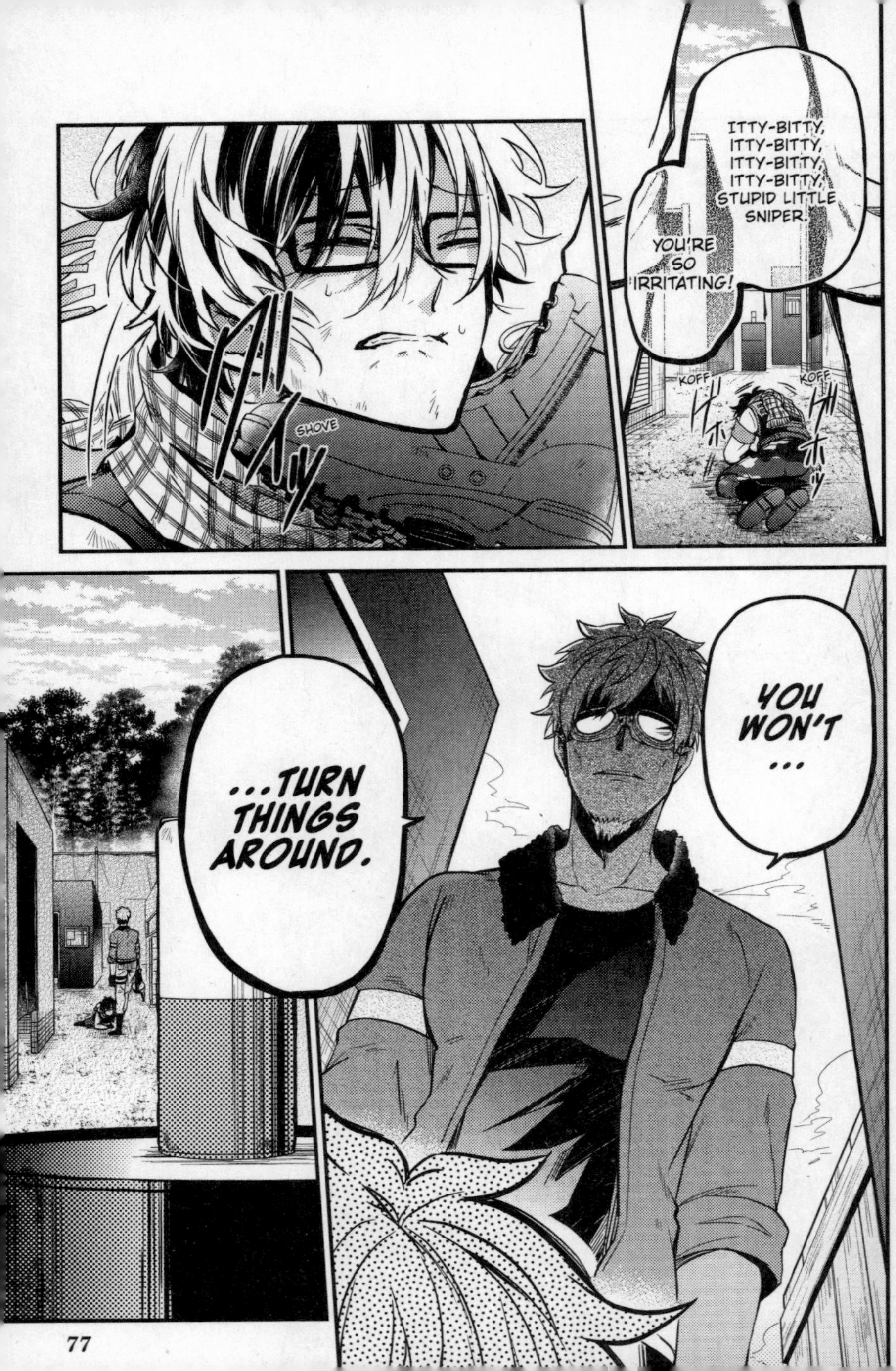

ITTY-BITTY, ITTY-BITTY, ITTY-BITTY, ITTY-BITTY, STUPID LITTLE SNIPER.
YOU'RE SO IRRITATING!
KOFF
KOFF
SHOVE
YOU WON'T ...
...TURN THINGS AROUND.

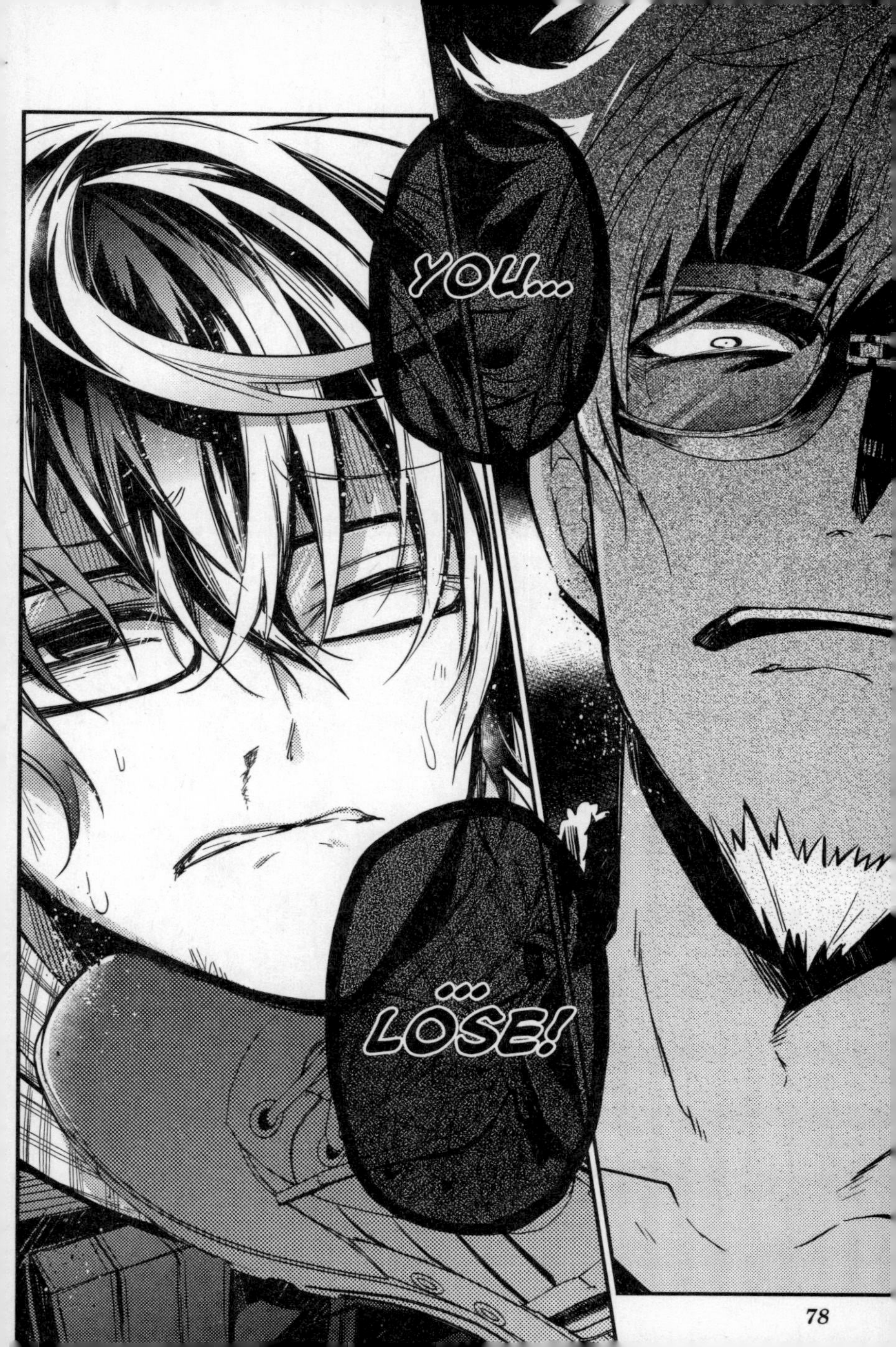
YOU...
...LÖSE!

*EXTRA VALENTINE'S STORY FROM TWITTER
~HARUKI EDITION~

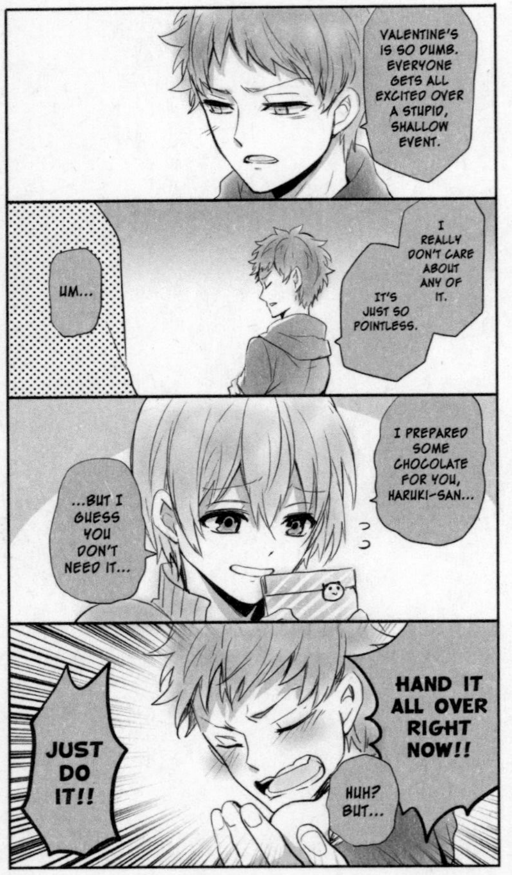
VALENTINE'S IS SO DUMB. EVERYONE GETS ALL EXCITED OVER A STUPID, SHALLOW EVENT.
I REALLY DON'T CARE ABOUT ANY OF IT.
IT'S JUST SO POINTLESS.
UM...
I PREPARED SOME CHOCOLATE FOR YOU, HARUKI-SAN...
...BUT I GUESS YOU DON'T NEED IT...
HAND IT ALL OVER RIGHT NOW!!
HUH? BUT...
JUST DO IT!!

*EXTRA VALENTINE'S STORY FROM TWITTER

~HARUKA EDITION~

(WHEN TACHIBANA TAKES A TRIP TO HOSHISHIRO GENERAL HOSPITAL)

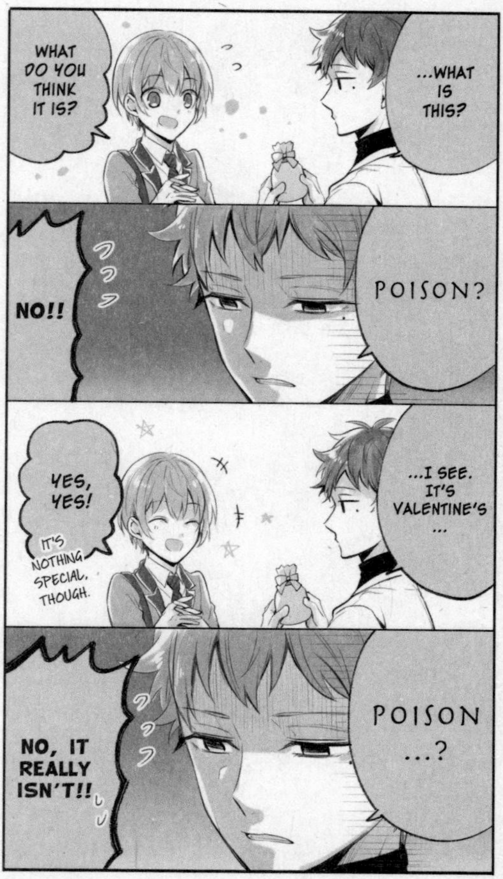
...WHAT IS THIS?
WHAT DO YOU THINK IT IS?
POISON?
NO!!
...I SEE. IT'S VALENTINE'S ...
YES, YES!
IT'S NOTHING SPECIAL, THOUGH.
POISON ...?
NO, IT REALLY ISN'T!!

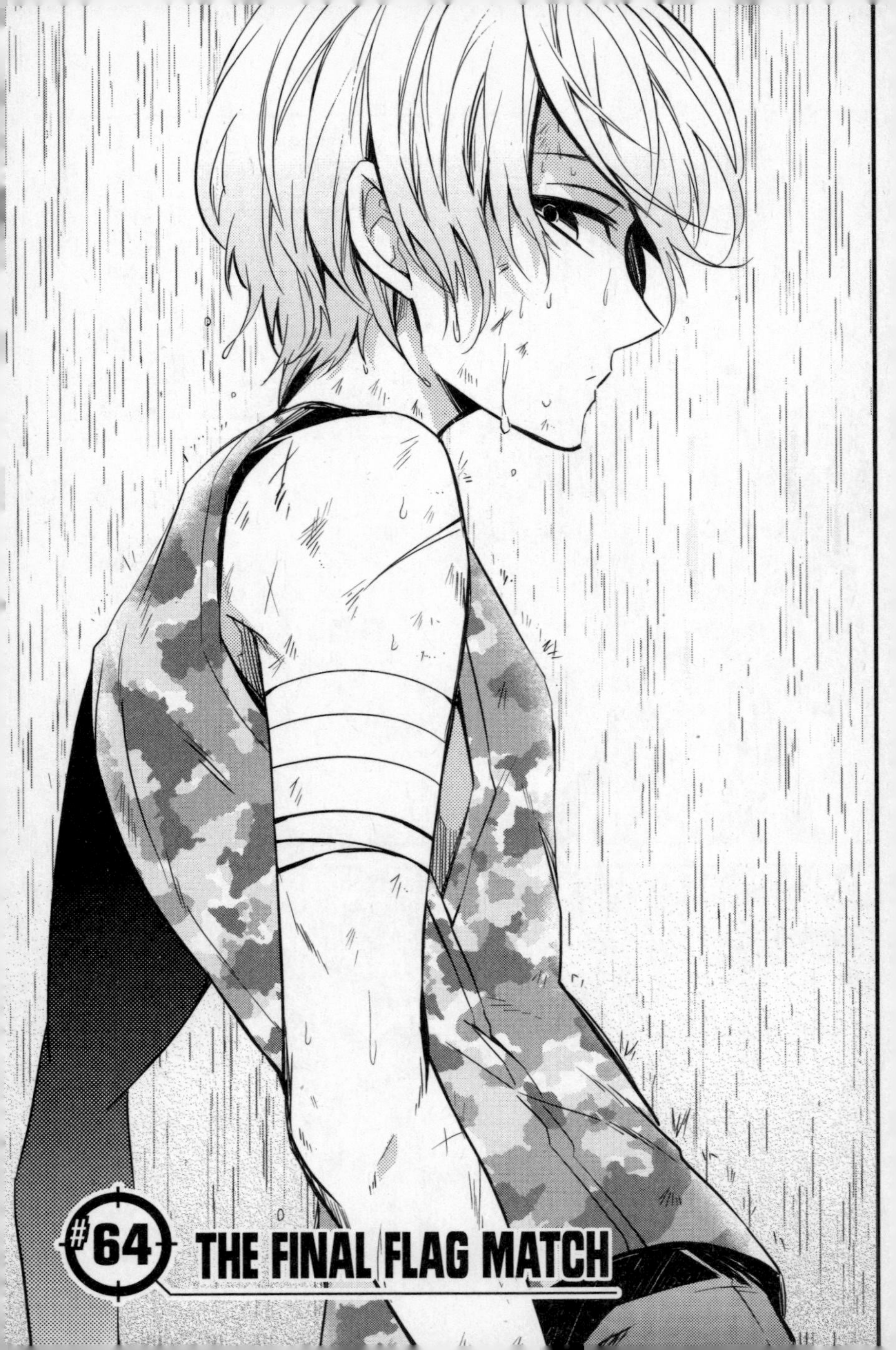
#64
THE FINAL FLAG MATCH

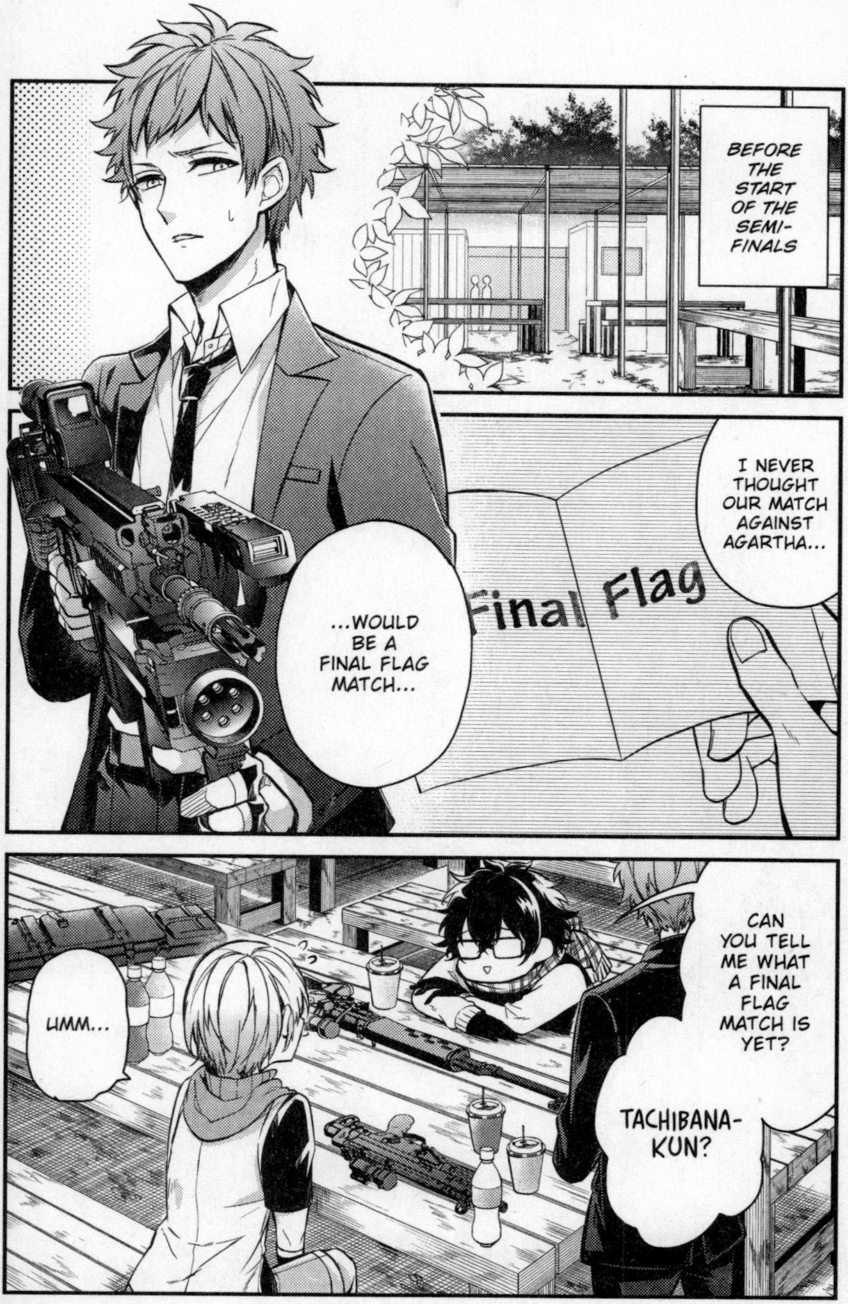
BEFORE THE START OF THE SEMI-FINALS
I NEVER THOUGHT OUR MATCH AGAINST AGARTHA...
Final Flag
...WOULD BE A FINAL FLAG MATCH...
CAN YOU TELL ME WHAT A FINAL FLAG MATCH IS YET?
TACHIBANA-KUN?
UMM...

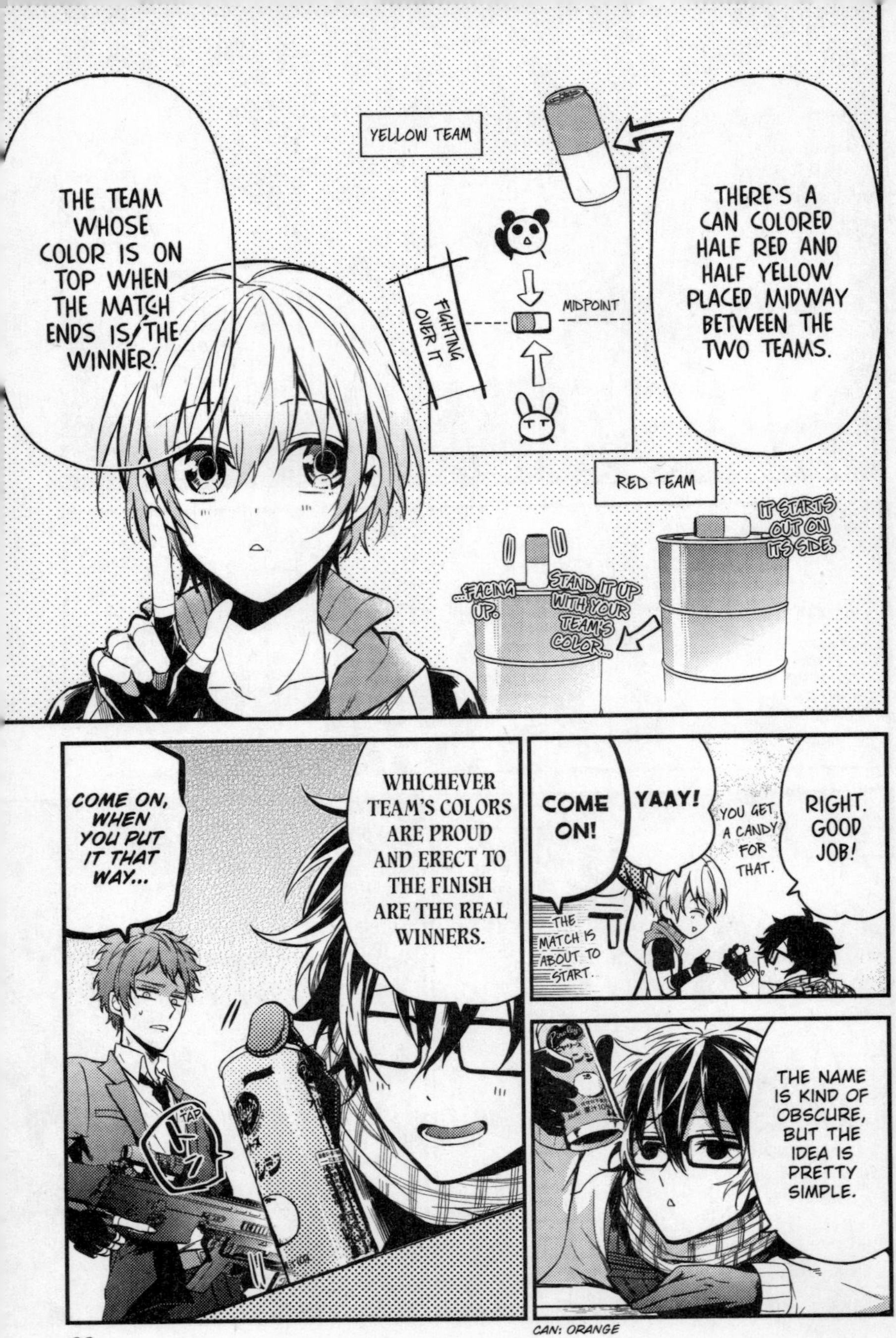
THERE'S A CAN COLORED HALF RED AND HALF YELLOW PLACED MIDWAY BETWEEN THE TWO TEAMS.
YELLOW TEAM
MIDPOINT
FIGHTING OVER IT
RED TEAM
IT STARTS OUT ON ITS SIDE.
STAND IT UP WITH YOUR TEAM'S COLOR...
...FACING UP.
THE TEAM WHOSE COLOR IS ON TOP WHEN THE MATCH ENDS IS THE WINNER!
RIGHT. GOOD JOB!
YOU GET A CANDY FOR THAT.
YAAY!
COME ON!
THE MATCH IS ABOUT TO START.
THE NAME IS KIND OF OBSCURE, BUT THE IDEA IS PRETTY SIMPLE.
WHICHEVER TEAM'S COLORS ARE PROUD AND ERECT TO THE FINISH ARE THE REAL WINNERS.
COME ON, WHEN YOU PUT IT THAT WAY...
TAP
CAN: ORANGE

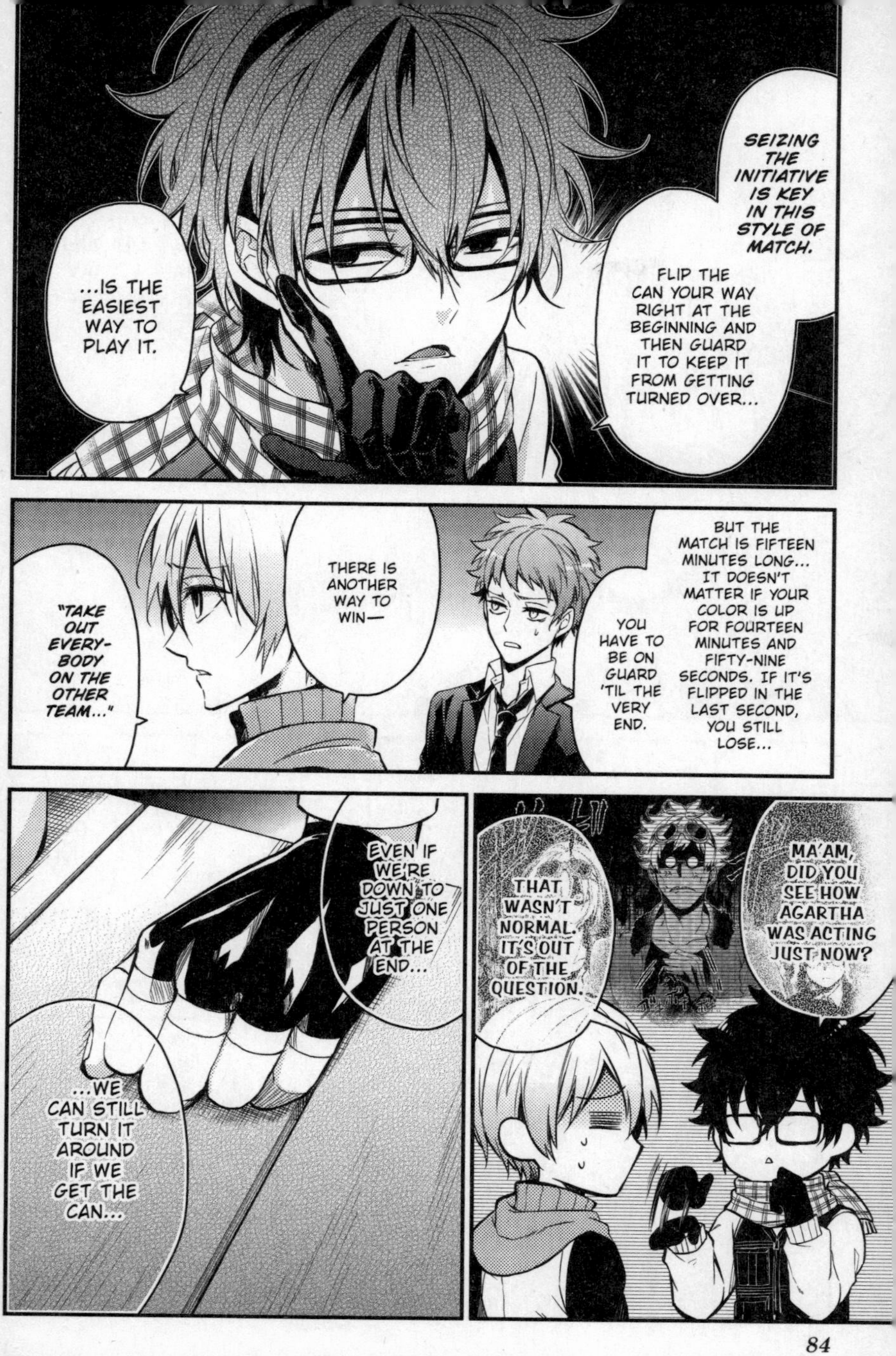
SEIZING THE INITIATIVE IS KEY IN THIS STYLE OF MATCH.
FLIP THE CAN YOUR WAY RIGHT AT THE BEGINNING AND THEN GUARD IT TO KEEP IT FROM GETTING TURNED OVER...
...IS THE EASIEST WAY TO PLAY IT.
BUT THE MATCH IS FIFTEEN MINUTES LONG... IT DOESN'T MATTER IF YOUR COLOR IS UP FOR FOURTEEN MINUTES AND FIFTY-NINE SECONDS. IF IT'S FLIPPED IN THE LAST SECOND, YOU STILL LOSE...
YOU HAVE TO BE ON GUARD 'TIL THE VERY END.
THERE IS ANOTHER WAY TO WIN—
"TAKE OUT EVERY-BODY ON THE OTHER TEAM..."
MA'AM, DID YOU SEE HOW AGARTHA WAS ACTING JUST NOW?
THAT WASN'T NORMAL. IT'S OUT OF THE QUESTION.
EVEN IF WE'RE DOWN TO JUST ONE PERSON AT THE END...
...WE CAN STILL TURN IT AROUND IF WE GET THE CAN...

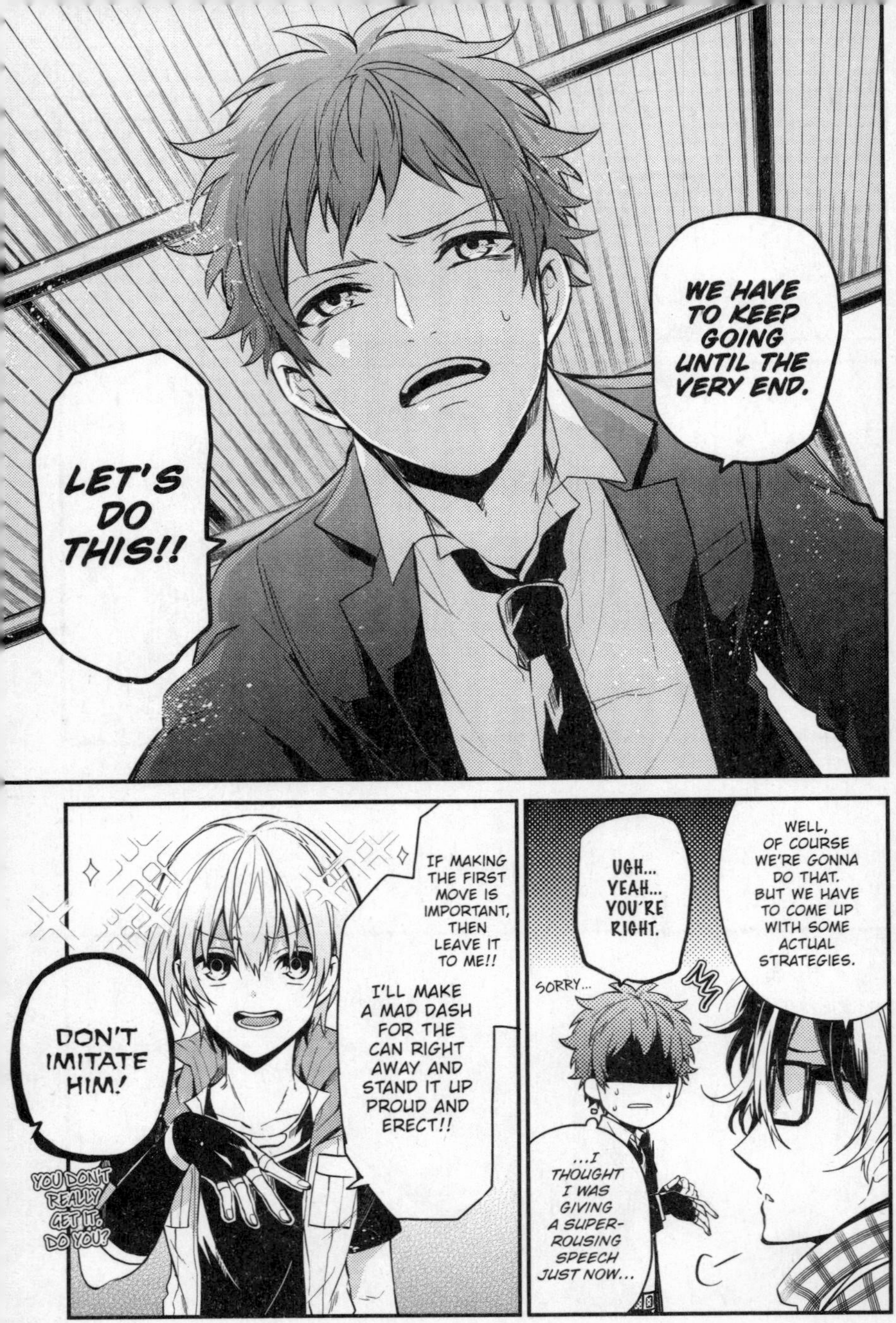
WE HAVE TO KEEP GOING UNTIL THE VERY END.
LET'S DO THIS!!
WELL, OF COURSE WE'RE GONNA DO THAT. BUT WE HAVE TO COME UP WITH SOME ACTUAL STRATEGIES.
UGH... YEAH... YOU'RE RIGHT.
SORRY...
...I THOUGHT I WAS GIVING A SUPER-ROUSING SPEECH JUST NOW...
IF MAKING THE FIRST MOVE IS IMPORTANT, THEN LEAVE IT TO ME!!
I'LL MAKE A MAD DASH FOR THE CAN RIGHT AWAY AND STAND IT UP PROUD AND ERECT!!
DON'T IMITATE HIM!
YOU DON'T REALLY GET IT, DO YOU?

WE SHOULD ASSUME THE OTHER TEAM IS ALREADY AWARE OF YOUR PHYSICAL ABILITIES.

MEANING...

...WE NEED TO THINK OF WHAT TO DO IF WE CAN'T GET THE UPPER HAND.

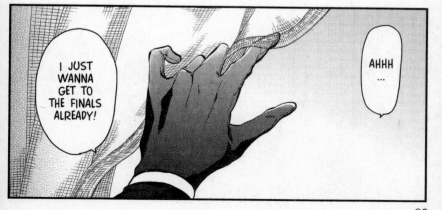

I JUST WANNA GET TO THE FINALS ALREADY!

AHHH...

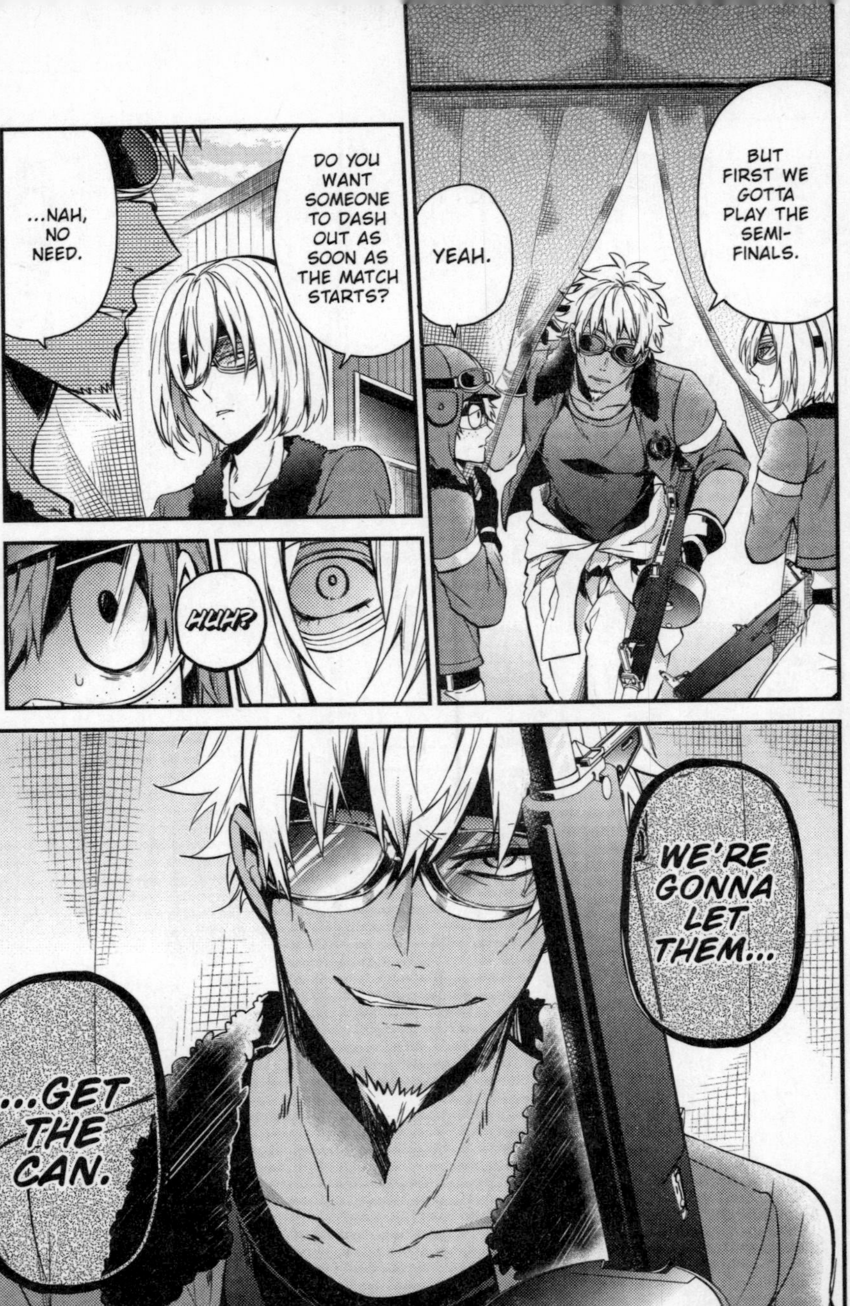

BUT FIRST WE GOTTA PLAY THE SEMI-FINALS.
YEAH.
DO YOU WANT SOMEONE TO DASH OUT AS SOON AS THE MATCH STARTS?
...NAH, NO NEED.
HUH?
WE'RE GONNA LET THEM...
...GET THE CAN.

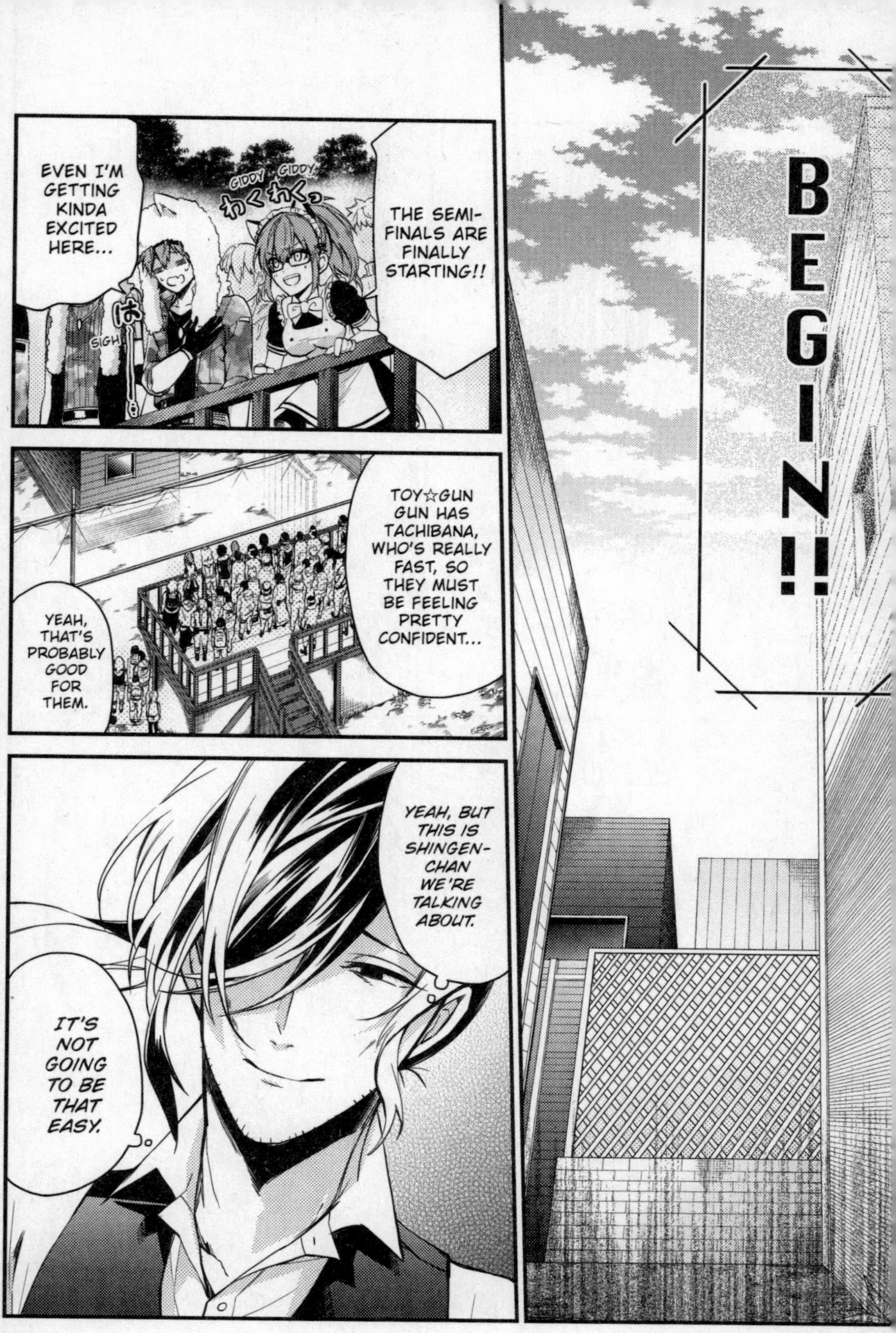
BEGIN!!
THE SEMI-FINALS ARE FINALLY STARTING!!
GIDDY GIDDY
わくわくっ
EVEN I'M GETTING KINDA EXCITED HERE...
は
SIGH
TOY☆GUN GUN HAS TACHIBANA, WHO'S REALLY FAST, SO THEY MUST BE FEELING PRETTY CONFIDENT...
YEAH, THAT'S PROBABLY GOOD FOR THEM.
YEAH, BUT THIS IS SHINGEN-CHAN WE'RE TALKING ABOUT.
IT'S NOT GOING TO BE THAT EASY.

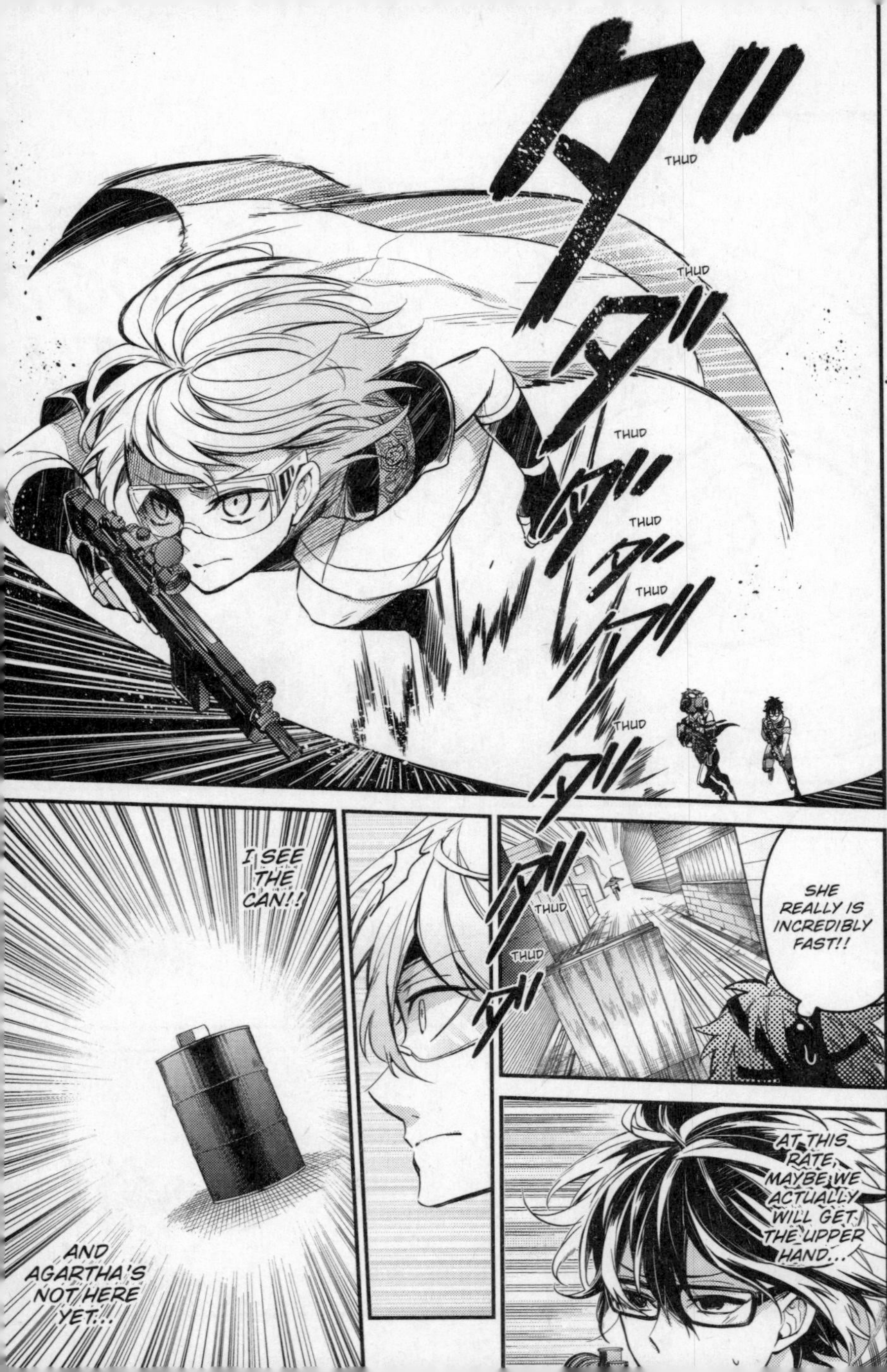
THUD
THUD
THUD
THUD
THUD
THUD
THUD
THUD
SHE REALLY IS INCREDIBLY FAST!!
AT THIS RATE, MAYBE WE ACTUALLY WILL GET THE UPPER HAND...
I SEE THE CAN!!
AND AGARTHA'S NOT HERE YET...

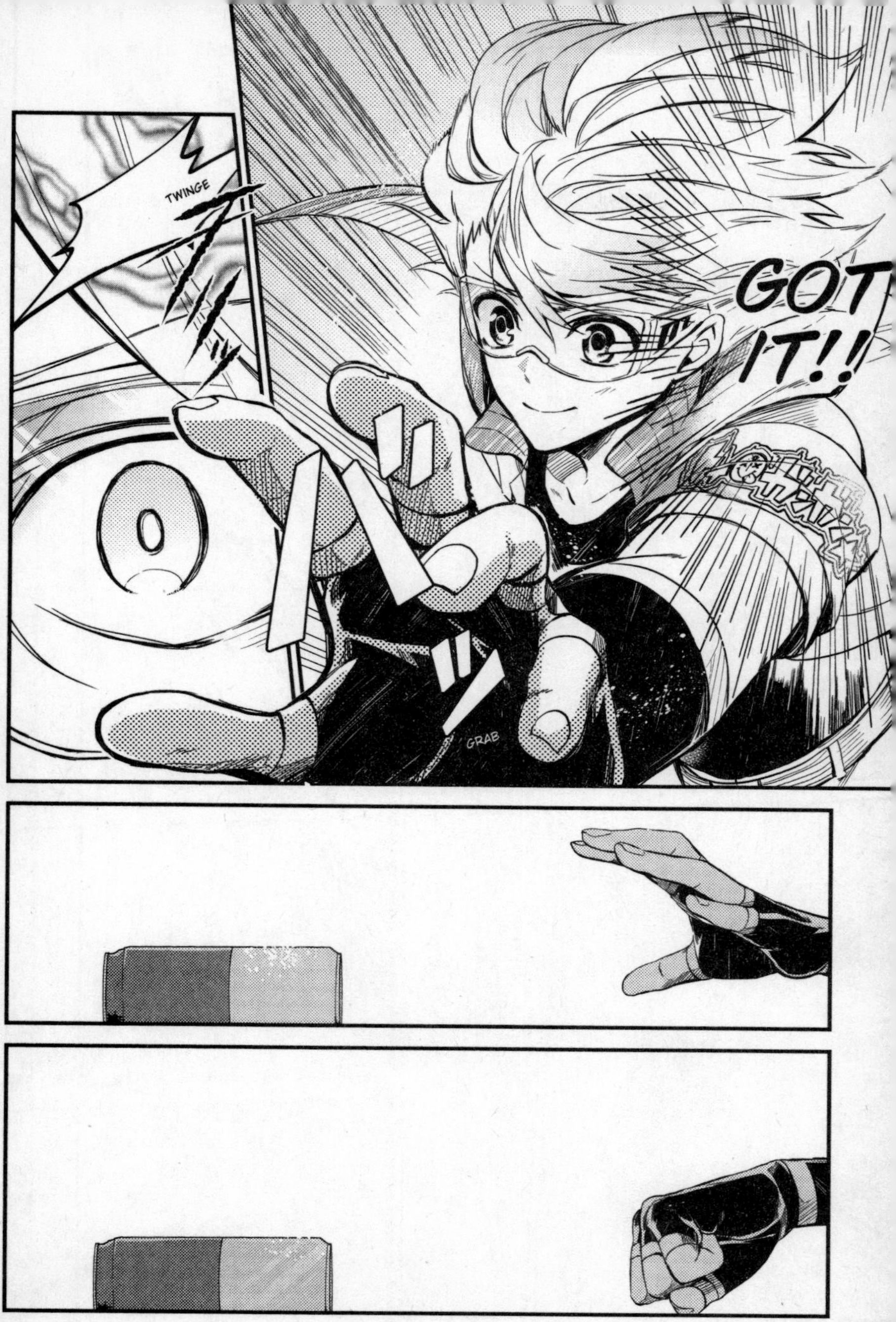
GOT IT!!
TWINGE
GRAB

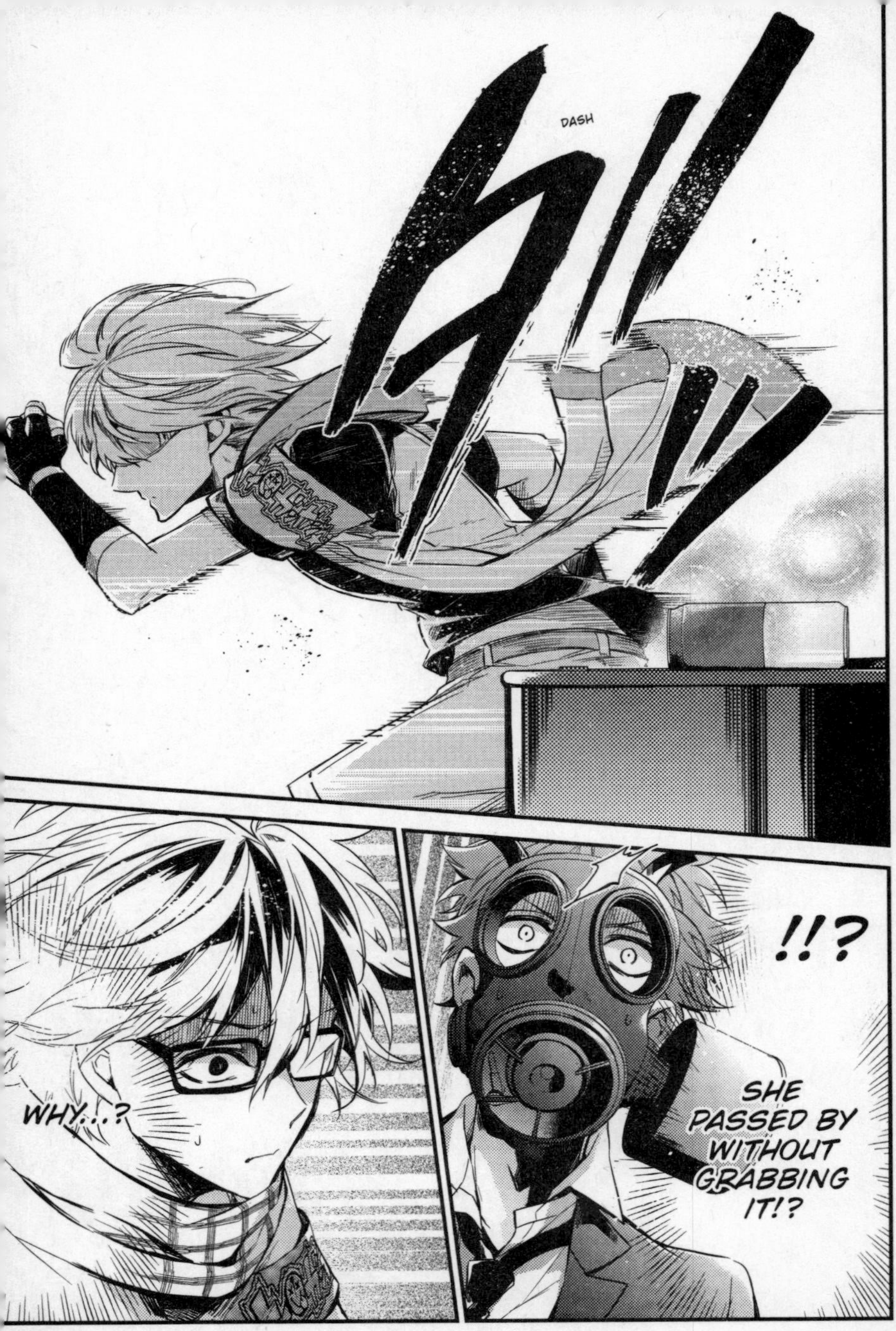
DASH
!!?
SHE PASSED BY WITHOUT GRABBING IT!?
WHY...?

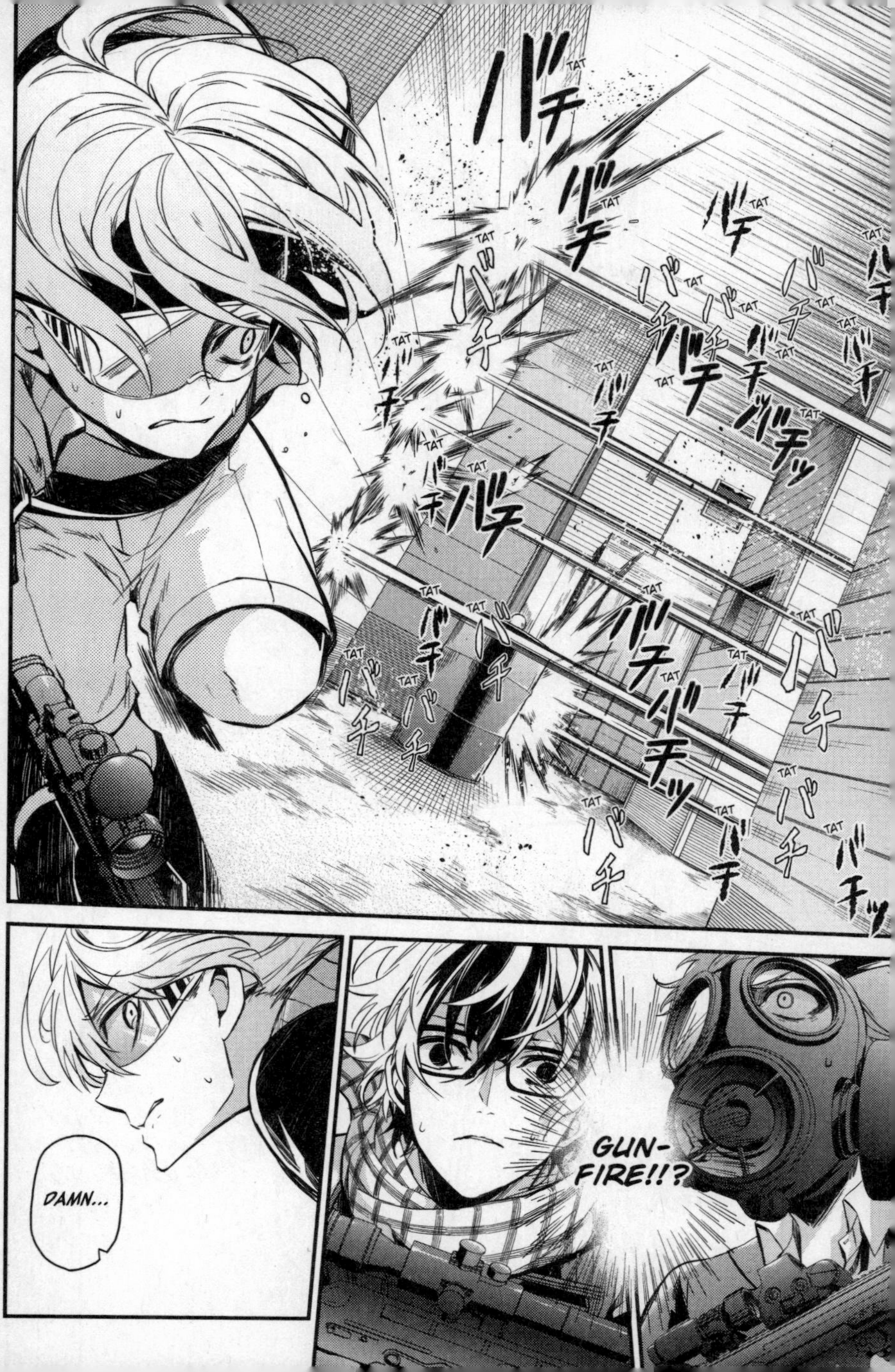

バチ TAT
バチ TAT
バチ TAT
バチッ TAT
バチバチバチッ TAT
GUN-FIRE!!?
DAMN...

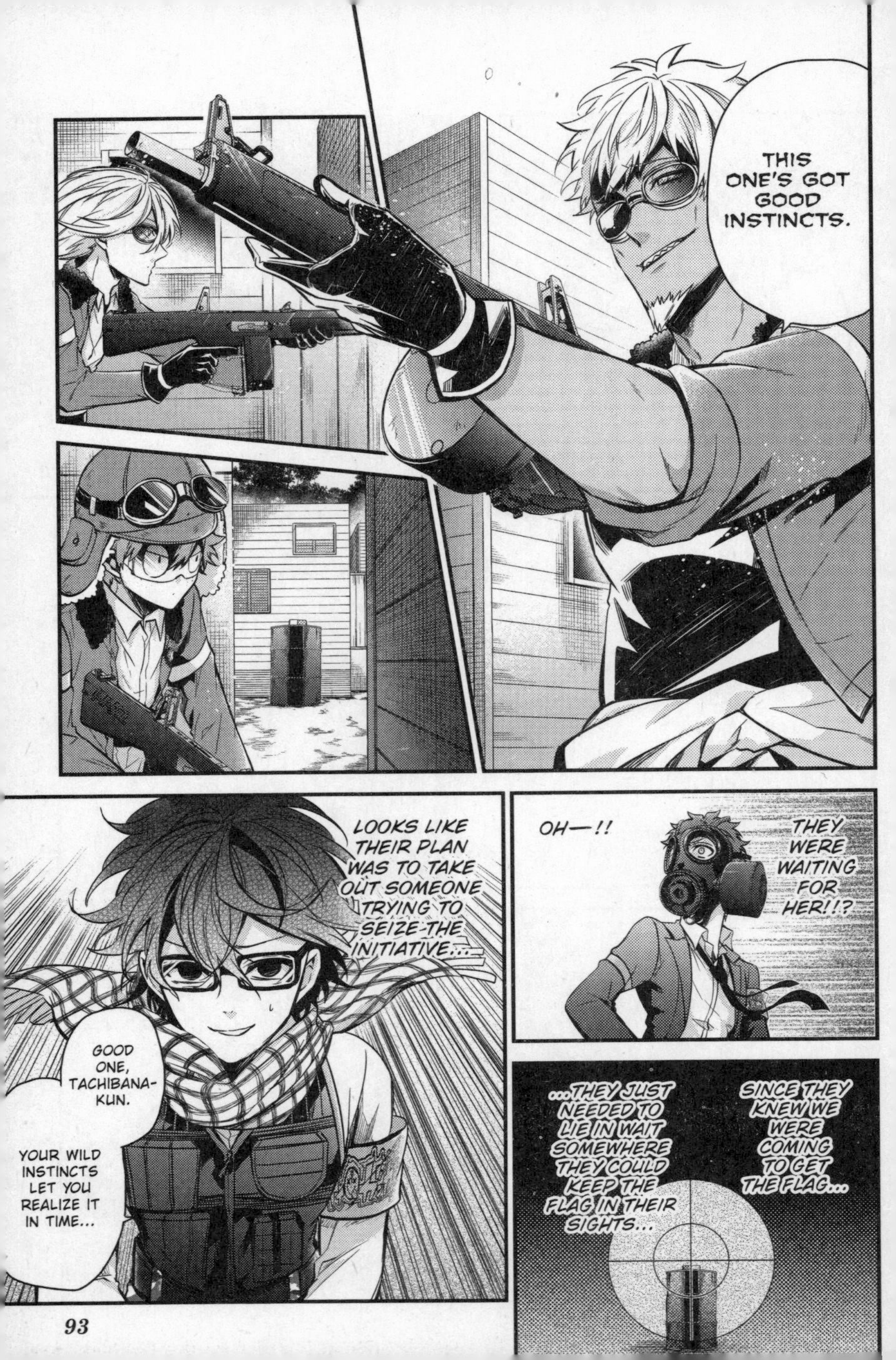
THIS ONE'S GOT GOOD INSTINCTS.
THEY WERE WAITING FOR HER!!?
OH—!!
SINCE THEY KNEW WE WERE COMING TO GET THE FLAG...
...THEY JUST NEEDED TO LIE IN WAIT SOMEWHERE THEY COULD KEEP THE FLAG IN THEIR SIGHTS...
LOOKS LIKE THEIR PLAN WAS TO TAKE OUT SOMEONE TRYING TO SEIZE THE INITIATIVE...
GOOD ONE, TACHIBANA-KUN.
YOUR WILD INSTINCTS LET YOU REALIZE IT IN TIME...

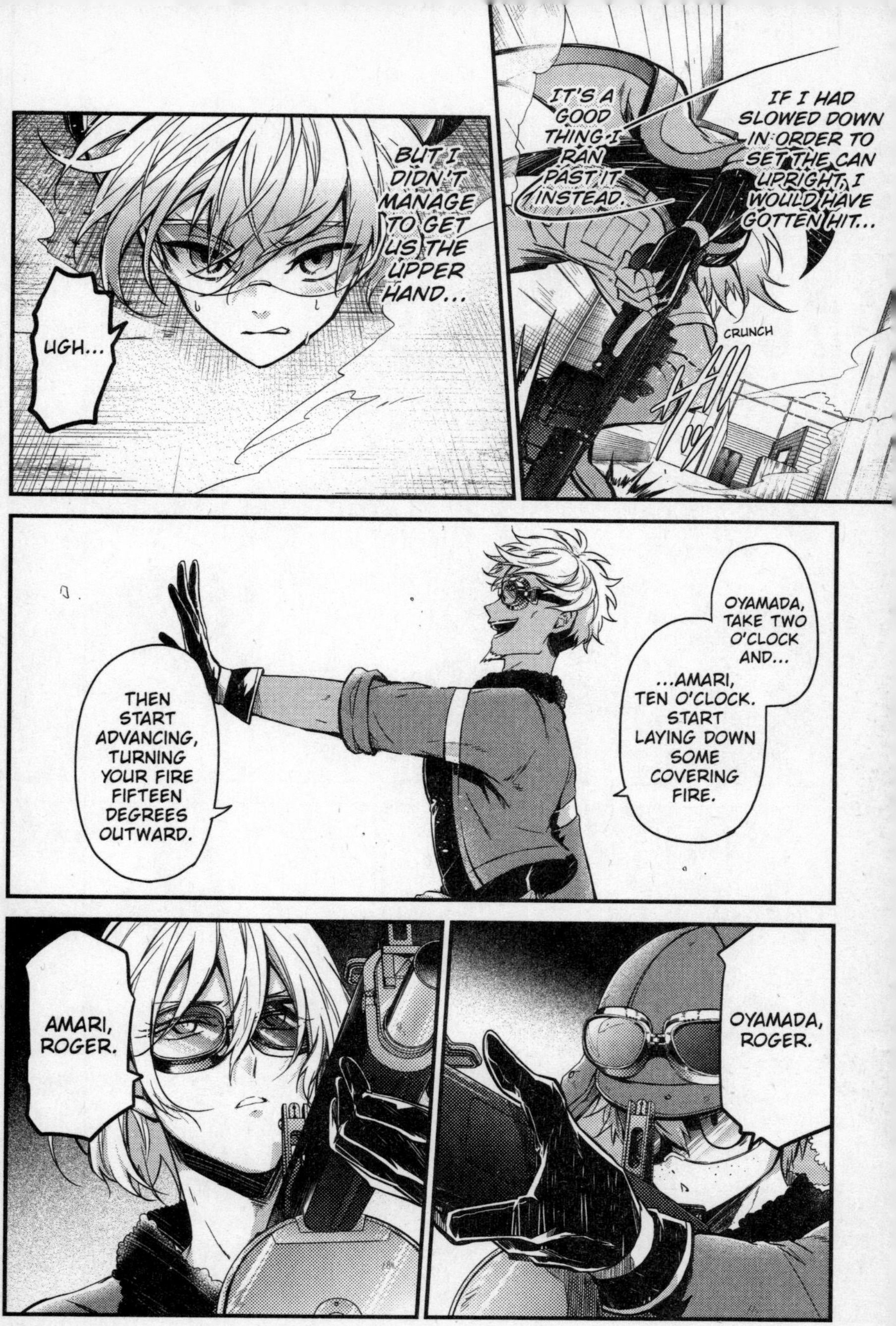
IF I HAD SLOWED DOWN IN ORDER TO SET THE CAN UPRIGHT, I WOULD HAVE GOTTEN HIT...
IT'S A GOOD THING I RAN PAST IT INSTEAD.
CRUNCH
BUT I DIDN'T MANAGE TO GET US THE UPPER HAND...
UGH...
OYAMADA, TAKE TWO O'CLOCK AND...
...AMARI, TEN O'CLOCK. START LAYING DOWN SOME COVERING FIRE.
THEN START ADVANCING, TURNING YOUR FIRE FIFTEEN DEGREES OUTWARD.
OYAMADA, ROGER.
AMARI, ROGER.

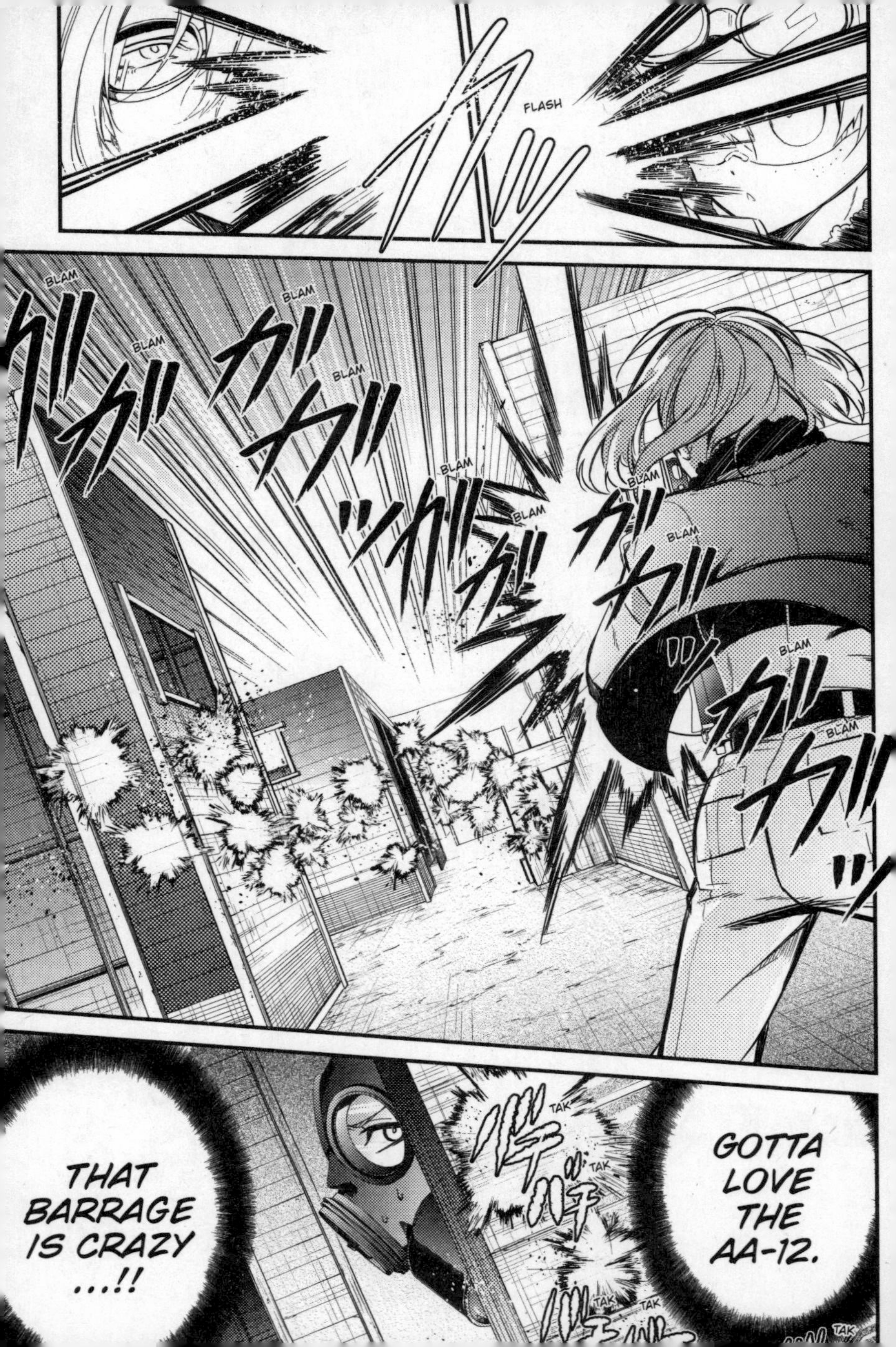
FLASH
BLAM
BLAM
BLAM
BLAM
BLAM
BLAM
BLAM
BLAM
BLAM
BLAM
GOTTA LOVE THE AA-12.
TAK
TAK
TAK
TAK
TAK
THAT BARRAGE IS CRAZY ...!!

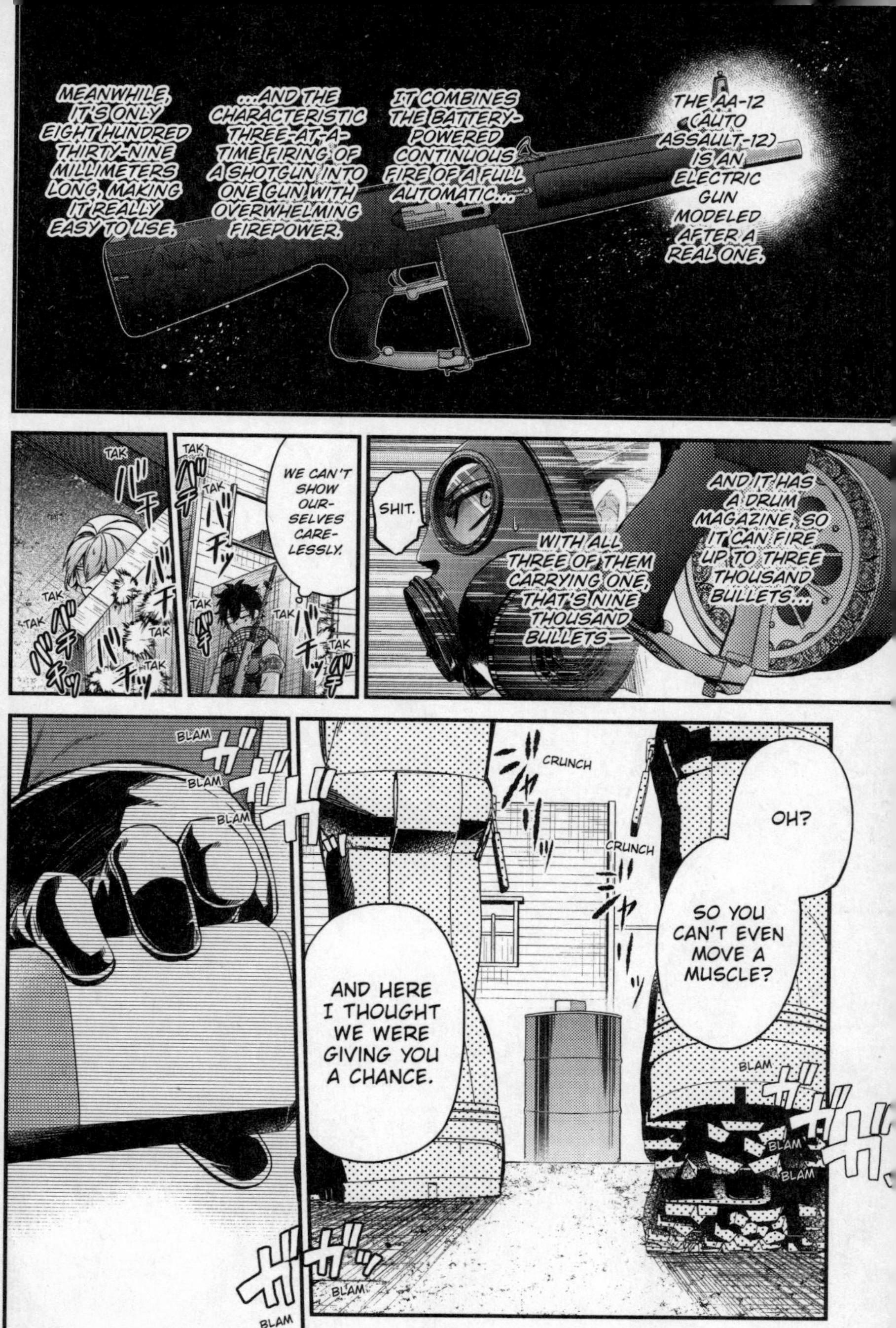

THE AA-12 (AUTO ASSAULT-12) IS AN ELECTRIC GUN MODELED AFTER A REAL ONE.
IT COMBINES THE BATTERY-POWERED CONTINUOUS FIRE OF A FULL AUTOMATIC...
...AND THE CHARACTERISTIC THREE-AT-A-TIME FIRING OF A SHOTGUN INTO ONE GUN WITH OVERWHELMING FIREPOWER.
MEANWHILE, IT'S ONLY EIGHT HUNDRED THIRTY-NINE MILLIMETERS LONG, MAKING IT REALLY EASY TO USE.
AND IT HAS A DRUM MAGAZINE, SO IT CAN FIRE UP TO THREE THOUSAND BULLETS...
WITH ALL THREE OF THEM CARRYING ONE, THAT'S NINE THOUSAND BULLETS—
SHIT.
TAK
TAK
TAK
TAK
WE CAN'T SHOW OURSELVES CARELESSLY.
TAK
TAK
TAK
TAK
TAK
CRUNCH
CRUNCH
OH?
SO YOU CAN'T EVEN MOVE A MUSCLE?
AND HERE I THOUGHT WE WERE GIVING YOU A CHANCE.
BLAM
BLAM
BLAM
BLAM
BLAM
BLAM
BLAM
BLAM

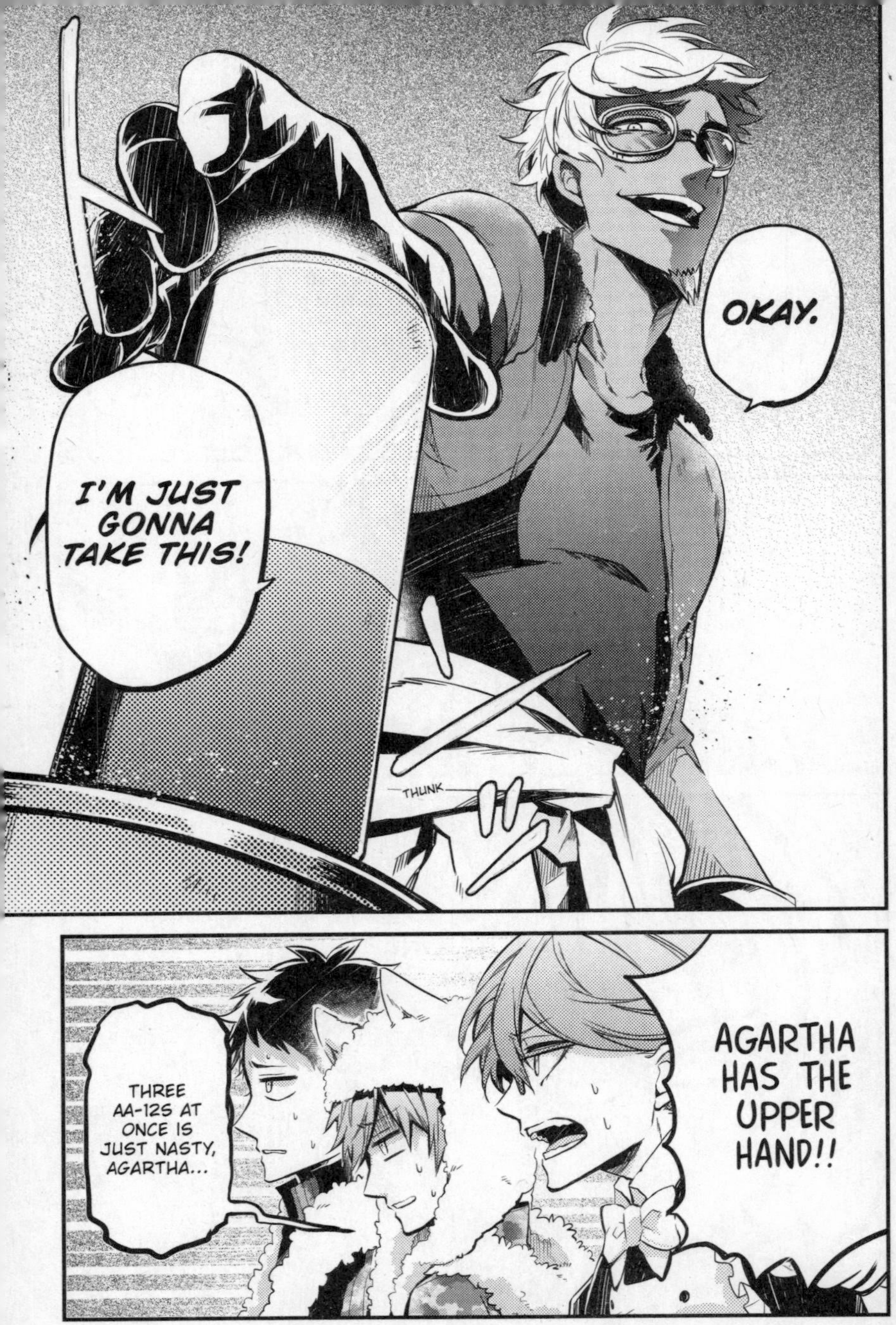
OKAY.
I'M JUST GONNA TAKE THIS!
THUNK
AGARTHA HAS THE UPPER HAND!!
THREE AA-12S AT ONCE IS JUST NASTY, AGARTHA...

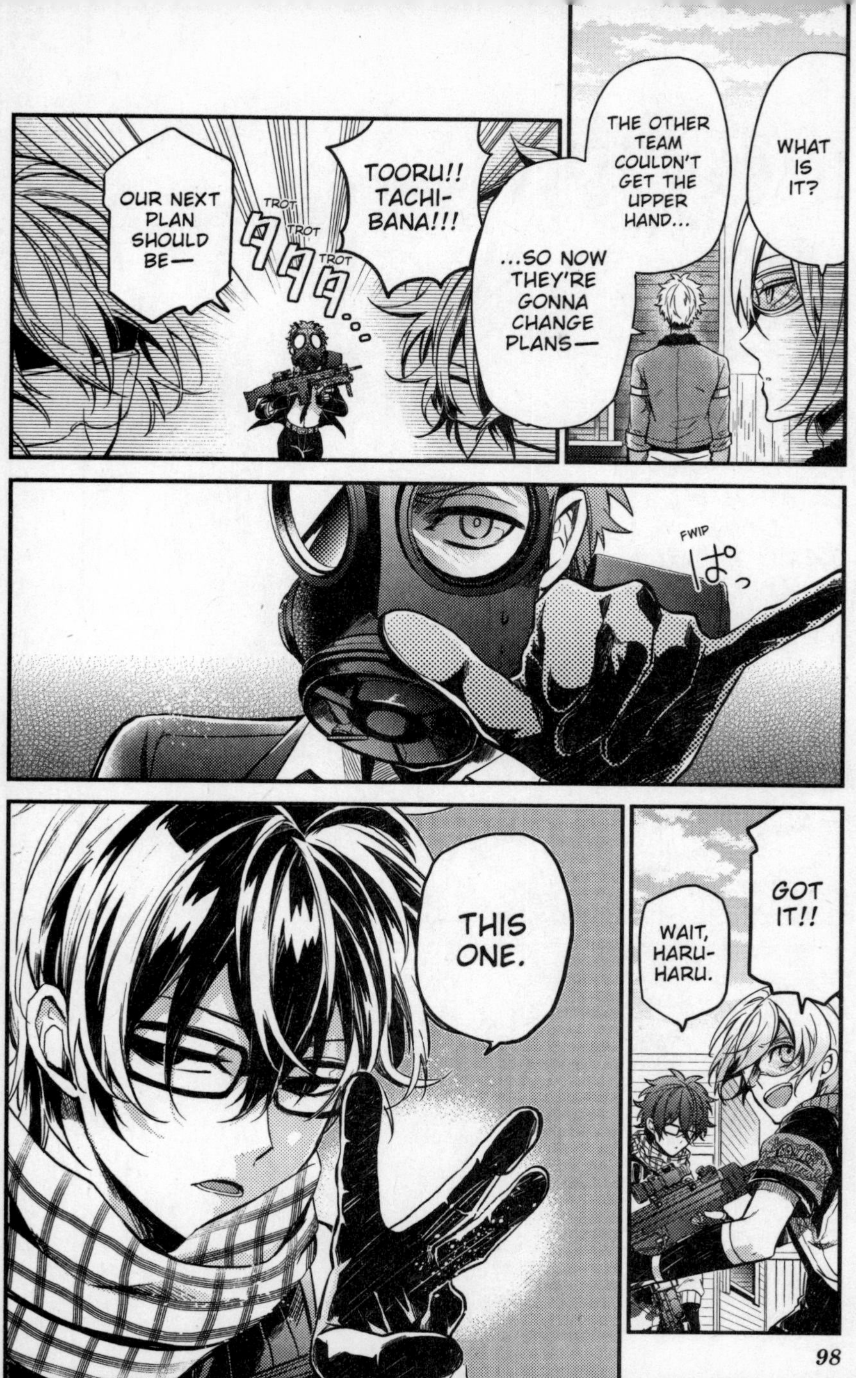
WHAT IS IT?
THE OTHER TEAM COULDN'T GET THE UPPER HAND...
...SO NOW THEY'RE GONNA CHANGE PLANS—
TOORU!! TACHIBANA!!!
TROT TROT TROT
OUR NEXT PLAN SHOULD BE—
FWIP
GOT IT!!
WAIT, HARUHARU.
THIS ONE.

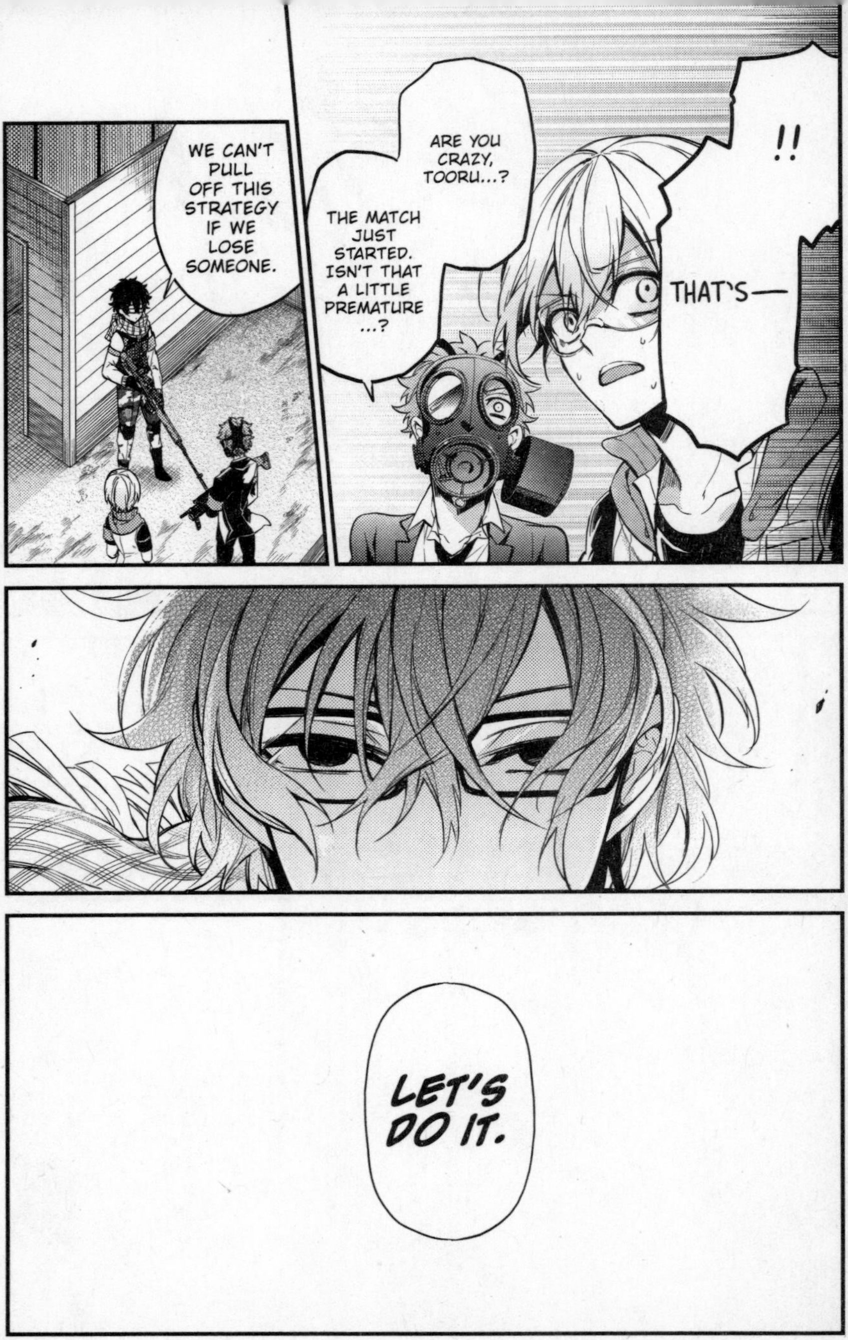
!!
THAT'S—
ARE YOU CRAZY, TOORU...?
THE MATCH JUST STARTED. ISN'T THAT A LITTLE PREMATURE ...?
WE CAN'T PULL OFF THIS STRATEGY IF WE LOSE SOMEONE.
LET'S DO IT.

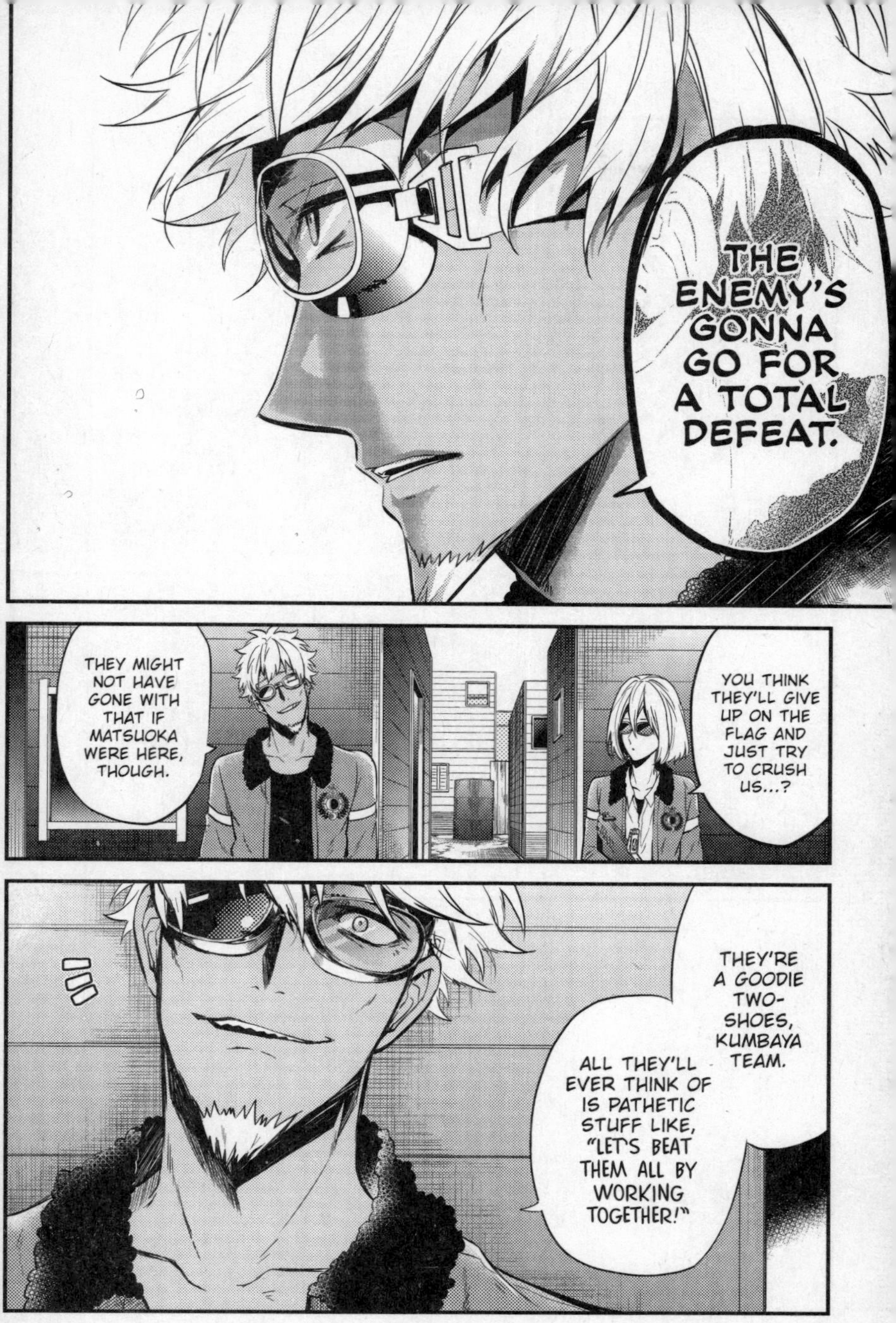
THE ENEMY'S GONNA GO FOR A TOTAL DEFEAT.
YOU THINK THEY'LL GIVE UP ON THE FLAG AND JUST TRY TO CRUSH US...?
THEY MIGHT NOT HAVE GONE WITH THAT IF MATSUOKA WERE HERE, THOUGH.
THEY'RE A GOODIE TWO-SHOES, KUMBAYA TEAM.
ALL THEY'LL EVER THINK OF IS PATHETIC STUFF LIKE, "LET'S BEAT THEM ALL BY WORKING TOGETHER!"

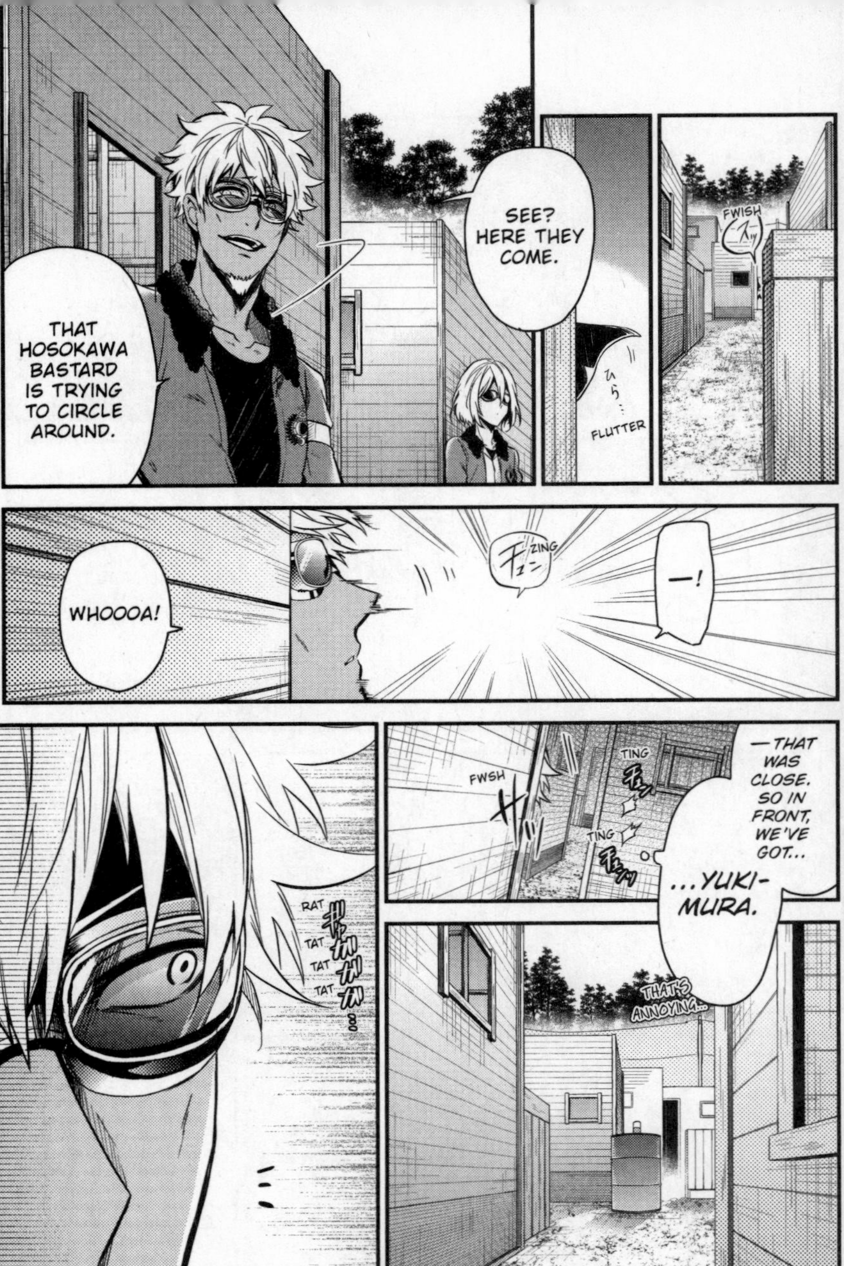
FWISH
SEE? HERE THEY COME.
FLUTTER
THAT HOSOKAWA BASTARD IS TRYING TO CIRCLE AROUND.
ZING
—!
WHOOOA!
—THAT WAS CLOSE. SO IN FRONT, WE'VE GOT...
TING
TING
FWSH
...YUKI-MURA.
THAT'S ANNOYING...
RAT
TAT
TAT
TAT

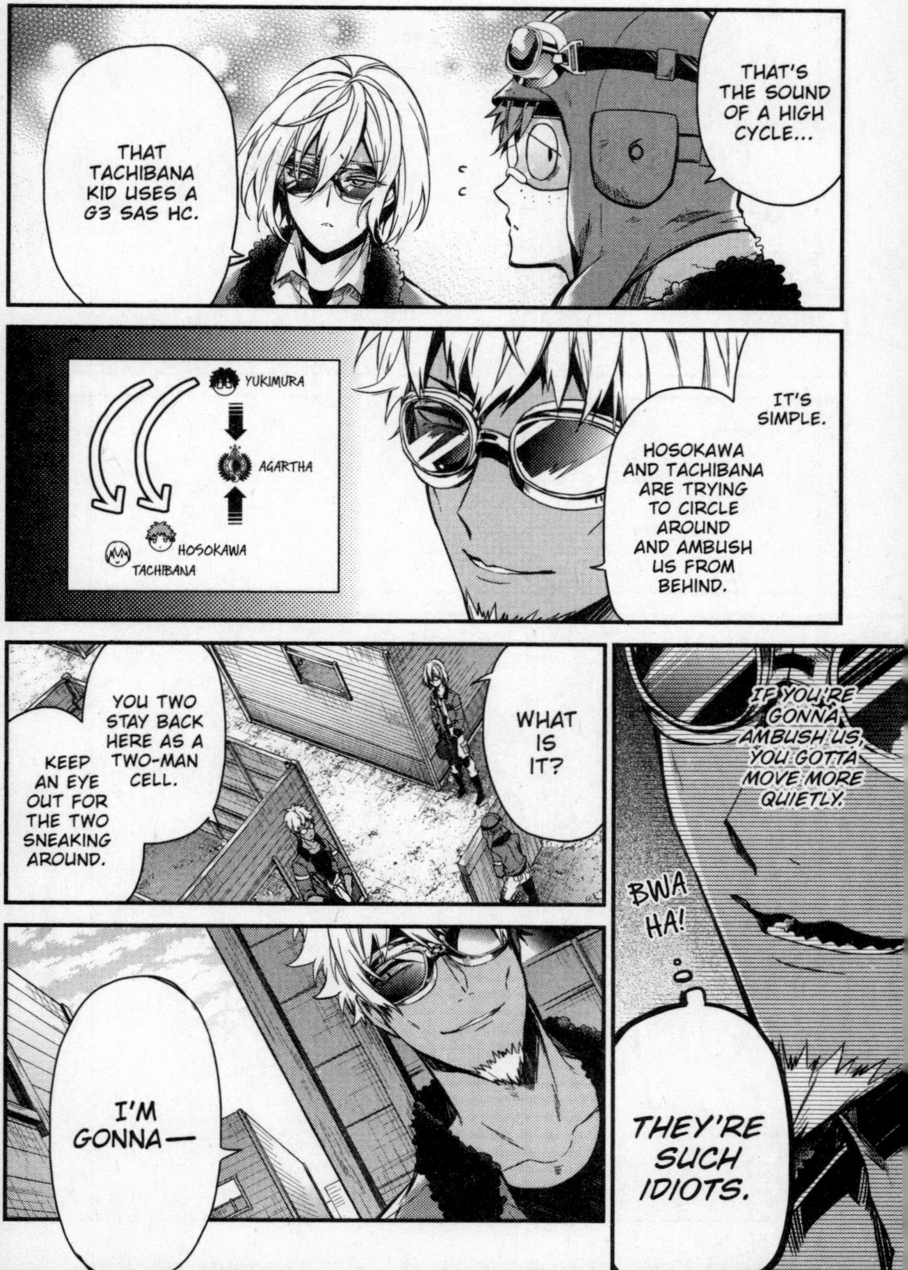
THAT'S THE SOUND OF A HIGH CYCLE...
THAT TACHIBANA KID USES A G3 SAS HC.
IT'S SIMPLE.
HOSOKAWA AND TACHIBANA ARE TRYING TO CIRCLE AROUND AND AMBUSH US FROM BEHIND.
YUKIMURA
AGARTHA
HOSOKAWA
TACHIBANA
IF YOU'RE GONNA AMBUSH US, YOU GOTTA MOVE MORE QUIETLY.
BWA HA!
THEY'RE SUCH IDIOTS.
WHAT IS IT?
YOU TWO STAY BACK HERE AS A TWO-MAN CELL.
KEEP AN EYE OUT FOR THE TWO SNEAKING AROUND.
I'M GONNA—

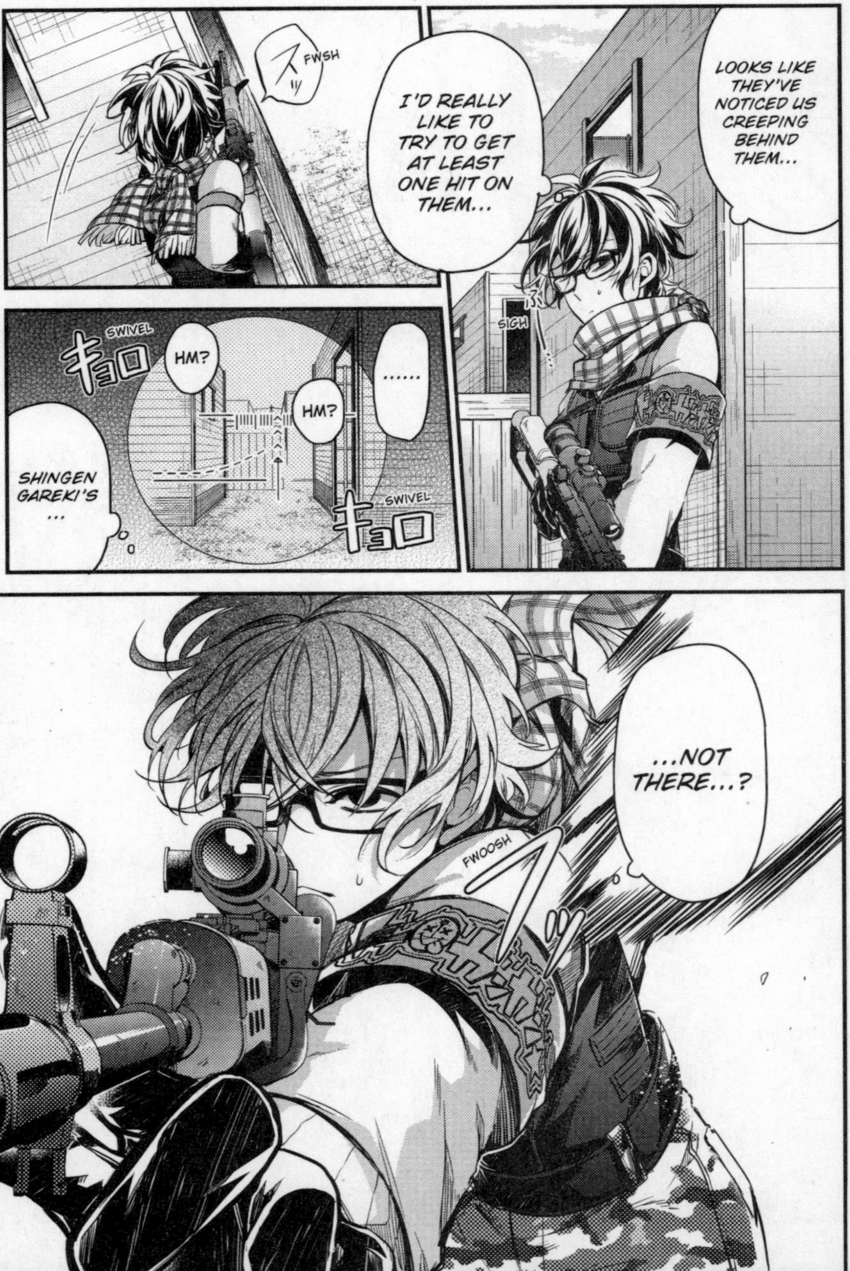
LOOKS LIKE THEY'VE NOTICED US CREEPING BEHIND THEM...
I'D REALLY LIKE TO TRY TO GET AT LEAST ONE HIT ON THEM...
SIGH
FWSH
......
HM?
HM?
SWIVEL
SWIVEL
SHINGEN GAREKI'S ...
...NOT THERE...?
FWOOSH

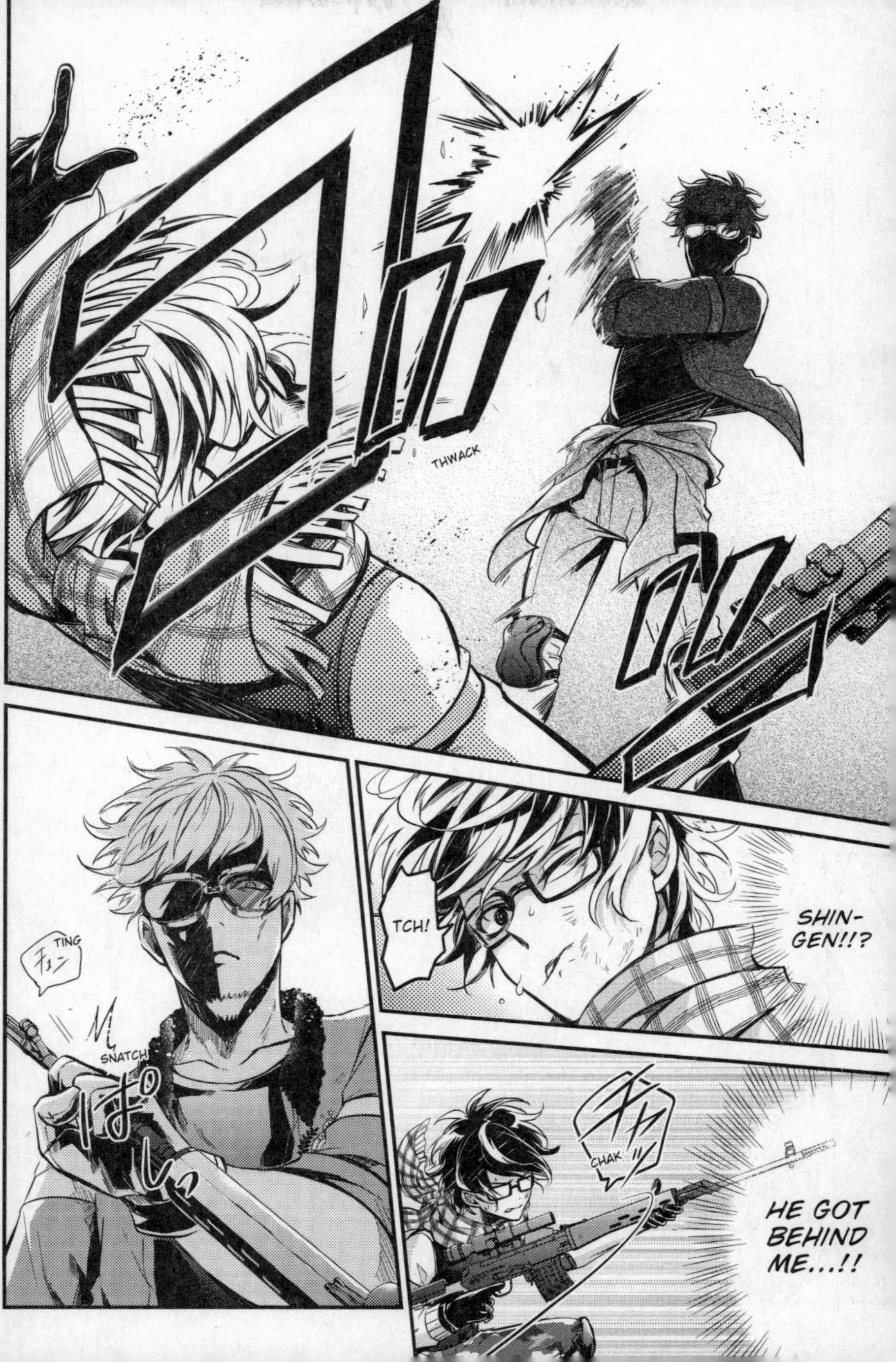
THWACK
SHIN-
GEN!!?
TCH!
CHAK
HE GOT
BEHIND
ME...!!
TING
SNATCH

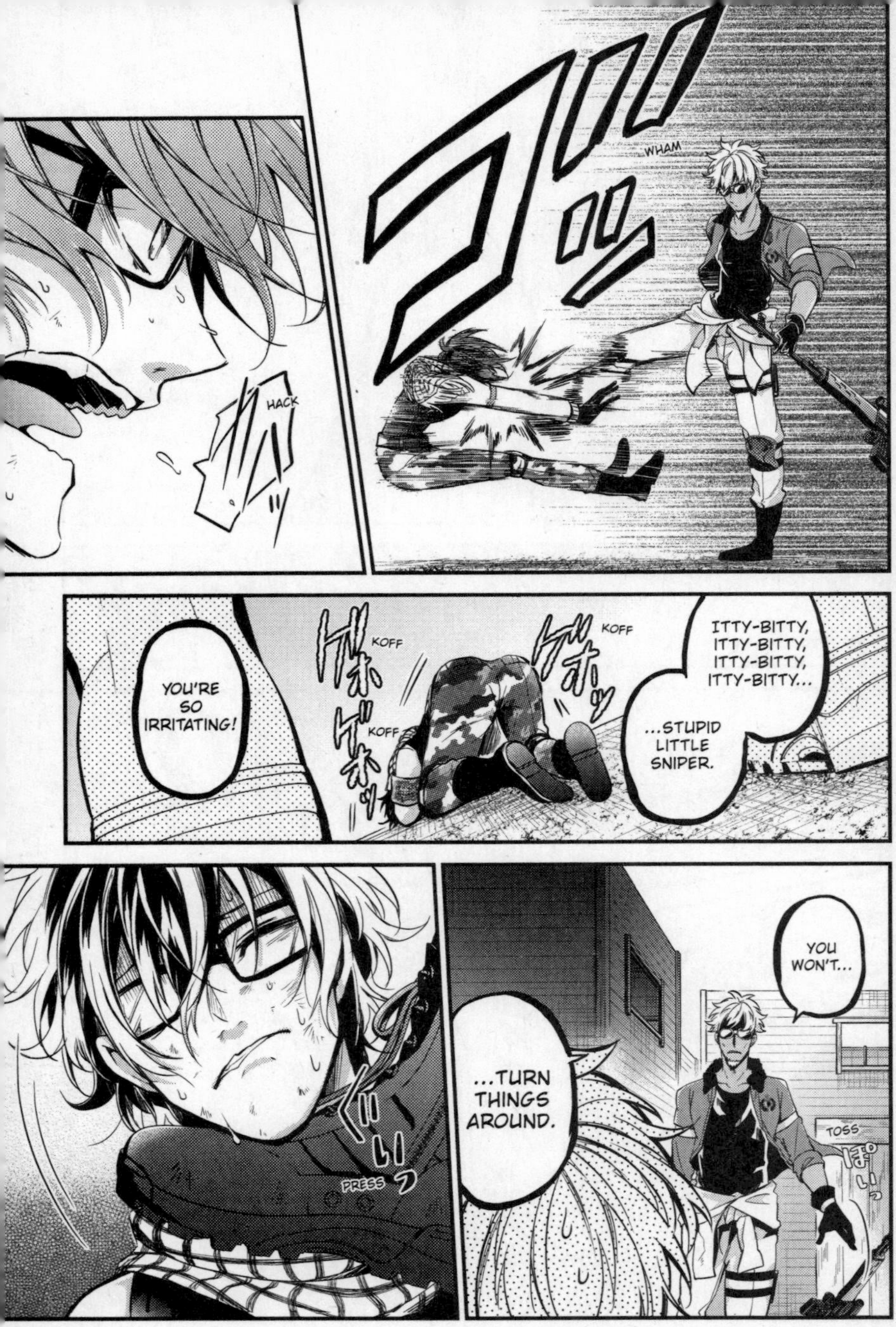
WHAM
HACK
KOFF
ITTY-BITTY, ITTY-BITTY, ITTY-BITTY, ITTY-BITTY...
...STUPID LITTLE SNIPER.
KOFF
KOFF
YOU'RE SO IRRITATING!
YOU WON'T...
...TURN THINGS AROUND.
TOSS
PRESS

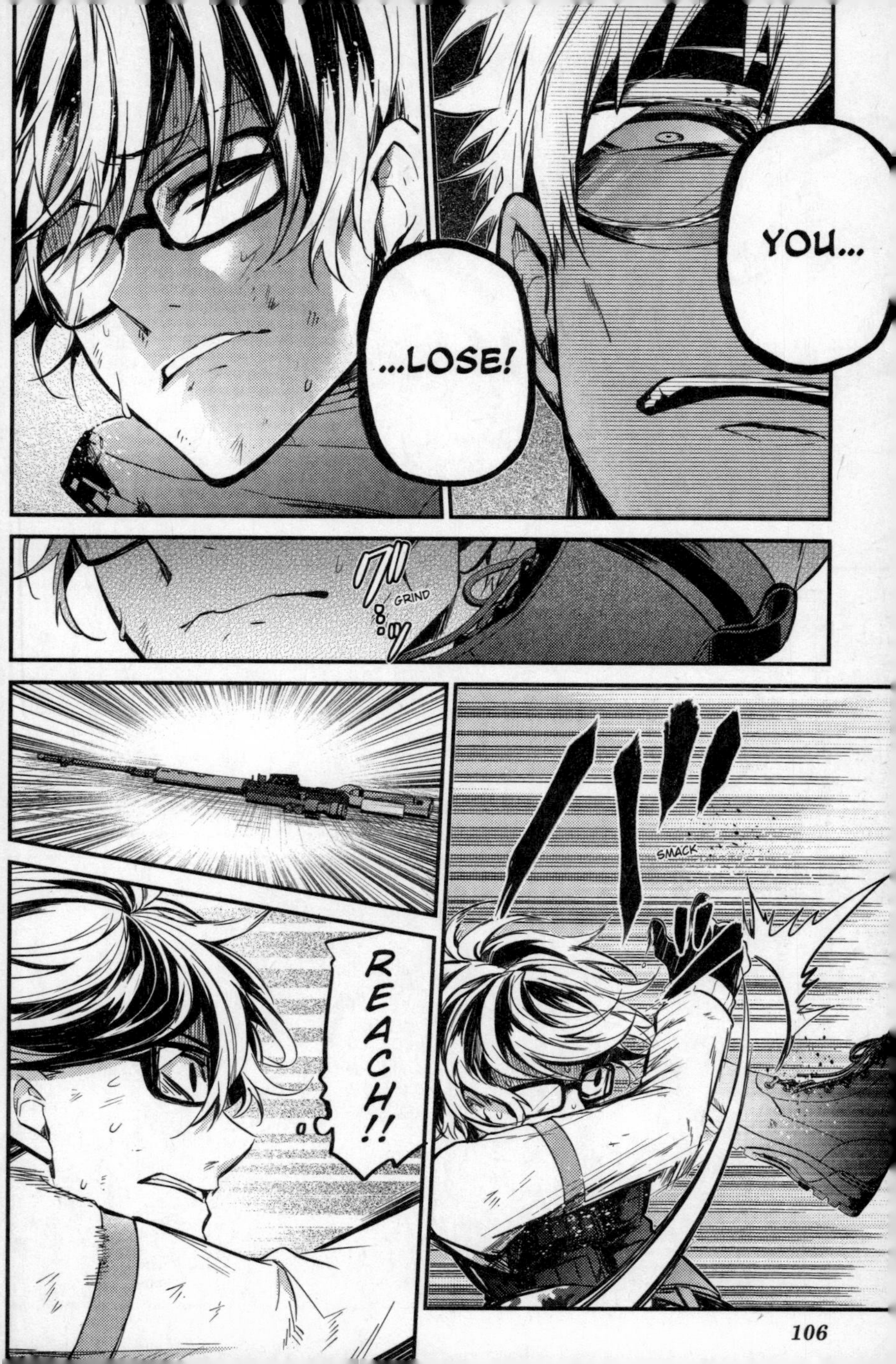
YOU...
...LOSE!
GRIND
SMACK
REACH!!

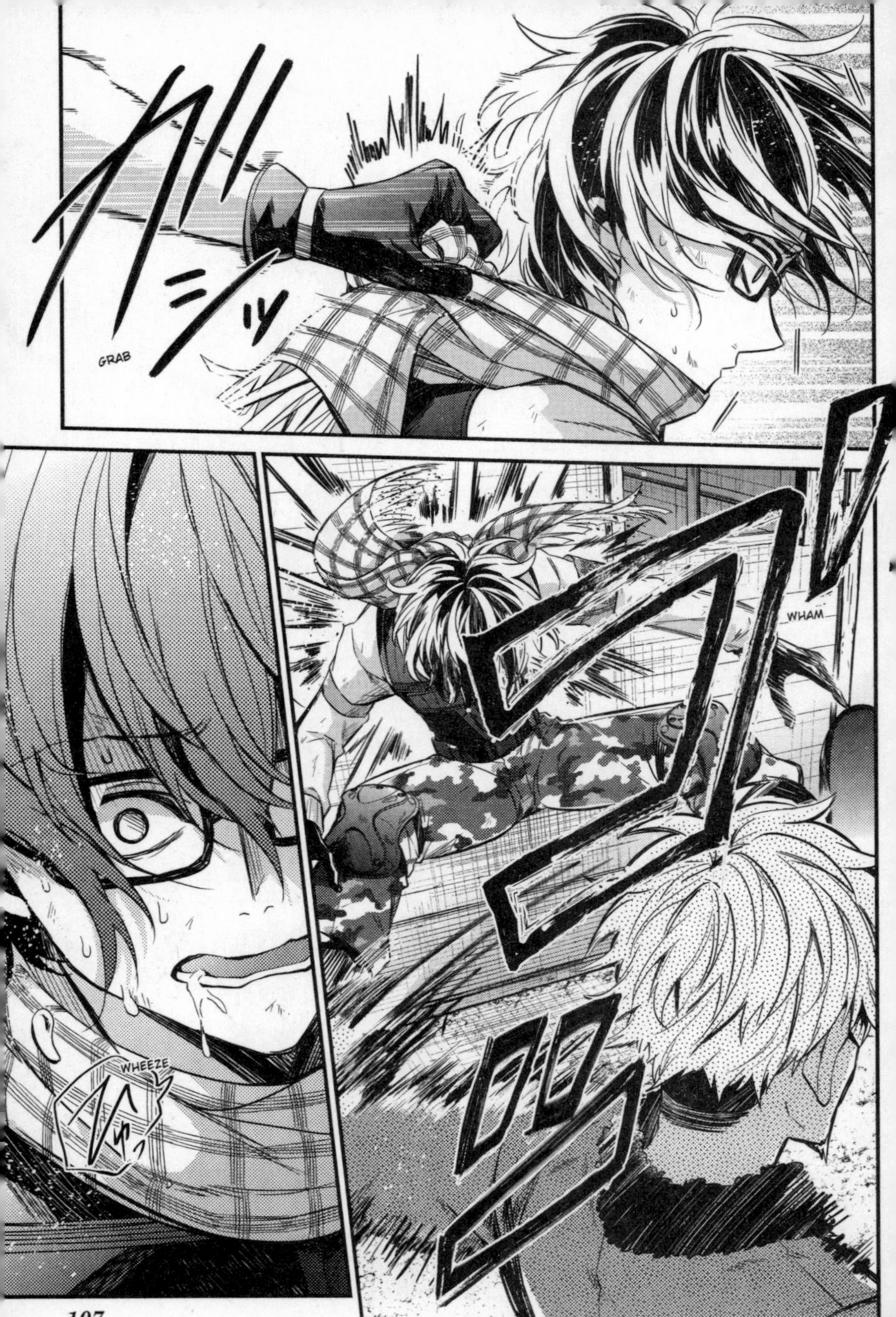
GRAB
WHAM
WHEEZE

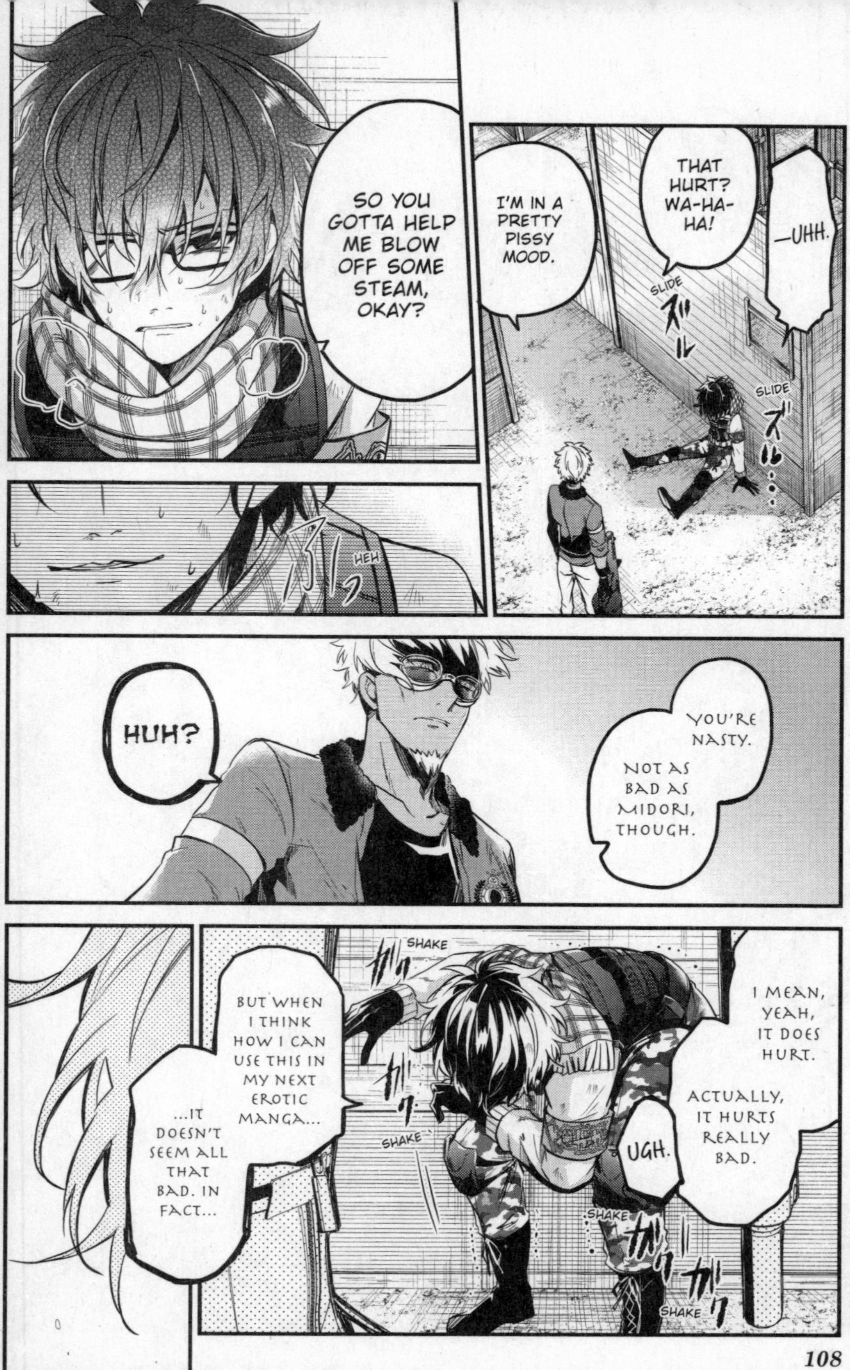
—UHH.
THAT HURT? WA-HA-HA!
SLIDE
SLIDE
I'M IN A PRETTY PISSY MOOD.
SO YOU GOTTA HELP ME BLOW OFF SOME STEAM, OKAY?
HEH
YOU'RE NASTY.
NOT AS BAD AS MIDORI, THOUGH.
HUH?
SHAKE
I MEAN, YEAH, IT DOES HURT.
ACTUALLY, IT HURTS REALLY BAD.
UGH.
SHAKE
SHAKE
SHAKE
BUT WHEN I THINK HOW I CAN USE THIS IN MY NEXT EROTIC MANGA...
...IT DOESN'T SEEM ALL THAT BAD. IN FACT...

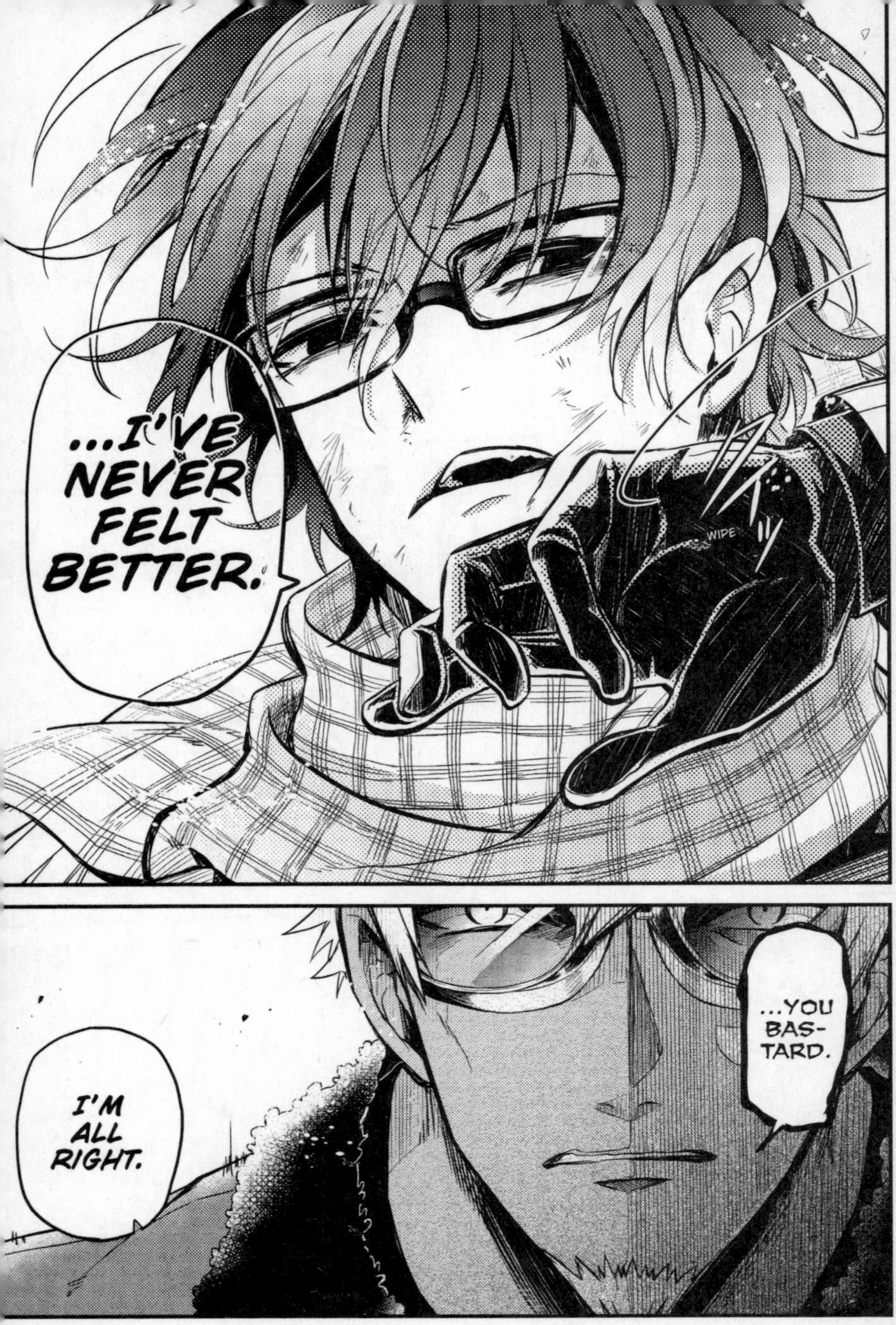
WIPE
...I'VE NEVER FELT BETTER.
...YOU BAS-TARD.
I'M ALL RIGHT.

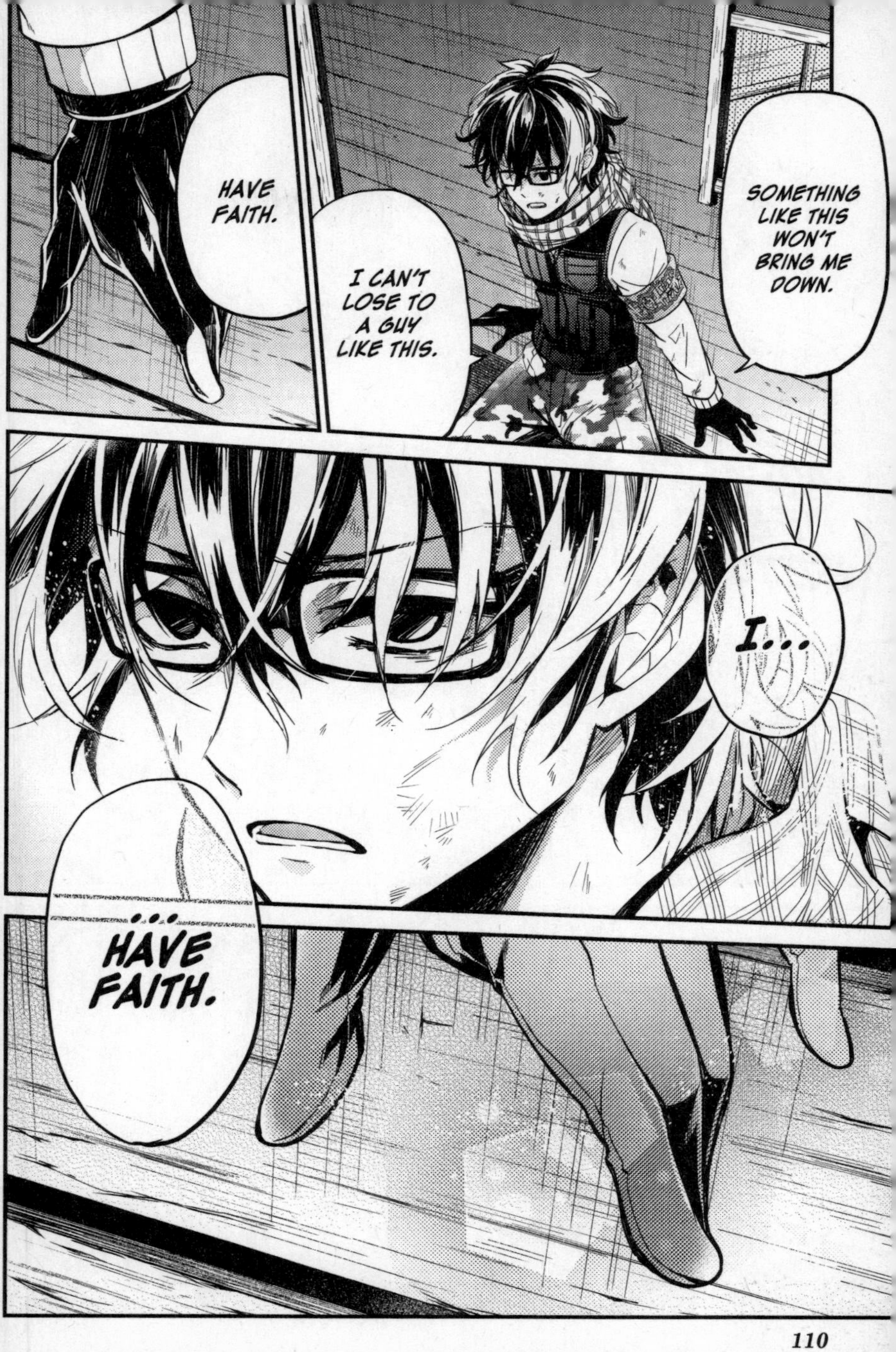
SOMETHING LIKE THIS WON'T BRING ME DOWN.
I CAN'T LOSE TO A GUY LIKE THIS.
HAVE FAITH.
I...
...HAVE FAITH.

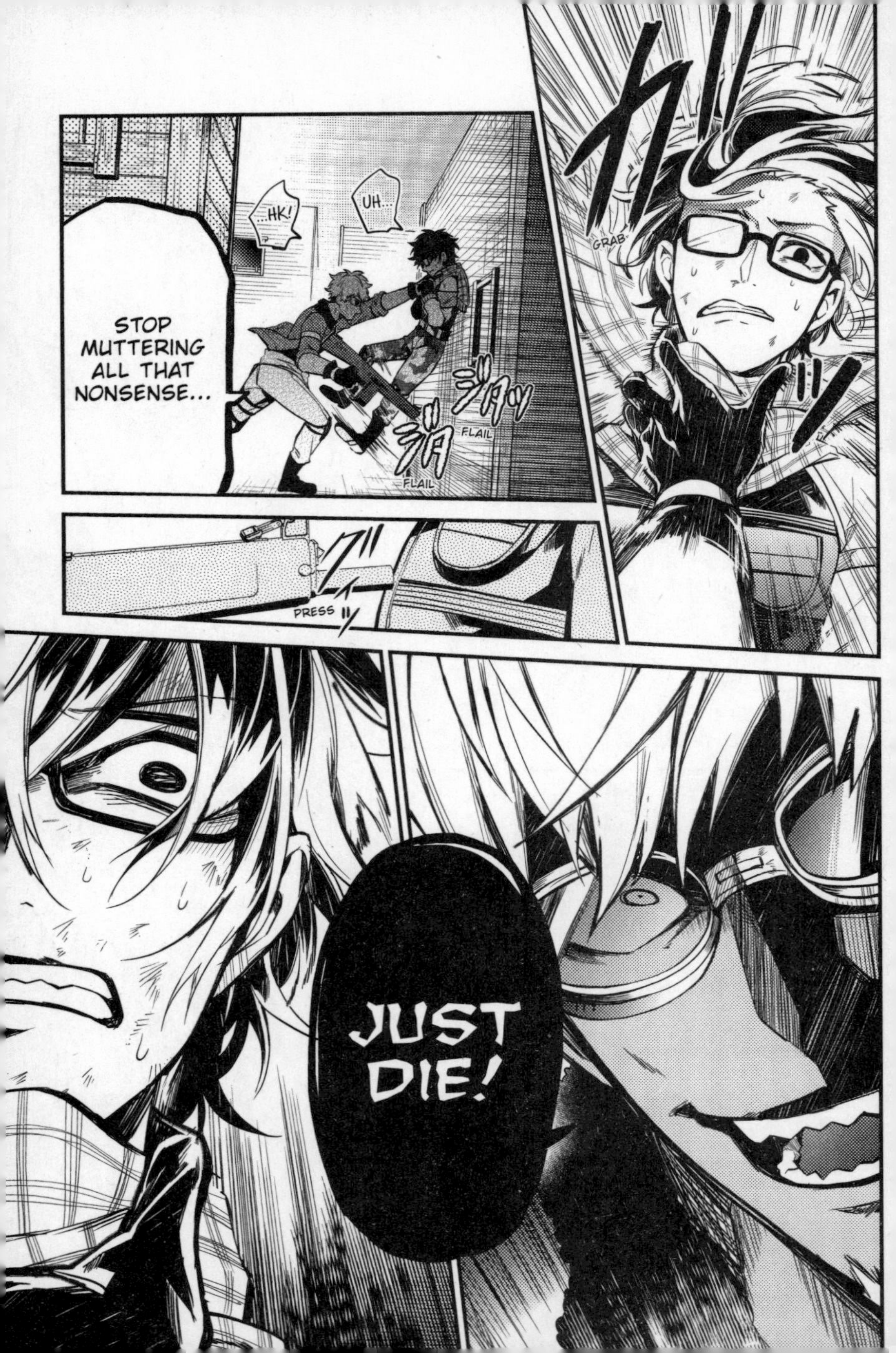
GRAB
UH...
...HK!
STOP MUTTERING ALL THAT NONSENSE...
FLAIL
FLAIL
PRESS
JUST DIE!

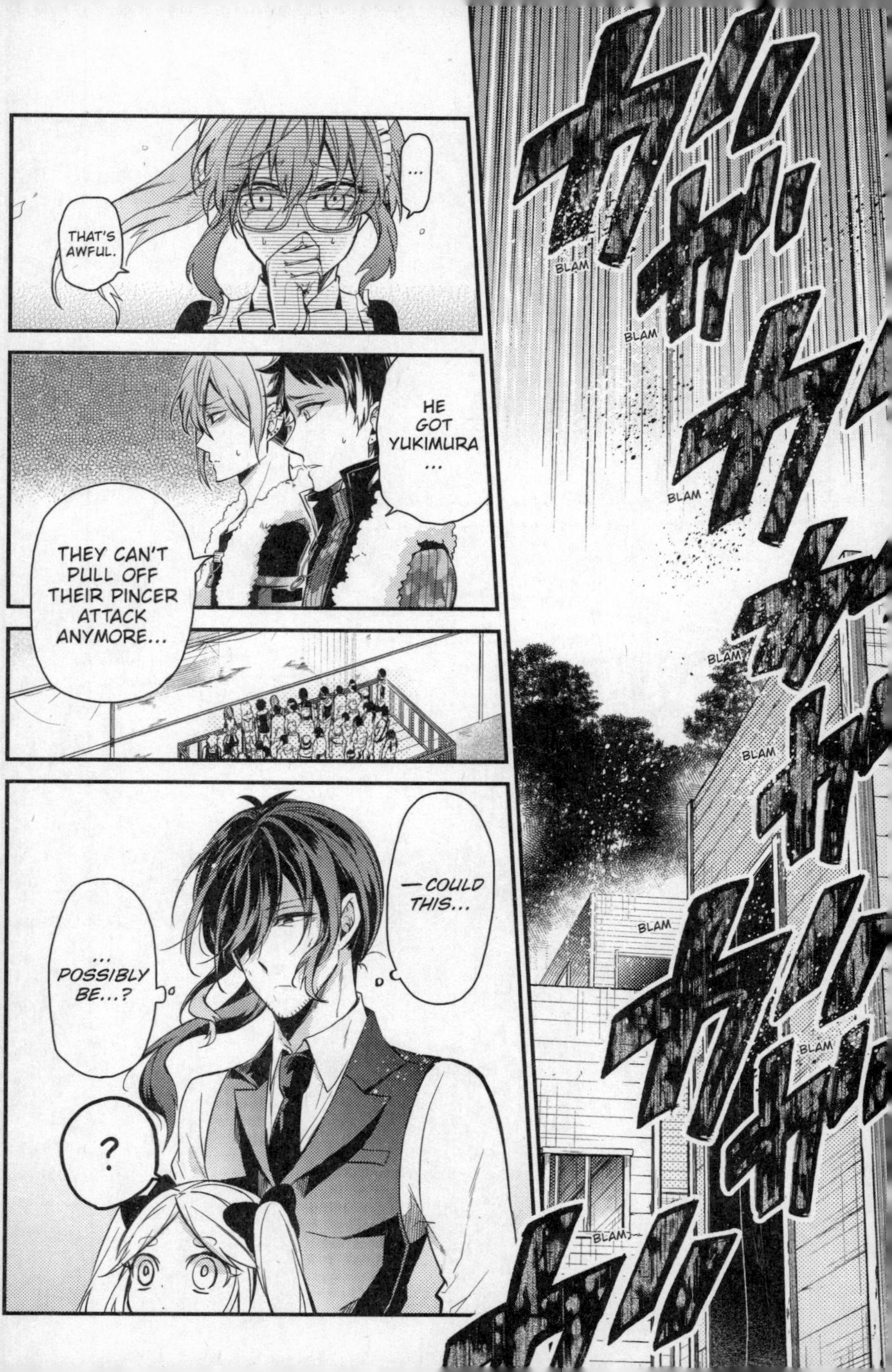
BLAM
BLAM
BLAM
BLAM
BLAM
BLAM
BLAM
BLAM
...
THAT'S AWFUL.
HE GOT YUKIMURA ...
THEY CAN'T PULL OFF THEIR PINCER ATTACK ANYMORE...
—COULD THIS...
... POSSIBLY BE...?
?

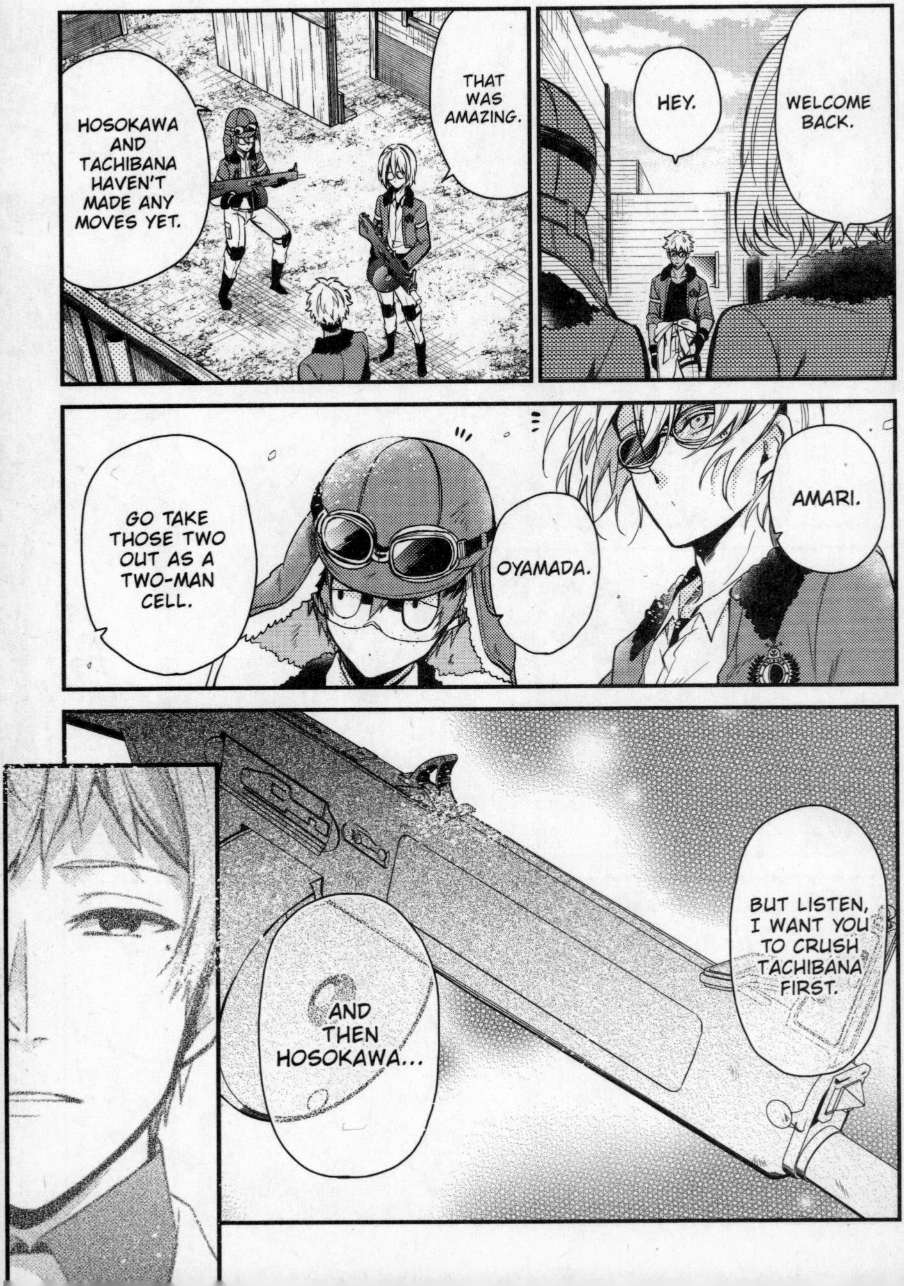
WELCOME BACK.
HEY.
THAT WAS AMAZING.
HOSOKAWA AND TACHIBANA HAVEN'T MADE ANY MOVES YET.
AMARI.
OYAMADA.
GO TAKE THOSE TWO OUT AS A TWO-MAN CELL.
BUT LISTEN, I WANT YOU TO CRUSH TACHIBANA FIRST.
AND THEN HOSOKAWA...

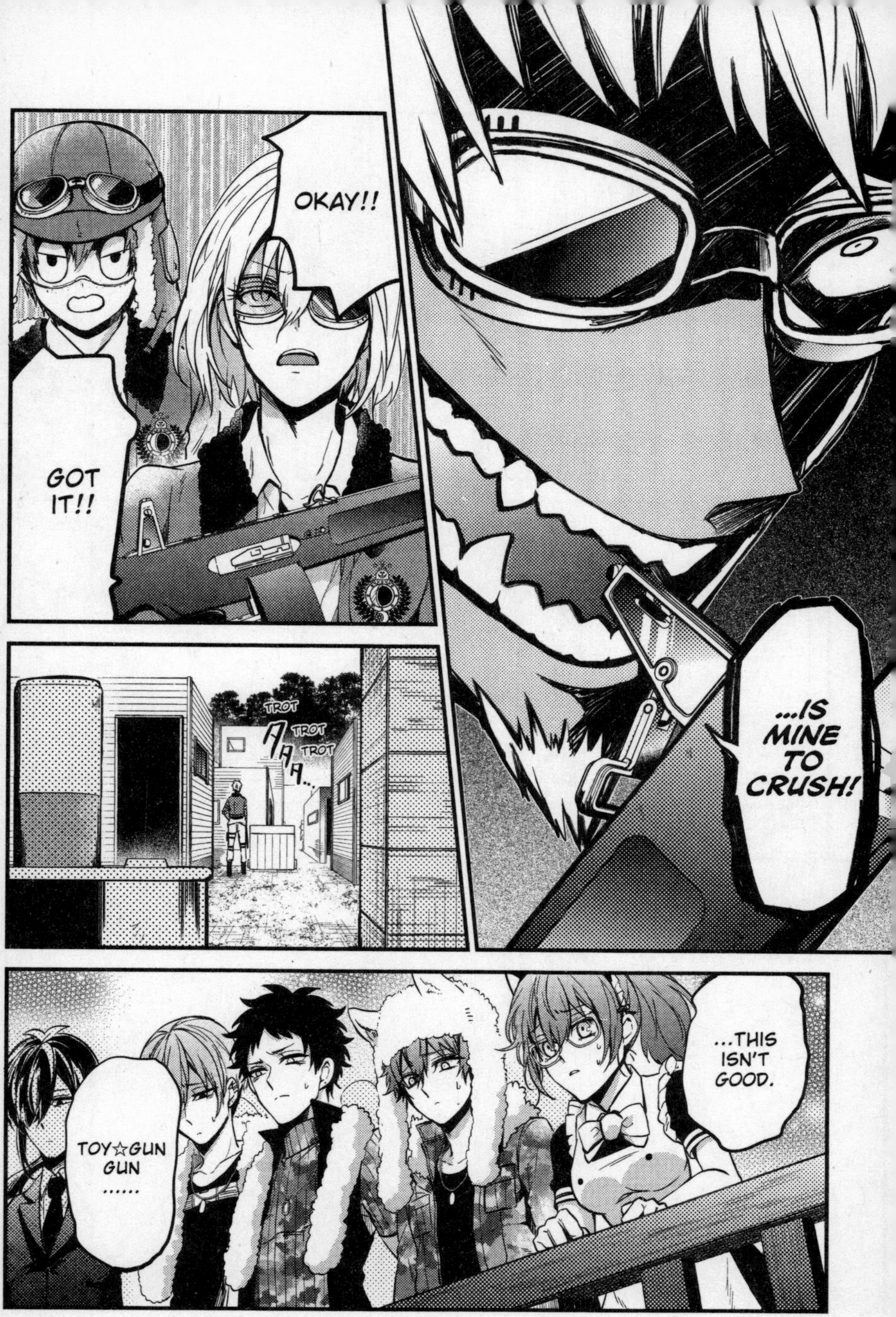
...IS MINE TO CRUSH!
OKAY!!
GOT IT!!
TROT
TROT
TROT
...THIS ISN'T GOOD.
TOY☆GUN GUN ....

*EXTRA VALENTINE'S STORY FROM TWITTER

~FUJIMOTO EDITION~

(WHEN TACHIBANA TAKES A TRIP TO HOSHISHIRO GENERAL HOSPITAL)

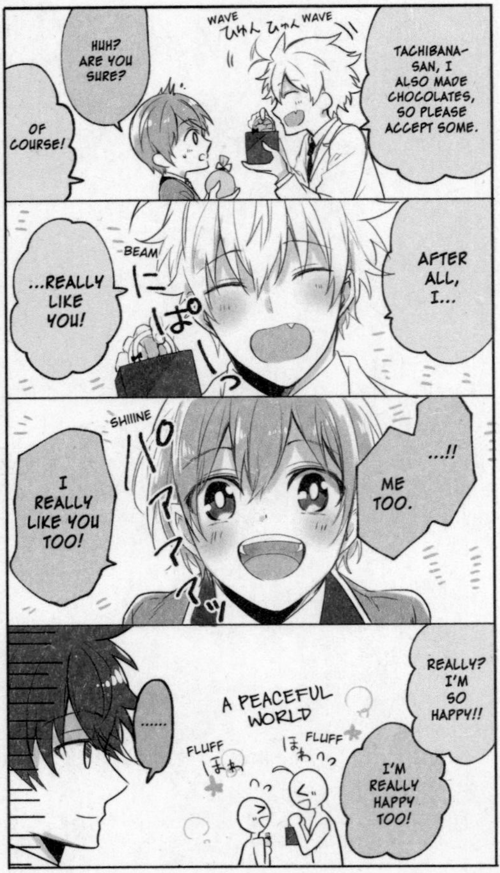
TACHIBANA-SAN, I ALSO MADE CHOCOLATES, SO PLEASE ACCEPT SOME.
WAVE
WAVE
HUH? ARE YOU SURE?
OF COURSE!
AFTER ALL, I...
BEAM
...REALLY LIKE YOU!
...!!
ME TOO.
SHIIINE
I REALLY LIKE YOU TOO!
REALLY? I'M SO HAPPY!!
I'M REALLY HAPPY TOO!
A PEACEFUL WORLD
FLUFF
FLUFF
......

*EXTRA VALENTINE'S STORY FROM TWITTER

~MIDORI EDITION~

(WHEN TACHIBANA TAKES A TRIP TO HOSHISHIRO GENERAL HOSPITAL)

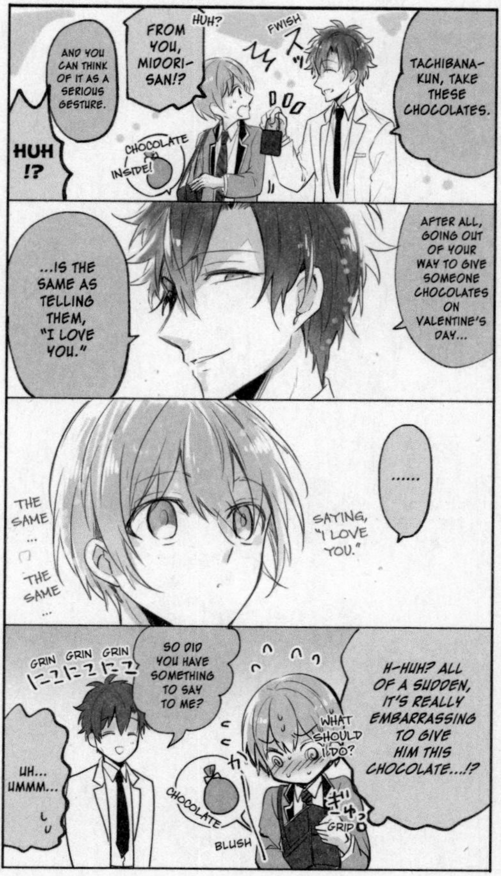
TACHIBANA-KUN, TAKE THESE CHOCOLATES.
FWISH
HUH?
FROM YOU, MIDORI-SAN!?
AND YOU CAN THINK OF IT AS A SERIOUS GESTURE.
CHOCOLATE INSIDE!
HUH !?
AFTER ALL, GOING OUT OF YOUR WAY TO GIVE SOMEONE CHOCOLATES ON VALENTINE'S DAY...
...IS THE SAME AS TELLING THEM, "I LOVE YOU."
......
SAYING, "I LOVE YOU."
THE SAME ...
THE SAME ...
H-HUH? ALL OF A SUDDEN, IT'S REALLY EMBARRASSING TO GIVE HIM THIS CHOCOLATE...!?
WHAT SHOULD I DO?
GRIP
SO DID YOU HAVE SOMETHING TO SAY TO ME?
GRIN GRIN GRIN
CHOCOLATE
BLUSH
UH... UMMM...

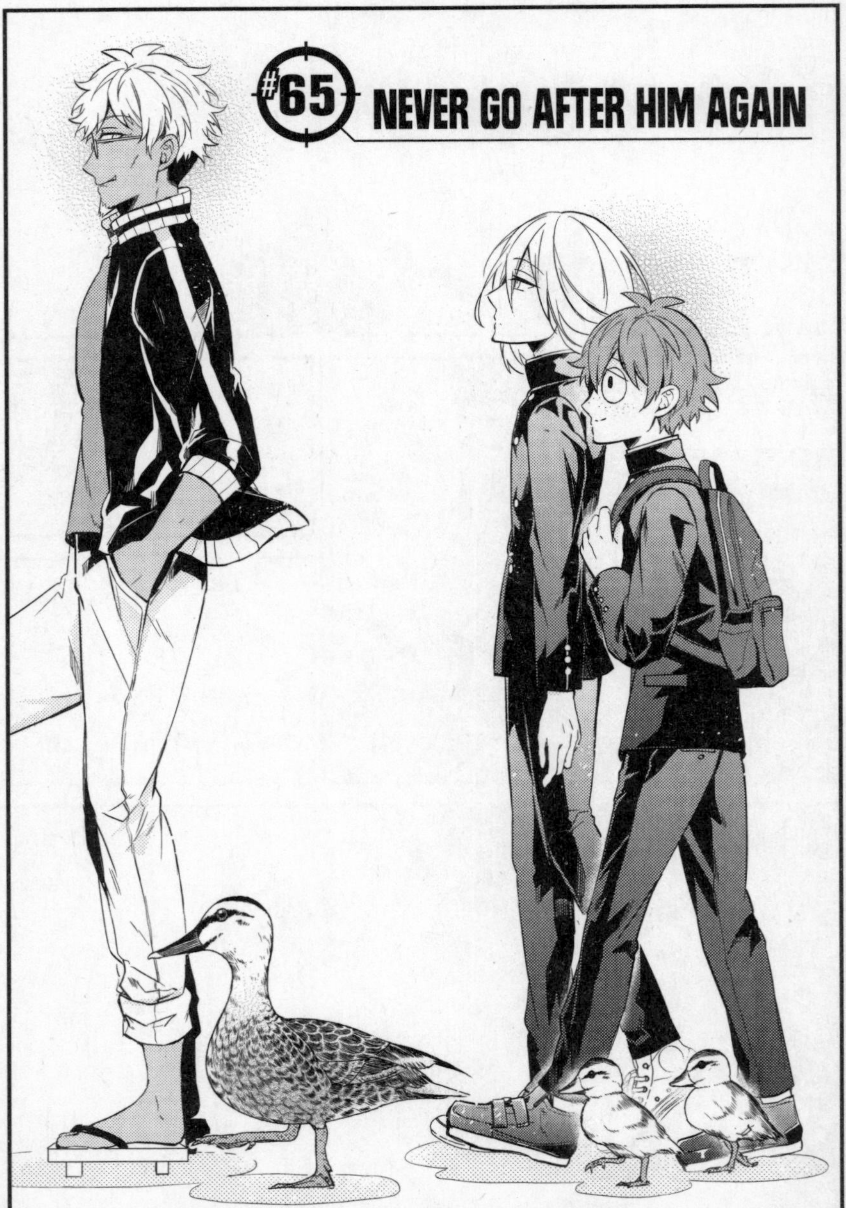
#65
NEVER GO AFTER HIM AGAIN

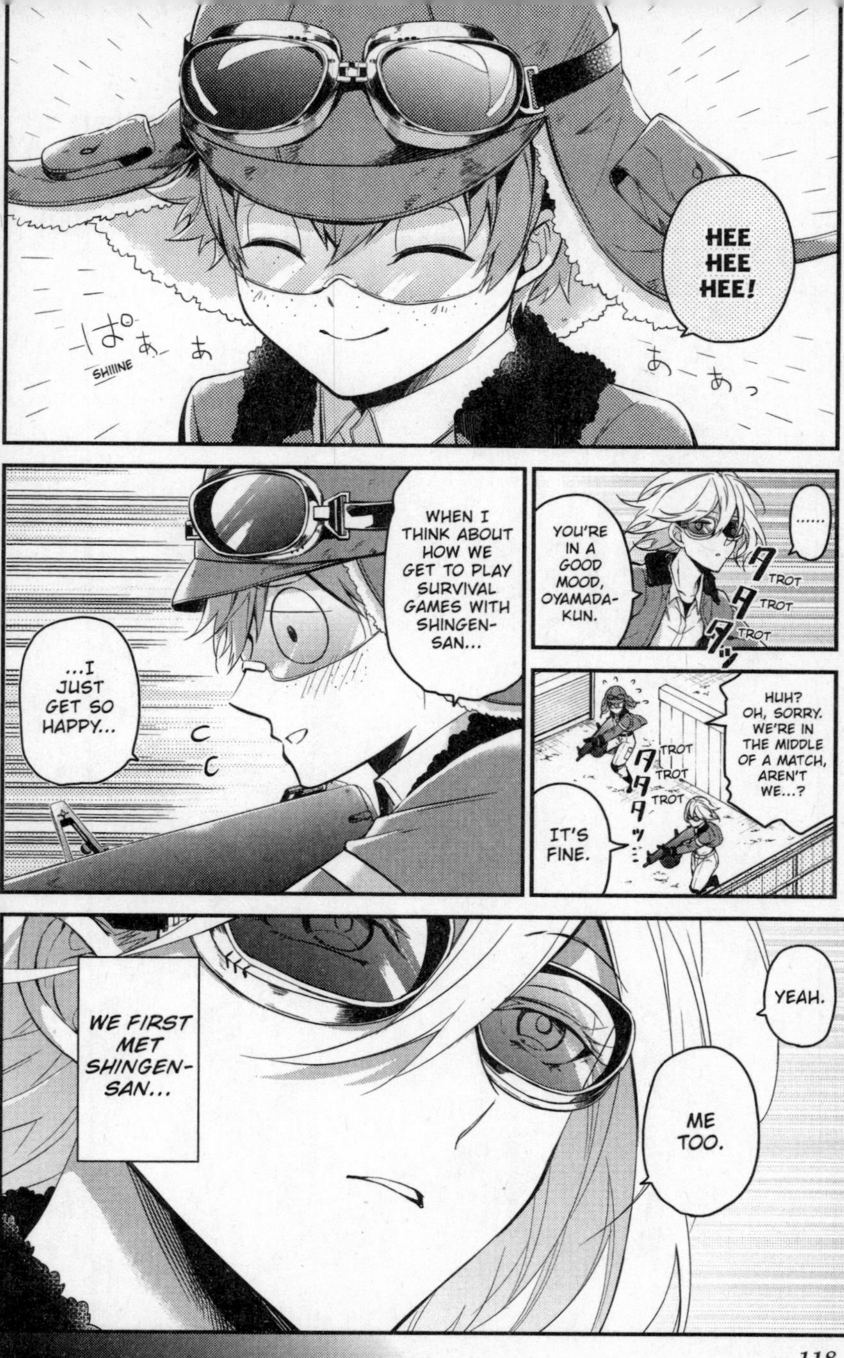
HEE HEE HEE!
あ あっ
ぱあ あ
SHIIINE
......
YOU'RE IN A GOOD MOOD, OYAMADA-KUN.
タタタッ
TROT TROT TROT
HUH? OH, SORRY. WE'RE IN THE MIDDLE OF A MATCH, AREN'T WE...?
タタタッ
TROT TROT TROT
IT'S FINE.
WHEN I THINK ABOUT HOW WE GET TO PLAY SURVIVAL GAMES WITH SHINGEN-SAN...
...I JUST GET SO HAPPY...
YEAH.
ME TOO.
WE FIRST MET SHINGEN-SAN...

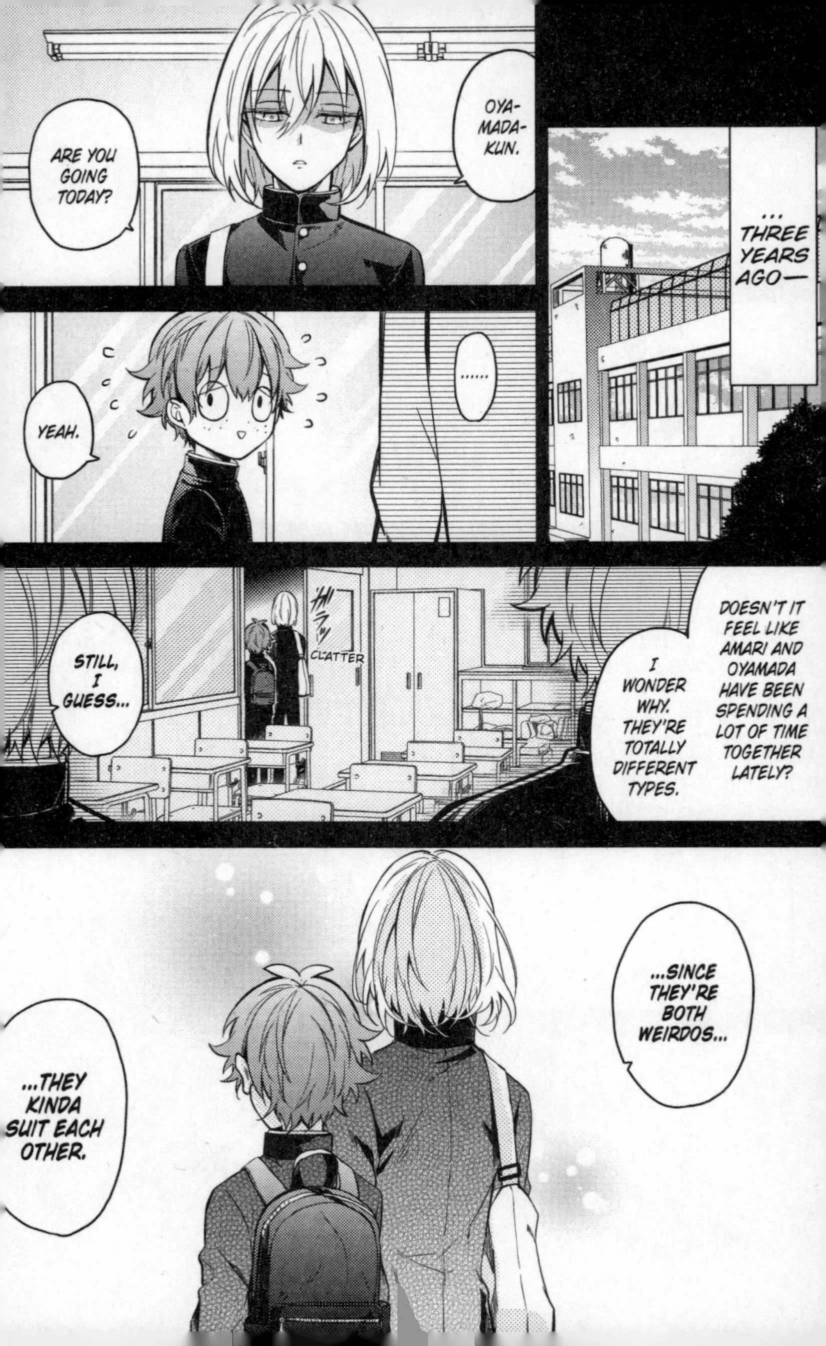
...THREE YEARS AGO—
OYA-MADA-KUN.
ARE YOU GOING TODAY?
......
YEAH.
DOESN'T IT FEEL LIKE AMARI AND OYAMADA HAVE BEEN SPENDING A LOT OF TIME TOGETHER LATELY?
I WONDER WHY. THEY'RE TOTALLY DIFFERENT TYPES.
CLATTER
STILL, I GUESS...
...SINCE THEY'RE BOTH WEIRDOS...
...THEY KINDA SUIT EACH OTHER.

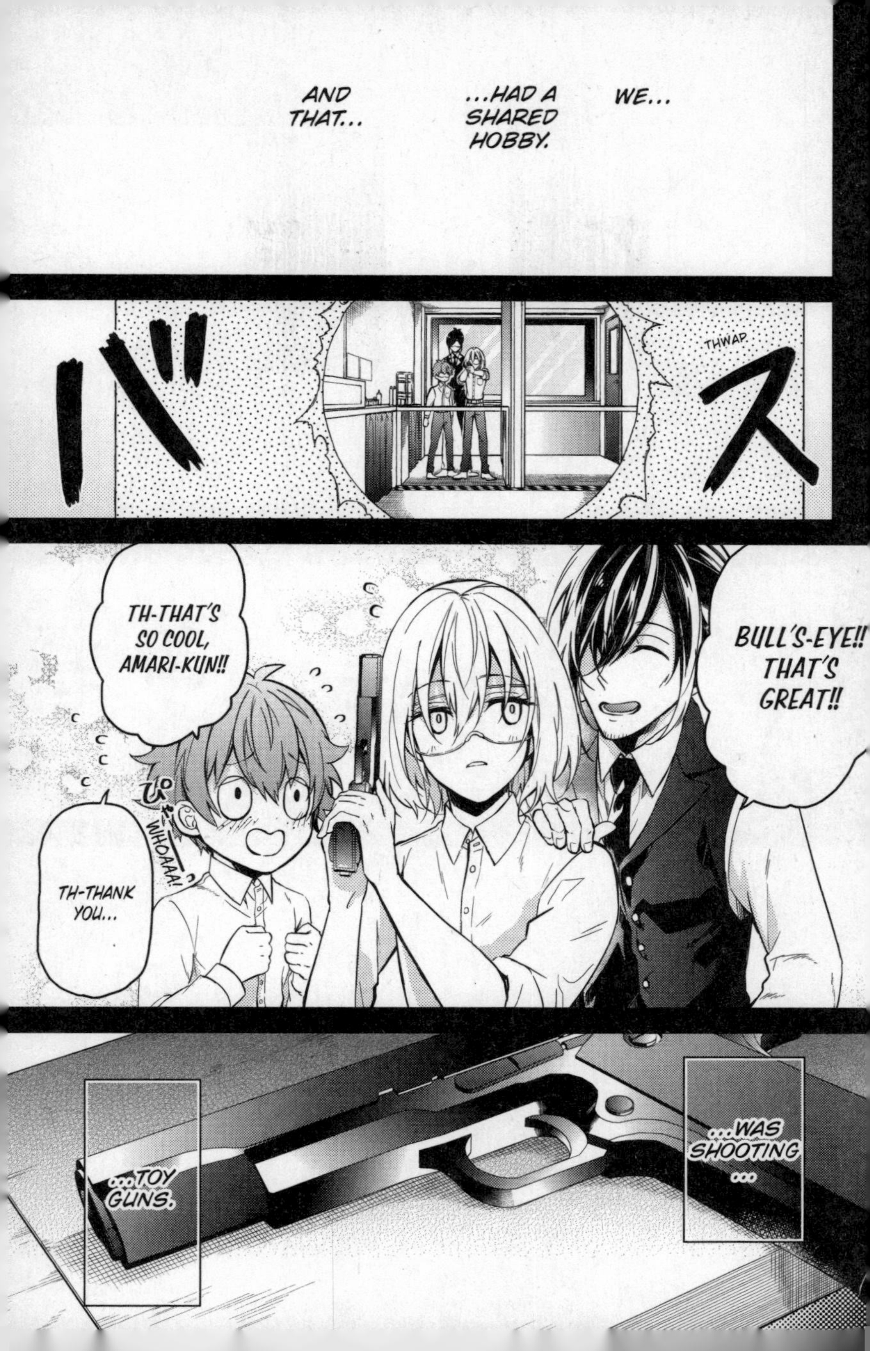
WE...
...HAD A SHARED HOBBY.
AND THAT...
バス
THWAP
BULL'S-EYE!! THAT'S GREAT!!
TH-THAT'S SO COOL, AMARI-KUN!!
WHOAAA!
TH-THANK YOU...
...WAS SHOOTING...
...TOY GUNS.

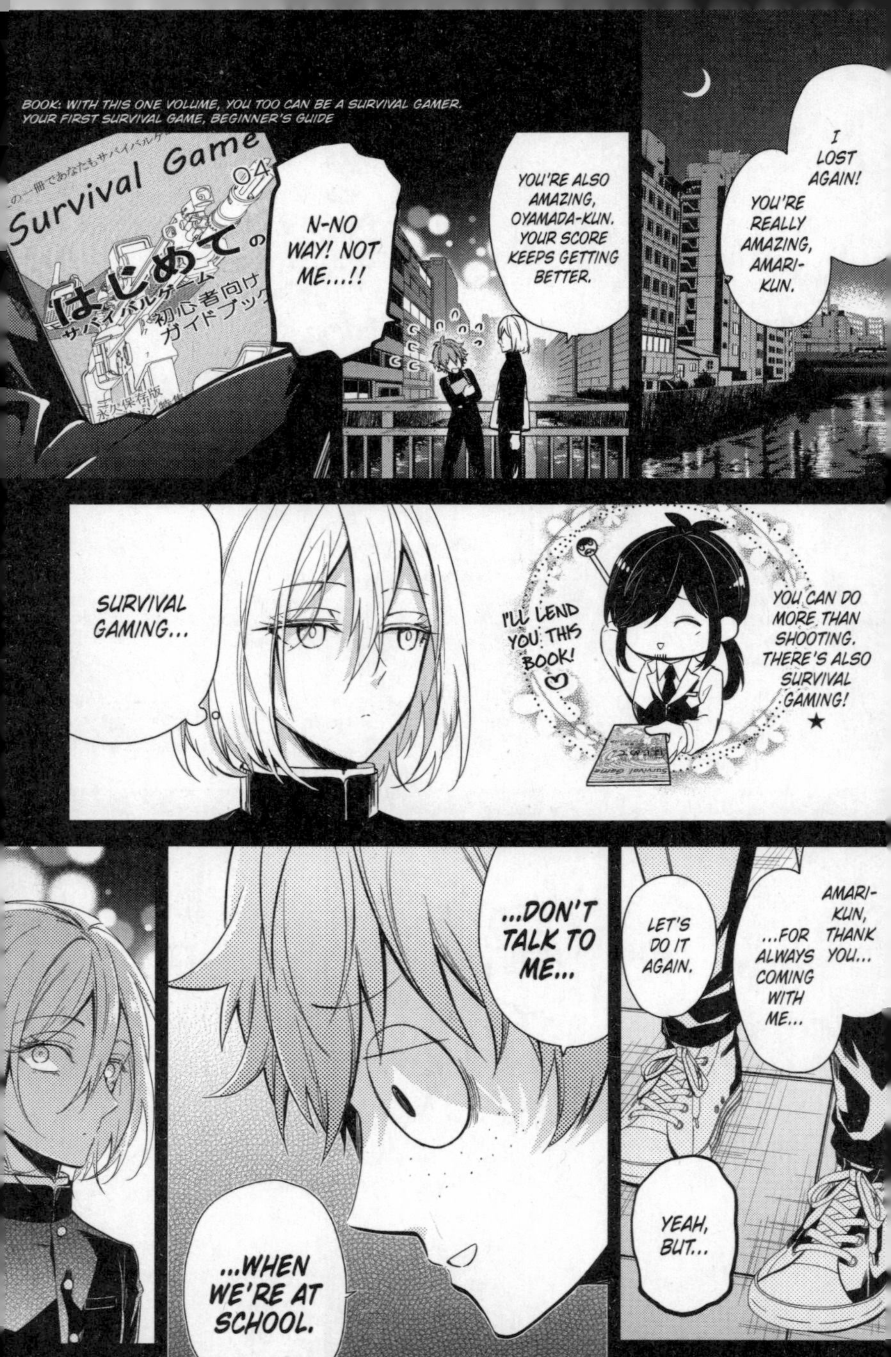
I LOST AGAIN! YOU'RE REALLY AMAZING, AMARI-KUN.
YOU'RE ALSO AMAZING, OYAMADA-KUN. YOUR SCORE KEEPS GETTING BETTER.
N-NO WAY! NOT ME...!!
BOOK: WITH THIS ONE VOLUME, YOU TOO CAN BE A SURVIVAL GAMER. YOUR FIRST SURVIVAL GAME, BEGINNER'S GUIDE
Survival Game
04
はじめてのサバイバルゲーム
初心者向けガイドブック
永久保存版
YOU CAN DO MORE THAN SHOOTING. THERE'S ALSO SURVIVAL GAMING! ★
I'LL LEND YOU THIS BOOK! ♡
SURVIVAL GAMING...
AMARI-KUN, THANK YOU...
...FOR ALWAYS COMING WITH ME...
LET'S DO IT AGAIN.
YEAH, BUT...
...DON'T TALK TO ME...
...WHEN WE'RE AT SCHOOL.

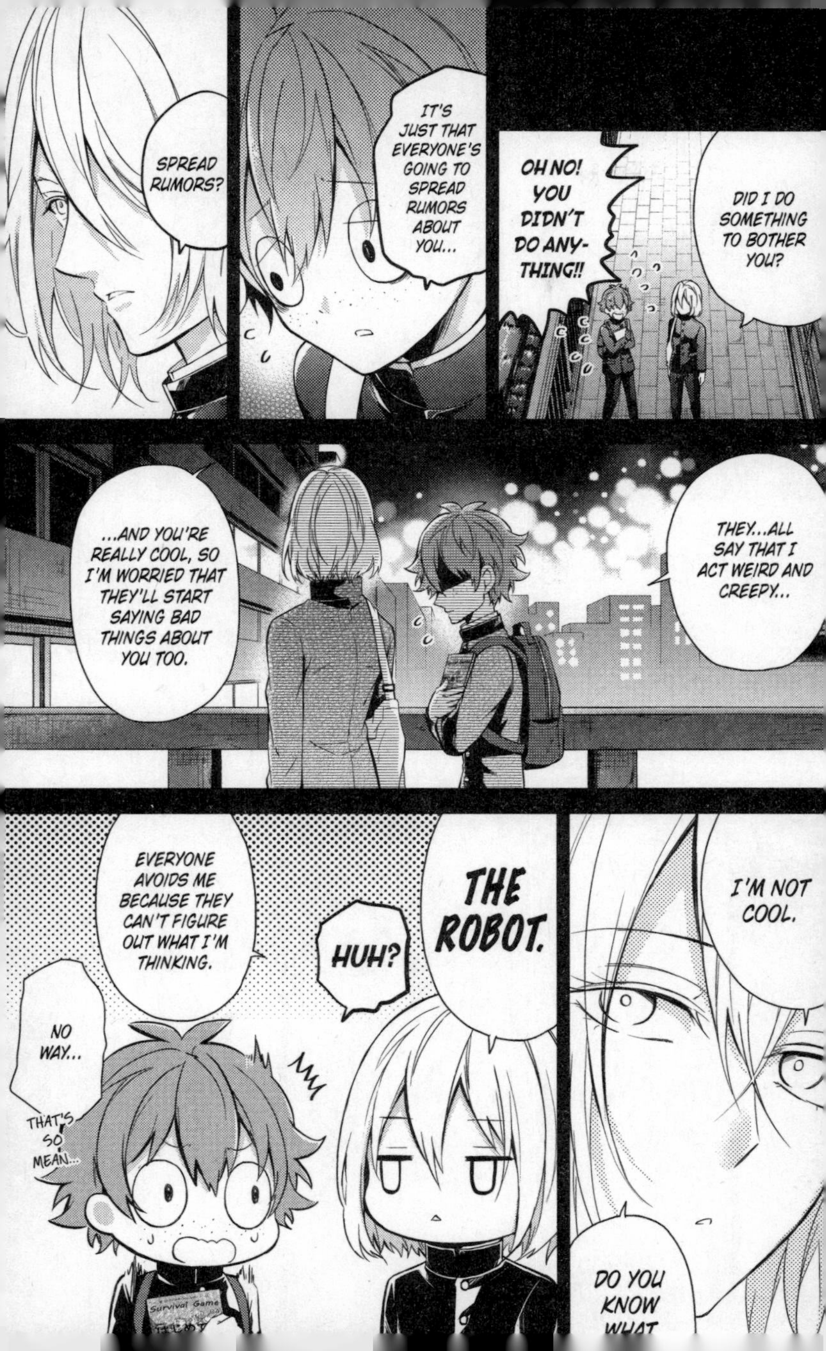
DID I DO SOMETHING TO BOTHER YOU?
OH NO! YOU DIDN'T DO ANY-THING!!
IT'S JUST THAT EVERYONE'S GOING TO SPREAD RUMORS ABOUT YOU...
SPREAD RUMORS?
THEY...ALL SAY THAT I ACT WEIRD AND CREEPY...
...AND YOU'RE REALLY COOL, SO I'M WORRIED THAT THEY'LL START SAYING BAD THINGS ABOUT YOU TOO.
I'M NOT COOL.
DO YOU KNOW WHAT
THE ROBOT.
HUH?
EVERYONE AVOIDS ME BECAUSE THEY CAN'T FIGURE OUT WHAT I'M THINKING.
NO WAY...
THAT'S SO MEAN...
Survival Game

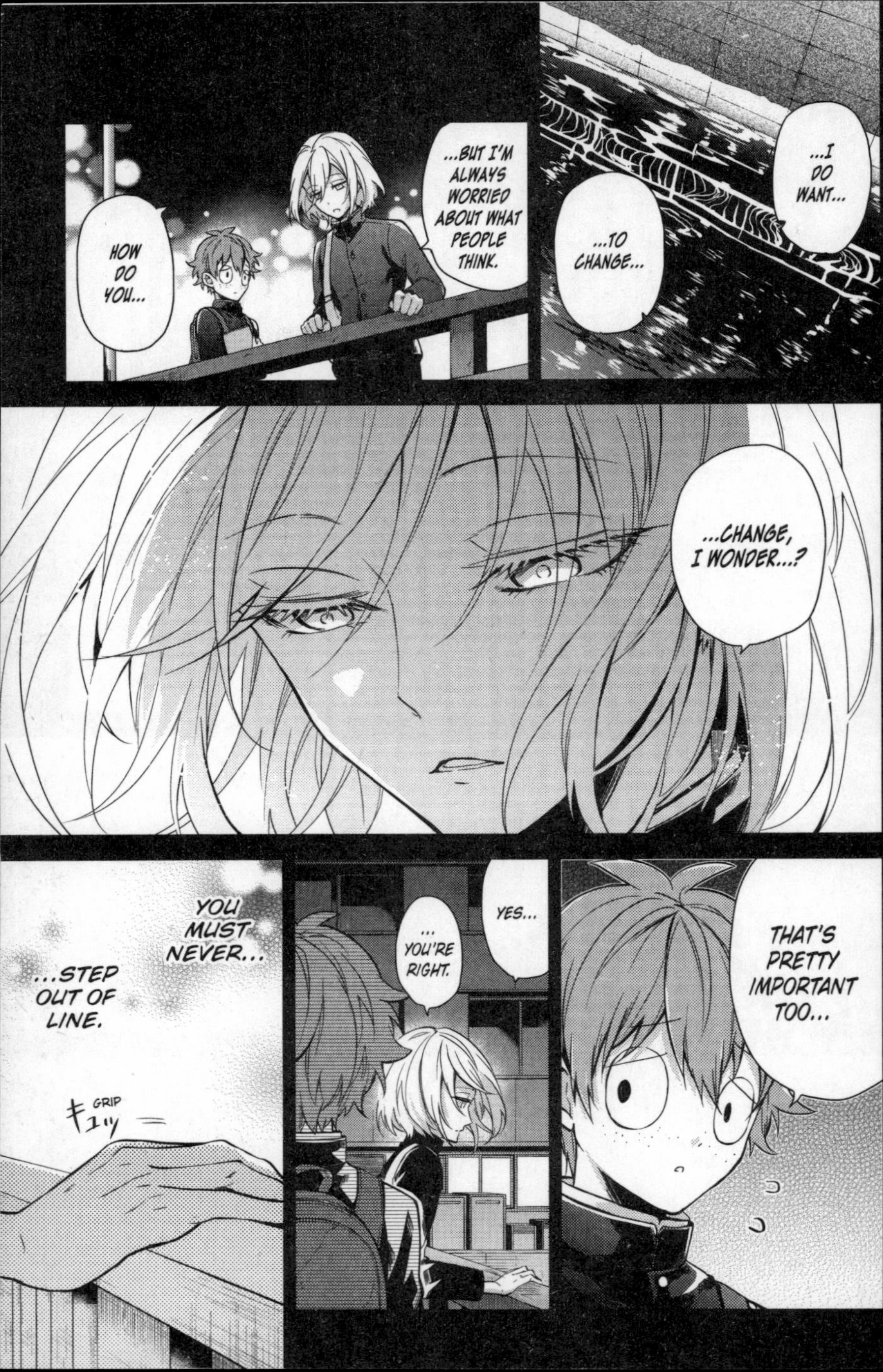
...I DO WANT...
...TO CHANGE...
...BUT I'M ALWAYS WORRIED ABOUT WHAT PEOPLE THINK.
HOW DO YOU...
...CHANGE, I WONDER...?
THAT'S PRETTY IMPORTANT TOO...
YES...
...YOU'RE RIGHT.
YOU MUST NEVER...
...STEP OUT OF LINE.
キュッ GRIP

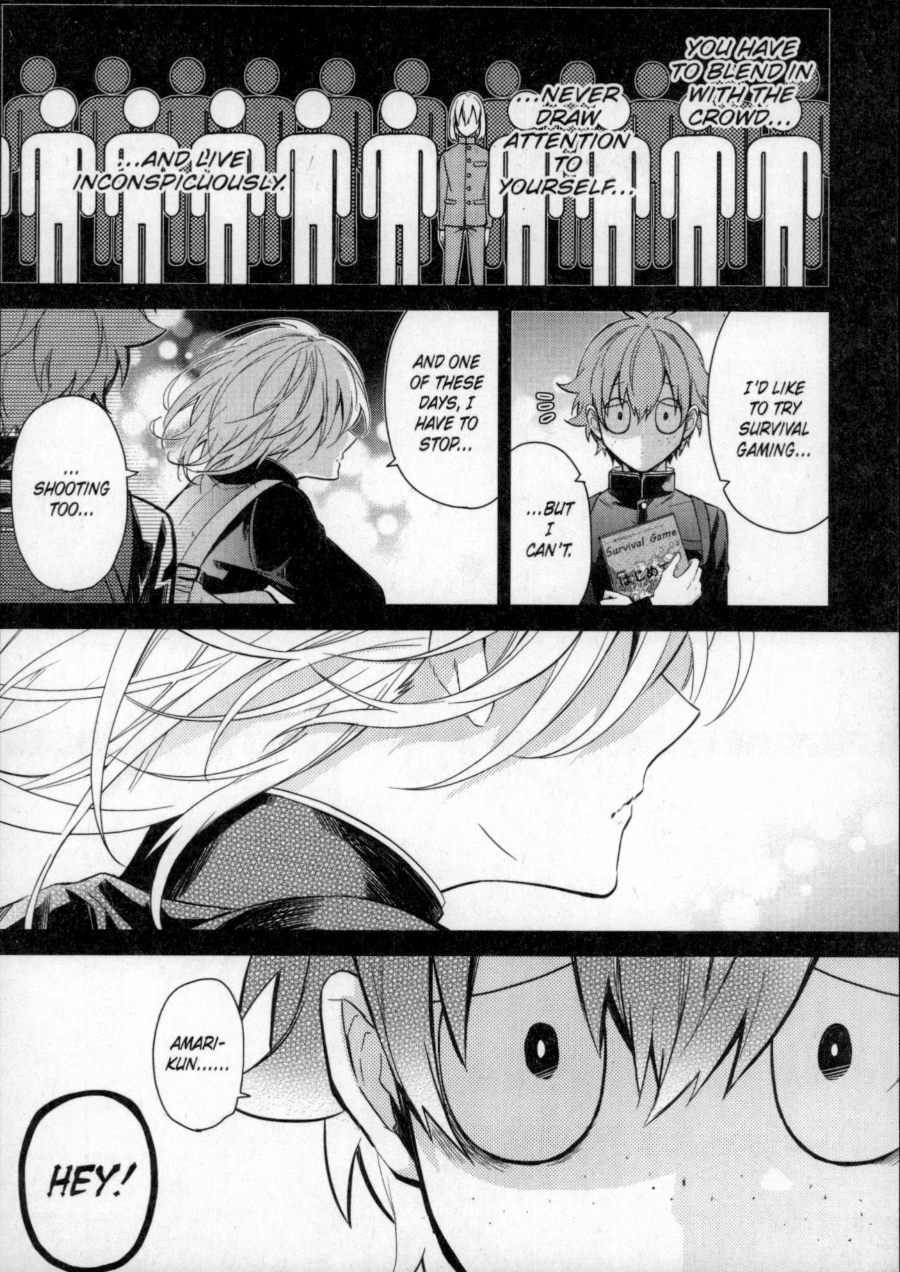
YOU HAVE TO BLEND IN WITH THE CROWD...
...NEVER DRAW ATTENTION TO YOURSELF...
...AND LIVE INCONSPICUOUSLY.
I'D LIKE TO TRY SURVIVAL GAMING...
Survival Game
...BUT I CAN'T.
AND ONE OF THESE DAYS, I HAVE TO STOP...
...SHOOTING TOO...
AMARI-KUN......
HEY!

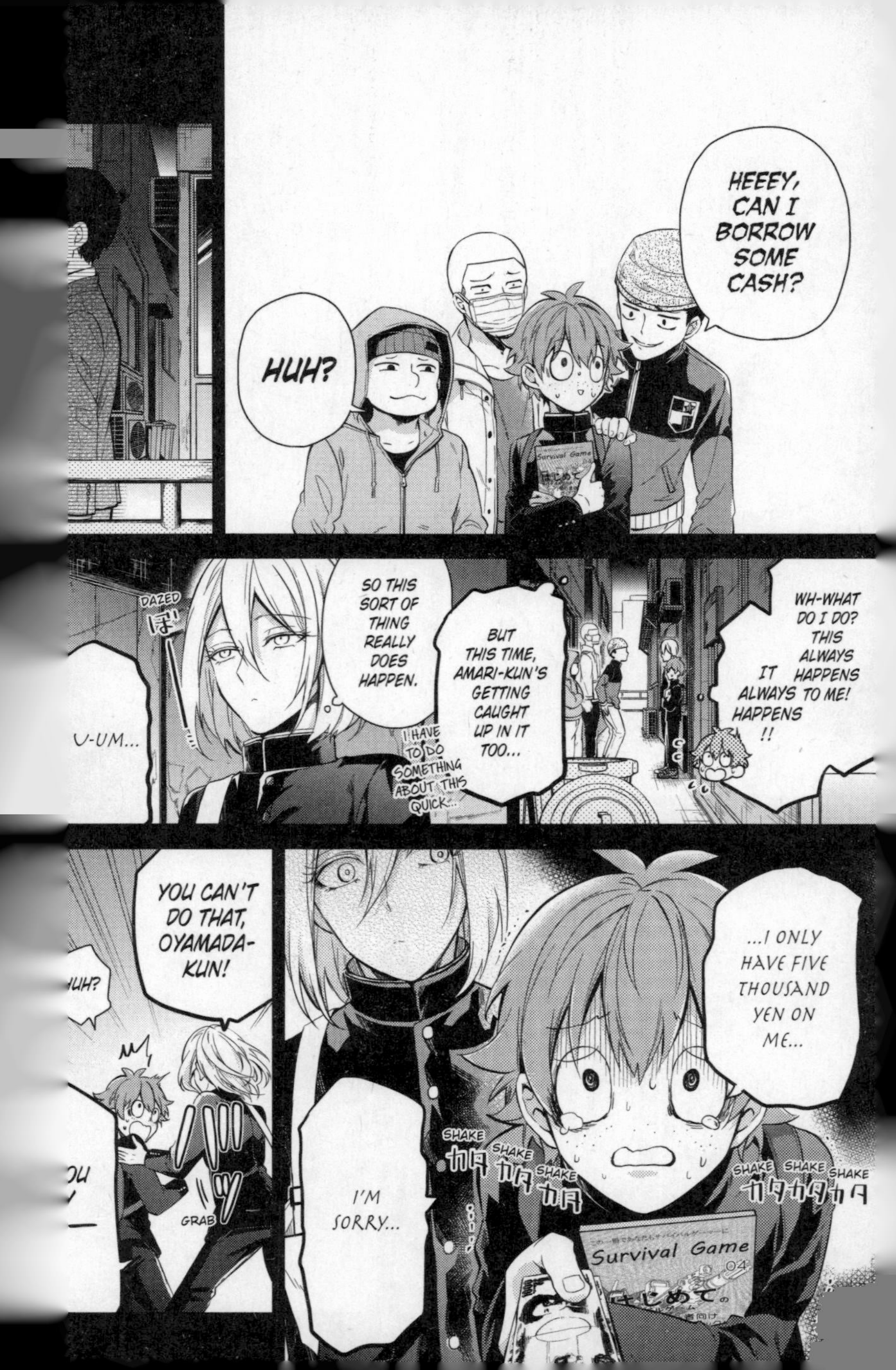
HEEEY, CAN I BORROW SOME CASH?
HUH?
Survival Game
WH-WHAT DO I DO? THIS ALWAYS HAPPENS TO ME!
IT ALWAYS HAPPENS !!
BUT THIS TIME, AMARI-KUN'S GETTING CAUGHT UP IN IT TOO...
I HAVE TO DO SOMETHING ABOUT THIS QUICK...
SO THIS SORT OF THING REALLY DOES HAPPEN.
DAZED
ぼー
U-UM...
...I ONLY HAVE FIVE THOUSAND YEN ON ME...
SHAKE SHAKE SHAKE
カタカタカタ
SHAKE SHAKE SHAKE
カタカタカタ
I'M SORRY...
Survival Game
04
はじめての
YOU CAN'T DO THAT, OYAMADA-KUN!
UH?
GRAB

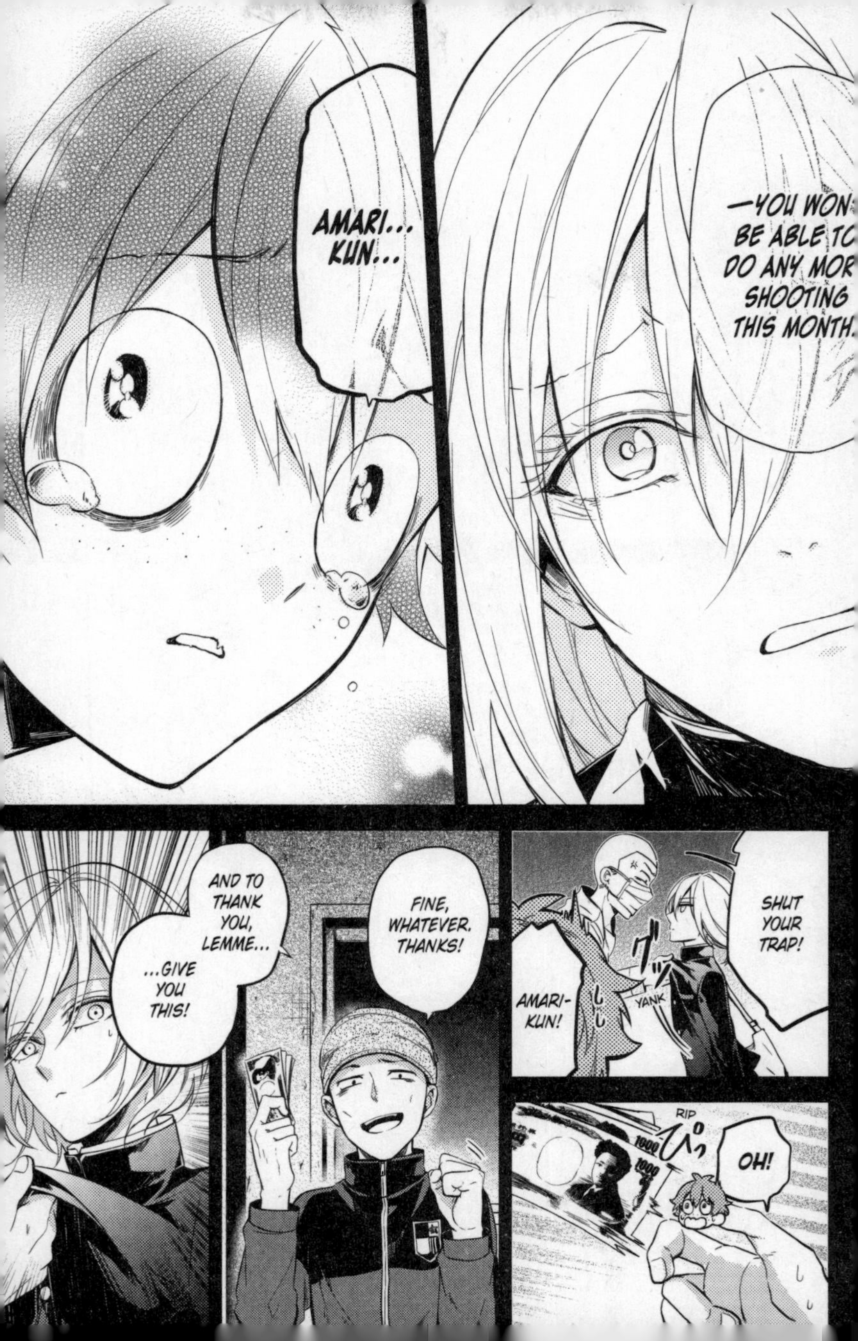
—YOU WON BE ABLE TO DO ANY MOR SHOOTING THIS MONTH.
AMARI... KUN...
SHUT YOUR TRAP!
AMARI-KUN!
YANK
RIP
OH!
FINE, WHATEVER. THANKS!
AND TO THANK YOU, LEMME...
...GIVE YOU THIS!

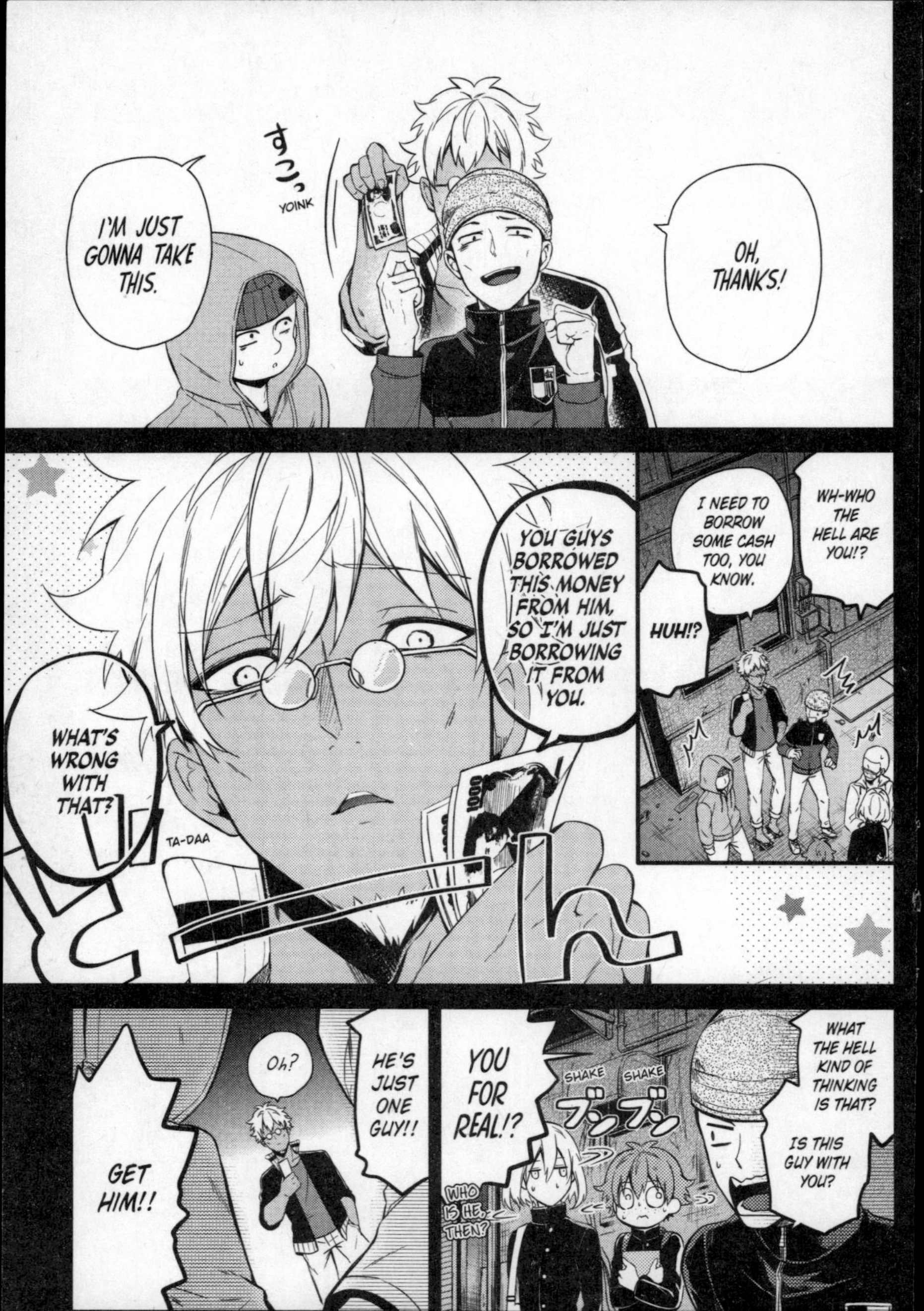
OH, THANKS!
すこっ
YOINK
I'M JUST GONNA TAKE THIS.
WH-WHO THE HELL ARE YOU!?
I NEED TO BORROW SOME CASH TOO, YOU KNOW.
HUH!?
YOU GUYS BORROWED THIS MONEY FROM HIM, SO I'M JUST BORROWING IT FROM YOU.
WHAT'S WRONG WITH THAT?
TA-DAA
WHAT THE HELL KIND OF THINKING IS THAT?
IS THIS GUY WITH YOU?
SHAKE SHAKE
ブンブン
YOU FOR REAL!?
WHO IS HE, THEN?
HE'S JUST ONE GUY!!
Oh?
GET HIM!!

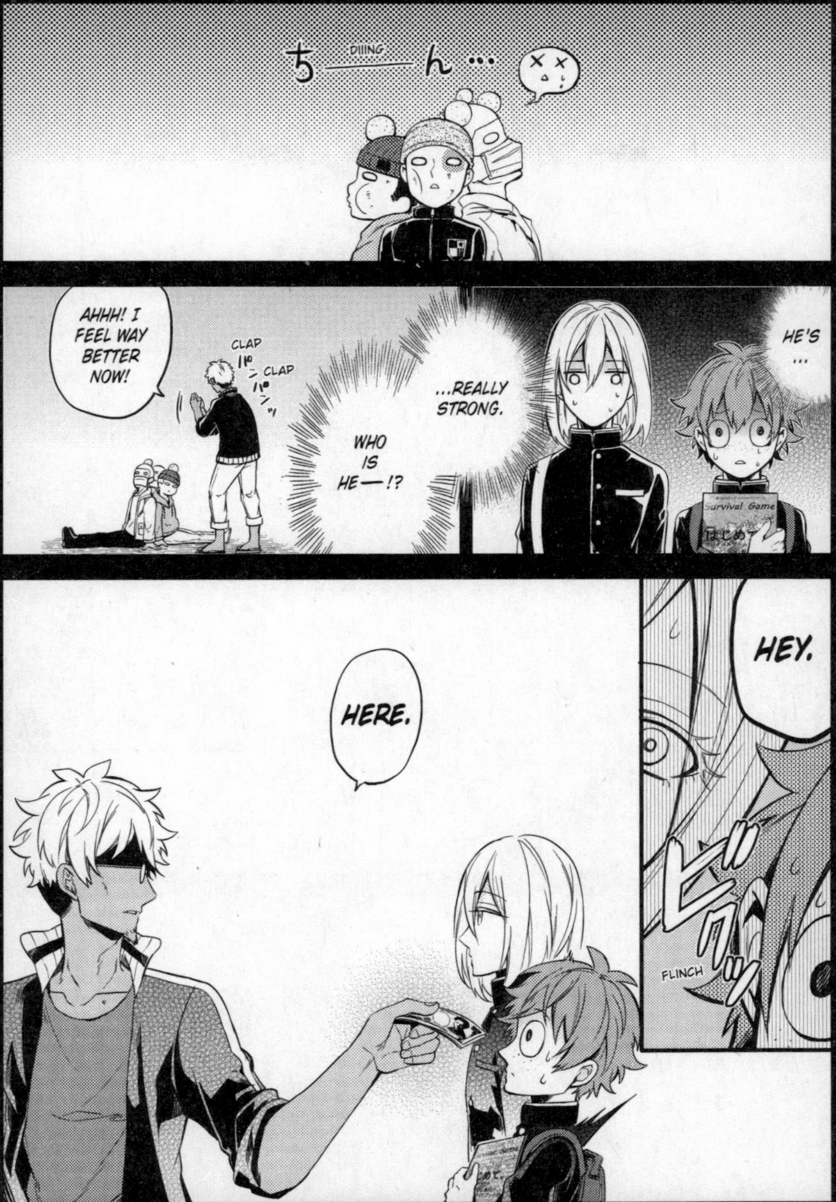

ち——ん…
DIIING
HE'S ...
...REALLY STRONG.
Survival Game
WHO IS HE—!?
AHHH! I FEEL WAY BETTER NOW!
CLAP
CLAP
HEY.
FLINCH
HERE.

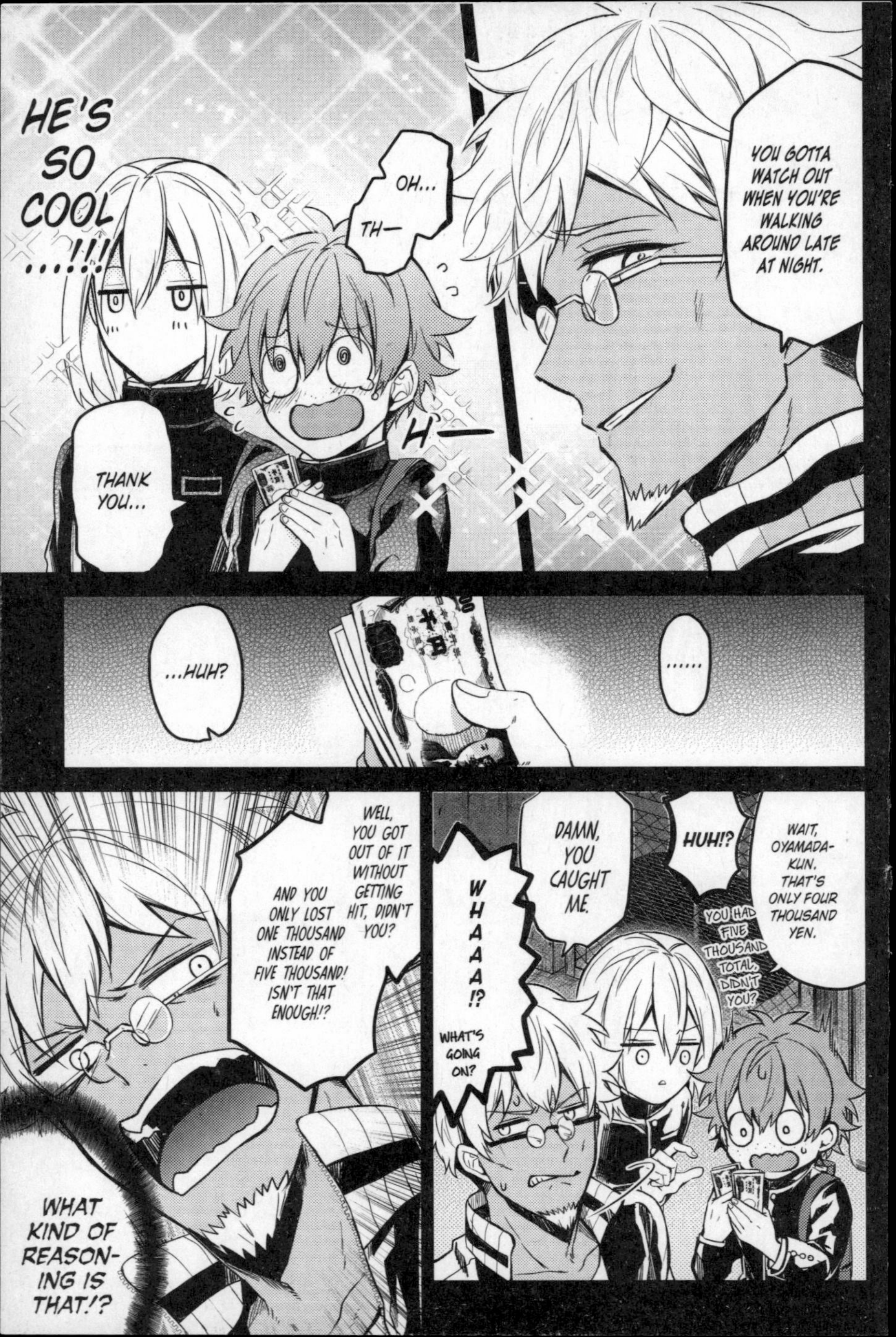
YOU GOTTA WATCH OUT WHEN YOU'RE WALKING AROUND LATE AT NIGHT.
OH... TH—
H—
THANK YOU...
HE'S SO COOL ......!!!
......
...HUH?
WAIT, OYAMADA-KUN. THAT'S ONLY FOUR THOUSAND YEN.
YOU HAD FIVE THOUSAND TOTAL, DIDN'T YOU?
HUH!?
DAMN, YOU CAUGHT ME.
WHAAAA!?
WHAT'S GOING ON?
WELL, YOU GOT OUT OF IT WITHOUT GETTING HIT, DIDN'T YOU?
AND YOU ONLY LOST ONE THOUSAND INSTEAD OF FIVE THOUSAND! ISN'T THAT ENOUGH!?
WHAT KIND OF REASONING IS THAT!?

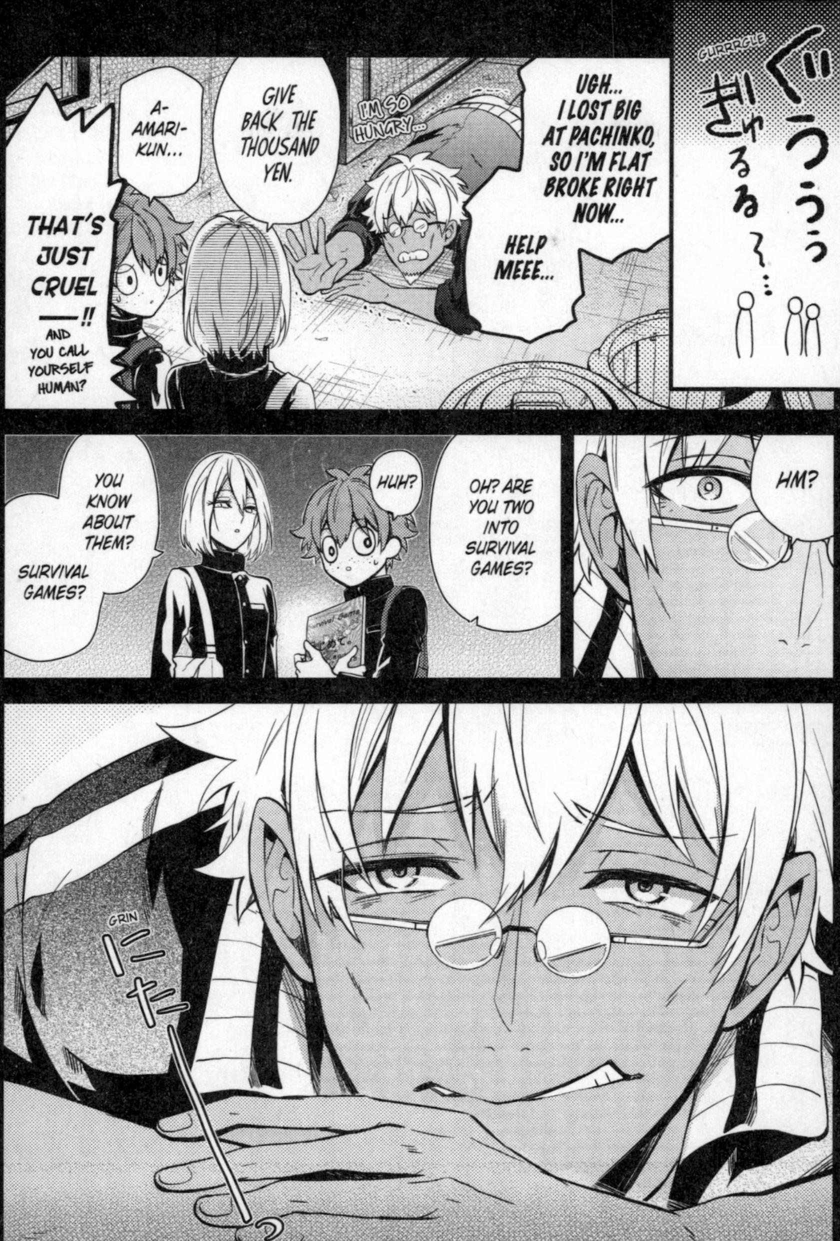
GURRRGLE
ぐうぅぅぎゅるる～…
UGH... I LOST BIG AT PACHINKO, SO I'M FLAT BROKE RIGHT NOW...
HELP MEEE...
I'M SO HUNGRY...
GIVE BACK THE THOUSAND YEN.
A-AMARI-KUN...
THAT'S JUST CRUEL——!!
AND YOU CALL YOURSELF HUMAN?
HM?
OH? ARE YOU TWO INTO SURVIVAL GAMES?
HUH?
YOU KNOW ABOUT THEM?
SURVIVAL GAMES?
GRIN
ニーたー

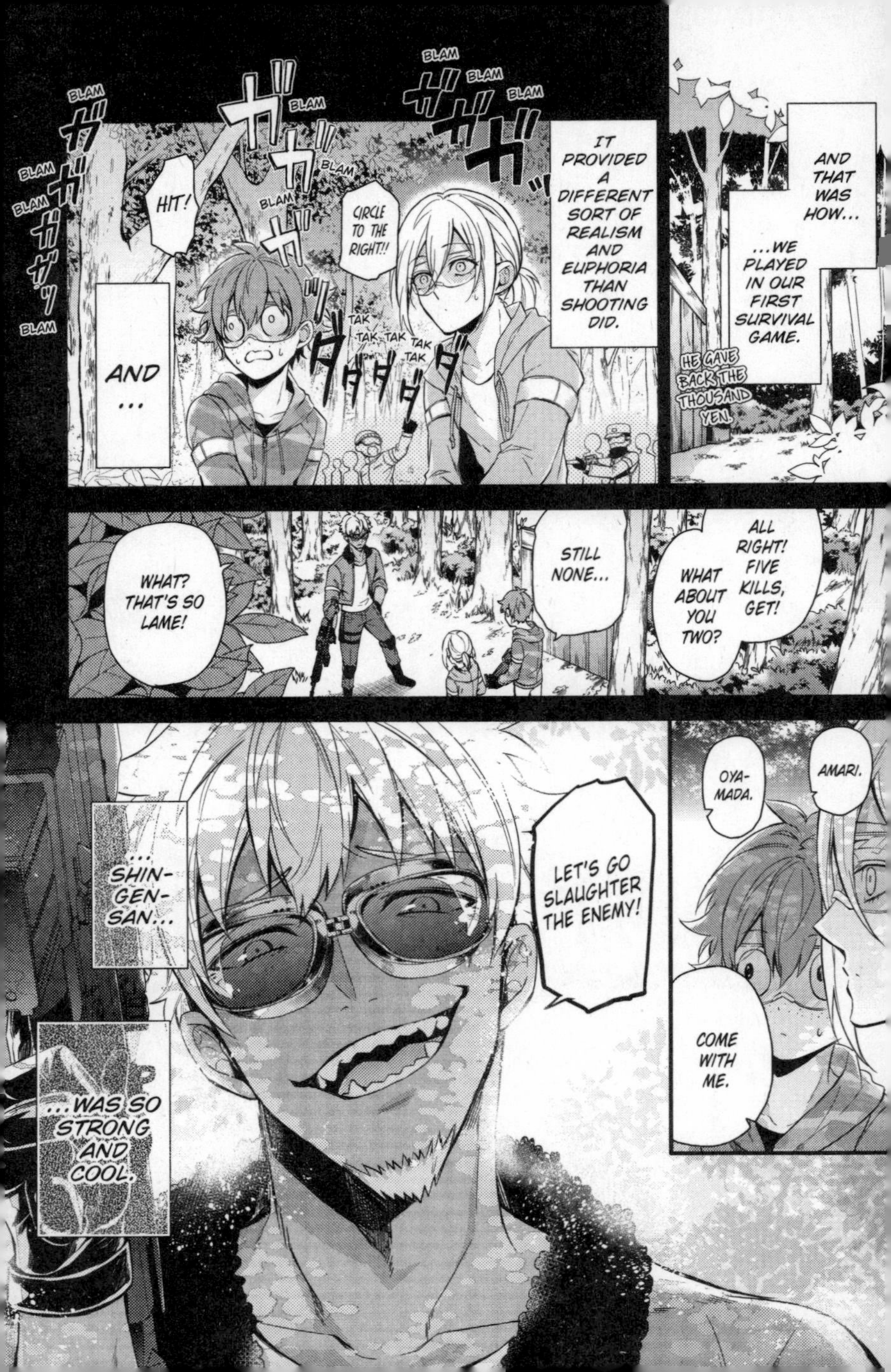
AND THAT WAS HOW...
...WE PLAYED IN OUR FIRST SURVIVAL GAME.
HE GAVE BACK THE THOUSAND YEN.
IT PROVIDED A DIFFERENT SORT OF REALISM AND EUPHORIA THAN SHOOTING DID.
BLAM BLAM BLAM
CIRCLE TO THE RIGHT!!
BLAM BLAM BLAM
HIT!
BLAM BLAM BLAM BLAM
TAK TAK TAK TAK TAK
AND...
ALL RIGHT! FIVE KILLS, GET!
WHAT ABOUT YOU TWO?
STILL NONE...
WHAT? THAT'S SO LAME!
AMARI.
OYA-MADA.
COME WITH ME.
LET'S GO SLAUGHTER THE ENEMY!
...SHIN-GEN-SAN...
...WAS SO STRONG AND COOL.

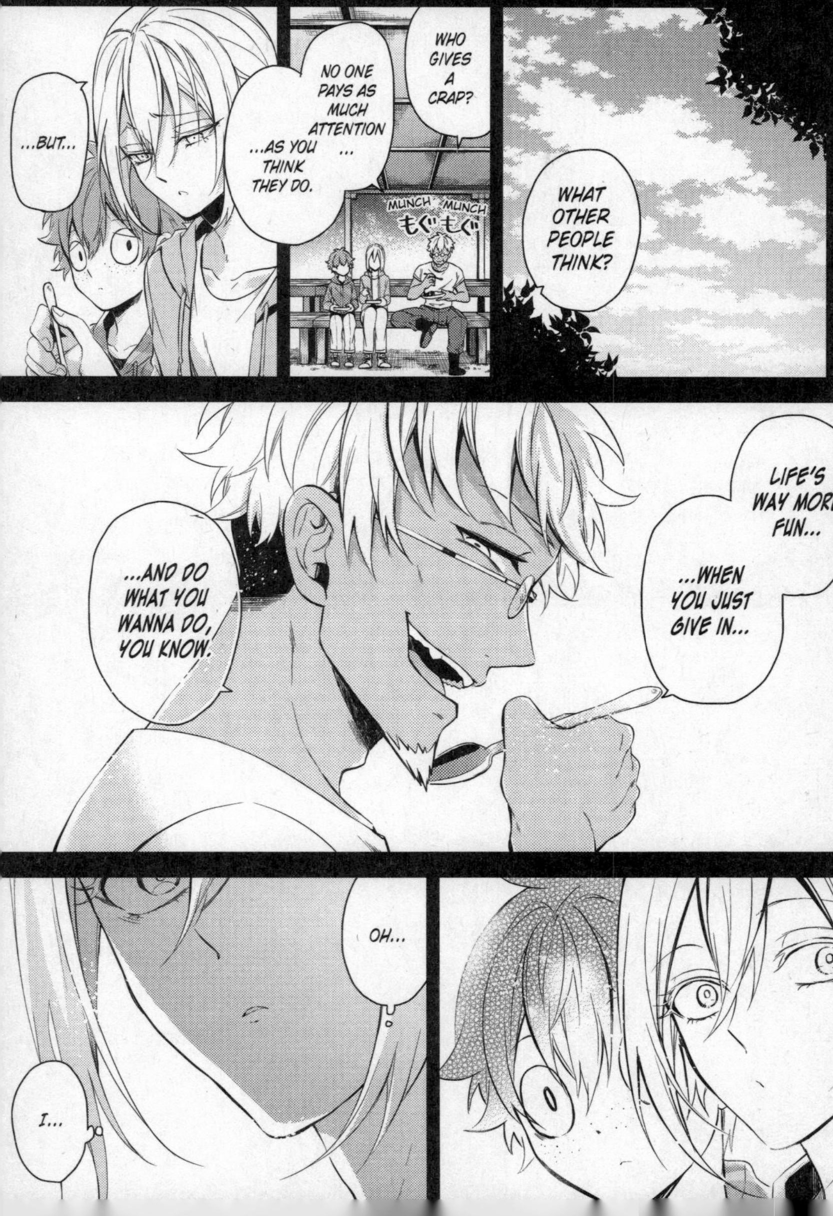
WHAT OTHER PEOPLE THINK?
WHO GIVES A CRAP?
NO ONE PAYS AS MUCH ATTENTION ...
...AS YOU THINK THEY DO.
MUNCH MUNCH
もぐもぐ
...BUT...
LIFE'S WAY MORE FUN...
...WHEN YOU JUST GIVE IN...
...AND DO WHAT YOU WANNA DO, YOU KNOW.
OH...
I...

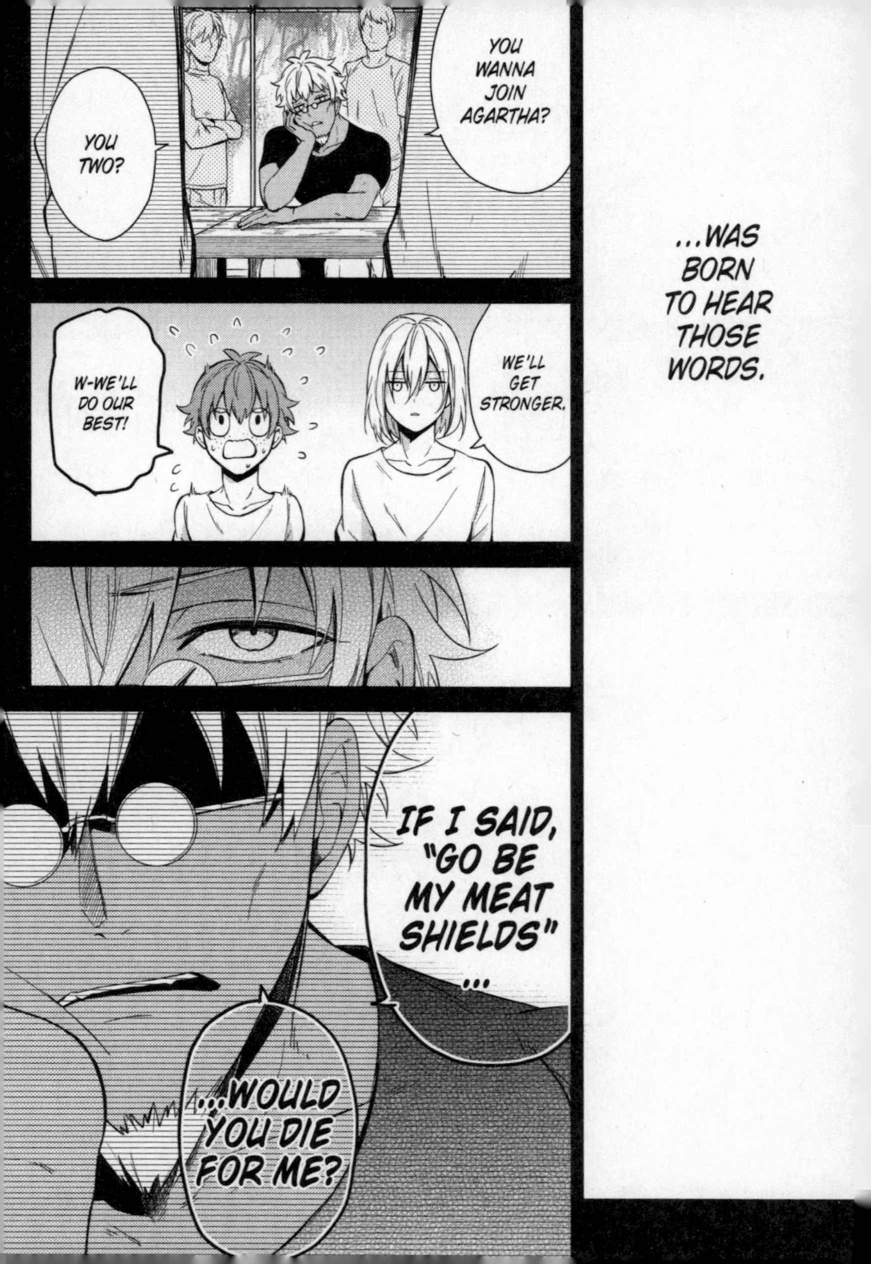
...WAS BORN TO HEAR THOSE WORDS.
YOU WANNA JOIN AGARTHA?
YOU TWO?
WE'LL GET STRONGER.
W-WE'LL DO OUR BEST!
IF I SAID, "GO BE MY MEAT SHIELDS" ...
...WOULD YOU DIE FOR ME?

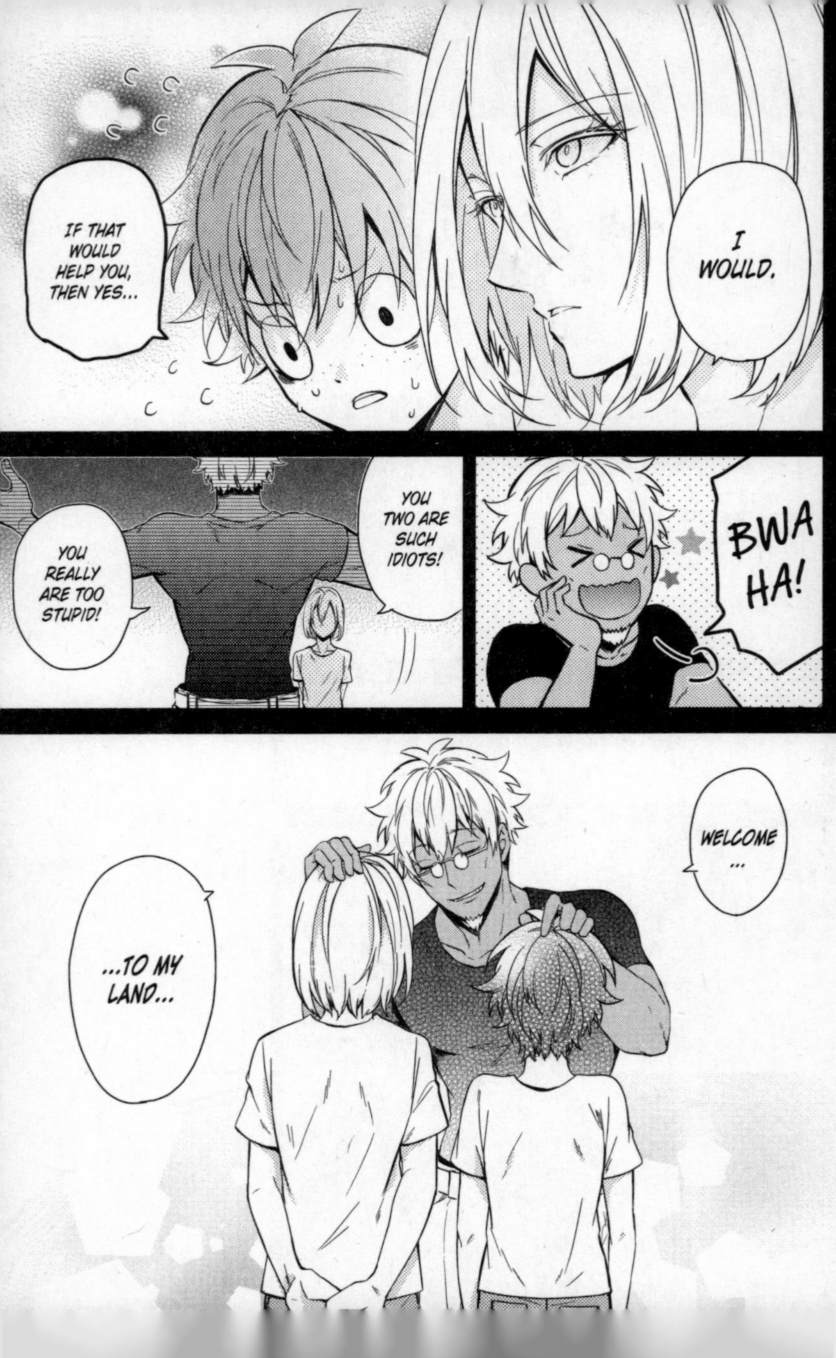
I WOULD.
IF THAT WOULD HELP YOU, THEN YES...
BWA HA!
YOU TWO ARE SUCH IDIOTS!
YOU REALLY ARE TOO STUPID!
WELCOME...
...TO MY LAND...

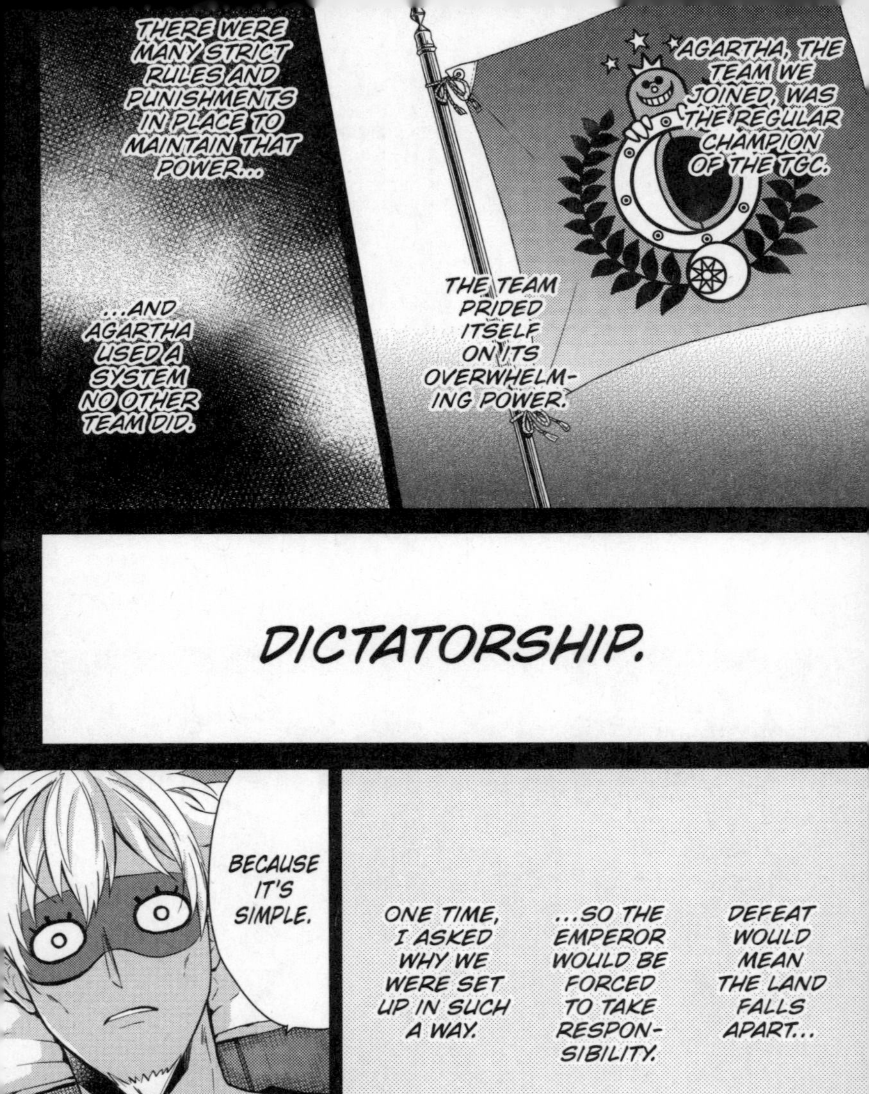
AGARTHA, THE TEAM WE JOINED, WAS THE REGULAR CHAMPION OF THE TGC.
THE TEAM PRIDED ITSELF ON ITS OVERWHELMING POWER.
THERE WERE MANY STRICT RULES AND PUNISHMENTS IN PLACE TO MAINTAIN THAT POWER...
...AND AGARTHA USED A SYSTEM NO OTHER TEAM DID.
DICTATORSHIP.
DEFEAT WOULD MEAN THE LAND FALLS APART...
...SO THE EMPEROR WOULD BE FORCED TO TAKE RESPONSIBILITY.
ONE TIME, I ASKED WHY WE WERE SET UP IN SUCH A WAY.
BECAUSE IT'S SIMPLE.

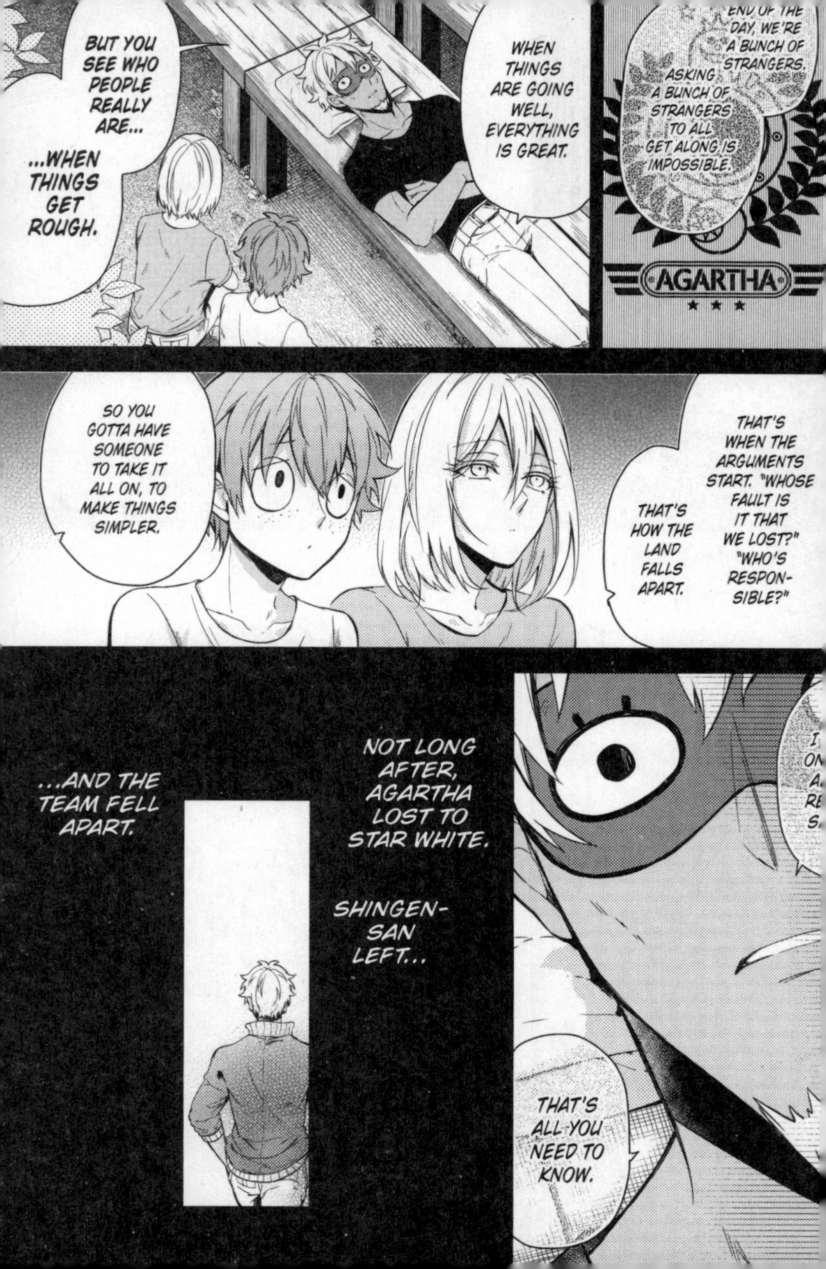
END OF THE DAY, WE'RE A BUNCH OF STRANGERS.
ASKING A BUNCH OF STRANGERS TO ALL GET ALONG IS IMPOSSIBLE.
AGARTHA
WHEN THINGS ARE GOING WELL, EVERYTHING IS GREAT.
BUT YOU SEE WHO PEOPLE REALLY ARE...
...WHEN THINGS GET ROUGH.
THAT'S WHEN THE ARGUMENTS START. "WHOSE FAULT IS IT THAT WE LOST?" "WHO'S RESPONSIBLE?"
THAT'S HOW THE LAND FALLS APART.
SO YOU GOTTA HAVE SOMEONE TO TAKE IT ALL ON, TO MAKE THINGS SIMPLER.
THAT'S ALL YOU NEED TO KNOW.
NOT LONG AFTER, AGARTHA LOST TO STAR WHITE.
SHINGEN-SAN LEFT...
...AND THE TEAM FELL APART.

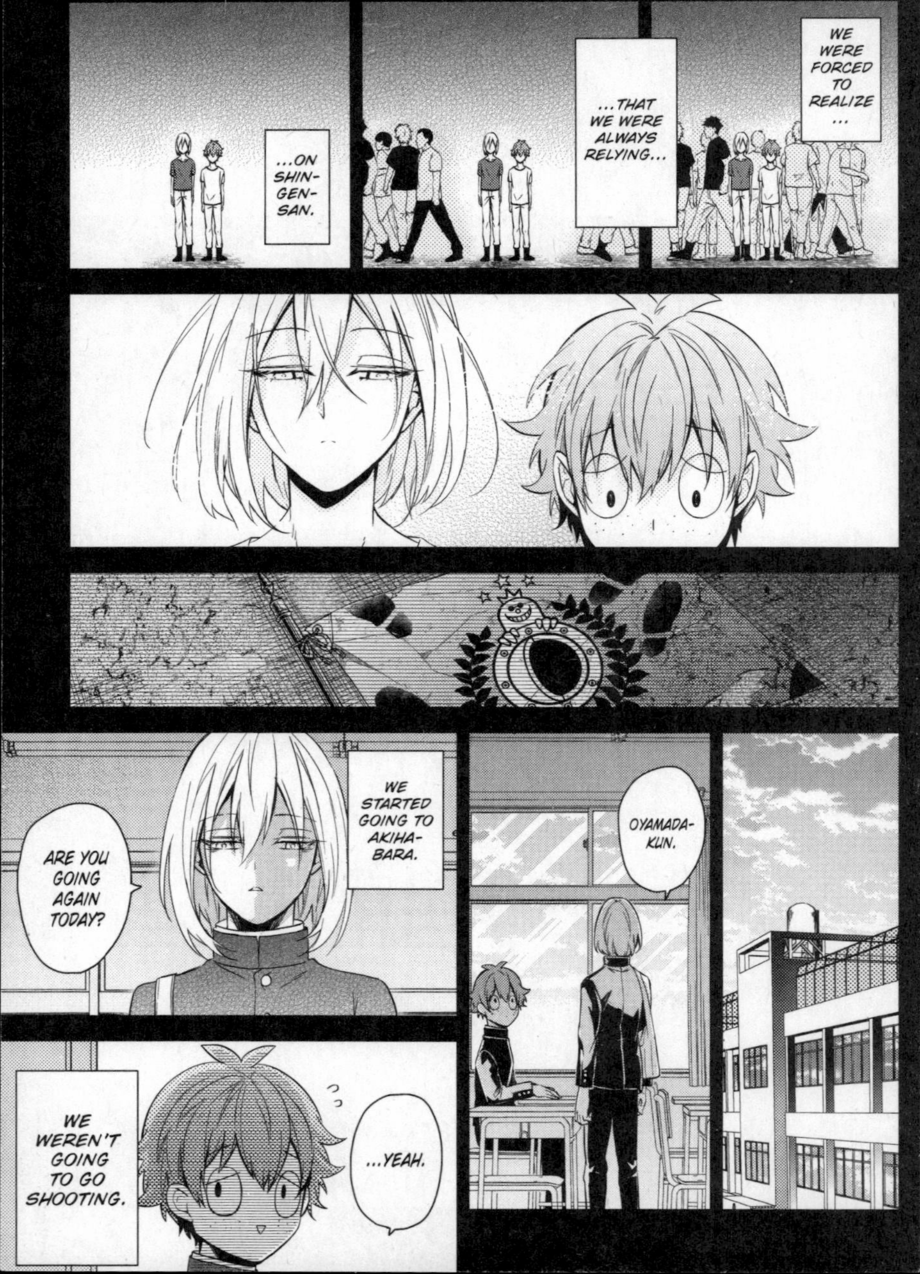
WE WERE FORCED TO REALIZE...
...THAT WE WERE ALWAYS RELYING...
...ON SHIN-GEN-SAN.
OYAMADA-KUN.
WE STARTED GOING TO AKIHA-BARA.
ARE YOU GOING AGAIN TODAY?
...YEAH.
WE WEREN'T GOING TO GO SHOOTING.

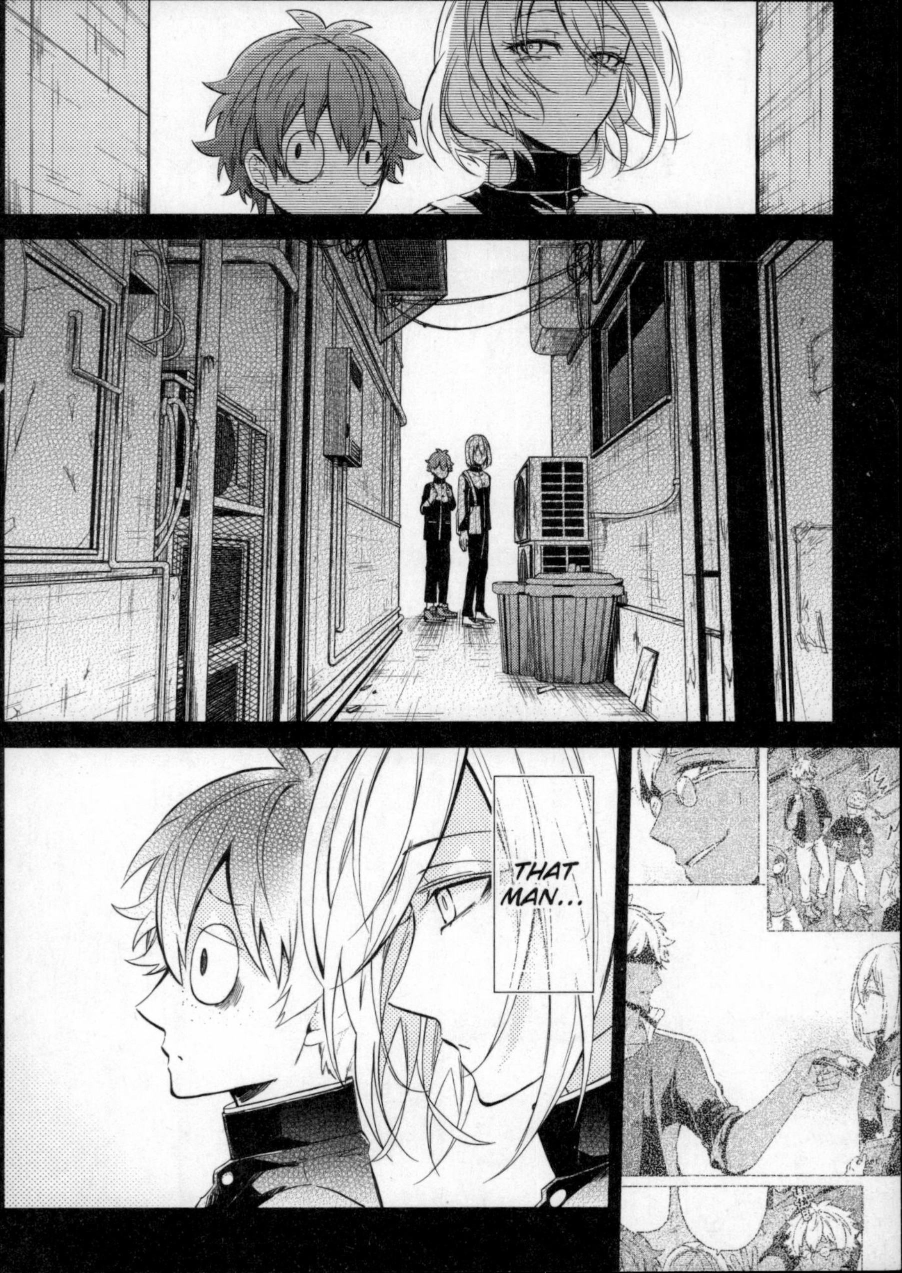
THAT MAN...

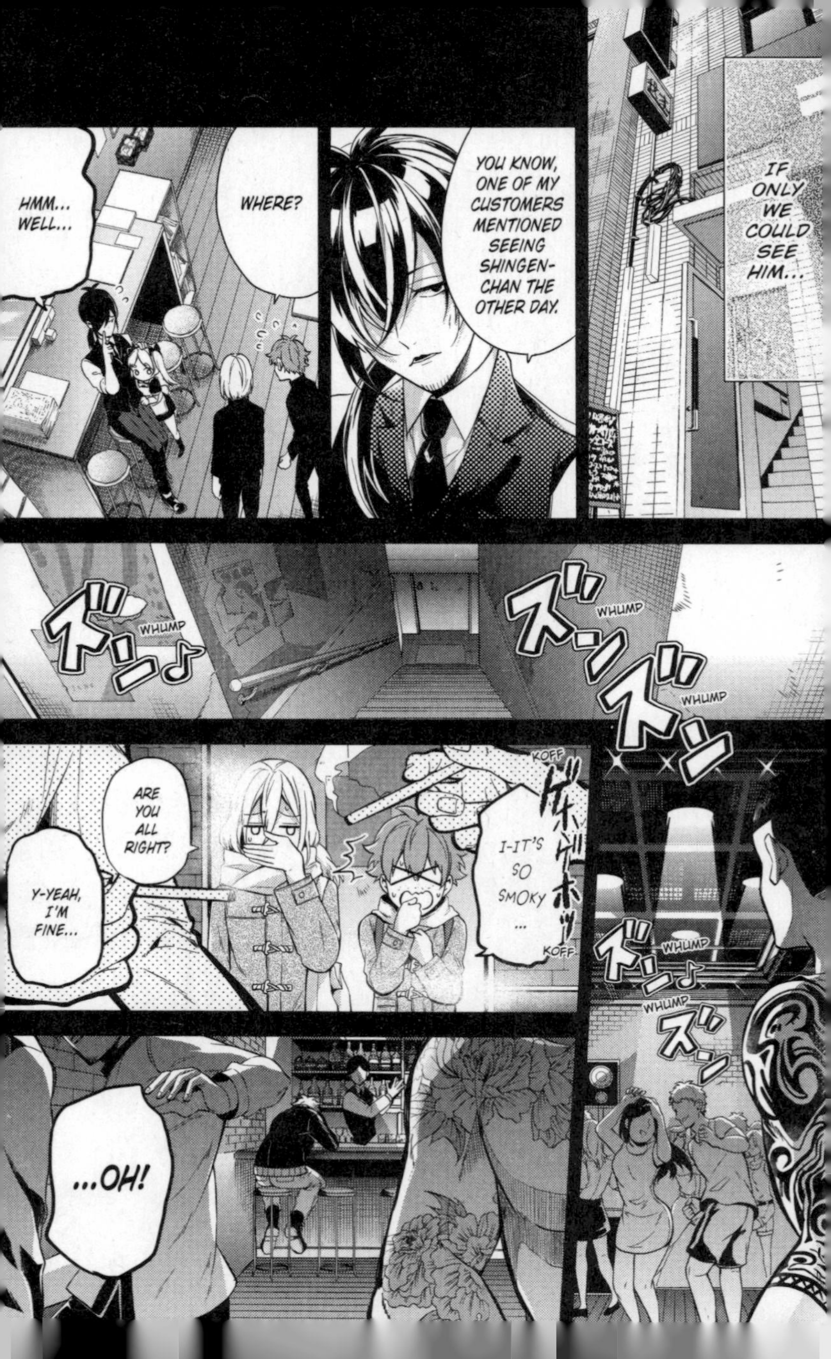
IF ONLY WE COULD SEE HIM...
YOU KNOW, ONE OF MY CUSTOMERS MENTIONED SEEING SHINGEN-CHAN THE OTHER DAY.
WHERE?
HMM... WELL...
WHUMP
WHUMP
WHUMP
WHUMP
WHUMP
KOFF
I-IT'S SO SMOKY...
KOFF
ARE YOU ALL RIGHT?
Y-YEAH, I'M FINE...
...OH!

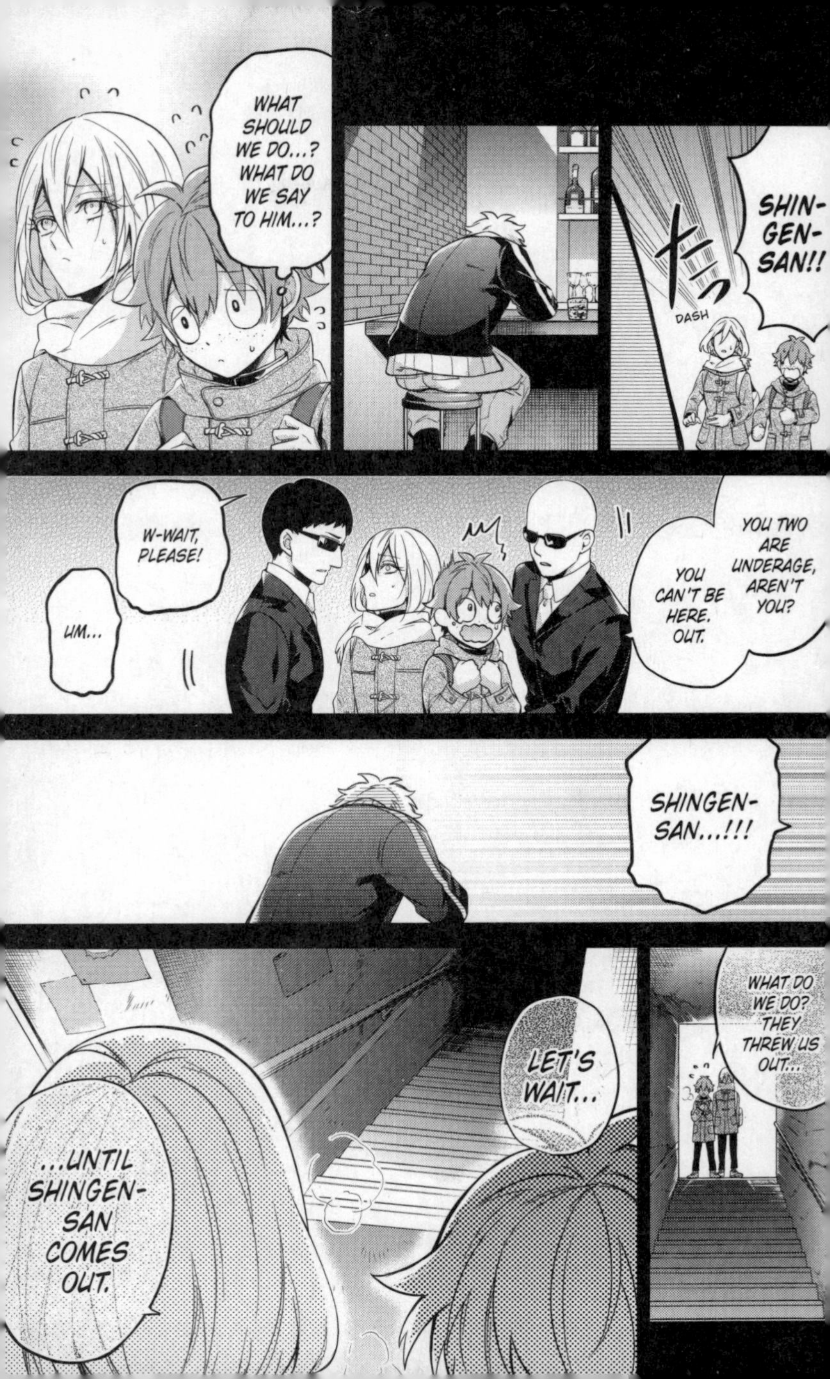
SHIN-GEN-SAN!!
DASH
WHAT SHOULD WE DO...? WHAT DO WE SAY TO HIM...?
YOU TWO ARE UNDERAGE, AREN'T YOU?
YOU CAN'T BE HERE. OUT.
W-WAIT, PLEASE!
UM...
SHINGEN-SAN...!!!
WHAT DO WE DO? THEY THREW US OUT...
LET'S WAIT...
...UNTIL SHINGEN-SAN COMES OUT.

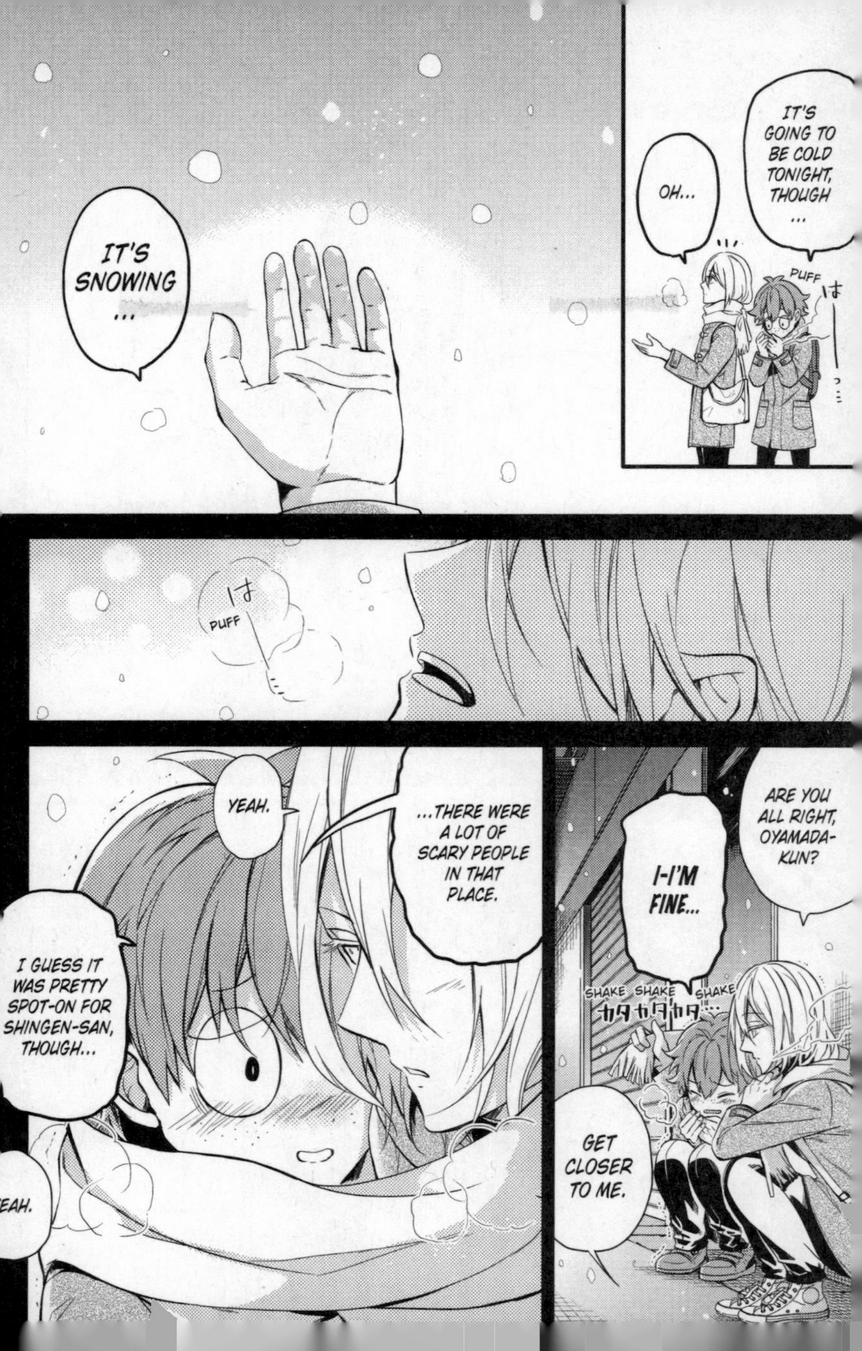
IT'S GOING TO BE COLD TONIGHT, THOUGH...
OH...
PUFF
は
IT'S SNOWING...
は
PUFF
ARE YOU ALL RIGHT, OYAMADA-KUN?
I-I'M FINE...
SHAKE SHAKE SHAKE
カタカタカタ...
GET CLOSER TO ME.
...THERE WERE A LOT OF SCARY PEOPLE IN THAT PLACE.
YEAH.
I GUESS IT WAS PRETTY SPOT-ON FOR SHINGEN-SAN, THOUGH...
EAH.

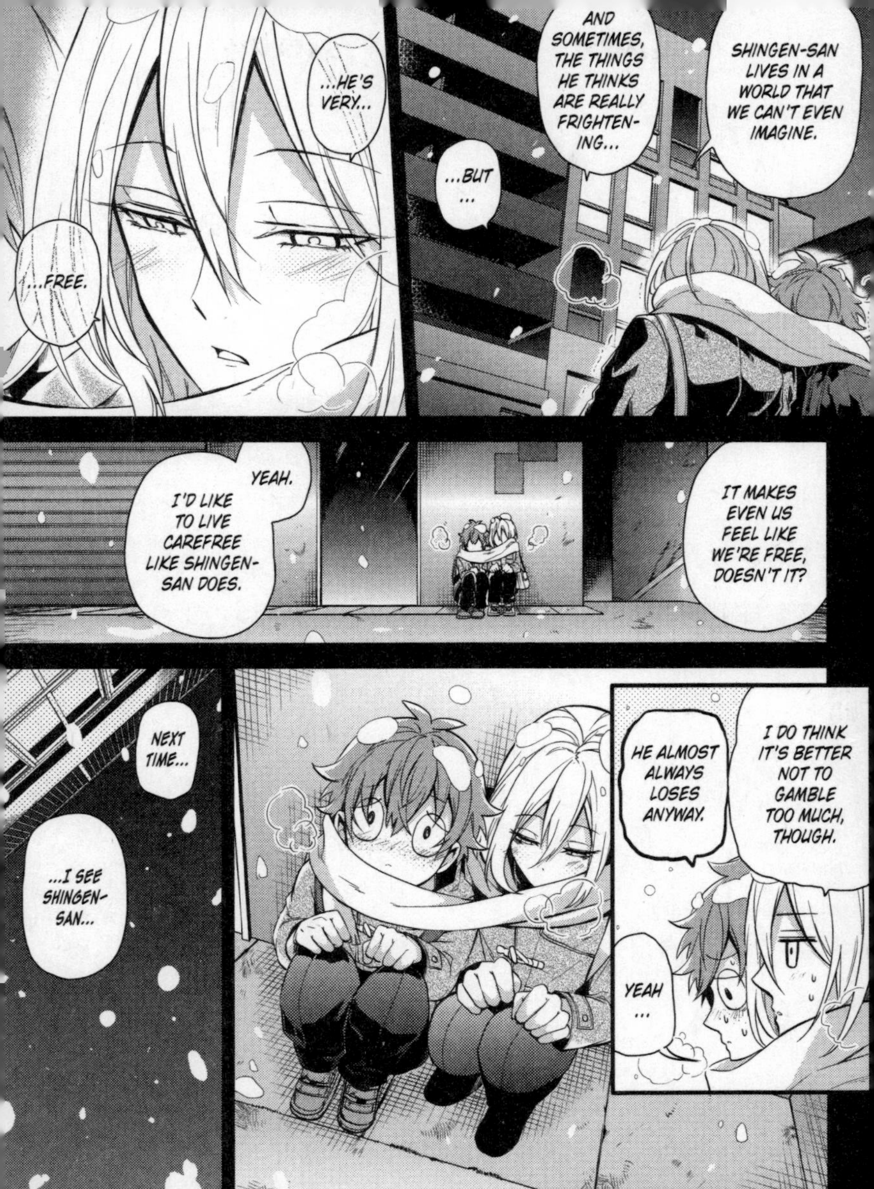
SHINGEN-SAN LIVES IN A WORLD THAT WE CAN'T EVEN IMAGINE.
AND SOMETIMES, THE THINGS HE THINKS ARE REALLY FRIGHTEN-ING...
...BUT ...
...HE'S VERY...
...FREE.
IT MAKES EVEN US FEEL LIKE WE'RE FREE, DOESN'T IT?
YEAH. I'D LIKE TO LIVE CAREFREE LIKE SHINGEN-SAN DOES.
I DO THINK IT'S BETTER NOT TO GAMBLE TOO MUCH, THOUGH.
HE ALMOST ALWAYS LOSES ANYWAY.
YEAH ...
NEXT TIME...
...I SEE SHINGEN-SAN...

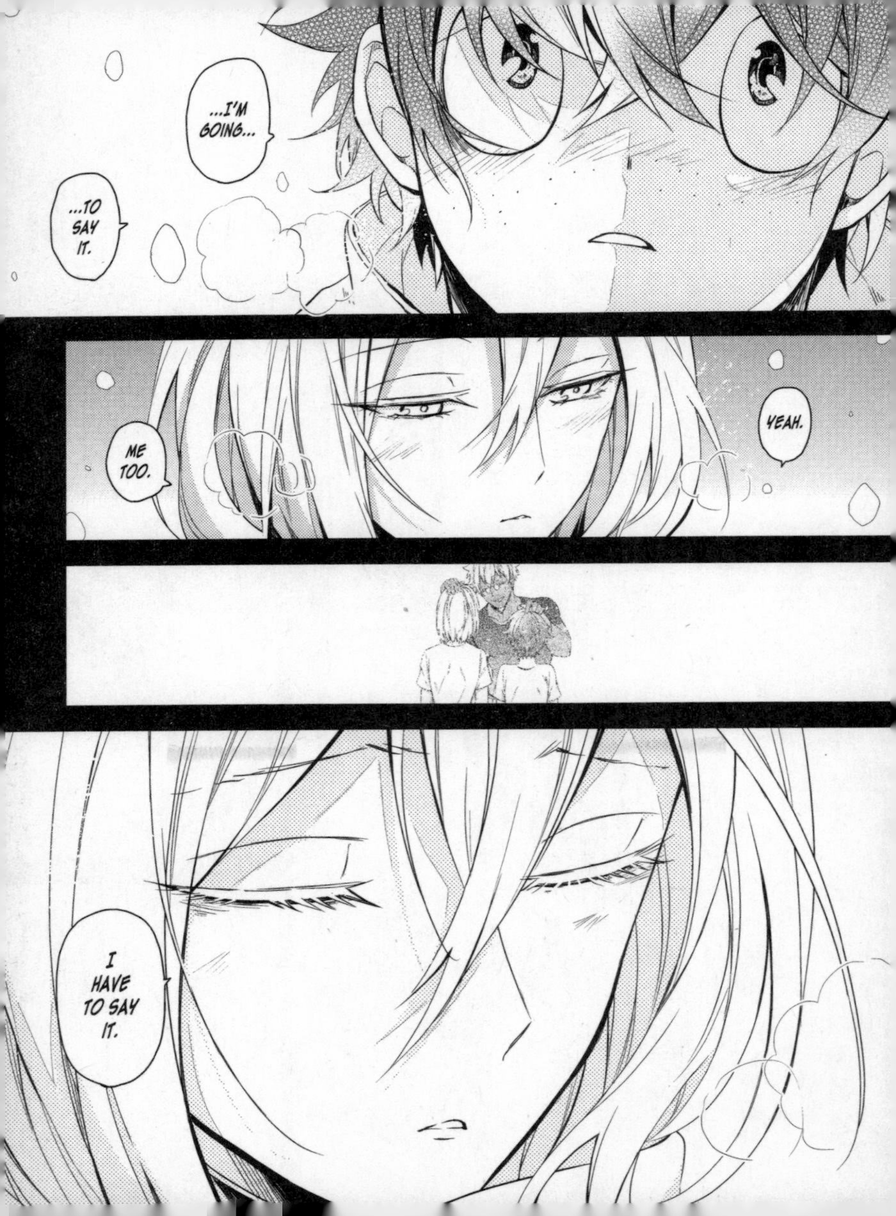
...I'M GOING...
...TO SAY IT.
YEAH.
ME TOO.
I HAVE TO SAY IT.

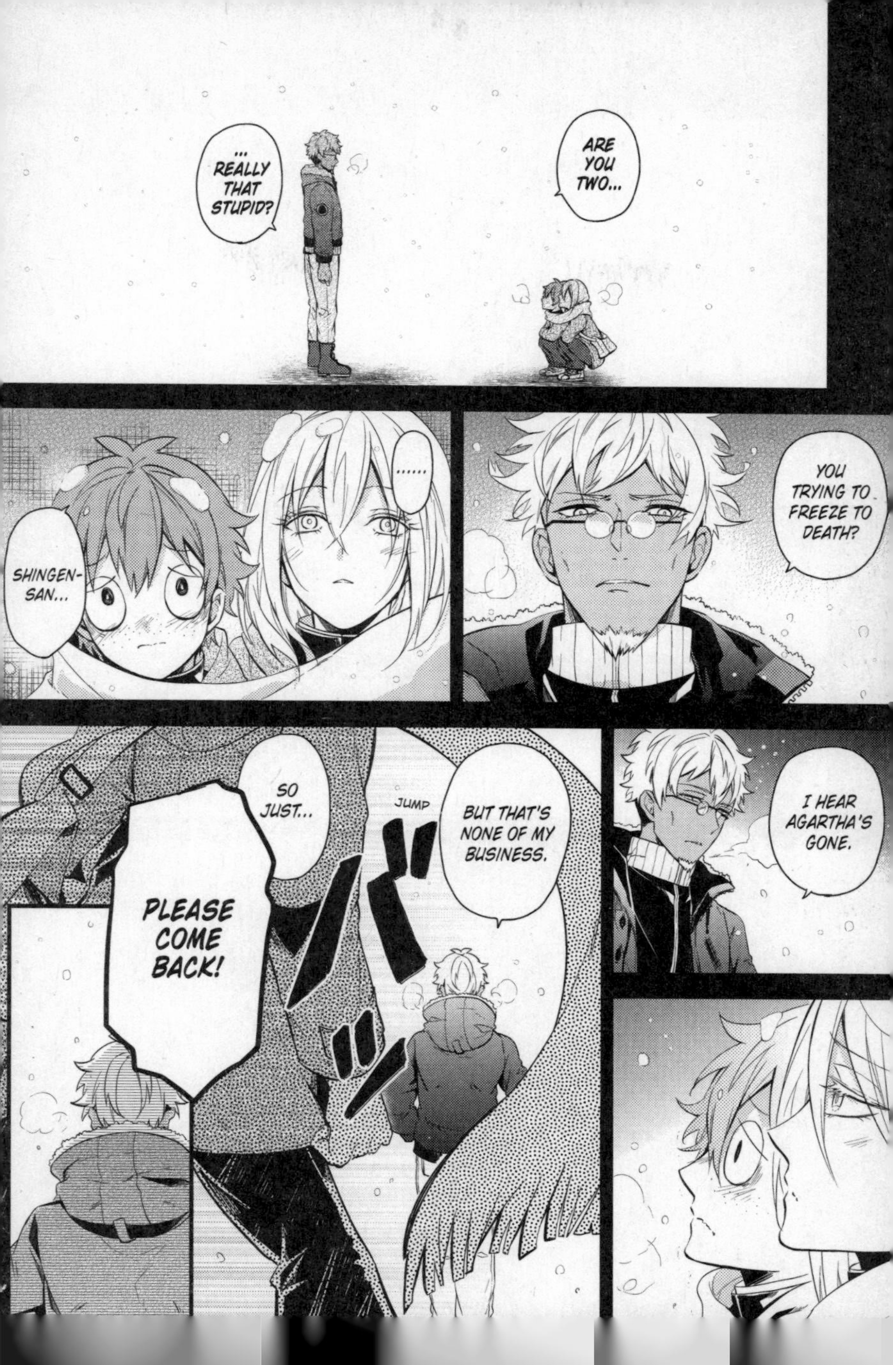
ARE YOU TWO...
...REALLY THAT STUPID?
YOU TRYING TO FREEZE TO DEATH?
......
SHINGEN-SAN...
I HEAR AGARTHA'S GONE.
BUT THAT'S NONE OF MY BUSINESS.
JUMP
SO JUST...
PLEASE COME BACK!

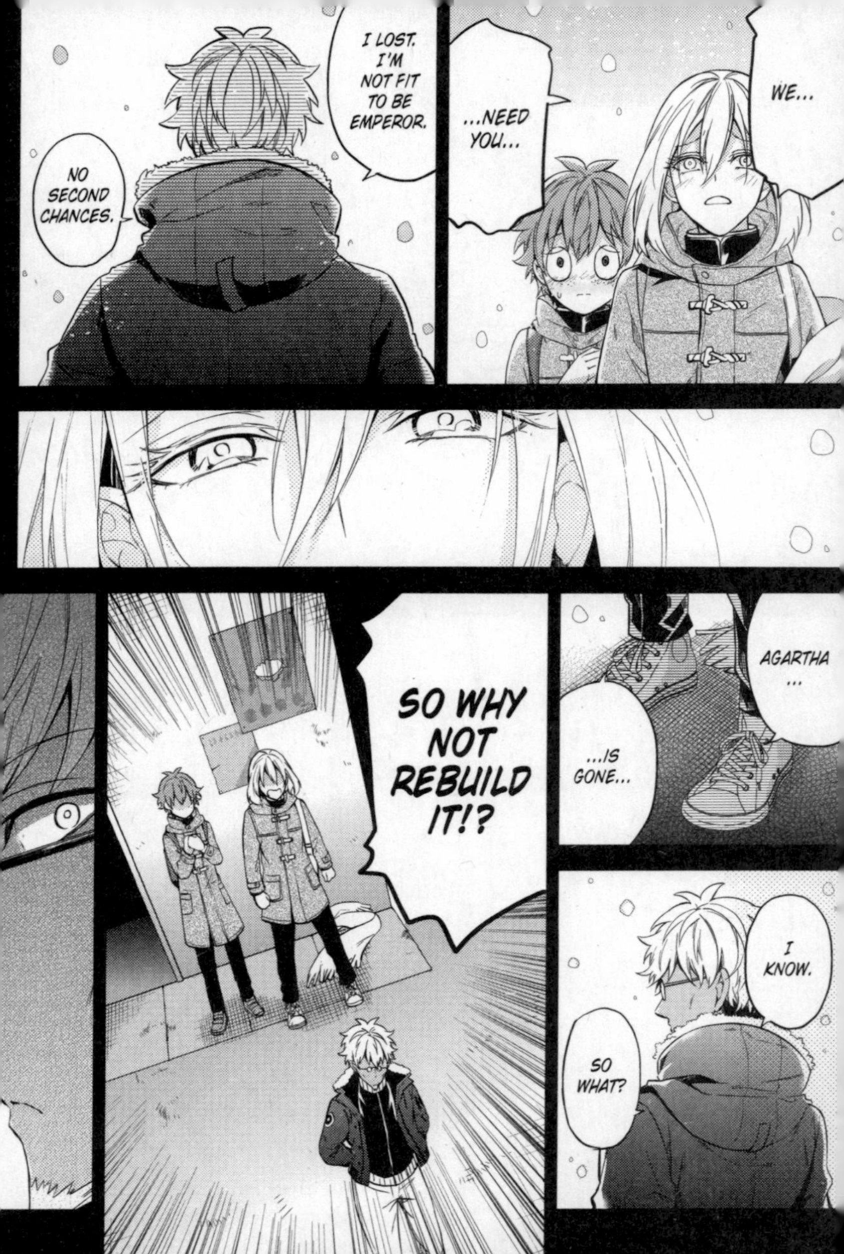
WE...
...NEED YOU...
I LOST. I'M NOT FIT TO BE EMPEROR.
NO SECOND CHANCES.
AGARTHA...
...IS GONE...
I KNOW.
SO WHAT?
SO WHY NOT REBUILD IT!?

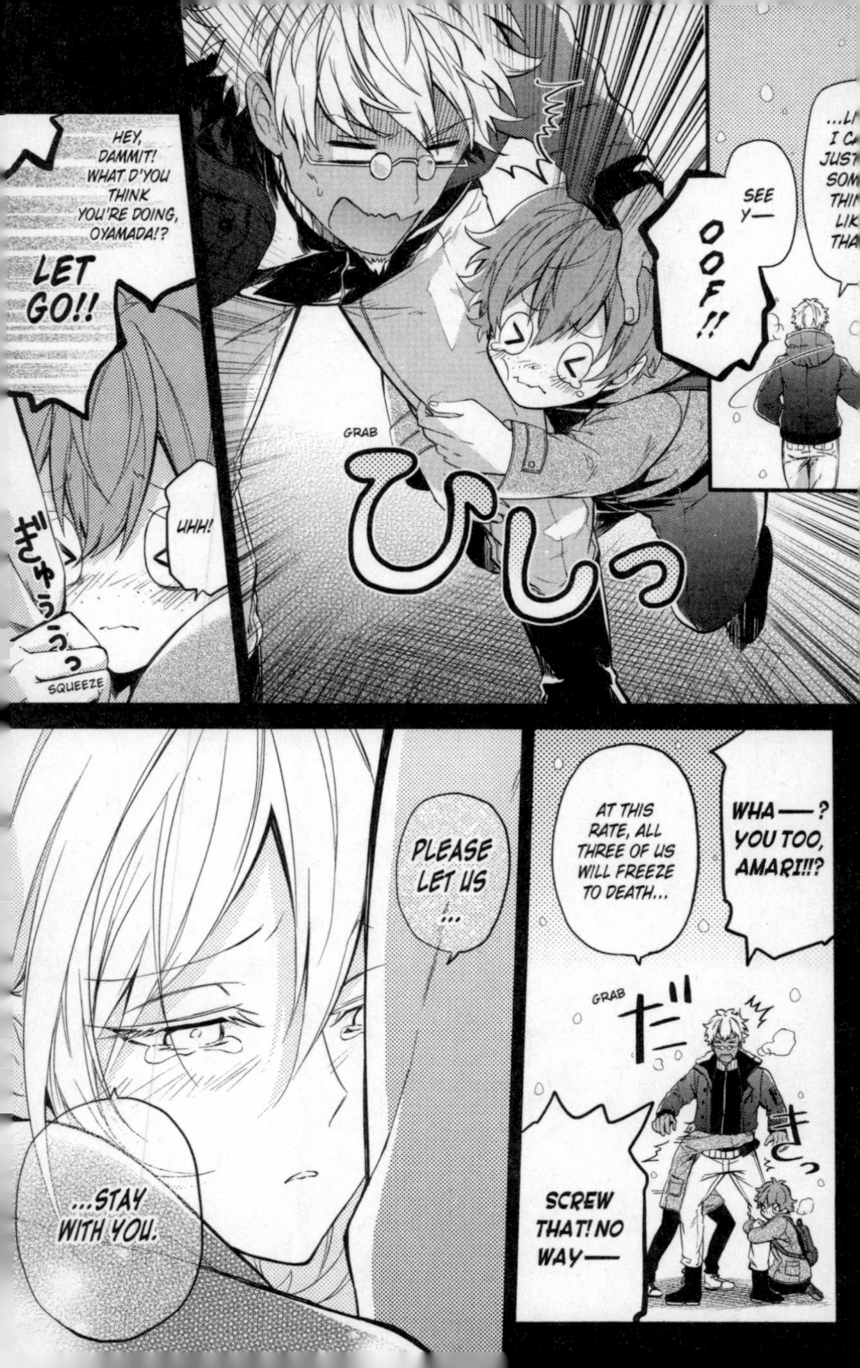
...LI I CA JUST SOM THIN LIK THA
SEE Y—
OOF!!
GRAB
ひしっ
HEY, DAMMIT! WHAT D'YOU THINK YOU'RE DOING, OYAMADA!?
LET GO!!
UHH!
ぎゅううっ
SQUEEZE
WHA—? YOU TOO, AMARI!!?
AT THIS RATE, ALL THREE OF US WILL FREEZE TO DEATH...
GRAB
だっ
きゅっ
SCREW THAT! NO WAY—
PLEASE LET US ...
...STAY WITH YOU.

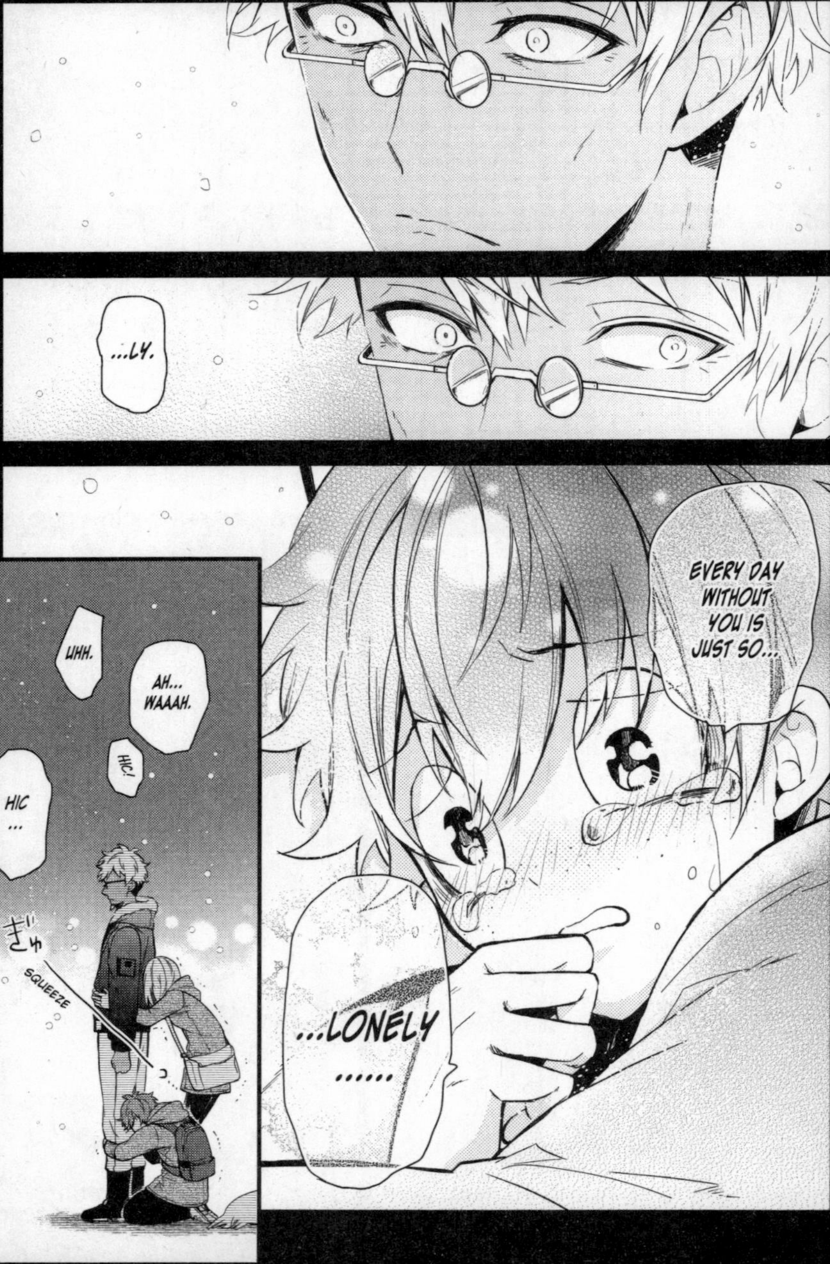
...LY.
EVERY DAY WITHOUT YOU IS JUST SO...
...LONELY ......
UHH.
AH... WAAAH.
HIC!
HIC ...
ぎゅ
SQUEEZE

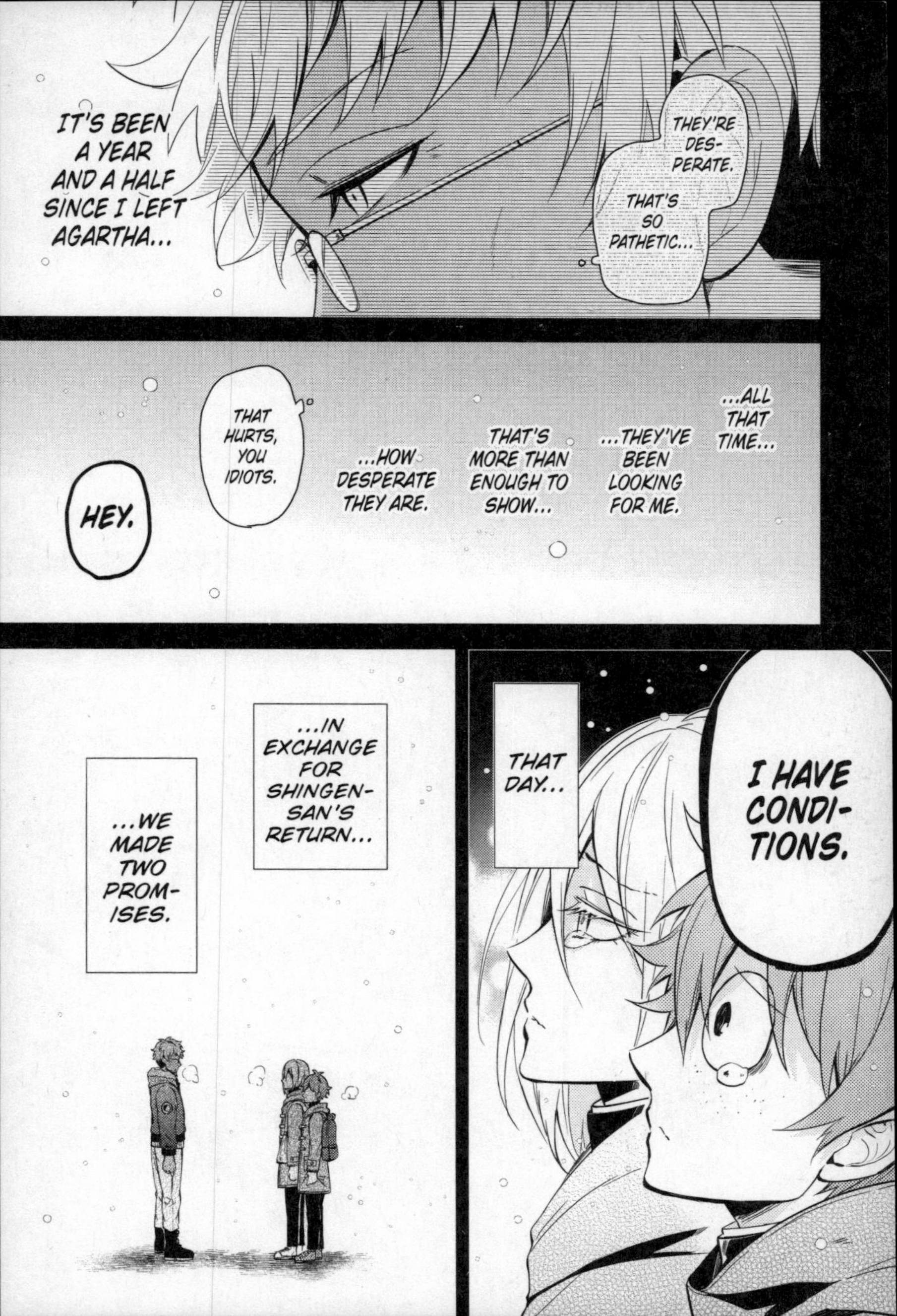
THEY'RE DES-PERATE.
THAT'S SO PATHETIC...
IT'S BEEN A YEAR AND A HALF SINCE I LEFT AGARTHA...
...ALL THAT TIME...
...THEY'VE BEEN LOOKING FOR ME.
THAT'S MORE THAN ENOUGH TO SHOW...
...HOW DESPERATE THEY ARE.
THAT HURTS, YOU IDIOTS.
HEY.
I HAVE CONDI-TIONS.
THAT DAY...
...IN EXCHANGE FOR SHINGEN-SAN'S RETURN...
...WE MADE TWO PROM-ISES.

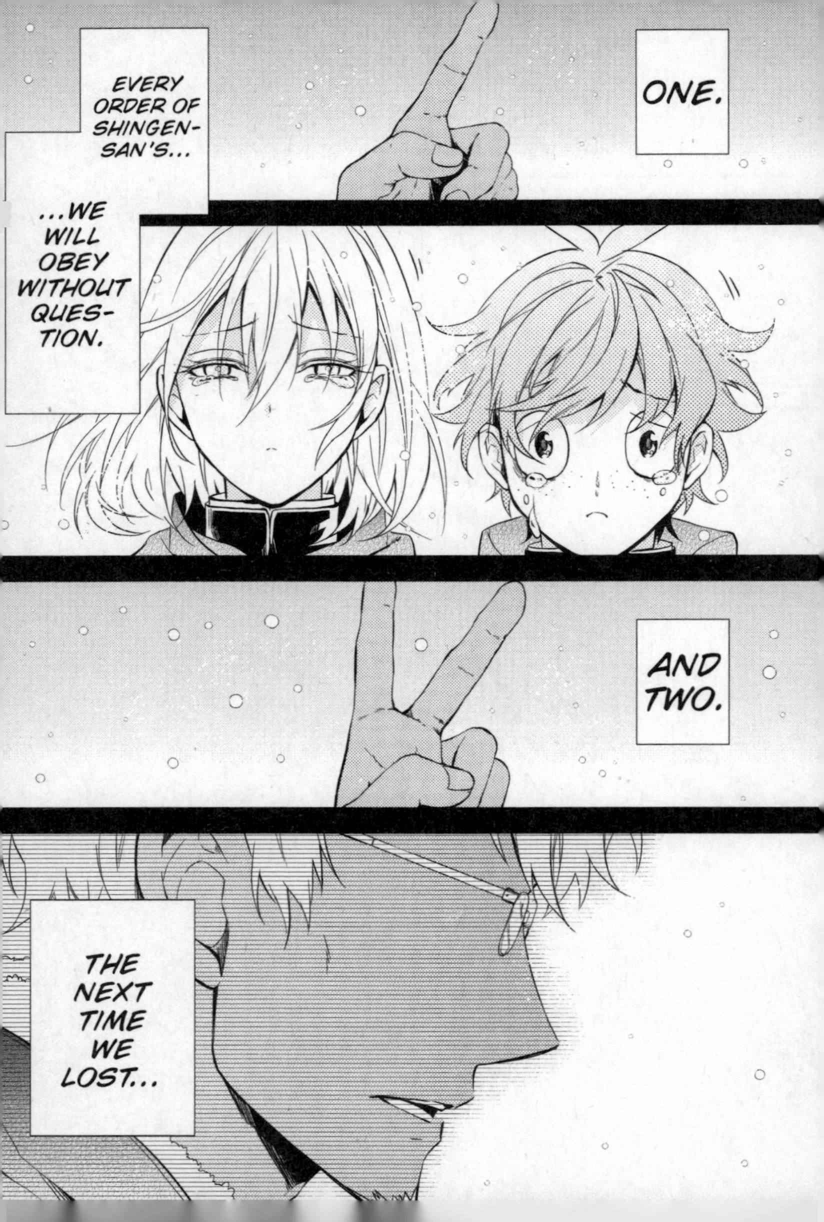
ONE.
EVERY ORDER OF SHINGEN-SAN'S...
...WE WILL OBEY WITHOUT QUES-TION.
AND TWO.
THE NEXT TIME WE LOST...

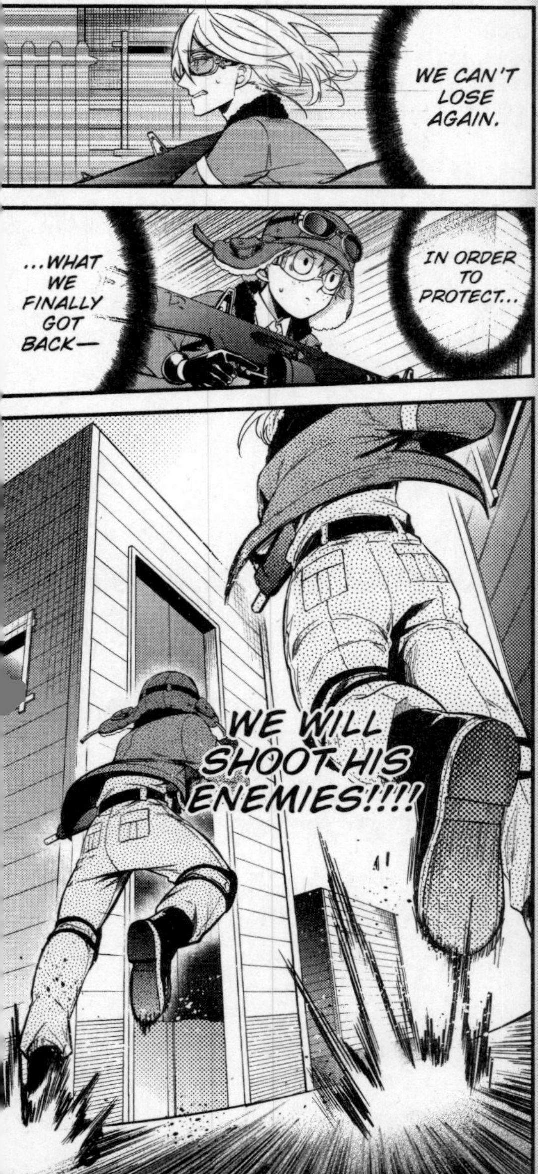
WE CAN'T LOSE AGAIN.
IN ORDER TO PROTECT...
...WHAT WE FINALLY GOT BACK—
WE WILL SHOOT HIS ENEMIES!!!!

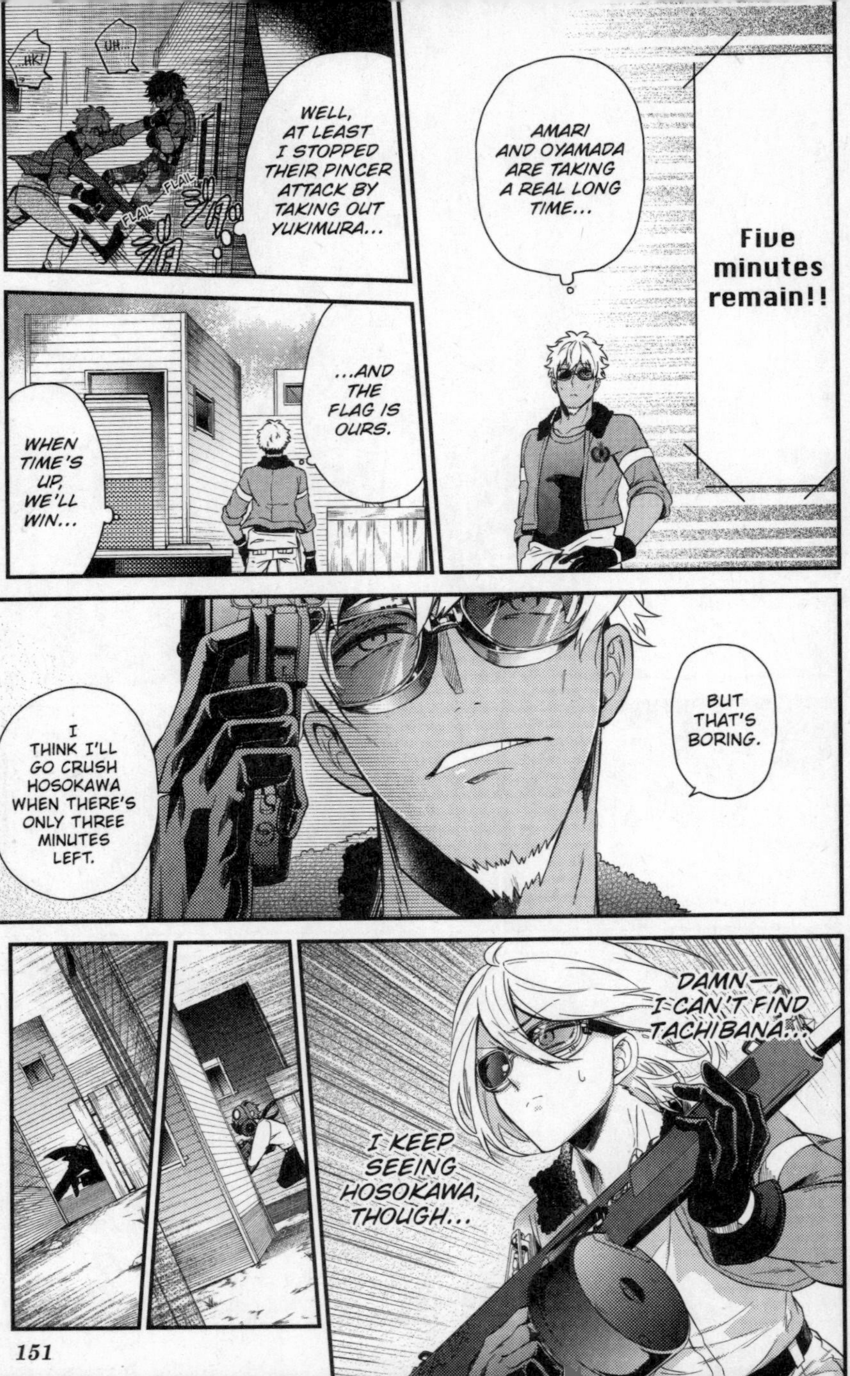
AMARI AND OYAMADA ARE TAKING A REAL LONG TIME...
Five minutes remain!!
WELL, AT LEAST I STOPPED THEIR PINCER ATTACK BY TAKING OUT YUKIMURA...
UH...
...HK!
FLAIL
FLAIL
...AND THE FLAG IS OURS.
WHEN TIME'S UP, WE'LL WIN...
BUT THAT'S BORING.
I THINK I'LL GO CRUSH HOSOKAWA WHEN THERE'S ONLY THREE MINUTES LEFT.
DAMN—I CAN'T FIND TACHIBANA...
I KEEP SEEING HOSOKAWA, THOUGH...

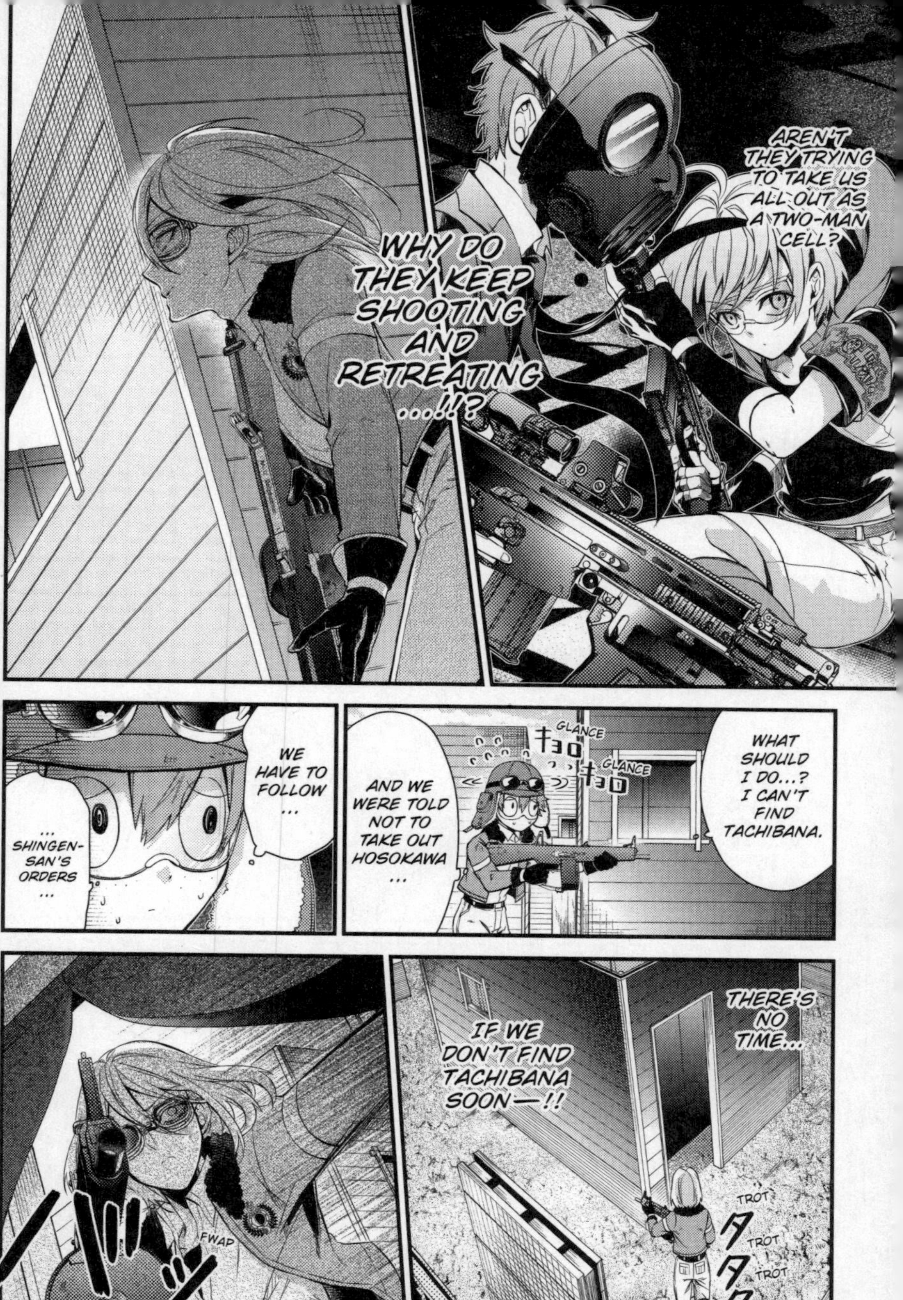
AREN'T THEY TRYING TO TAKE US ALL OUT AS A TWO-MAN CELL?
WHY DO THEY KEEP SHOOTING AND RETREATING ...!!?
WHAT SHOULD I DO...? I CAN'T FIND TACHIBANA.
GLANCE
GLANCE
AND WE WERE TOLD NOT TO TAKE OUT HOSOKAWA ...
WE HAVE TO FOLLOW ...
... SHINGEN-SAN'S ORDERS ...
THERE'S NO TIME...
IF WE DON'T FIND TACHIBANA SOON—!!
TROT
TROT
TROT
FWAP

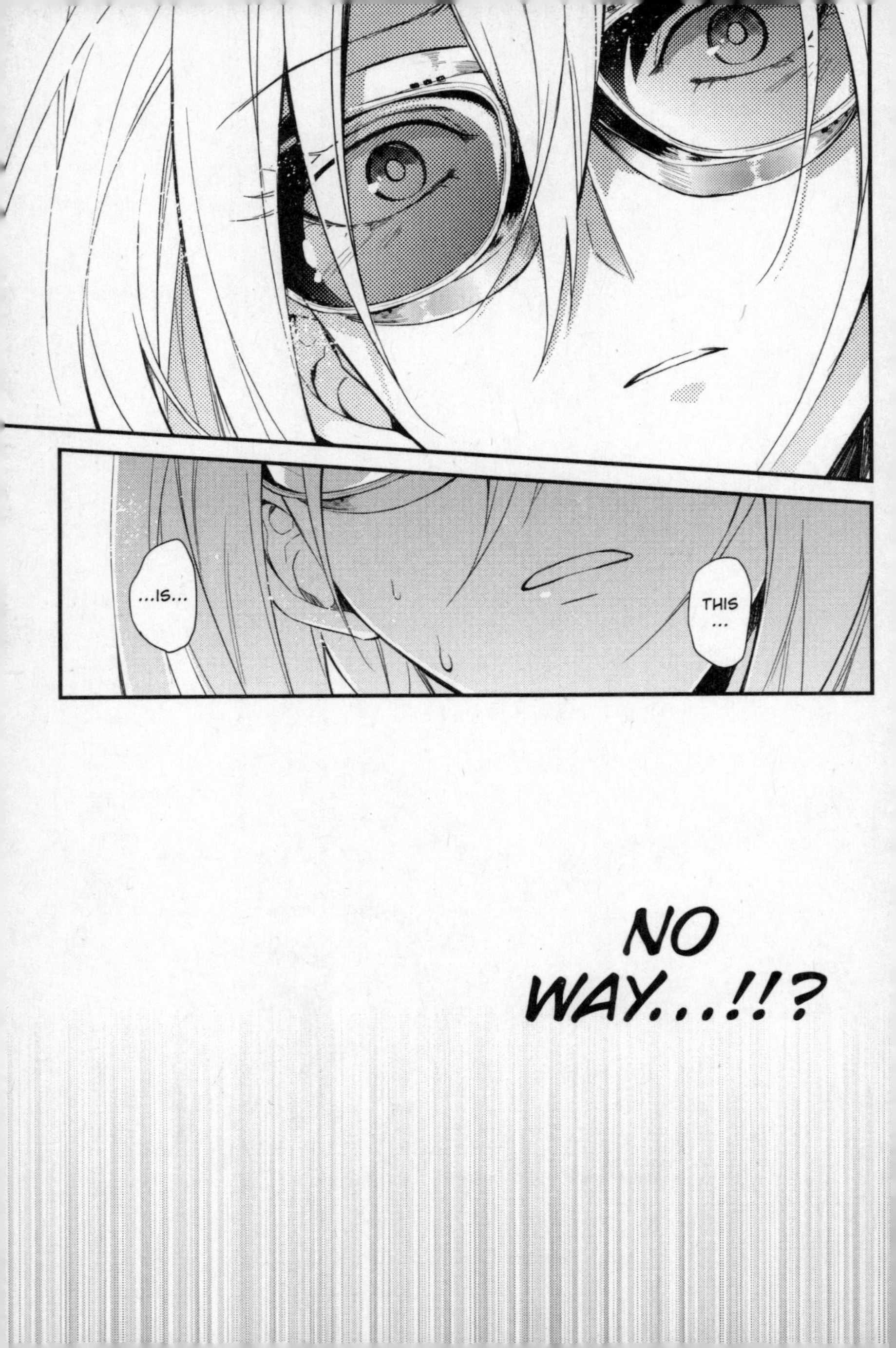
THIS...
...IS...
NO WAY...!!?

AOHARU×MACHINEGUN

A DAY WITH AGARTHA

THESE TWO ARE COMPLETE LIGHTWEIGHTS WHEN IT COMES TO ALCOHOL.
NO MORE LETTING THEM DRINK... WHAT A WASTE.
URRRGH
UHHH
SURPRIS-INGLY REPEN-TANT

*ATTENTION!!
NO DRINKING UNTIL YOU'RE OF AGE!!

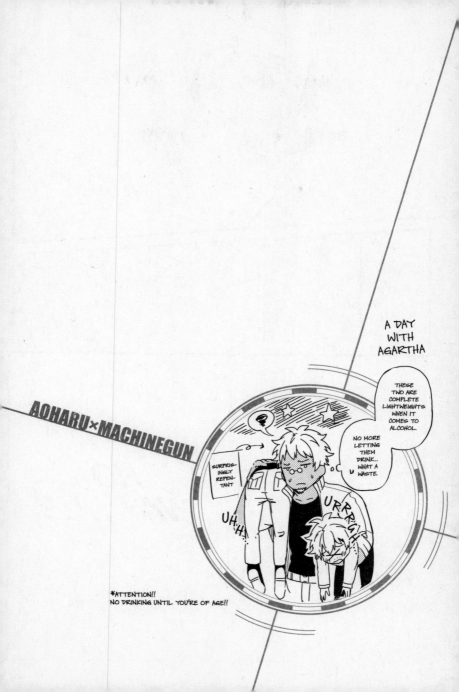

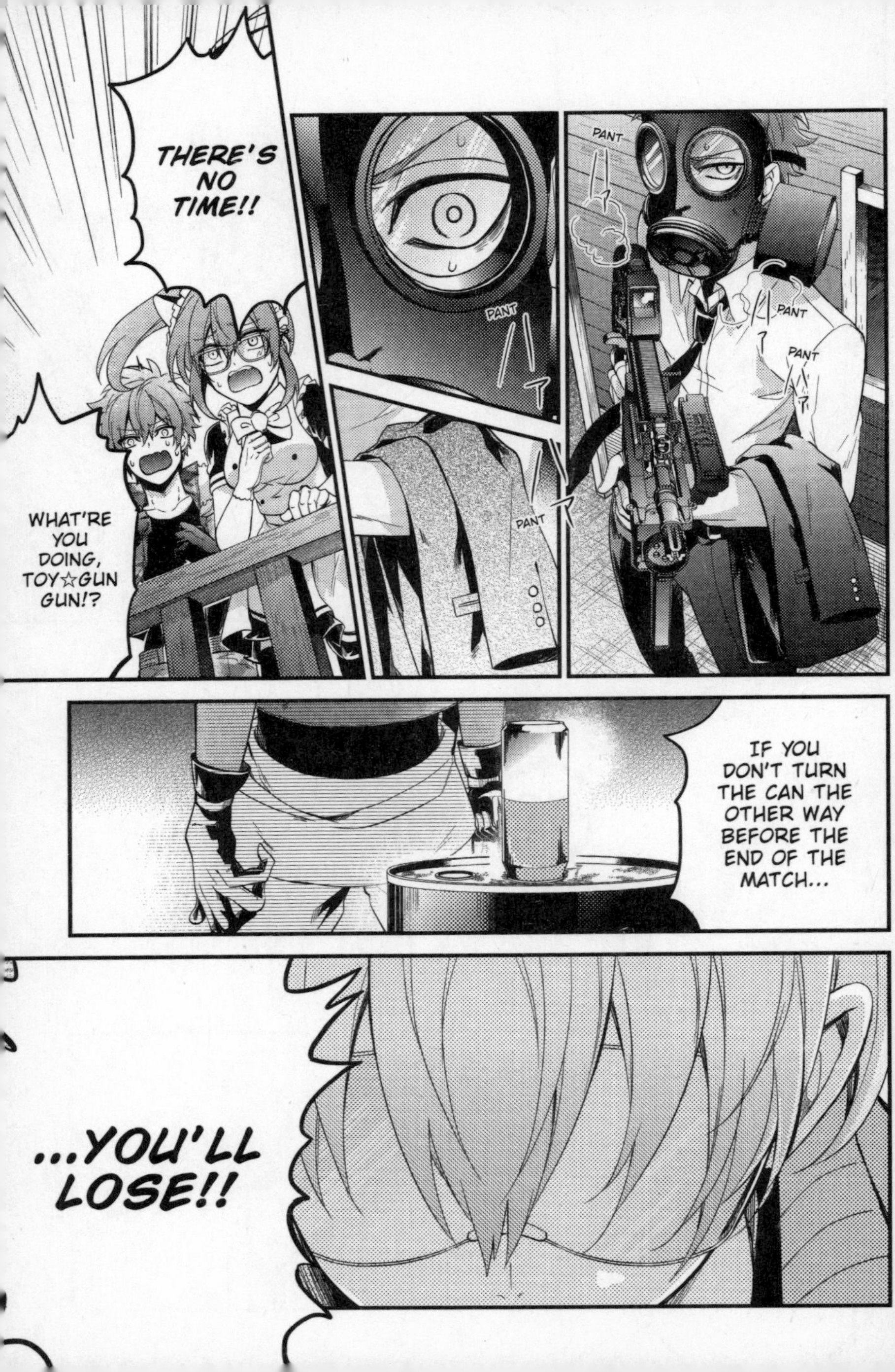
PANT
PANT
PANT
PANT
PANT
THERE'S NO TIME!!
WHAT'RE YOU DOING, TOY☆GUN GUN!?
IF YOU DON'T TURN THE CAN THE OTHER WAY BEFORE THE END OF THE MATCH...
...YOU'LL LOSE!!

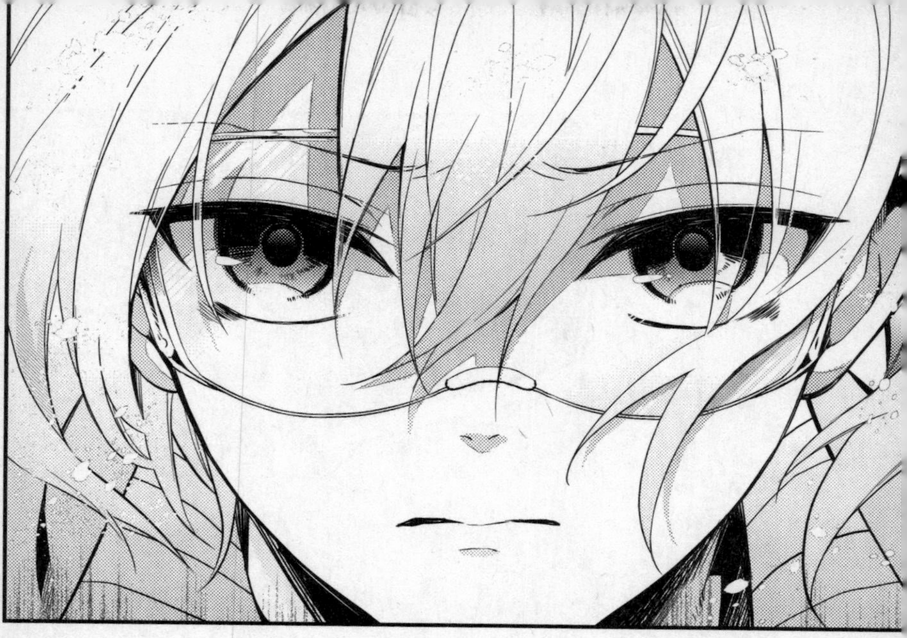

#66 PROMISE

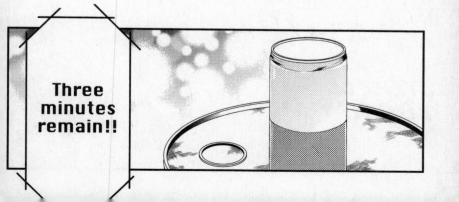

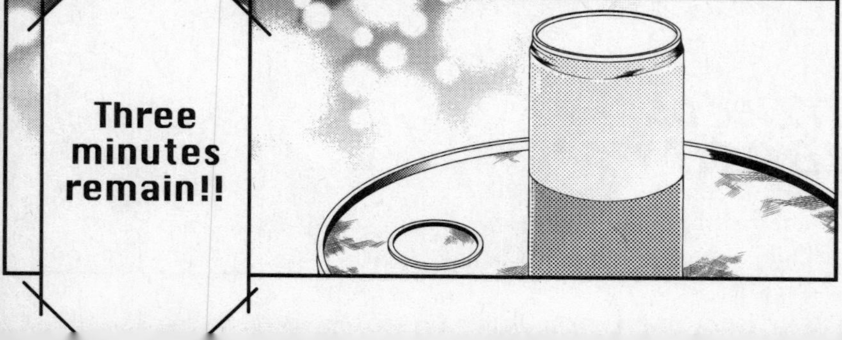
Three minutes remain!!

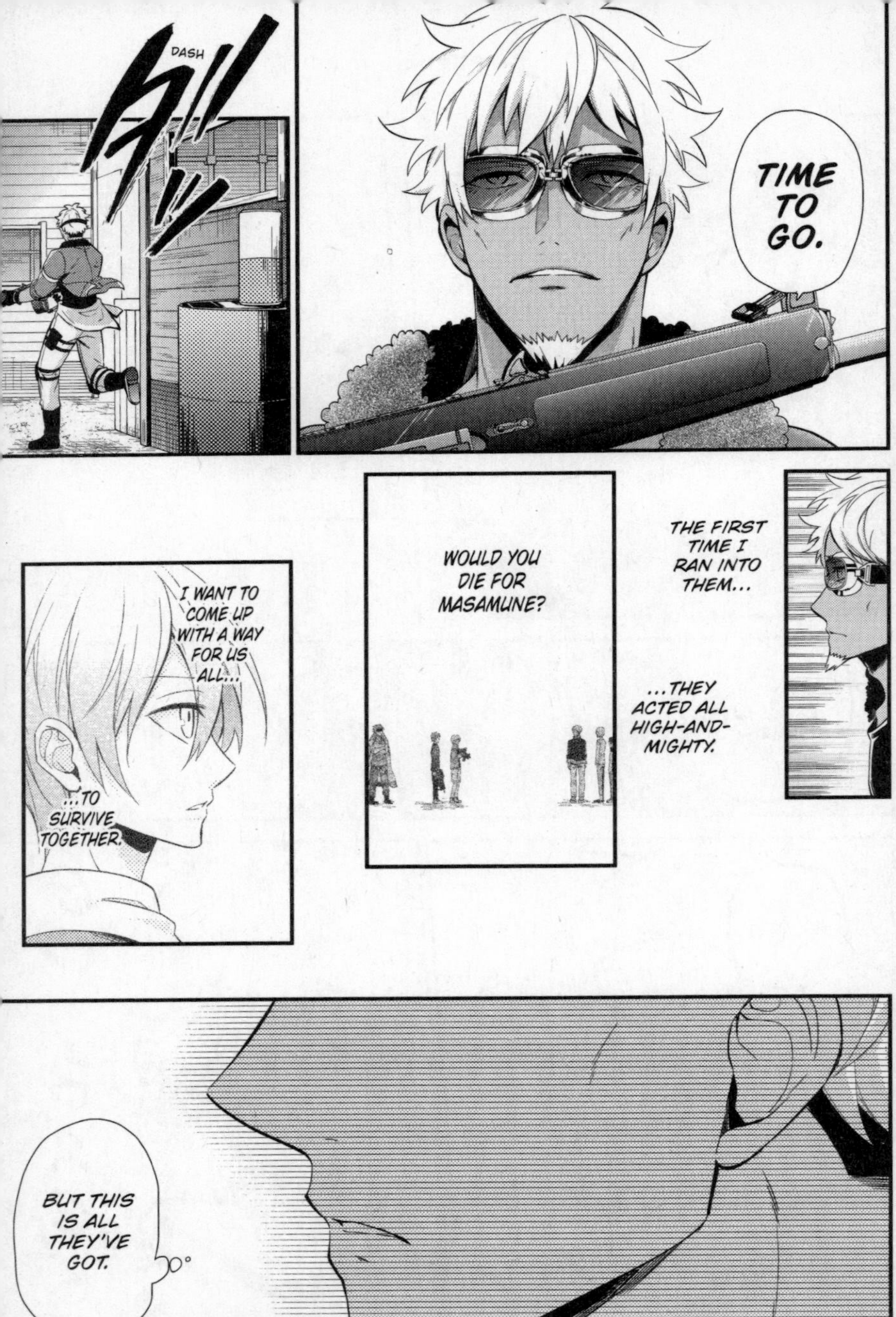
TIME TO GO.
DASH
THE FIRST TIME I RAN INTO THEM...
...THEY ACTED ALL HIGH-AND-MIGHTY.
WOULD YOU DIE FOR MASAMUNE?
I WANT TO COME UP WITH A WAY FOR US ALL...
...TO SURVIVE TOGETHER.
BUT THIS IS ALL THEY'VE GOT.

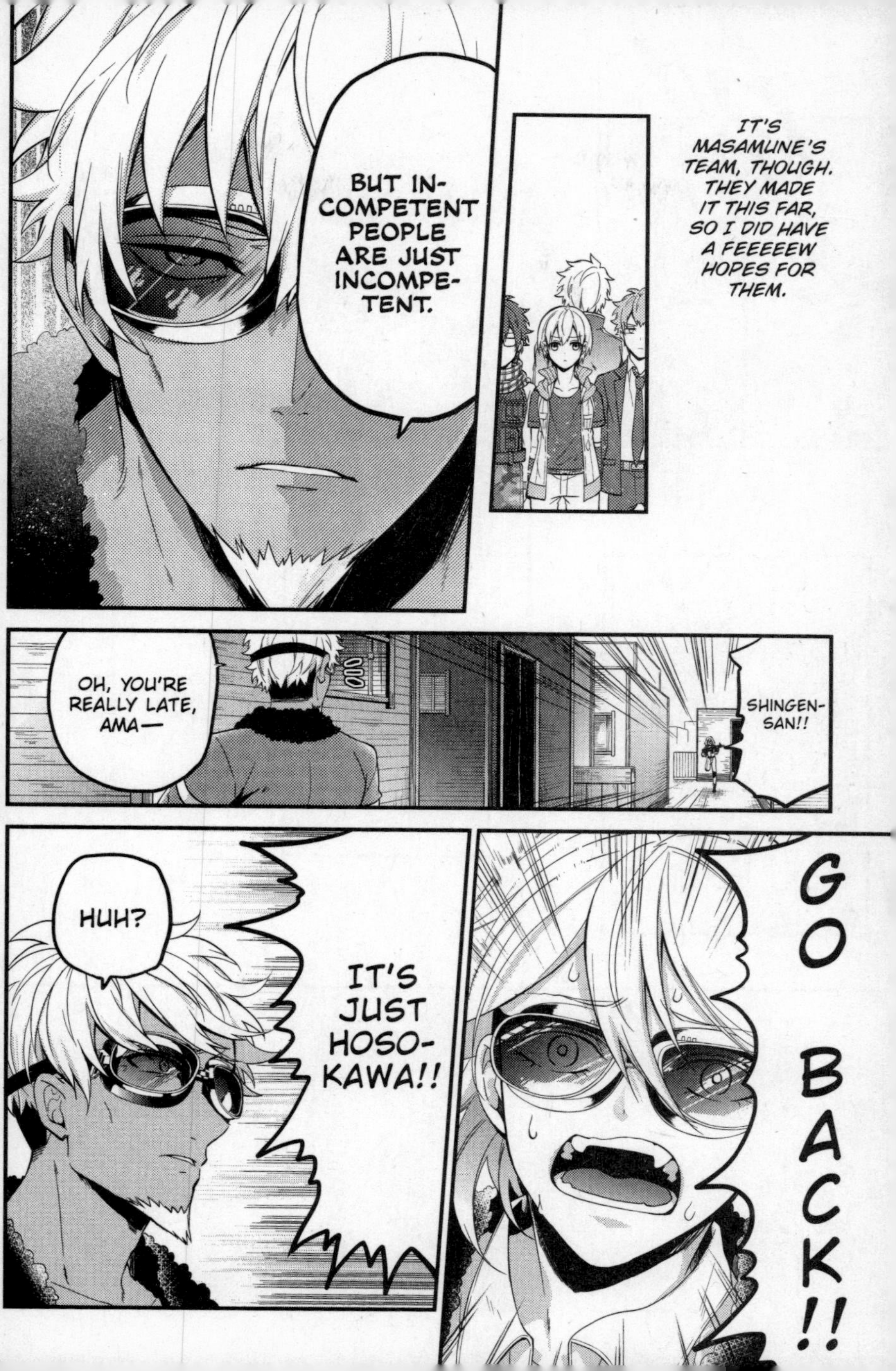
IT'S MASAMUNE'S TEAM, THOUGH. THEY MADE IT THIS FAR, SO I DID HAVE A FEEEEEW HOPES FOR THEM.
BUT IN-COMPETENT PEOPLE ARE JUST INCOMPE-TENT.
OH, YOU'RE REALLY LATE, AMA—
SHINGEN-SAN!!
GO BACK!!
HUH?
IT'S JUST HOSO-KAWA!!

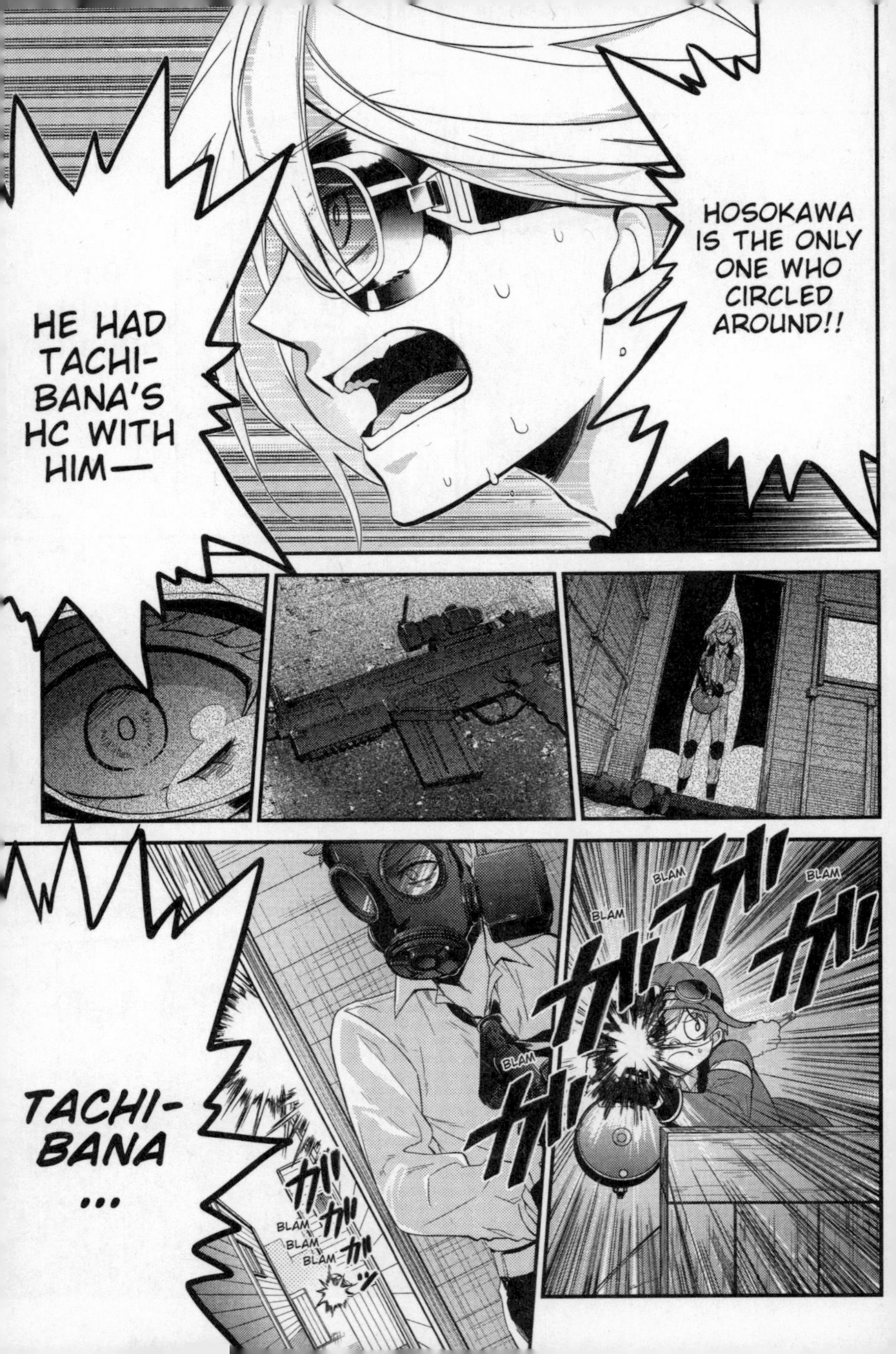
HOSOKAWA IS THE ONLY ONE WHO CIRCLED AROUND!!
HE HAD TACHIBANA'S HC WITH HIM—
BLAM
BLAM
BLAM
BLAM
TACHIBANA...
BLAM
BLAM
BLAM

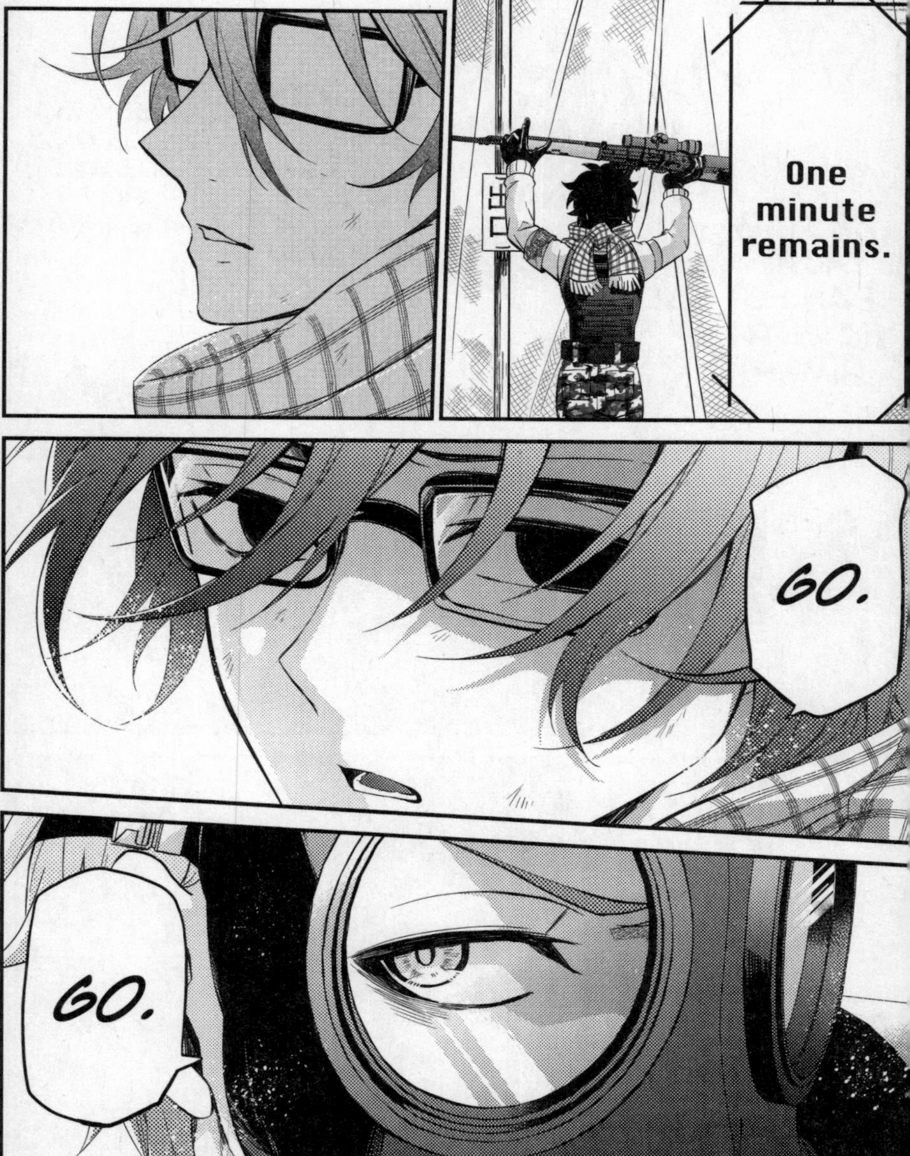
One minute remains.
GO.
GO.

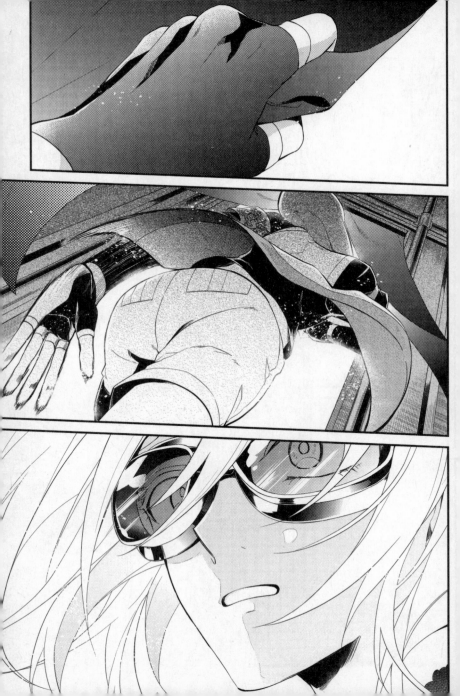

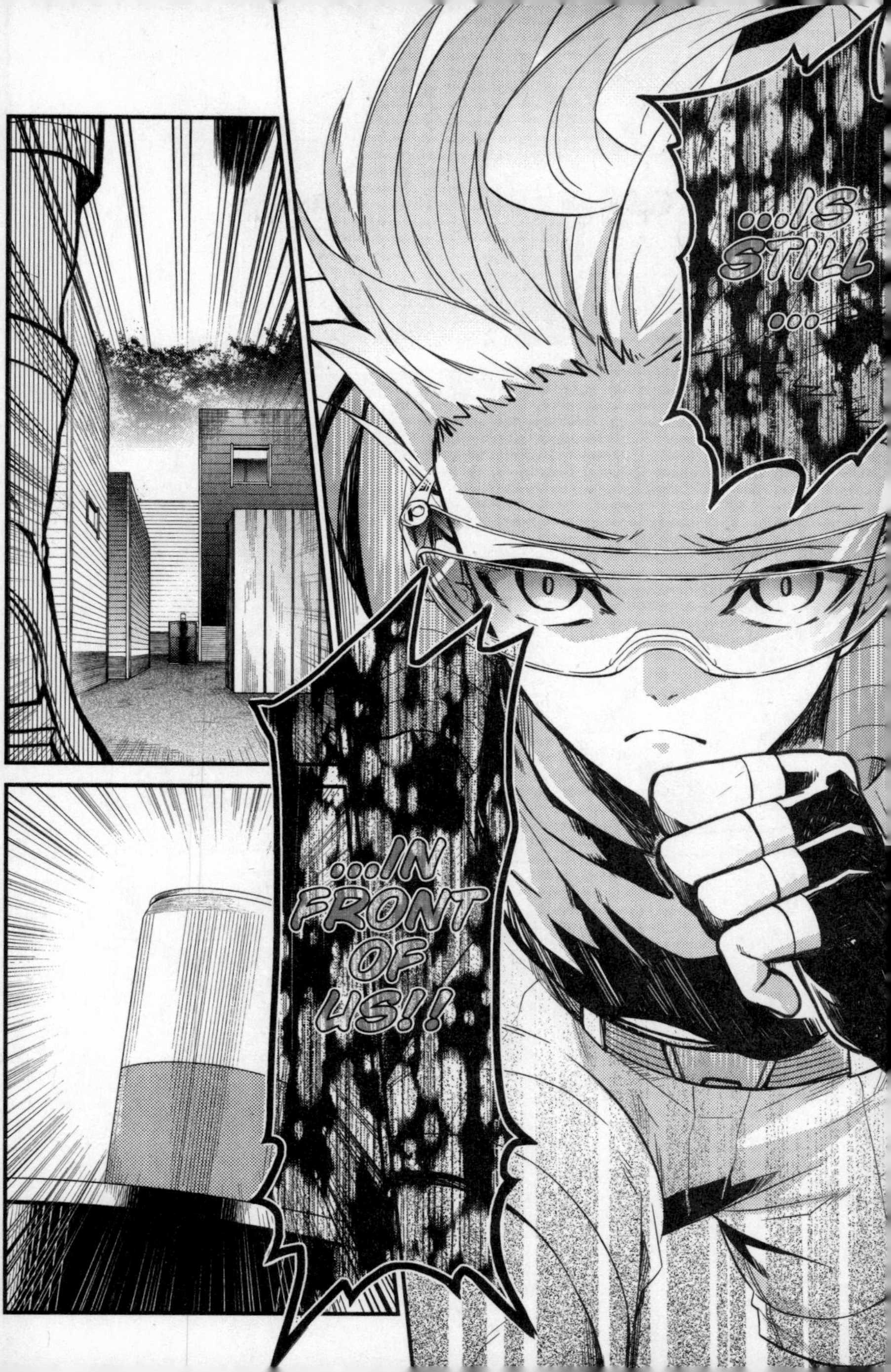
...IS STILL...
...IN FRONT OF US!!

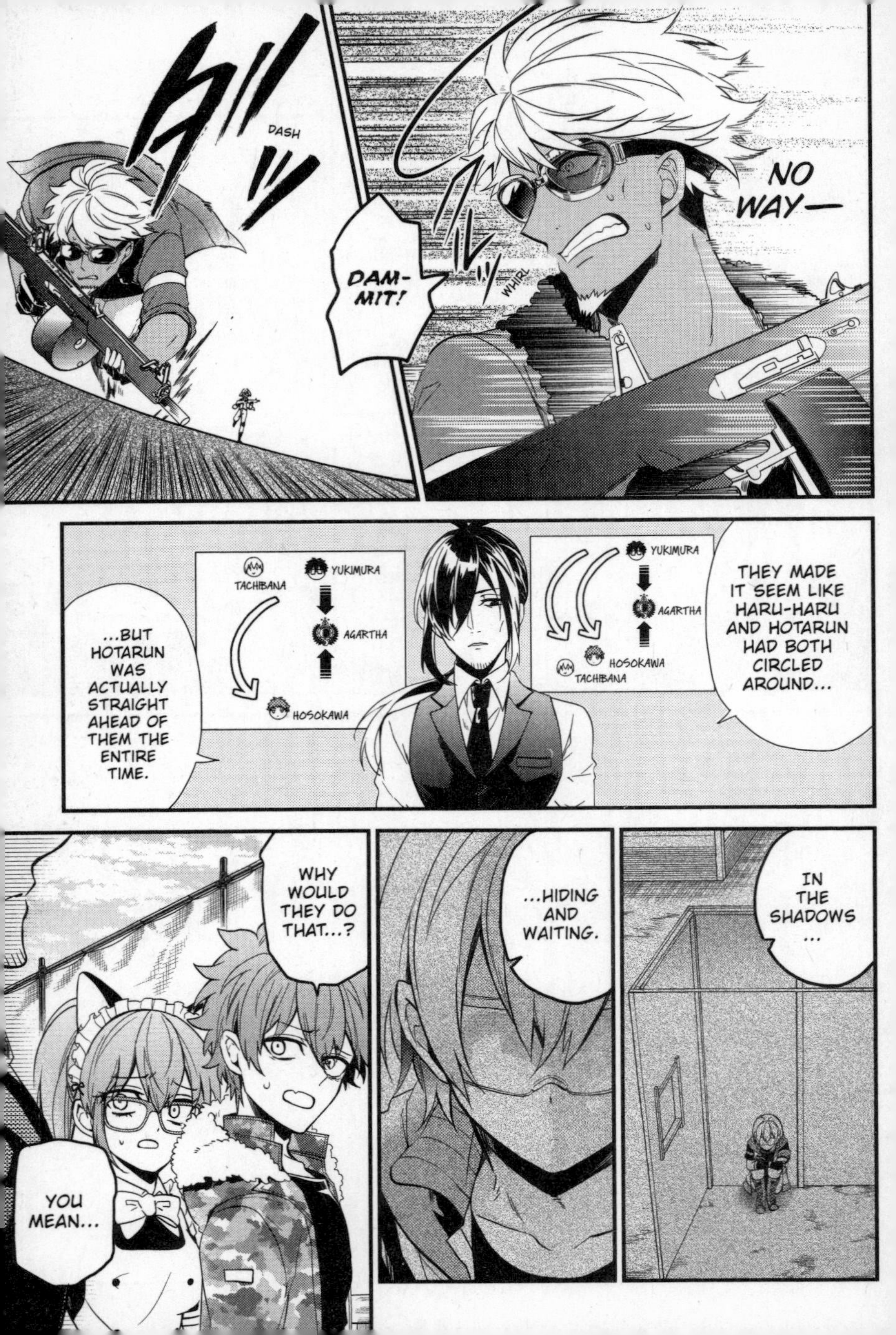
NO WAY—
DAMMIT!
WHIRL
DASH
THEY MADE IT SEEM LIKE HARU-HARU AND HOTARUN HAD BOTH CIRCLED AROUND...
YUKIMURA
AGARTHA
HOSOKAWA
TACHIBANA
TACHIBANA
YUKIMURA
AGARTHA
HOSOKAWA
...BUT HOTARUN WAS ACTUALLY STRAIGHT AHEAD OF THEM THE ENTIRE TIME.
IN THE SHADOWS...
...HIDING AND WAITING.
WHY WOULD THEY DO THAT...?
YOU MEAN...

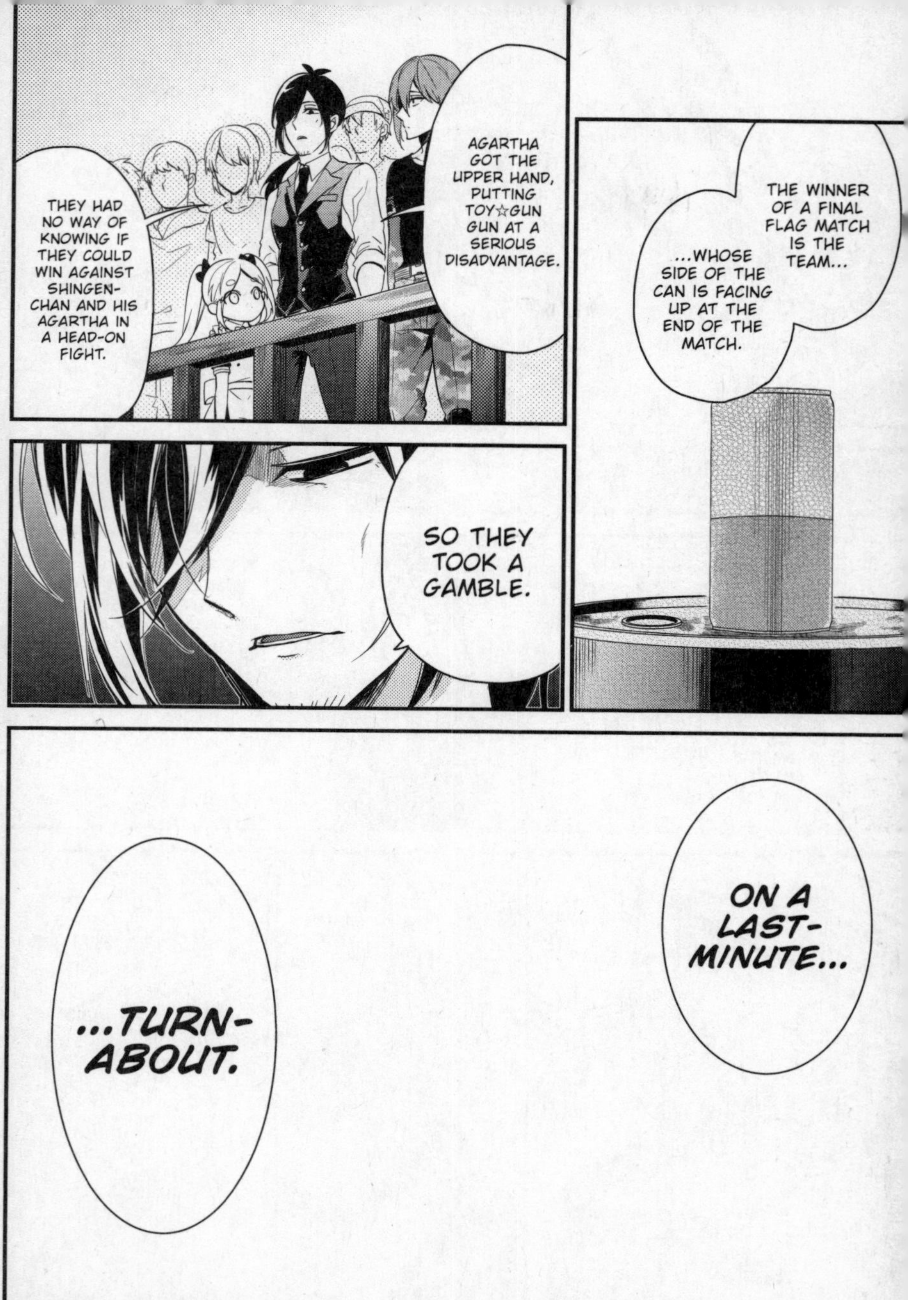
THE WINNER OF A FINAL FLAG MATCH IS THE TEAM...
...WHOSE SIDE OF THE CAN IS FACING UP AT THE END OF THE MATCH.
AGARTHA GOT THE UPPER HAND, PUTTING TOY☆GUN GUN AT A SERIOUS DISADVANTAGE.
THEY HAD NO WAY OF KNOWING IF THEY COULD WIN AGAINST SHINGEN-CHAN AND HIS AGARTHA IN A HEAD-ON FIGHT.
SO THEY TOOK A GAMBLE.
ON A LAST-MINUTE...
...TURN-ABOUT.

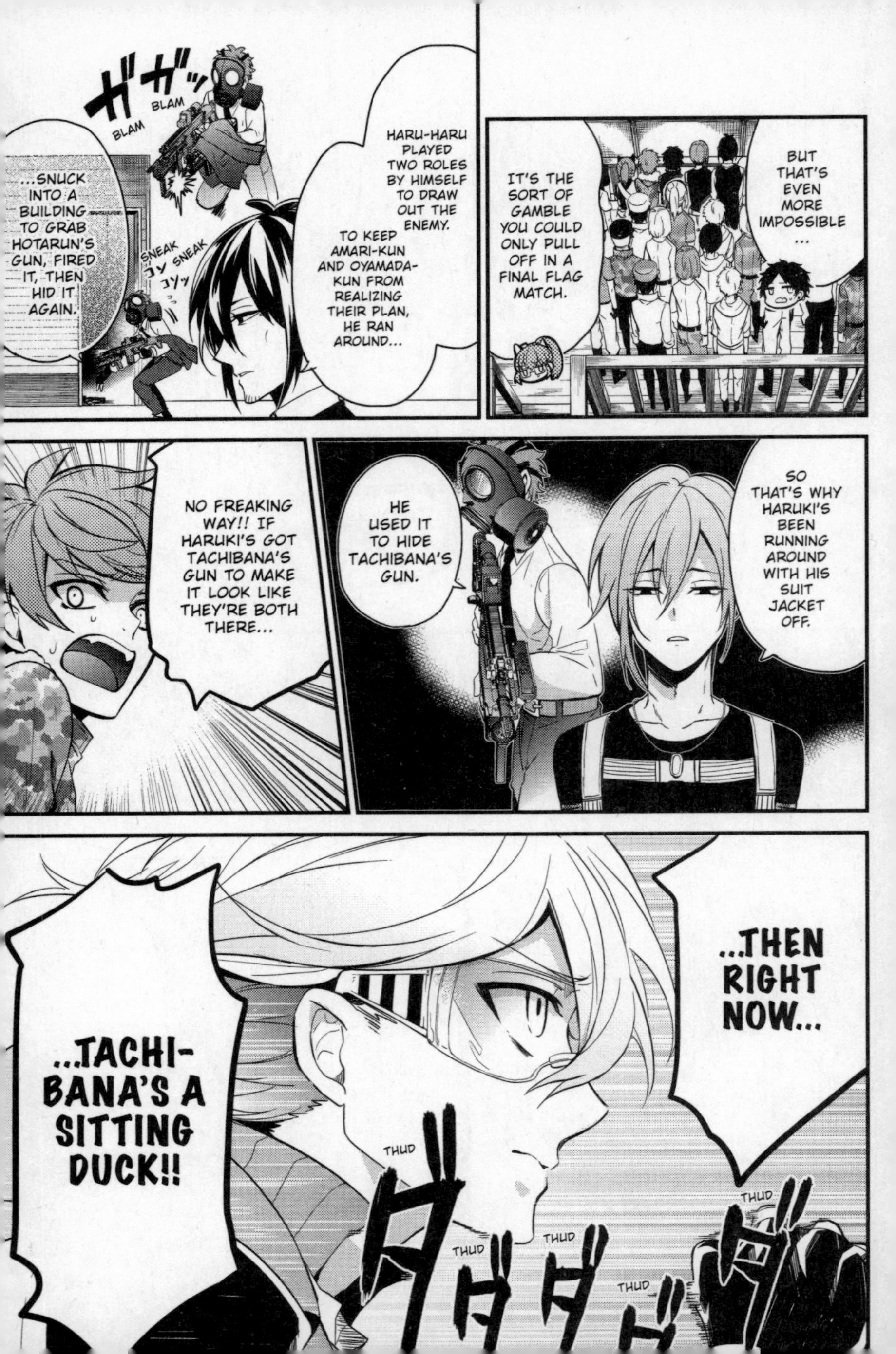

BUT THAT'S EVEN MORE IMPOSSIBLE...
IT'S THE SORT OF GAMBLE YOU COULD ONLY PULL OFF IN A FINAL FLAG MATCH.
HARU-HARU PLAYED TWO ROLES BY HIMSELF TO DRAW OUT THE ENEMY.
TO KEEP AMARI-KUN AND OYAMADA-KUN FROM REALIZING THEIR PLAN, HE RAN AROUND...
ガガッ
BLAM BLAM
...SNUCK INTO A BUILDING TO GRAB HOTARUN'S GUN, FIRED IT, THEN HID IT AGAIN.
SNEAK SNEAK
SO THAT'S WHY HARUKI'S BEEN RUNNING AROUND WITH HIS SUIT JACKET OFF.
HE USED IT TO HIDE TACHIBANA'S GUN.
NO FREAKING WAY!! IF HARUKI'S GOT TACHIBANA'S GUN TO MAKE IT LOOK LIKE THEY'RE BOTH THERE...
...THEN RIGHT NOW...
...TACHIBANA'S A SITTING DUCK!!
THUD THUD THUD THUD THUD

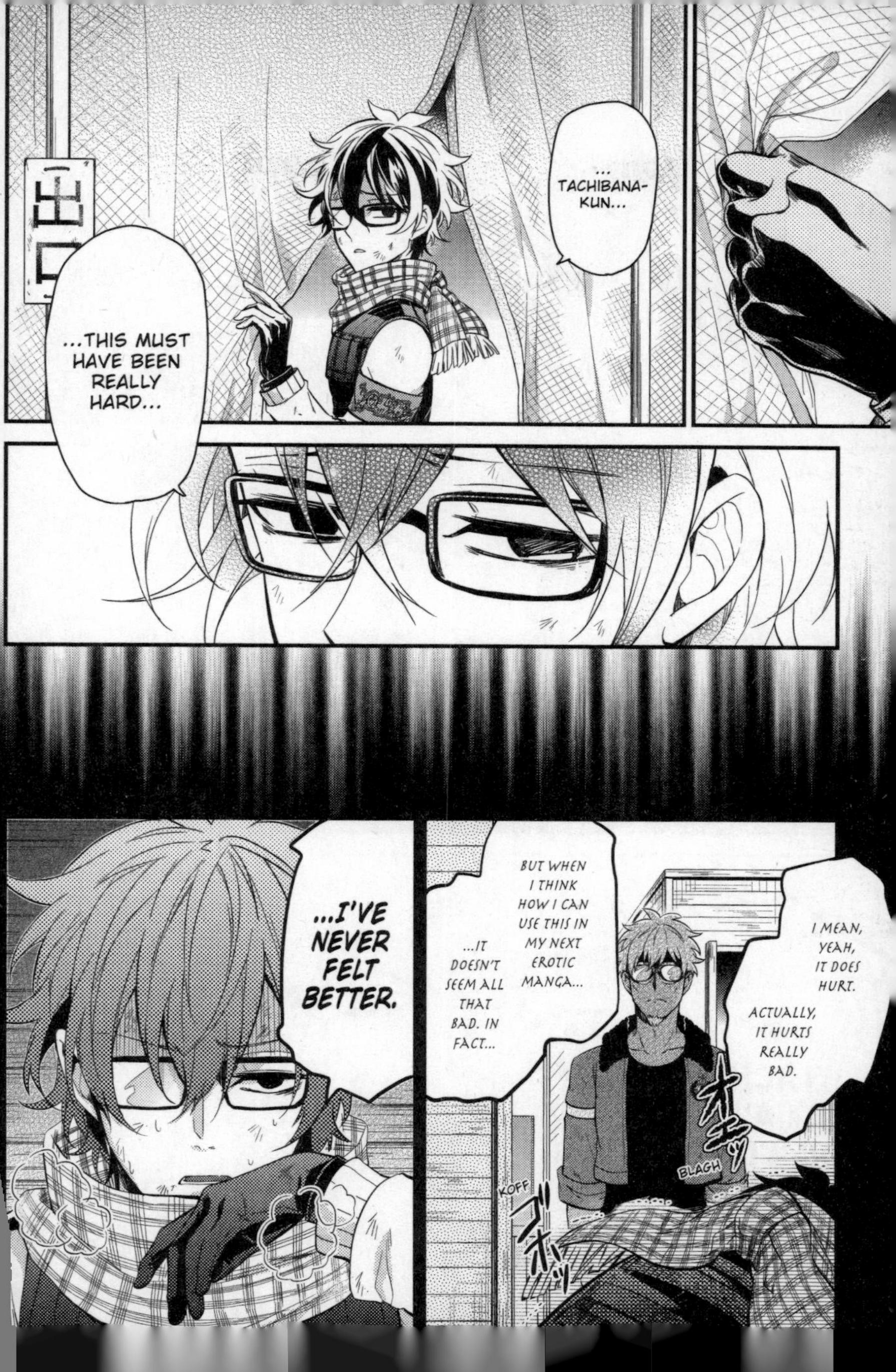
...TACHIBANA-KUN...
...THIS MUST HAVE BEEN REALLY HARD...
I MEAN, YEAH, IT DOES HURT.
ACTUALLY, IT HURTS REALLY BAD.
BLAGH
KOFF
BUT WHEN I THINK HOW I CAN USE THIS IN MY NEXT EROTIC MANGA...
...IT DOESN'T SEEM ALL THAT BAD. IN FACT...
...I'VE NEVER FELT BETTER.

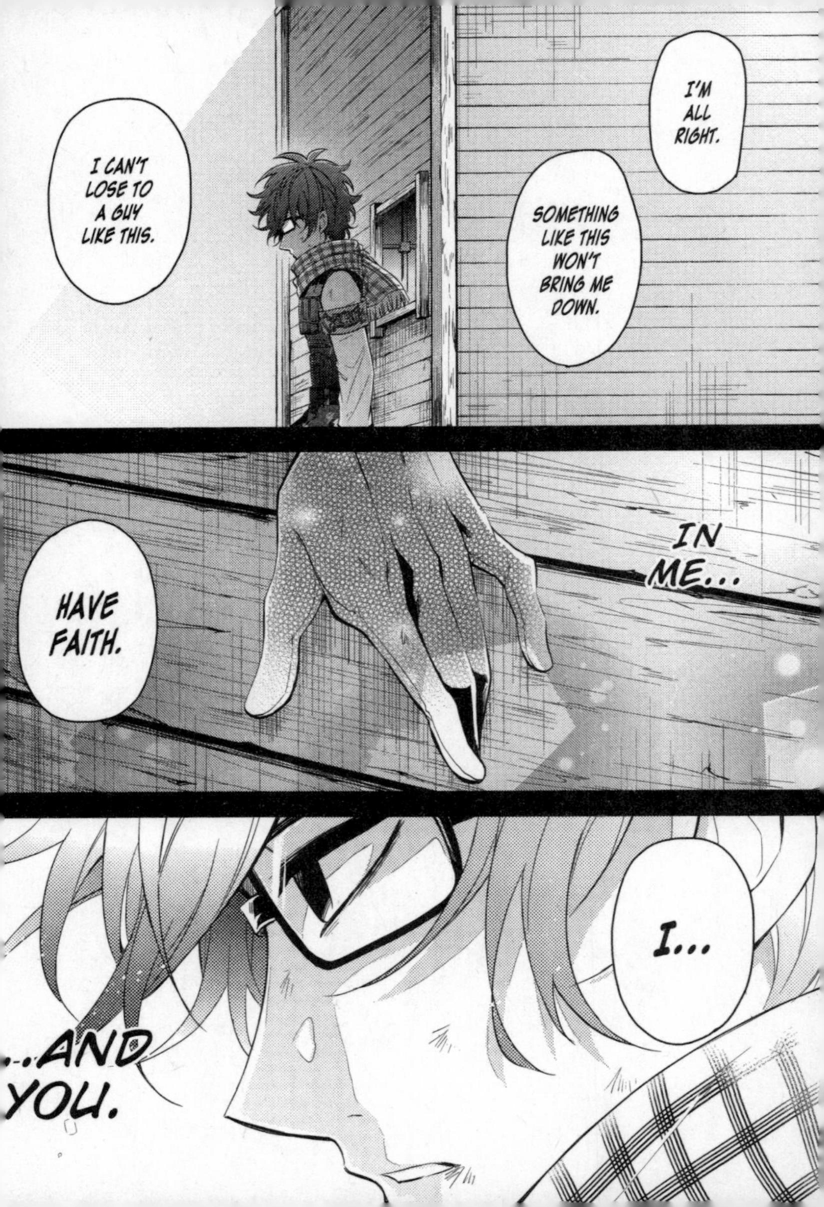
I'M ALL RIGHT.
SOMETHING LIKE THIS WON'T BRING ME DOWN.
I CAN'T LOSE TO A GUY LIKE THIS.
IN ME...
HAVE FAITH.
I...
...AND YOU.

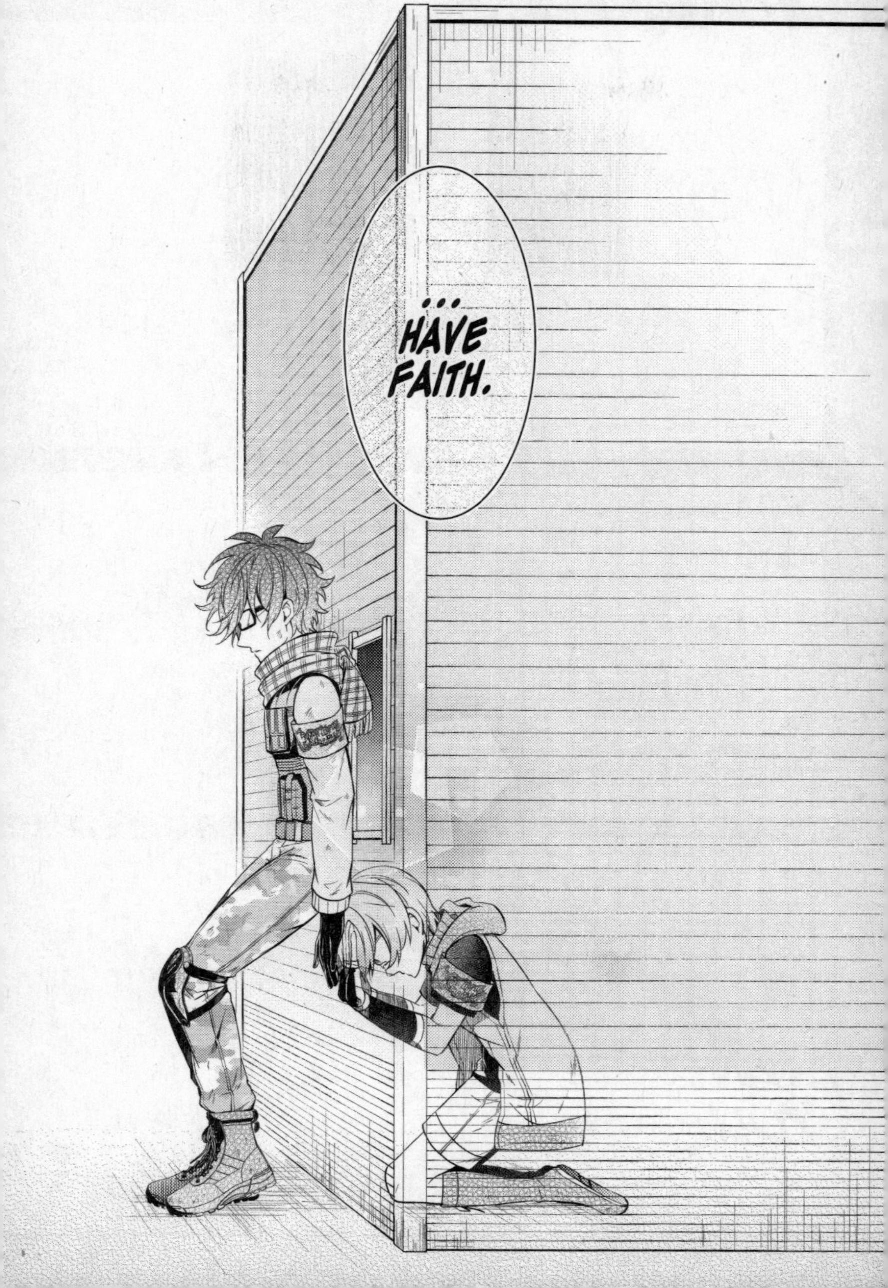
...HAVE FAITH.

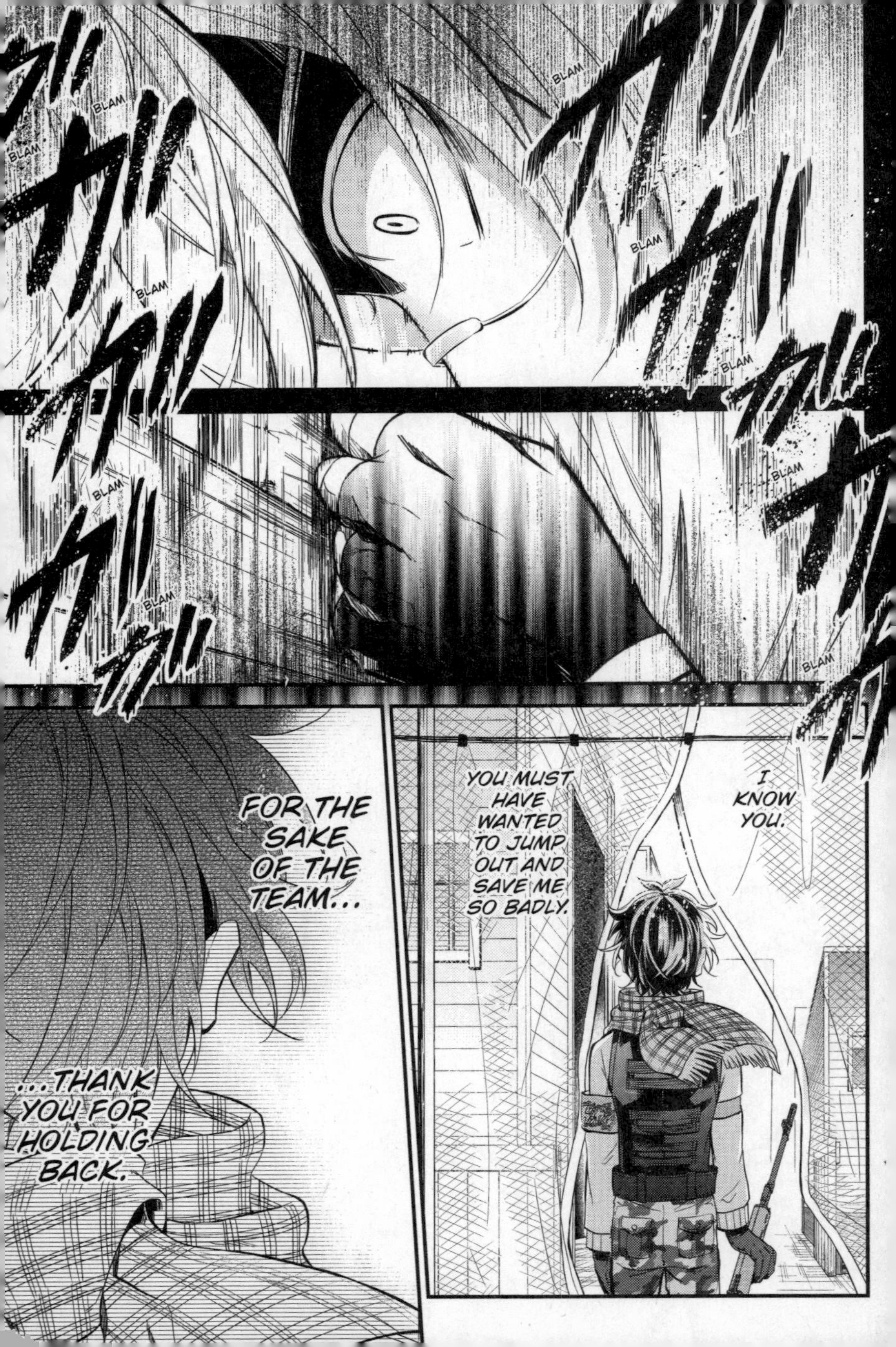
BLAM
BLAM
BLAM
BLAM
BLAM
BLAM
BLAM
BLAM
BLAM
BLAM
I KNOW YOU.
YOU MUST HAVE WANTED TO JUMP OUT AND SAVE ME SO BADLY.
FOR THE SAKE OF THE TEAM...
...THANK YOU FOR HOLDING BACK.

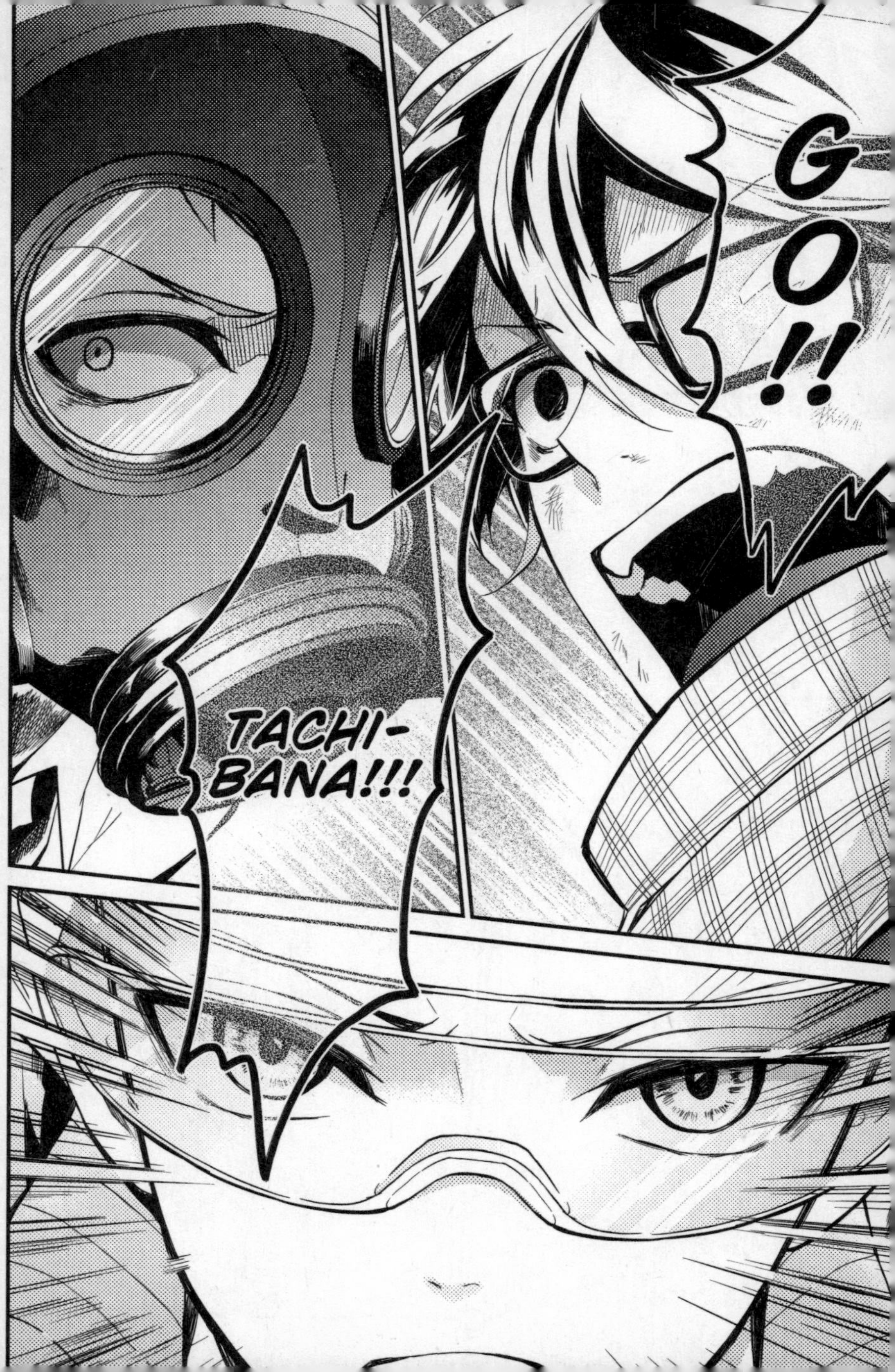
GO!!
TACHI-BANA!!!

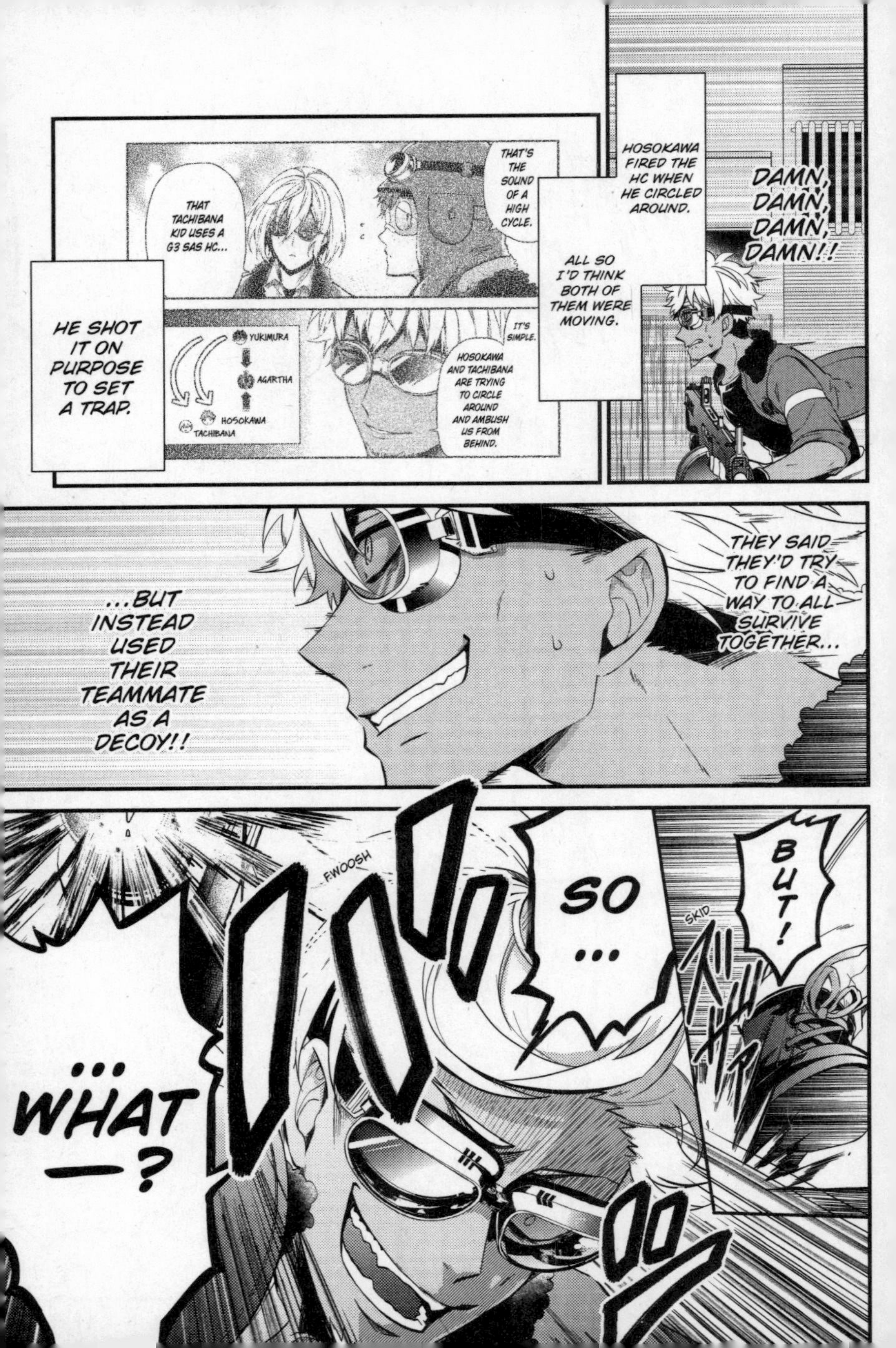
DAMN, DAMN, DAMN, DAMN!!
HOSOKAWA FIRED THE HC WHEN HE CIRCLED AROUND.
ALL SO I'D THINK BOTH OF THEM WERE MOVING.
THAT'S THE SOUND OF A HIGH CYCLE.
THAT TACHIBANA KID USES A G3 SAS HC...
IT'S SIMPLE.
HOSOKAWA AND TACHIBANA ARE TRYING TO CIRCLE AROUND AND AMBUSH US FROM BEHIND.
YUKIMURA
AGARTHA
HOSOKAWA
TACHIBANA
HE SHOT IT ON PURPOSE TO SET A TRAP.
THEY SAID THEY'D TRY TO FIND A WAY TO ALL SURVIVE TOGETHER...
...BUT INSTEAD USED THEIR TEAMMATE AS A DECOY!!
BUT!
SKID
SO...
FWOOSH
...WHAT—?

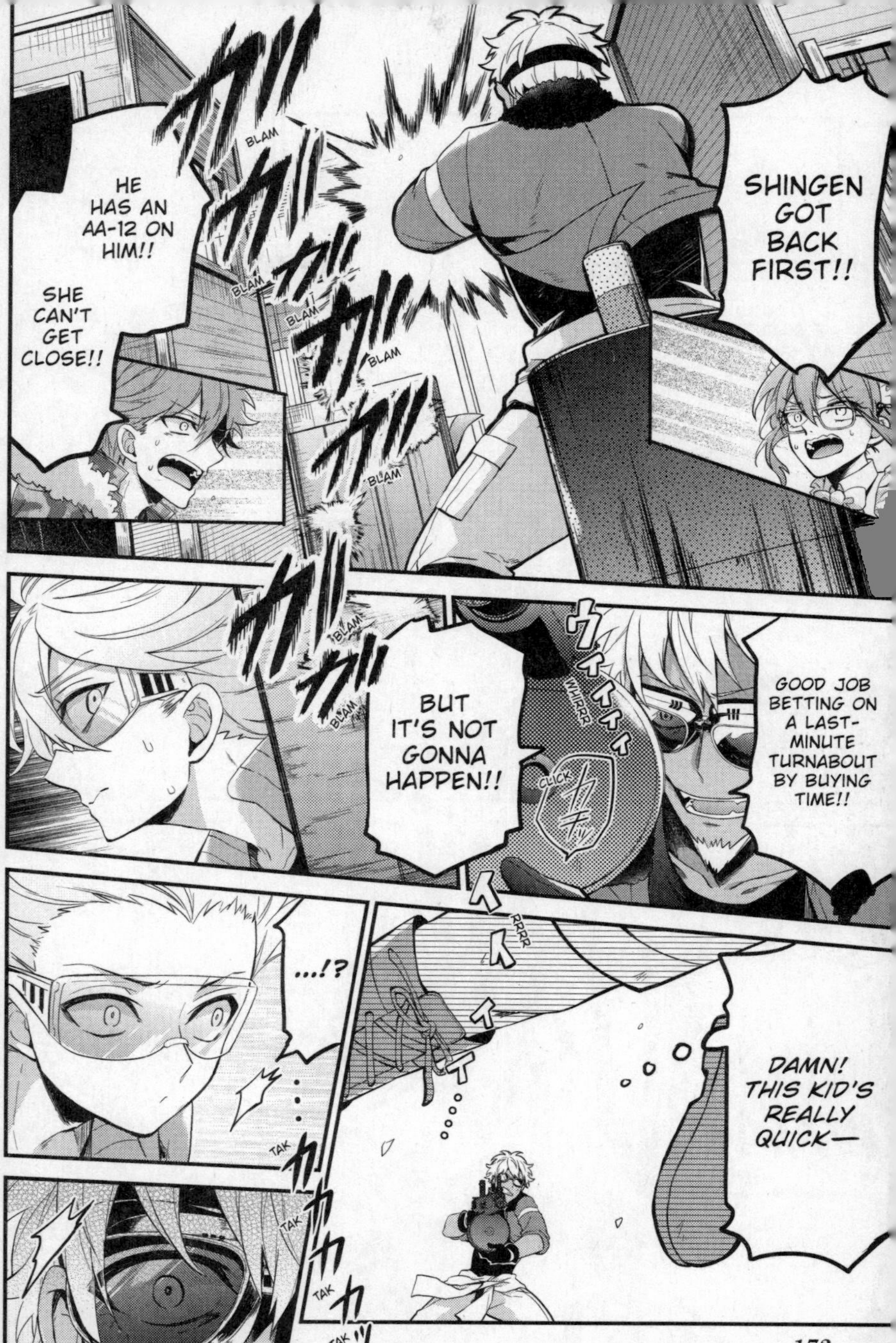
SHINGEN GOT BACK FIRST!!
BLAM
HE HAS AN AA-12 ON HIM!!
SHE CAN'T GET CLOSE!!
BLAM
BLAM
BLAM
BLAM
GOOD JOB BETTING ON A LAST-MINUTE TURNABOUT BY BUYING TIME!!
WHIRRR
CLICK
BUT IT'S NOT GONNA HAPPEN!!
BLAM
BLAM
DAMN! THIS KID'S REALLY QUICK—
RRRR
...!?
...
TAK
TAK
TAK
TAK

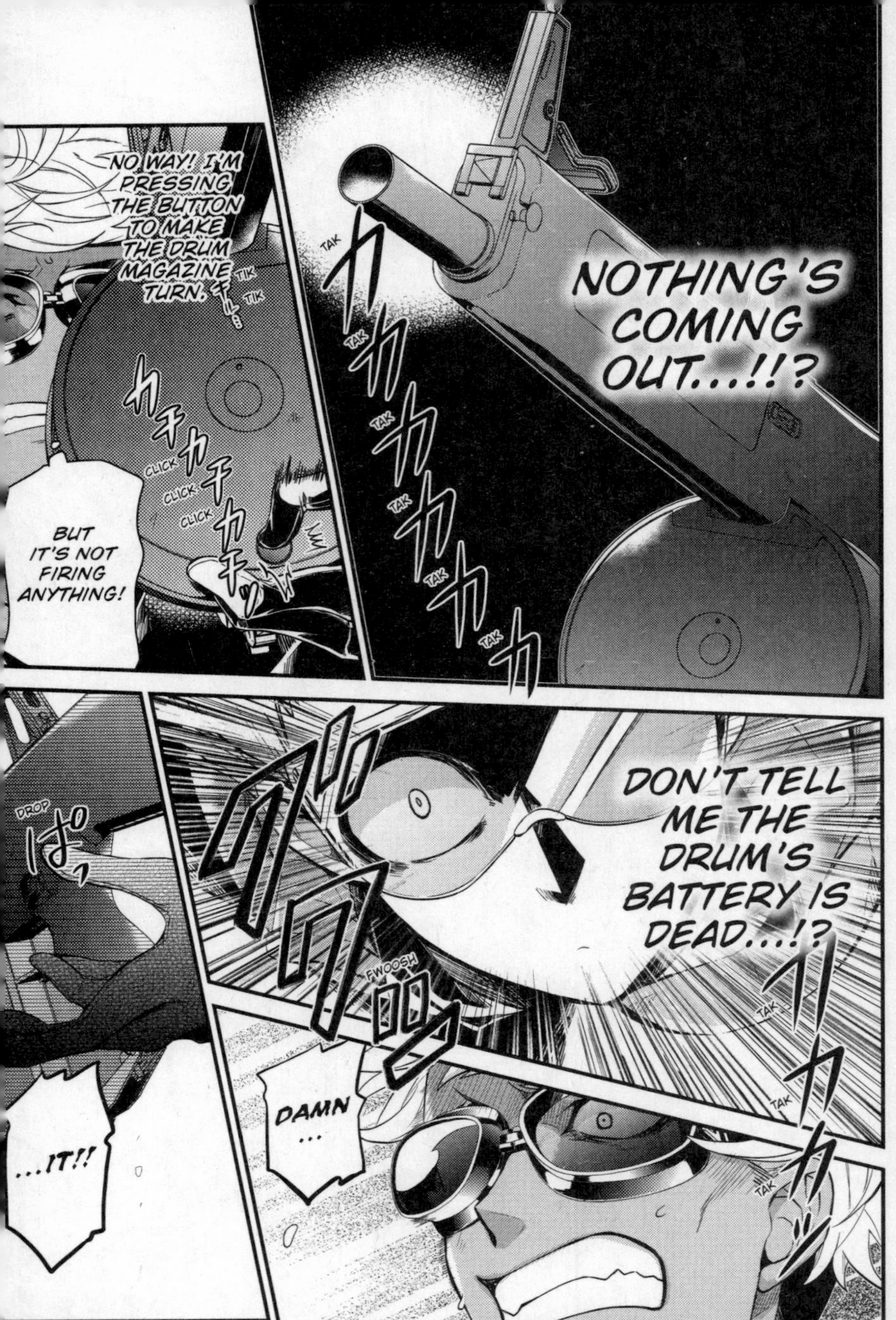

TAK
TAK
TAK
TAK
TAK
TAK
NOTHING'S COMING OUT...!!?
NO WAY! I'M PRESSING THE BUTTON TO MAKE THE DRUM MAGAZINE TURN.
TIK
TIK
CLICK
CLICK
CLICK
BUT IT'S NOT FIRING ANYTHING!
DON'T TELL ME THE DRUM'S BATTERY IS DEAD...!?
FWOOSH
TAK
TAK
TAK
DAMN...
DROP
...IT!!

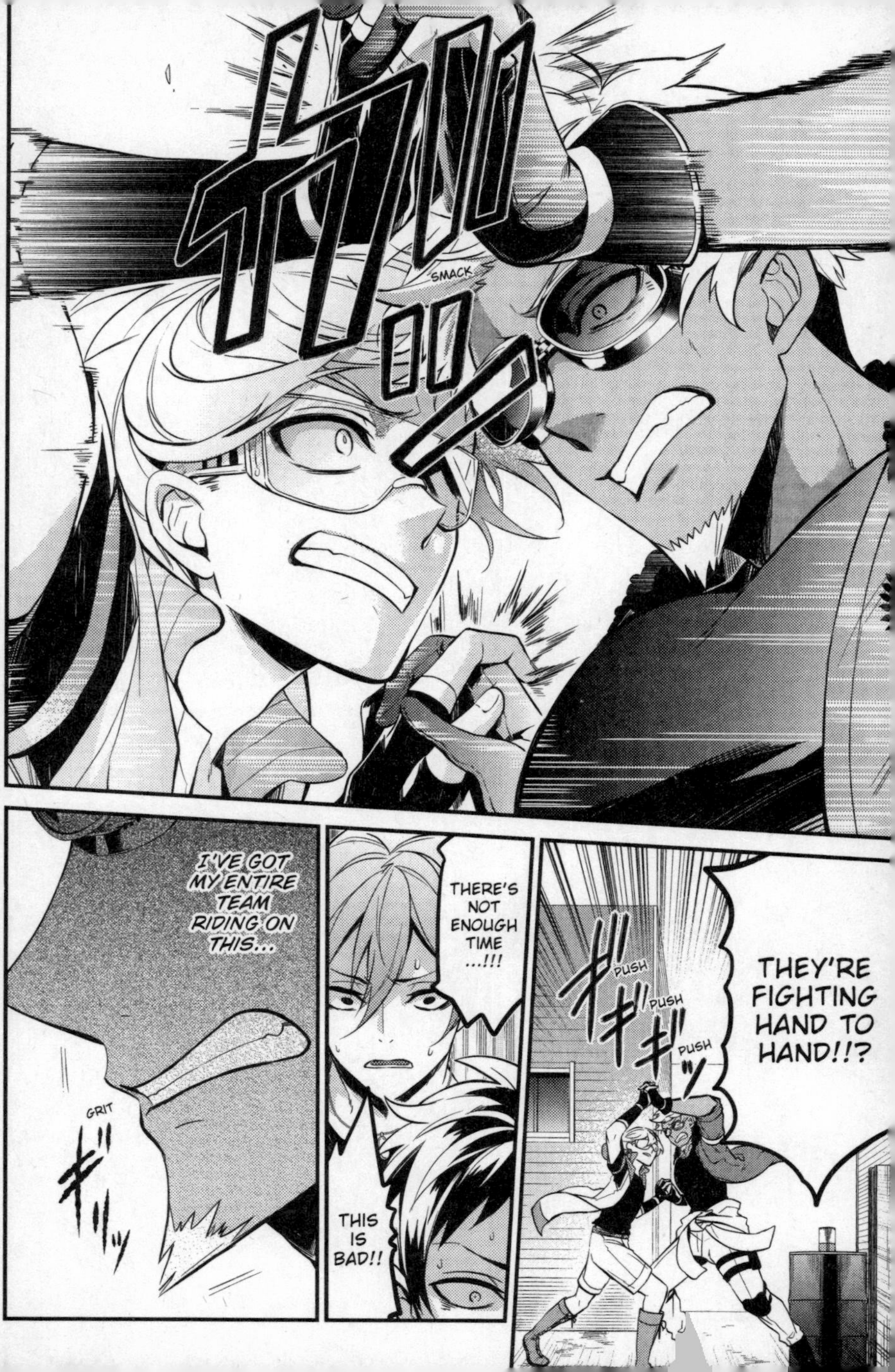
SMACK
PUSH
PUSH
PUSH
THEY'RE FIGHTING HAND TO HAND!!?
THERE'S NOT ENOUGH TIME ...!!!
THIS IS BAD!!
I'VE GOT MY ENTIRE TEAM RIDING ON THIS...
GRIT

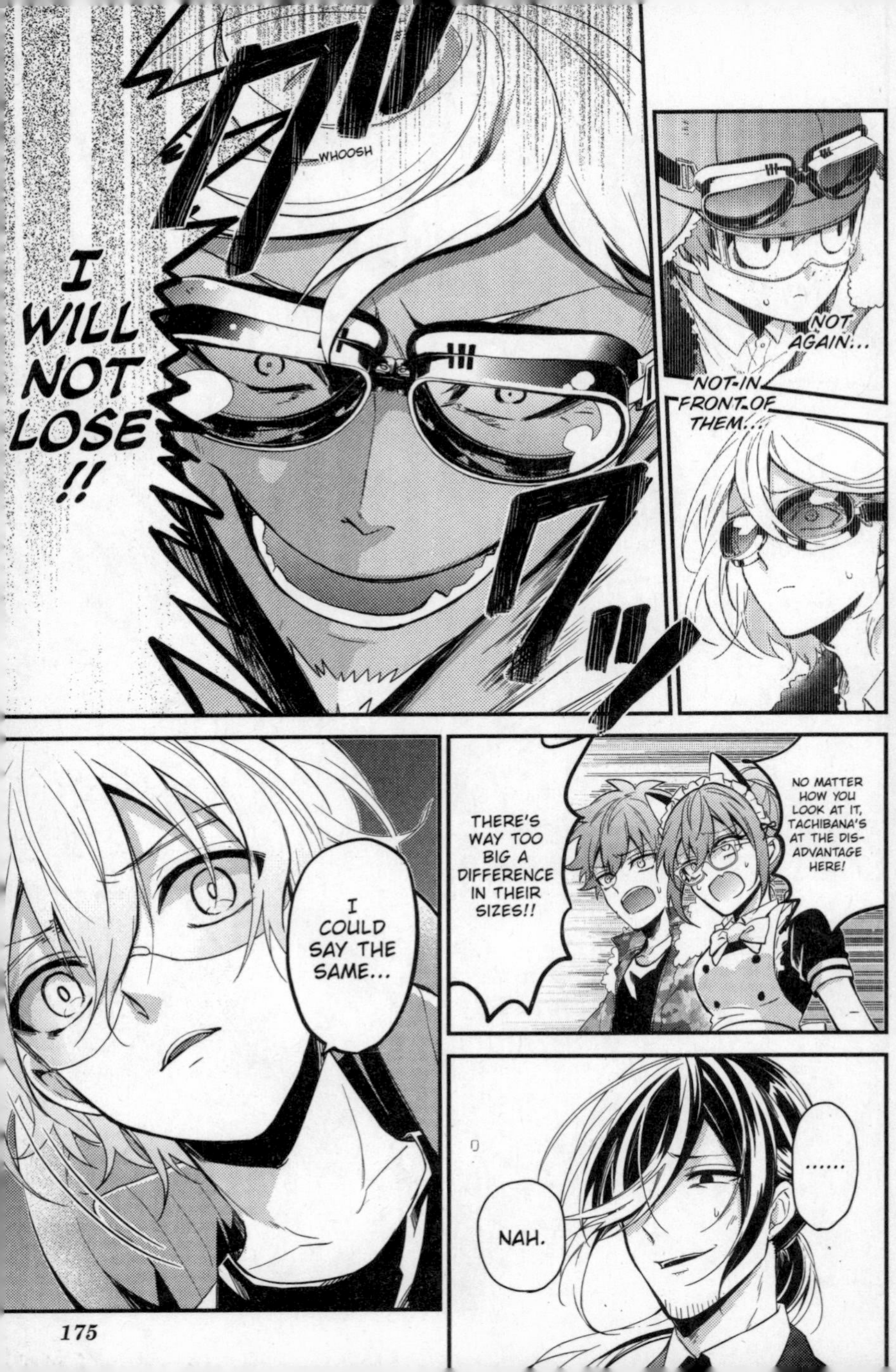
NOT AGAIN...
NOT IN FRONT OF THEM...
WHOOSH
I WILL NOT LOSE!!
NO MATTER HOW YOU LOOK AT IT, TACHIBANA'S AT THE DIS-ADVANTAGE HERE!
THERE'S WAY TOO BIG A DIFFERENCE IN THEIR SIZES!!
......
NAH.
I COULD SAY THE SAME...

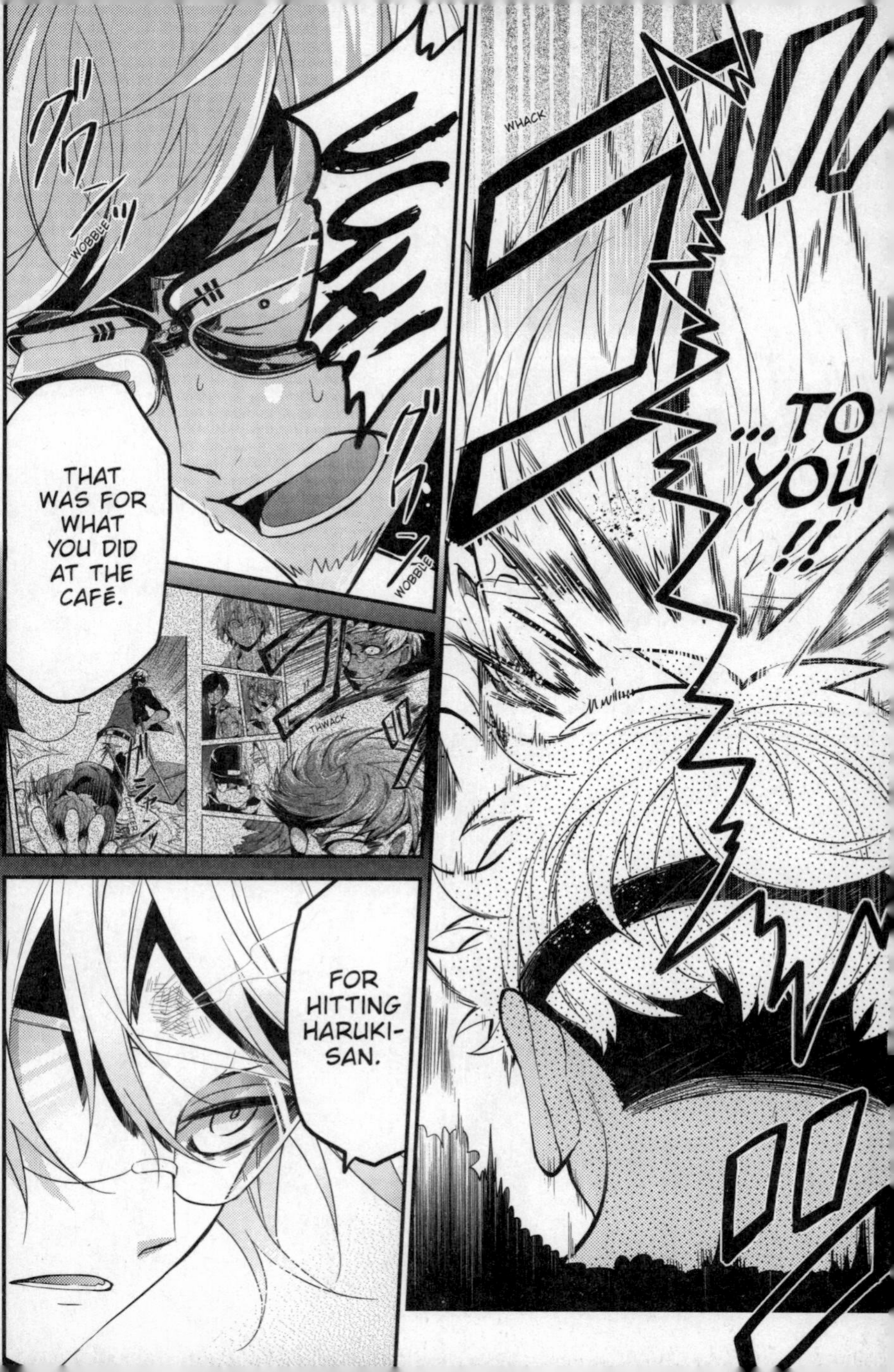
WHACK
...TO YOU!!
WOBBLE
WOBBLE
THAT WAS FOR WHAT YOU DID AT THE CAFÉ.
THWACK
FOR HITTING HARUKI-SAN.

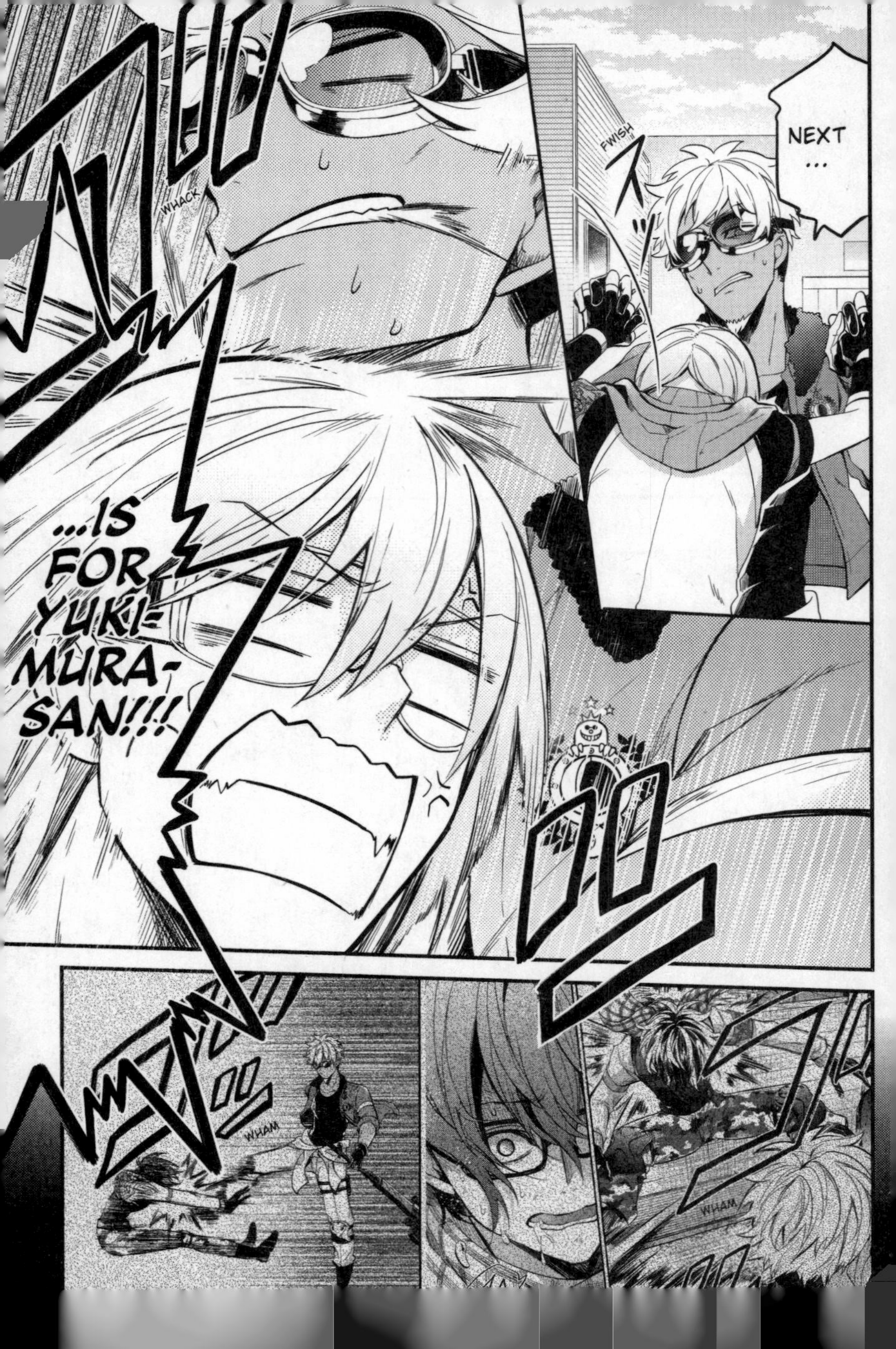

FWISH
NEXT ...
WHACK
...IS FOR YUKI-MURA-SAN!!!
WHAM
WHAM

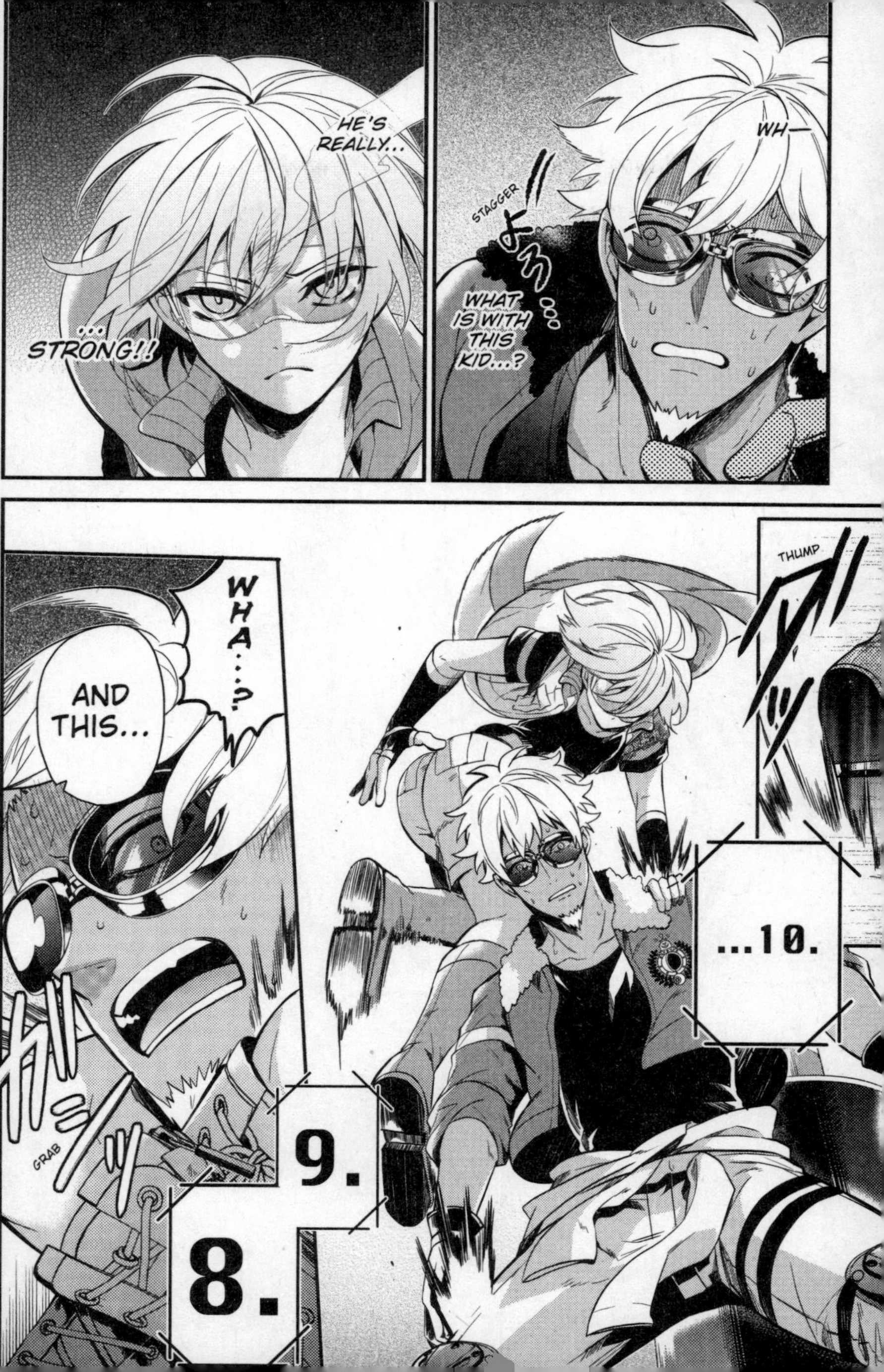
WH—
STAGGER
WHAT IS WITH THIS KID...?
HE'S REALLY...
...STRONG!!
THUMP
...10.
WHA...?
AND THIS...
GRAB
9.
8.

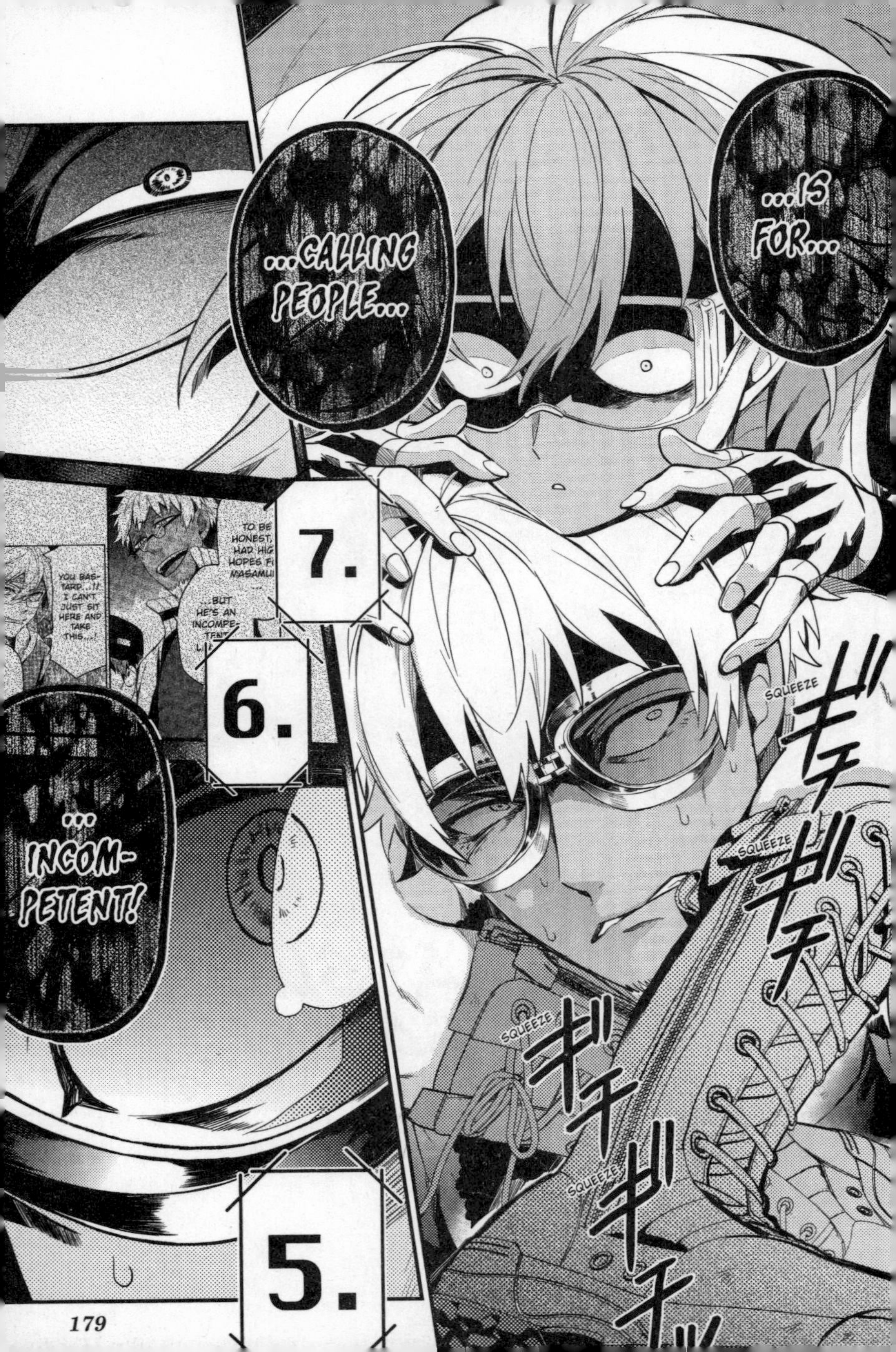
...IS FOR...
...CALLING PEOPLE...
7.
TO BE HONEST, HAD HIG HOPES F MASAMU ...
...BUT HE'S AN INCOMPE-TENT LI
YOU BAS-TARD...!! I CAN'T JUST SIT HERE AND TAKE THIS...!
6.
... INCOM-PETENT!
SQUEEZE
SQUEEZE
SQUEEZE
SQUEEZE
5.

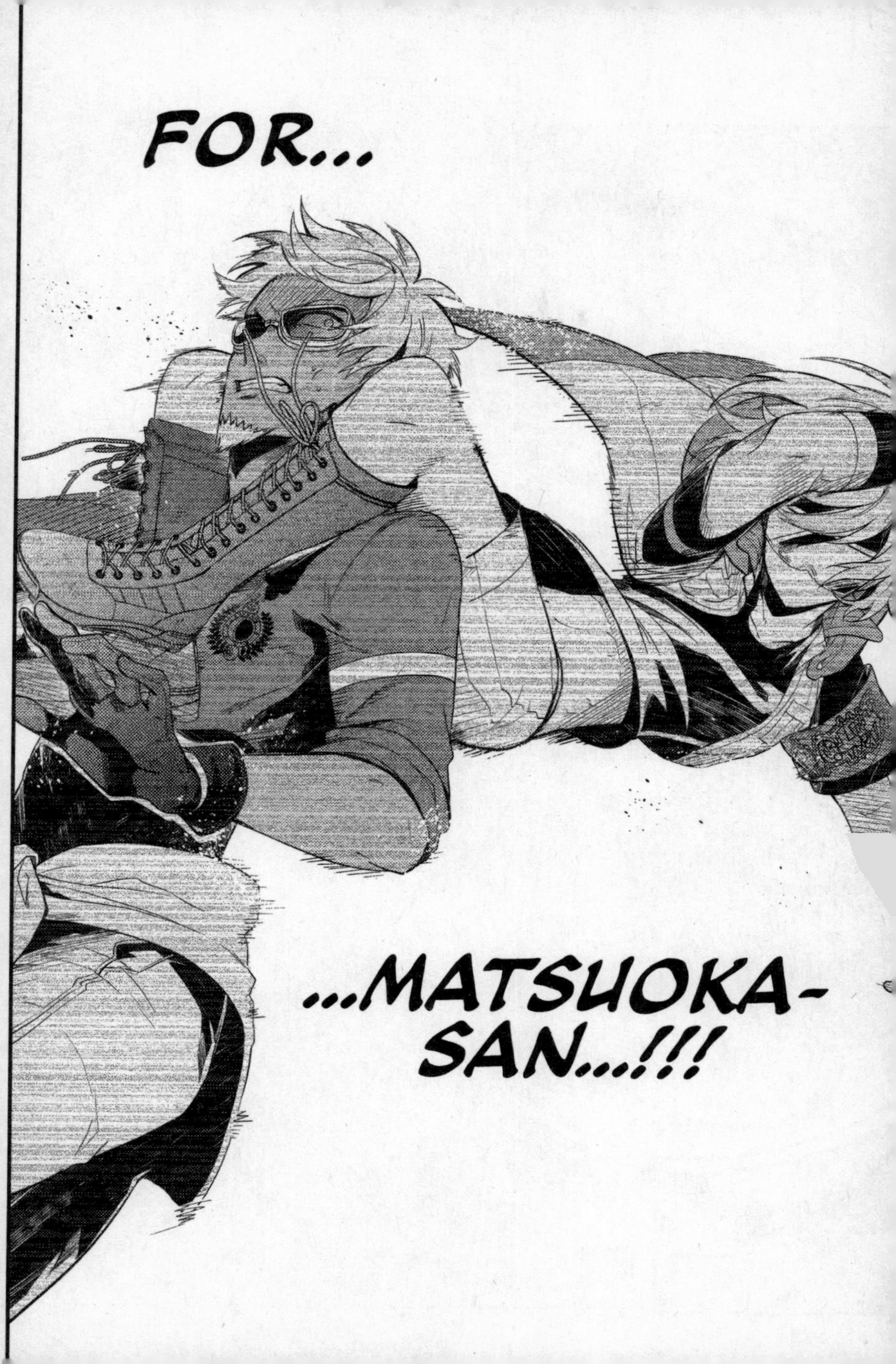
FOR...
...MATSUOKA-SAN...!!!

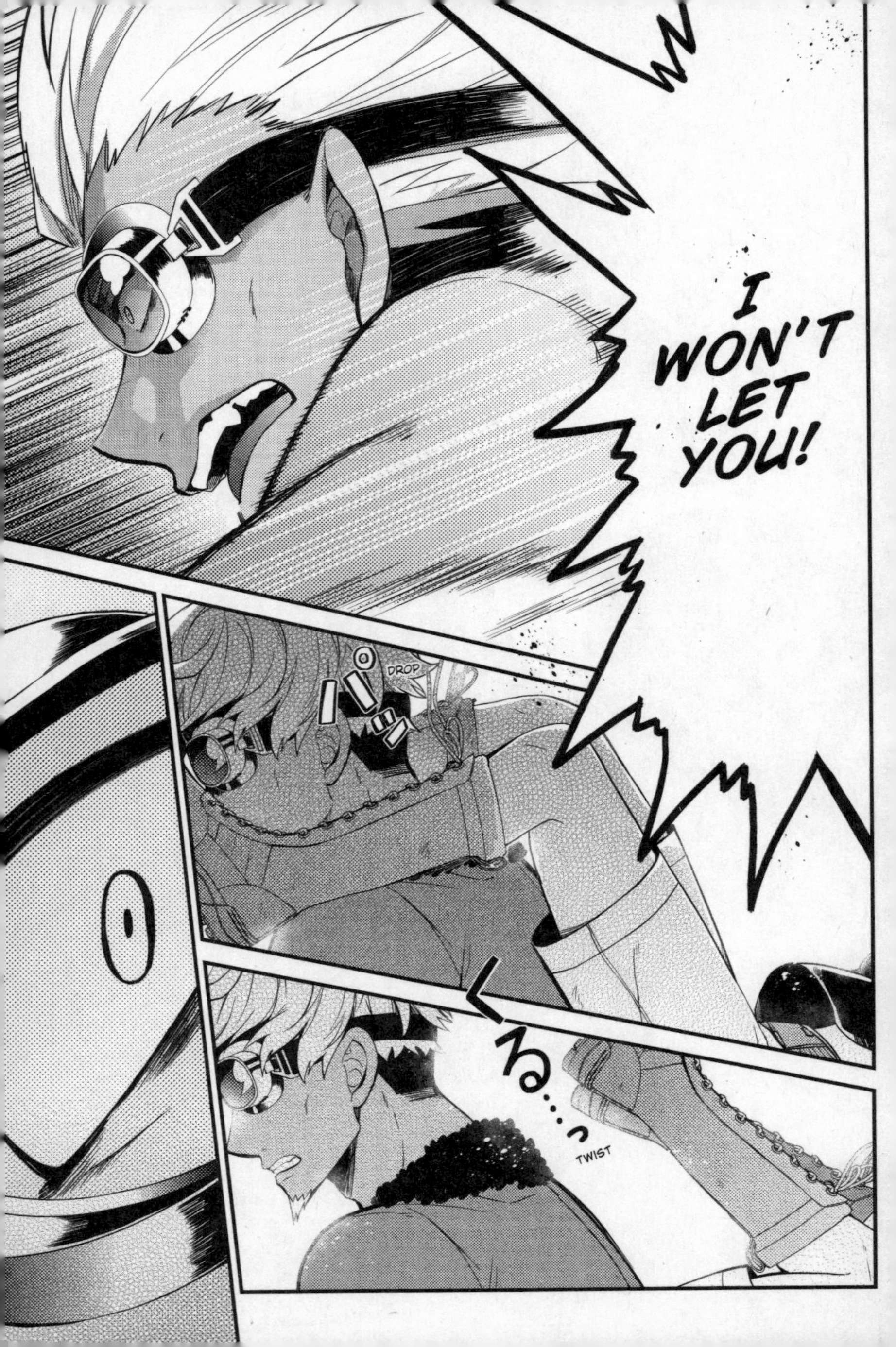

I WON'T LET YOU!
DROP
くる…っ
TWIST

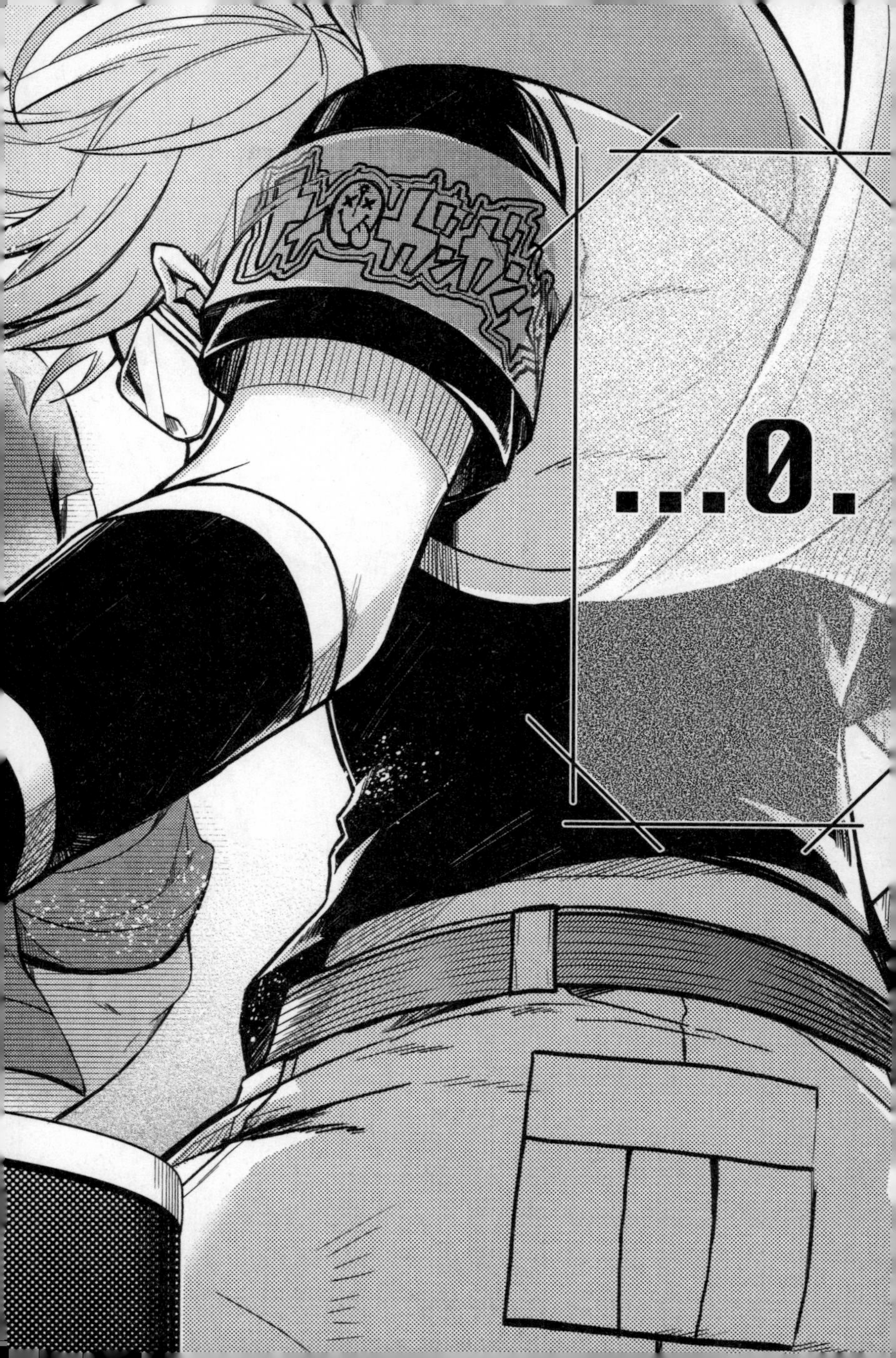
...0.

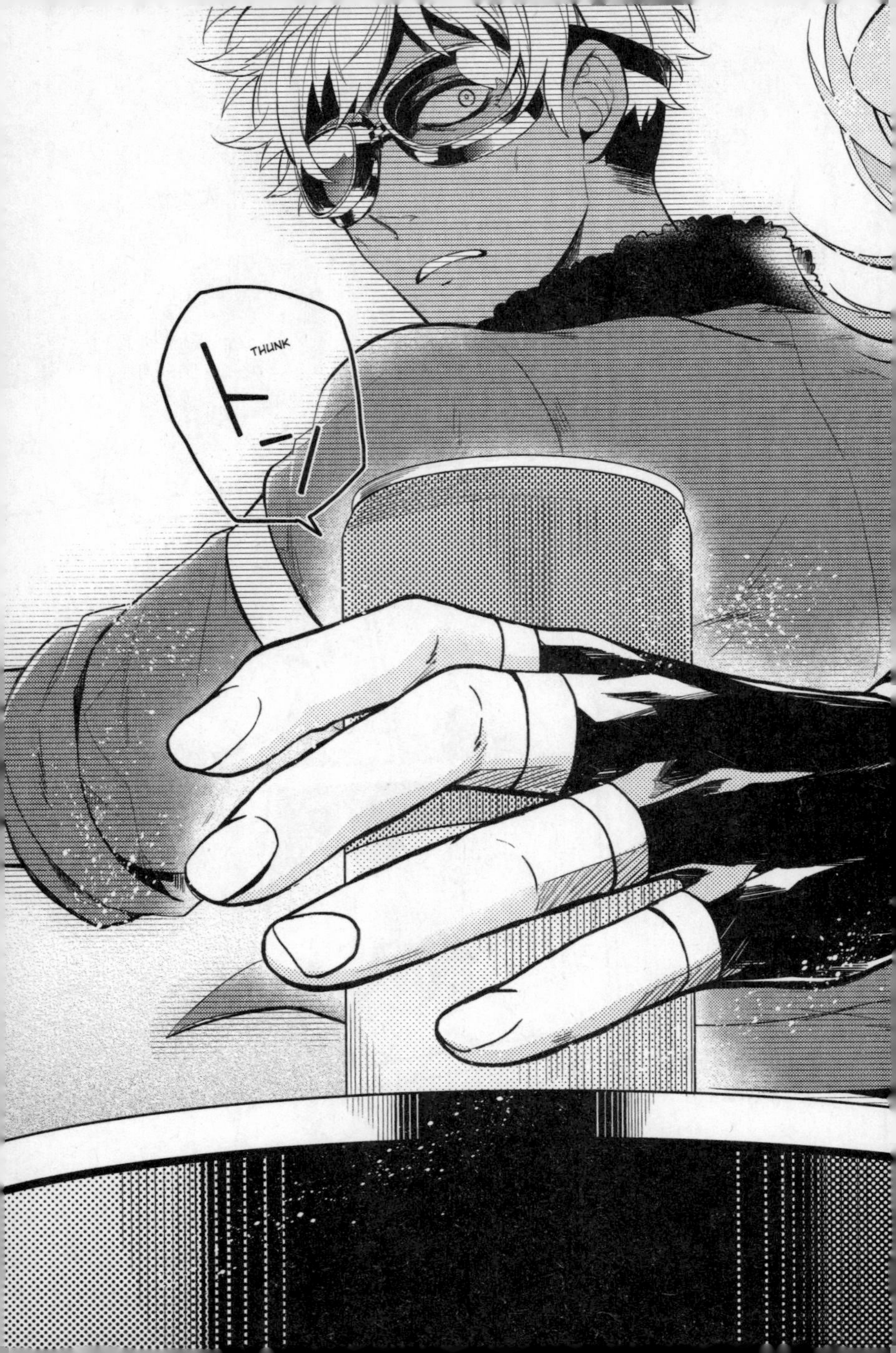
THUNK

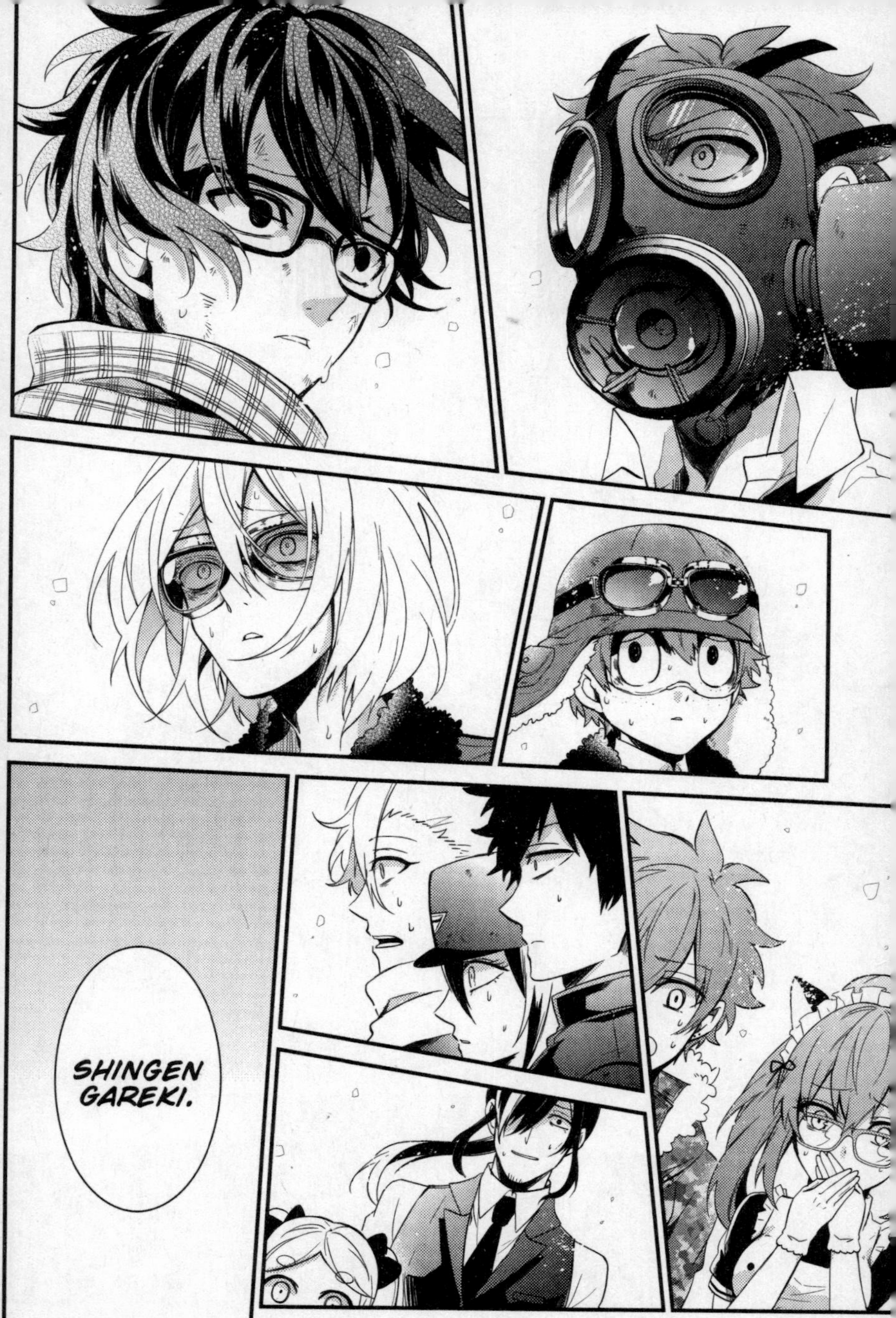
SHINGEN GAREKI.

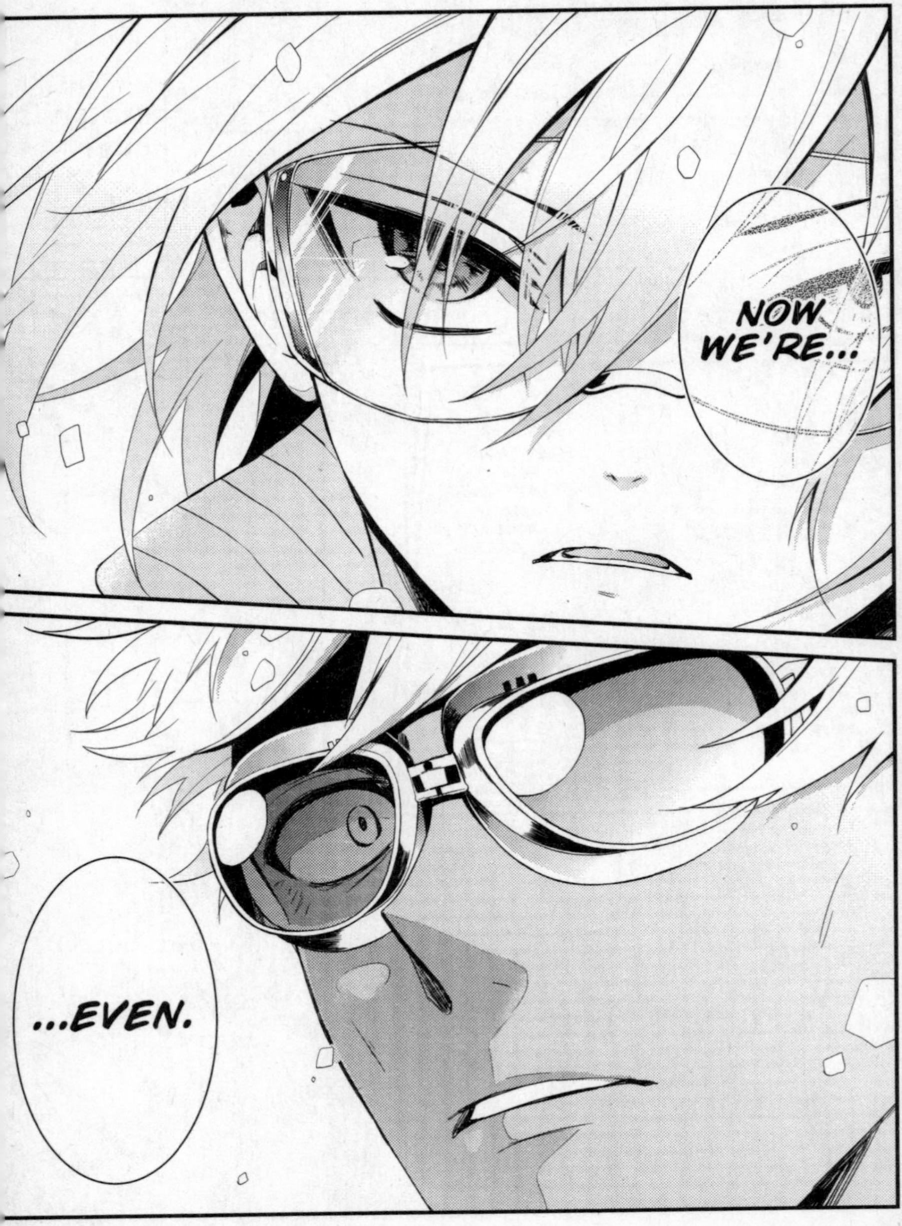
NOW WE'RE...
...EVEN.

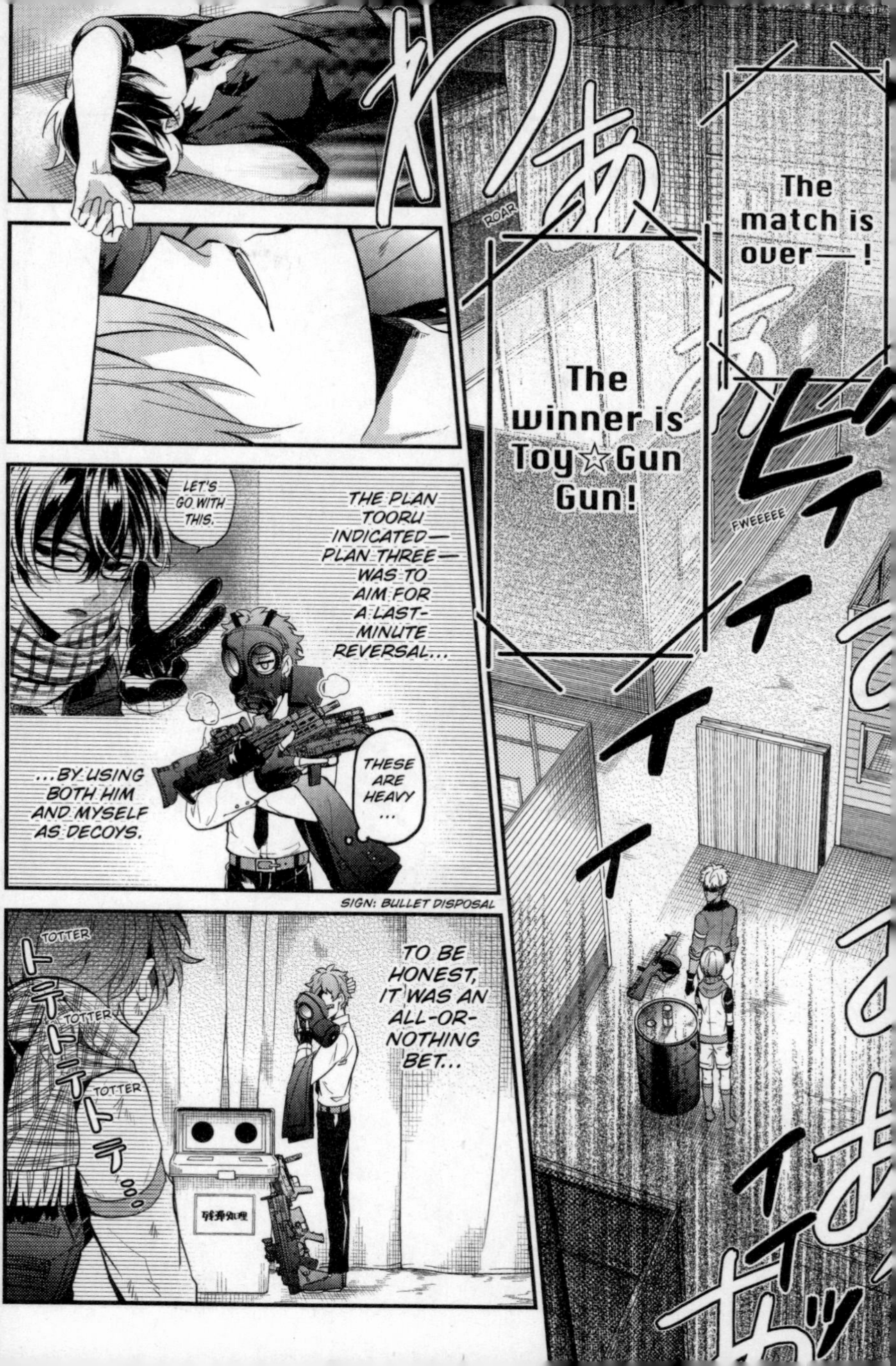

The match is over—!
The winner is Toy☆Gun Gun!
ROAR
FWEEEEE
THE PLAN TOORU INDICATED—PLAN THREE—WAS TO AIM FOR A LAST-MINUTE REVERSAL...
LET'S GO WITH THIS.
THESE ARE HEAVY...
...BY USING BOTH HIM AND MYSELF AS DECOYS.
SIGN: BULLET DISPOSAL
TO BE HONEST, IT WAS AN ALL-OR-NOTHING BET...
TOTTER
TOTTER
TOTTER

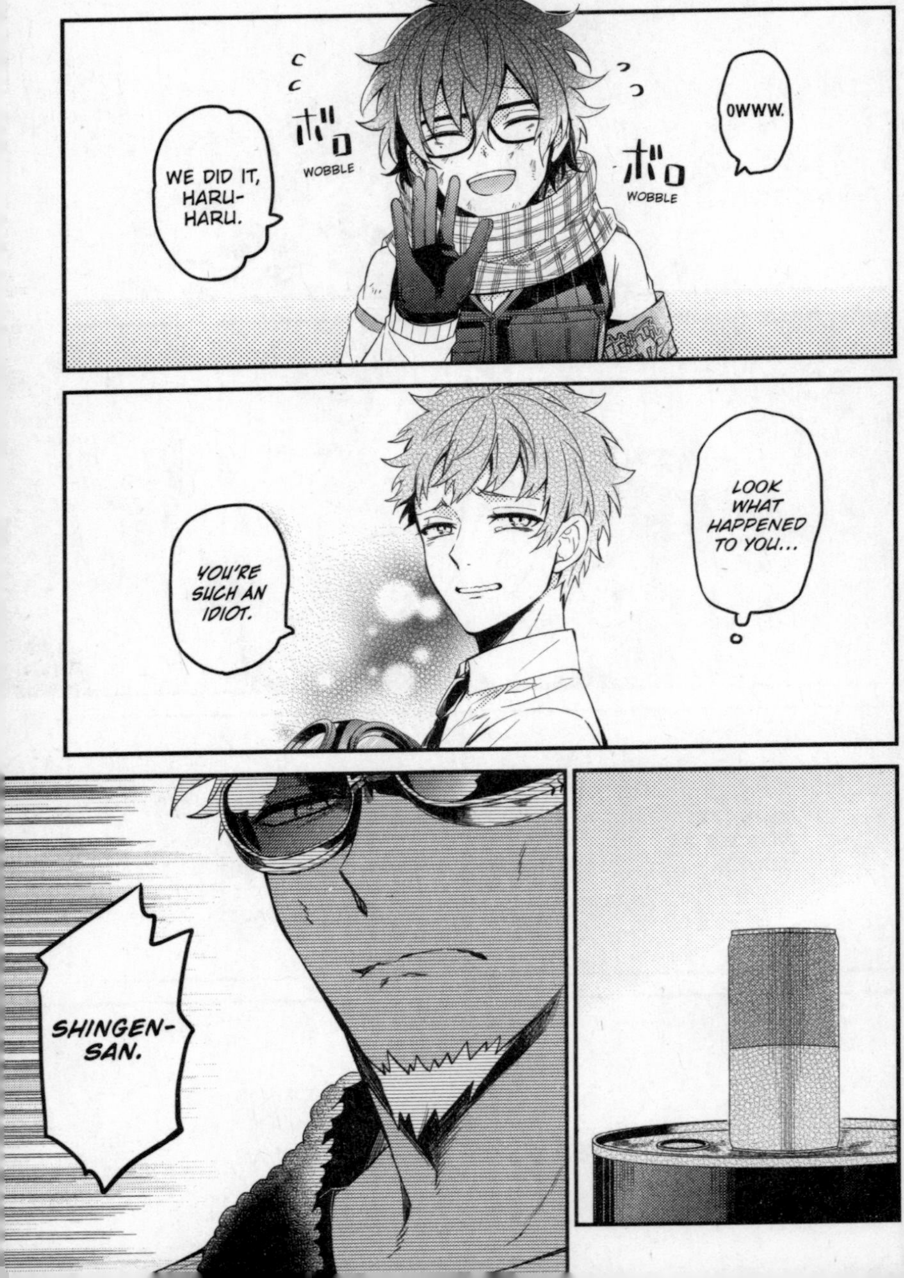
OWWW.
ボロ
WOBBLE
ボロ
WOBBLE
WE DID IT, HARU-HARU.
LOOK WHAT HAPPENED TO YOU...
YOU'RE SUCH AN IDIOT.
SHINGEN-SAN.

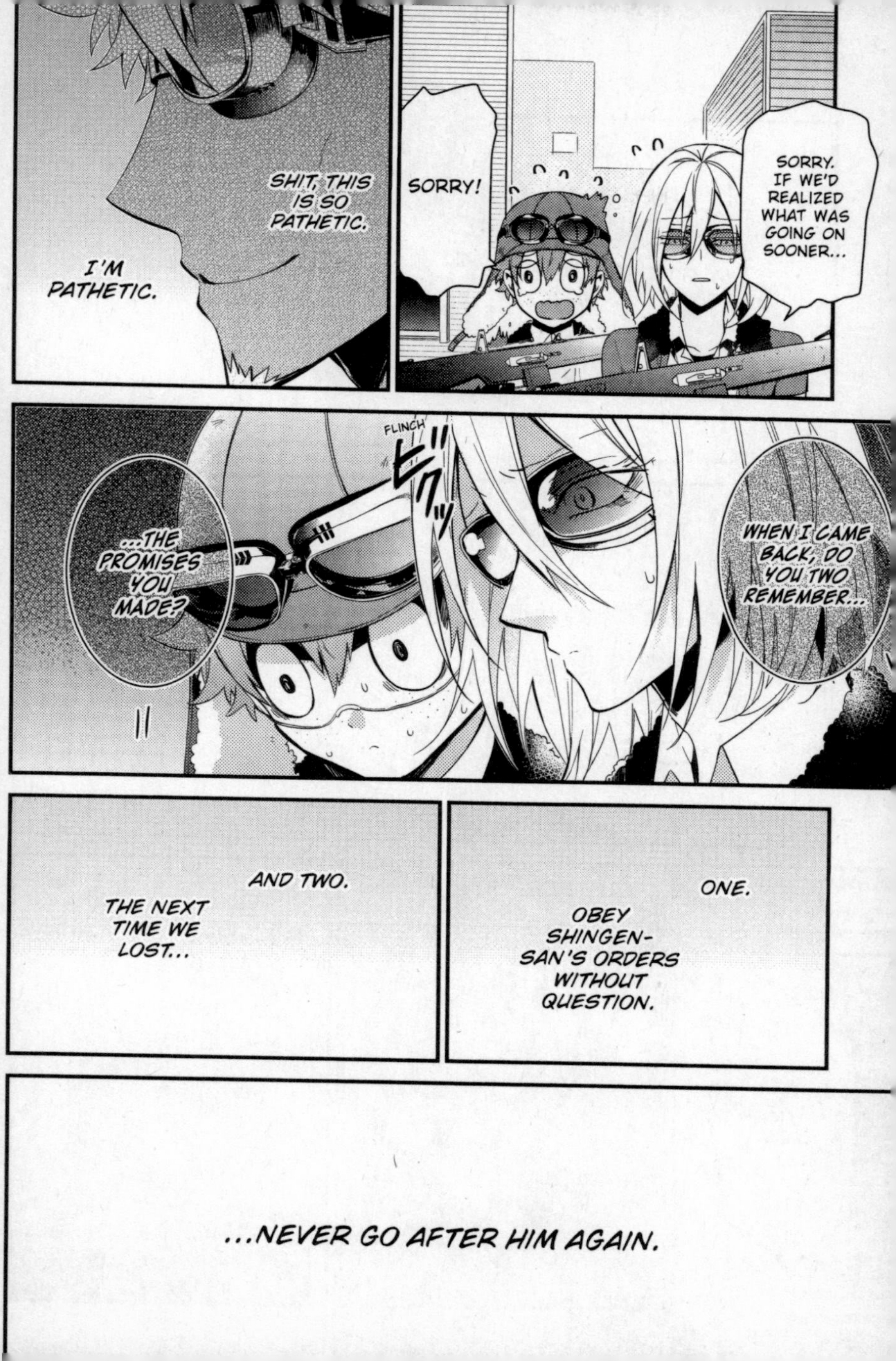
SORRY. IF WE'D REALIZED WHAT WAS GOING ON SOONER...
SORRY!
SHIT, THIS IS SO PATHETIC.
I'M PATHETIC.
WHEN I CAME BACK, DO YOU TWO REMEMBER...
FLINCH
...THE PROMISES YOU MADE?
ONE.
OBEY SHINGEN-SAN'S ORDERS WITHOUT QUESTION.
AND TWO.
THE NEXT TIME WE LOST...
...NEVER GO AFTER HIM AGAIN.

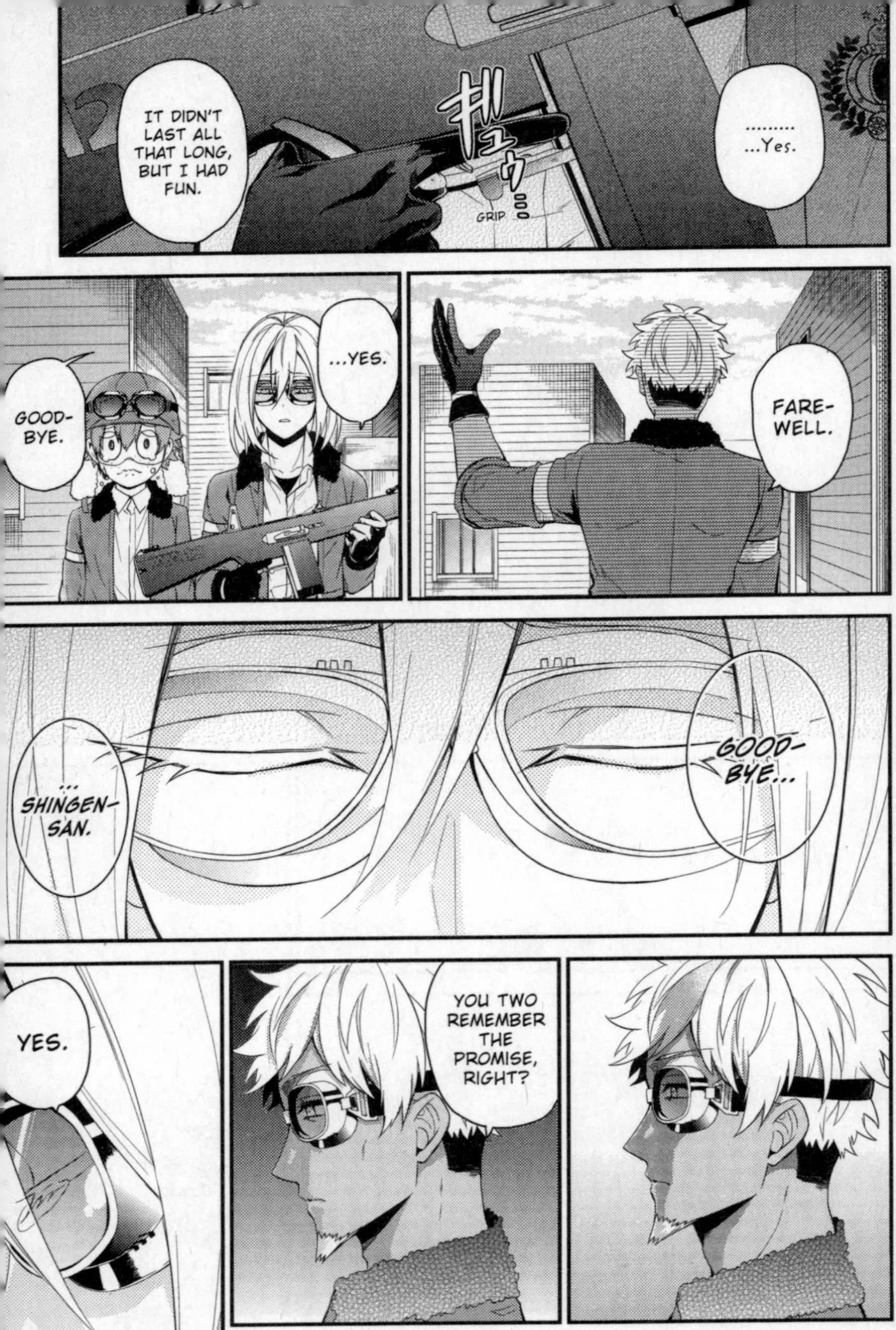

....
...Yes.
ギュゥ
GRIP
IT DIDN'T LAST ALL THAT LONG, BUT I HAD FUN.
FARE-WELL.
...YES.
GOOD-BYE.
GOOD-BYE...
... SHINGEN-SAN.
YOU TWO REMEMBER THE PROMISE, RIGHT?
YES.

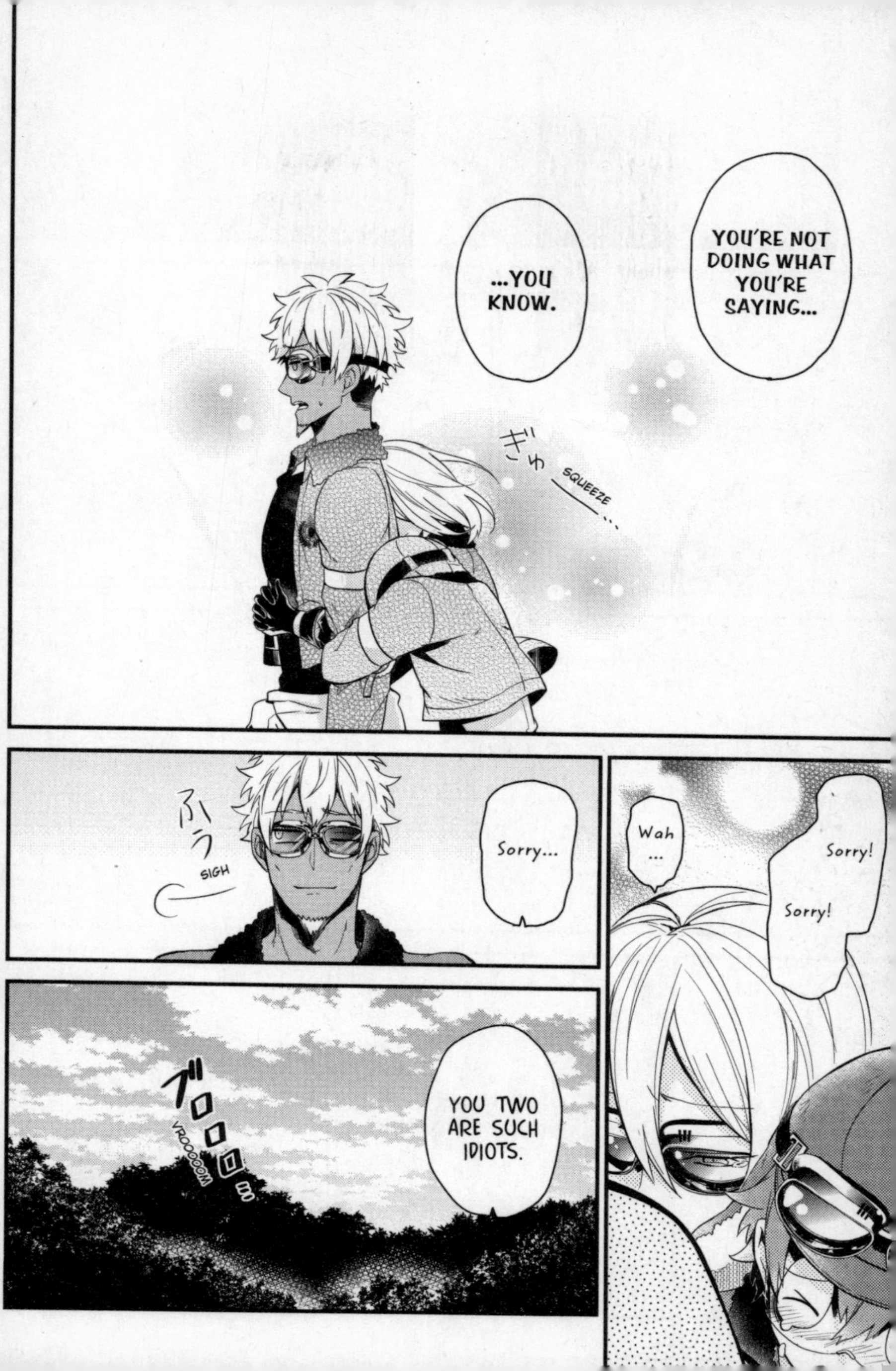
YOU'RE NOT DOING WHAT YOU'RE SAYING...
...YOU KNOW.
ぎゅ
SQUEEZE
Sorry!
Sorry!
Wah ...
Sorry...
ふう
SIGH
YOU TWO ARE SUCH IDIOTS.
ブロロロ
VROOOOOM

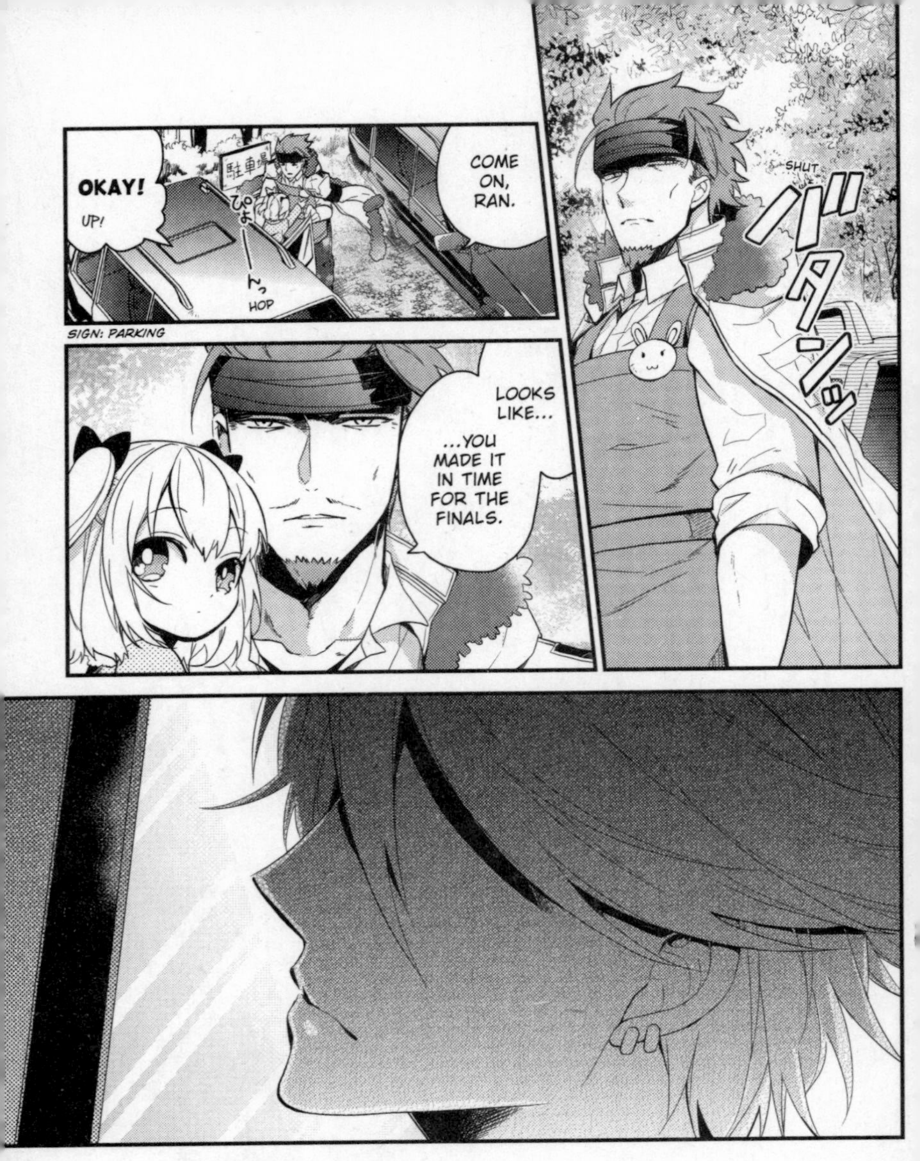
SHUT
バタンッ
COME ON, RAN.
OKAY!
UP!
駐車場
ぴょーんっ
HOP
SIGN: PARKING
LOOKS LIKE...
...YOU MADE IT IN TIME FOR THE FINALS.

AOHARU×MACHINEGUN ⑯ END

AOHARU×MACHINEGUN

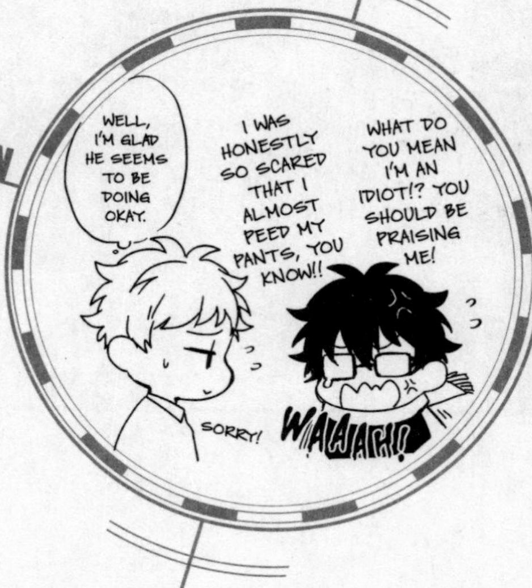
WHAT DO YOU MEAN I'M AN IDIOT!? YOU SHOULD BE PRAISING ME!
I WAS HONESTLY SO SCARED THAT I ALMOST PEED MY PANTS, YOU KNOW!!
WELL, I'M GLAD HE SEEMS TO BE DOING OKAY.
WAAAAH!
SORRY!

Special Thanks

My editor S-sama...
......You get "dog" in personality tests.
My editor S-sama...
......You get "sloth" in personality tests.

The sales staff, the designers.

Tokyo Marui, Deka Shimamura-sama...
......Everyone's so ripped.
Hirano-sama......Are you doing well——!?
Tajima-sama......Thanks for the New Year's card.

[Collaborators]
Friendly Fire-sama......I'm obsessed with this place.
Morizou-sama......Thank you for all your help.

[Emblem design]
Shishihime-sama......We may have passed by
each other on the street sometime. ②

[Background assistants] (pen names)

Waka Sanada-sama (Dokuganryuu)...
......I had yellowtail sashimi! It was really good!
Yuusuke Murayama-sama (Yumeko Sakurai)...
......Sneezing, runny nose Con'c.

My father, my mother, my brother.
And you!!

THAT'S RIGHT.

BOYS AND GIRLS, NO HITTING, KICKING, OR PUSHING PEOPLE AGAINST SURVIVAL WALLS WHEN SURVIVAL GAMING!! ABSOLUTELY NOT AT ALL!!

NADE

b

T

Lettering: Alexis Eckerman

AOHARU×KIKANJU Volume 16 ©2019 NAOE/ SQUARE ENIX CO., LTD. First published in Japan in 2019 by SQUARE ENIX CO., LTD. English translation rights arranged with SQUARE ENIX CO., LTD. and Yen Press, LLC through Tuttle-Mori Agency, Inc., Tokyo.

English Translation ©2020 by SQUARE ENIX CO., LTD.

Yen Press
150 West 30th St
New York, NY 100

Visit us at yenpre
facebook.com/ye
twitter.com/yenp
yenpress.tumblr.c
instagram.com/ye

First Yen Press Print Edition: January 2020
Originally published as an ebook in January 2020 by Yen Press.

Yen Press is an imprint of Yen Press, LLC.
The Yen Press name and logo are trademarks of Yen Press, LLC.

The publisher is not responsible for websites (or their content) that are not owned by the publisher.

Library of Congress Control Number: 2016946057

ISBN: 978-1-9753-3284-6 (paperback)
     978-1-9753-3303-4 (ebook)

10 9 8 7 6 5 4 3 2 1

WOR

Printed in the United States of America